Management for Professionals

The Springer series *Management for Professionals* comprises high-level business and management books for executives. The authors are experienced business professionals and renowned professors who combine scientific background, best practice, and entrepreneurial vision to provide powerful insights into how to achieve business excellence.

More information about this series at https://link.springer.com/bookseries/10101

B Rajesh Kumar

Project Finance

Structuring, Valuation and Risk Management for Major Projects

B Rajesh Kumar
Dubai International Academic City
Institute of Management Technology
Dubai, United Arab Emirates

ISSN 2192-8096   ISSN 2192-810X (electronic)
Management for Professionals
ISBN 978-3-030-96727-7   ISBN 978-3-030-96725-3 (eBook)
https://doi.org/10.1007/978-3-030-96725-3

© The Editor(s) (if applicable) and The Author(s), under exclusive license to Springer Nature Switzerland AG 2022
This work is subject to copyright. All rights are solely and exclusively licensed by the Publisher, whether the whole or part of the material is concerned, specifically the rights of translation, reprinting, reuse of illustrations, recitation, broadcasting, reproduction on microfilms or in any other physical way, and transmission or information storage and retrieval, electronic adaptation, computer software, or by similar or dissimilar methodology now known or hereafter developed.
The use of general descriptive names, registered names, trademarks, service marks, etc. in this publication does not imply, even in the absence of a specific statement, that such names are exempt from the relevant protective laws and regulations and therefore free for general use.
The publisher, the authors and the editors are safe to assume that the advice and information in this book are believed to be true and accurate at the date of publication. Neither the publisher nor the authors or the editors give a warranty, expressed or implied, with respect to the material contained herein or for any errors or omissions that may have been made. The publisher remains neutral with regard to jurisdictional claims in published maps and institutional affiliations.

This Springer imprint is published by the registered company Springer Nature Switzerland AG
The registered company address is: Gewerbestrasse 11, 6330 Cham, Switzerland

*To my beloved
Lakshmi and Appu*

Preface

Modern infrastructure is critical to economic development. Large projects have a significant impact on the social and economic development of any country. Policy leadership and supportive financing environment are major determinants for infrastructure to facilitate the economic growth and well-being of a nation. Studies have estimated that the global infrastructure investment requirement will exceed $94 trillion for the next 25 years. China, the USA, India, and Japan would account for more than half of the global infrastructure investment requirement by the year 2040. The OECD reports suggest that infrastructural investment demands in four key sectors of telecommunications, electricity, surface transport, and water were estimated at US $ 53 trillion by the year 2030. Technological trends are also shaping the infrastructure industry. The trend observed is that the developed economies (OECD) consumed more than 50% of the world's energy resources though having only 20% of the population.

In the context of rapid technological changes, demographic trends, and environmental factors, infrastructural planners ought to design and develop infrastructural projects which are futuristic in nature. Sustainability has become the central theme of infrastructure innovations. In modern perspective, infrastructure developers must give attention to all-round sustainability including financial sustainability, operational sustainability, funding, and technological sustainability. There has been an increasing involvement of institutional investors like pension funds and insurance funds in infrastructural projects with debt and equity financing after the 2008 economic crisis.

This book focuses on the world's largest infrastructural, industrial, and public service projects through the lens of structuring, financing, valuing, and managing risks. The book discusses the cases of 50 mega projects undertaken in different parts of the world. Infrastructure funding requires high upfront costs with long asset life requiring substantial financing. It is also characterized by a lack of liquidity. Infrastructure projects are highly risky due to the costs incurred during the predevelopment and construction stage. Infrastructure projects may not generate positive cash flows during the early phases of the project. The first chapter discusses the trends and challenges faced by the infrastructure industry. COVID-19 has introduced a new set of challenges for infrastructure industry. The following chapters focus on the different financing instruments and risks inherent in financing large projects. The fourth chapter focuses on various aspects of structuring and implementation of the project.

The cases covered in this book are based on the largest projects undertaken by countries and corporates. The Chuo Shinkansen project is a major rail transportation project in Japan based on magnetic levitation system to connect the whole of Japan though rail network. Airbus A3XX, the world's largest passenger aircraft, is the most researched product launch in history. The South North Water Transfer project is the most expensive and expansive infrastructure project in China which brought fundamental changes to the hydrology and ecology of the Yellow and Yangtze river system. Dubailand is one of the most ambitious leisure development projects in the world being built in Dubai. The International Space Station is the largest technology project of all time and is often described as the most expensive project ever constructed at a cost of $160 billion dollars.

Al Maktoum International Airport will be the world's largest global gateway with a capacity to handle 160–260 million passengers. California High Speed Rail is a publicly funded high speed rail system under construction in the US State of California which will connect San Francisco to Los Angeles basin under three hours with speeds of over 200 miles per hour. Crossrail is one of the landmark infrastructure projects ever undertaken in the UK which aims to offer better connections from east to west region. The iconic starfish structure of Beijing Daxing International Airport is the largest single structure airport terminal in the world spanning 7.5 million square feet. Jubail Industrial City is the largest civil engineering project in the world today. The Hong Kong Zhuhai Macao Bridge is the longest bridge cum tunnel sea crossing in the world.

Gotthard Base Tunnel is the world's longest and deepest rail tunnel in Switzerland. Channel Tunnel UK is the longest undersea tunnel in the world with a length of 37.9 km. Doha Metro is designed as one of the most advanced rail transit systems in the world developed by Qatar Railways Development Company. The American Society of Civil Engineers had ranked the Panama Canal as one of the seven wonders of the modern world. Three Gorges Dam is the largest hydroelectric dam in the world in terms of electricity production. One World Trade Center (One WTC) is the main building of the rebuilt World Trade Center complex in Lower Manhattan, New York City. Burj Khalifa, the iconic structure in the UAE, is the tallest man-made structure in the world. The Shanghai World Financial Center is one of the tallest mixed-use skyscraper in the world. The Dolphin Gas project is one of the largest trans-border energy projects in the GCC region. Bhadla Solar Park and Tengger Desert Solar Park are two of the largest solar parks in the world.

Millau viaduct is the tallest bridge in the world. Jiaozhou Bay Bridge in the eastern China's Shandong province is the longest sea bridge in the world. Trans-Siberian Railway is the longest single rail system in the world which spans across three countries and crosses the two continents of Europe and Asia. The Pan American Highway, the longest road on earth, is a network of roads which stretches across the Americas and measures approximately 48,000 km in total length.

Yangshan Deepwater port project made the Port of Shanghai the biggest and busiest terminal in the world. Sakhalin II is termed as one of the largest integrated export-oriented oil and gas projects in the world. Ichthys project is one of the most complex liquefied natural gas projects in the world with the longest subsea pipeline in the Southern Hemisphere. The Kashagan oil field is the first major offshore oil and gas development project in Kazakhstan with one of the largest oil discoveries. Barzan gas project is a joint venture between Qatar gas and Exxon Mobil. The Australian Japan Cable Network (AJCN) is a subsea cable system which offers connectivity and bandwidth options with diverse landings in Australia, Guam, and Japan. Addis Ababa–Djibouti Railway is the first electrified standard gauge railway project in Africa which is a part of the Belt and Road Initiative. Port Mann Bridge, Vancouver, is the widest long span bridge in the world measuring 65 m. Chernobyl's New Safe Confinement is a unique design and construction project in the context that such a huge structure was constructed for the first time at a heavily contaminated site. Kashiwazaki-Kariwa nuclear station is the largest nuclear power station in the world. Kudankulam Nuclear Power Plant is the largest nuclear power plant in India. Boundary Dam power station became the first power station in the world to successfully use the CCS technology.

The Boeing 787-9 Dreamliner is one of the world's most technologically advanced aircraft. It is the first airplane in which the composite materials form approximately 50% of the primary structure. Shanghai Metro system is the biggest metro system by route length with 743 km. The Sao Francisco River Basin project is strategically important for Brazil on account of its potential in agriculture, hydropower, tourism, and urban and industrial water supply. Kazan smart city project is a greenfield development project which is being developed using the latest advancements in urban planning and engineering. Masdar City is the sustainable city project in Abu Dhabi, UAE. Delhi–Mumbai Industrial Corridor (DMIC) is a mega infrastructure project in India covering a distance of 1438 km between the political capital (Delhi) and the business capital (Mumbai) of India. Golden Quadrilateral Highway is the fifth longest highway project in the world with a total length of 5846 km. Hong Kong Disneyland is a US$3.6 billion theme park complex in Hong Kong. Jamnagar Refinery is the world's largest refinery and petrochemicals complex owned by Reliance Industries. The Big Dig (Central Artery/Tunnel Project) was a mega road infrastructure project which was undertaken in Boston, Massachusetts, USA, to improve the flow of traffic and avoid travel congestion across Boston. The North South Corridor program is a multimodal (road, rail, and ports) transcontinental interconnector project which basically aims to connect Cape Town in the south and Cairo in the north. Libya's Great Man-Made River project is one of the largest civil engineering projects in the world, involving the abstraction of ancient groundwater from the Sahara Desert and the transportation of water over hundreds of kilometers to the coast of Libya.

Dubai, United Arab Emirates   B Rajesh Kumar

Acknowledgments

I would like to thank the production and editorial staff at Springer who guided this book through the publishing process. I wish to acknowledge the valuable guidance and support of Rocio Torregrosa, Associate Editor at Springer. I thank Parthiban Kannan, Project Coordinator, and his team for all the support. I acknowledge the content of various websites and sources of information to which I referred. I acknowledge the permission granted by OECD library and IJ Global to use their data in my book.

Contents

1	Trends in Infrastructure Industry	1
2	Infrastructure Financing Instruments	31
3	Risks Inherent in Project Finance and Its Mitigation	55
4	Structuring and Implementation of the Project	81
5	Case 1: The Chuo Shinkansen Project, Japan	87
6	Case 2: Developing the World's Largest Passenger Aircraft-Airbus A3XX	91
7	Case 3: South North Water Transfer Project China	101
8	Case 4: Dubailand Project	107
9	Case 5: International Space Station	111
10	Case 6: Al Maktoum International Airport	117
11	Case 7: California High Speed Rail Project	123
12	Case 8: London Cross Rail Project	131
13	Case 9: Beijing Daxing International Airport	139
14	Case: 10 Jubail II Industrial City	145
15	Case 11: Hong Kong Zhuhai Macao Bridge (HZMB)	151
16	Case 12: Gotthard Base Tunnel (GBT)	157
17	Case 13: Channel Tunnel UK	163
18	Case 14: Doha Metro	171
19	Case 15: Panama Canal Expansion	177
20	Case 16: Three Gorges Dam—The World's Largest Hydroelectric Plant	183

21	Case 17: One World Trade Center	187
22	Case 18: Making of the Tallest Building—Burj Khalifa	191
23	Case 19: Shanghai World Financial Center	195
24	Case 20: Dolphin Gas Project	199
25	Case 21: Bhadla Solar Park	205
26	Case 22: Tengger Desert Solar Park China	209
27	Case 23: Millau Viaduct—The Tallest Bridge, France	211
28	Case 24: Jiaozhou Bay Bridge	215
29	Case 25: Trans-Siberian Railway	219
30	Case 26: Pan-American Highway	223
31	Case 27: Port of Shanghai	227
32	Case 28: Sakhalin Project–II	233
33	Case 29: Ichthys LNG Project	237
34	Case 30: Kashagan Oil Field Development Project	241
35	Case 31: Barzan Gas Project	247
36	Case 32: Australian Japan Cable	251
37	Case 33: Addis Ababa–Djibouti Railway	255
38	Case 34: Port Mann Bridge Vancouver	259
39	Case 35: Chernobyl New Safe Confinement Project	263
40	Case 36: Kashiwazaki Kariwa Nuclear Project, Japan	267
41	Case 37: Kudankulam Nuclear Power Plant, India	271
42	Case 38: Boundary Dam Power Station	275
43	Case 39: Boeing 787 Dreamliner Project	279
44	Case 40: Shanghai Metro System	285
45	Case 41: São Francisco River Basin Project	289
46	Case 42: Kazan Smart City Project	293
47	Case 43: Masdar City	297
48	Case 44: Delhi Mumbai Industrial Corridor Project	301
49	Case 45: Golden Quadrilateral Highway, India	305

50	Case 46: Hong Kong Disney Land Project	309
51	Case 47: Jamnagar Refinery Project, India	315
52	Case 48: Big Dig Project	319
53	Case 49: North-South Corridor Road/Rail Project	325
54	Case 50: Great Man Made River Water Supply Project, Libya	329

Trends in Infrastructure Industry   1

Modern Infrastructure is critical to economic development which affects the quality of life. Right information, policy leadership and supportive financing environments are determinants for infrastructure to improve economic growth and community wellbeing. The global infrastructure study report by Oxford Economics estimate that global infrastructure investment requirement will amount to $94 trillion during the period 2016–2040. To achieve this target, nations have to increase the proportion of GDP to infrastructure funding to 3.5% compared to 3%. Global infrastructure spending had been around 3% of the world GDP over the last decade. According to World Economic Forum, worldwide investment in infrastructure is expected to be US$79 trillion by 2040.

Infrastructure have become the mainstream part of the alternatives industry and has grown substantially during the past decade. The total assets under management for infrastructure industry have increased from $129 billion in 2009 to $582 billion by 2019. There are about 707 active infrastructure fund managers with about 4000 institutions making allocations to infrastructure. Preqin 2020 global infrastructure report suggest that Europe needs to invest about EUR 270bn a year between now and 2030 to build new infrastructure.

Asia region accounts for the lion share of approximately 54% of global infrastructure needs by 2040. China, US, India and Japan would account for more than half of the global infrastructure investment requirement by 2040. A further investment of $3.5 trillion would be required to meet the United Nations' Sustainable Development Goals for electricity and water. Infrastructure investment is of paramount importance for sustainable development in both developed and developing economies. The focus on infrastructure through construction and operation of new and upgraded infrastructure projects facilitates economic activity through job creation and increased demand for goods and services. Infrastructure investment underpins productivity.

There are issues of underinvestment in infrastructure even in developed countries with strong financial system. Infrastructure requires huge up-front investments and returns are expected after many years. The risk of uncertain returns in the context of changing technologies creates huge challenges for financing the projects even in well-functioning capital market. These risks can be mitigated to some extent through government regulation or through means such as direct government provision of infrastructure. Infrastructure projects provide positive externalities for society in the form of benefits which is greater than the private benefits generated for operators.

Demographic changes are central factors which determine infrastructure demand. For example, African region's population is expected to exceed 2 billion by the year 2040. The total infrastructure investment forecast for Africa is estimated to be \$4.3 trillion by 2040 or \$174 billion per year (Oxford Economics Report). The population in the Oceania region is expected to reach 54 million by the year 2040. In African region, over 20% of total fixed investment is dedicated to infrastructure compared to 9% in Americas. US is expected to invest \$8.5 trillion in infrastructure during the period 2016–2040 to account for expected economic and demographic growth. During the period 2007–2015, China had initiated huge infrastructure investment which accounted for 30% of all global infrastructure investment (Oxford Economics Report). By 2040, China is expected to spend over \$26 trillion as part of infrastructure investment which translates into \$1.1 trillion per year. The population growth in India is expected to propel significant demand for infrastructure in India over the next 25 years with investment needs of over \$3.9 trillion. Europe is expected to invest \$12.8 trillion in infrastructure during the period 2016–2040. The Oceania region representing Australia and New Zealand will invest approximately \$1.7 trillion during the period 2016–2040. By 2016, developing economies accounted for 62% of total infrastructure spending. China accounts for 29% of the world's infrastructure expenditure.

The Paris Agreement aims to keep the global temperature rise in this century well below 2 °C above the pre-industrial levels. International Renewable Energy Agency (IEA) 2017 report suggest that to maintain the above limit in terms of temperature, approximately \$39.6 trillion of investment in power sector is required during the period 2016–2050.

Infrastructure investments aim to produce predictable and stable cash flows over the long term. The current scenario indicates that infrastructure investment decisions are facing new challenges in the context of fracturing of societies, markets and institutions. This trend suggests increasing gap between the protectionists and free-marketers.

In Asian region, massive cross border projects such as Kuala Lumpur-Singapore high speed rail (MyHSR), Thailand's Eastern Economic Corridor, the China Thailand high speed railway project and the China–Pakistan Economic Corridor are gaining momentum.

Infrastructure planners must adapt to the new changes in the context that technology is undergoing rapid and fundamental innovative changes. Similar drastic changes are also witnessed with respect to social norms, demographic trends and environmental factors. In the changing scenario, infrastructure planners must focus on designing and development of infrastructure projects which are futuristic in nature. For example, for the development of new high speed rail network, impetus ought to be given on application of technologies such as hyper loops or drones for more feasible solutions. Transport planners must consider introduction of Autonomous Vehicles (AV) as a part of transport investments and spatial planning. The concept of AVs has the potential to create new opportunities for business to adopt innovative practices on import of goods and distribution of products. Artificial intelligence will have a major role to play with respect to health infrastructure development.

Sustainability have become the central theme of infrastructure innovations. In modern perspective, infrastructure developers must give attention to all round sustainability including financial sustainability, operational sustainability, funding and technological sustainability. The pace of infrastructure development is showing distinct patterns in developing and developed nations. In developed mature markets, the replacement and upgrades for infrastructural development are slow to emerge, whereas in some developing nations, the infrastructure projects are being completed at great speed. For example, development of high speed rail in China and infrastructure projects in Middle East. Asset management techniques of infrastructural projects have become more sophisticated in a digital environment and its enhanced security is of paramount importance. Governments need to identify these strategically important assets and develop guidelines to protect them.

Another trend observed is the emergence of dynamic pricing in a wide variety of infrastructure services. For decades, firms have been using variable pricing which facilitated managing demand and ration capacity for infrastructure owners and operators. In energy sector, it helped institutions to manage peak versus off peak times, while in transport sector, it helped commuters to shift their travel times. For example, rail travel was cheaper outside rush hours. Recent trends suggest the emergence of dynamic pricing wherein charges are adjusted in real time to reflect actual capacity, supply and demand. Dynamic pricing models are adopted by low cost airlines, railway companies and app based companies such as Uber and Grab. The availability of real time data, sophisticated algorithms have enhanced firms' capability to calibrate their prices more efficiently. Increasing private equity investment in infrastructural projects is another trend which is observed.

1.1 Sustainability in Infrastructure Industry

The global urban population which is currently around 3.9 billion will increase to approximately 6.3 billion by the year 2050 which will constitute around 70% of the total global population. In this scenario, it will be a herculean task for urban planning, construction, water and waste management projects to cater to the needs of ever burgeoning urban population. Another challenge in terms of sustainability is due to problems which arises due to climate change. UN Habitat report suggest that cities consume 78% of the world energy and produce more than 60% of greenhouse gas emissions. Almost 90% of urban areas are located along coastlines which lead to predicted rise in sea levels. Studies find that climate driven disasters account for approximately 91% of the 7255 major disasters which occurred during the period 1999–2017. Cities in emerging economies pose huge challenges in terms of sustainability due to its characteristics such as informal settlements which lack infrastructure and services. The European Union has earmarked EUR 100 billion as a part of the European Green Deal to make Europe the first climate neutral country.

The International Monetary Fund Report estimates that emerging market and low income developing countries require investments to a tune of US$2.6 trillion to meet the UN Sustainable Development Goals by 2030. This will be representing approximately 2.5% of the 2030 world GDP. The World Bank estimates that new climate smart infrastructure would cost low and middle income countries in the range of 2–8% of their GDP per year through 2030. In terms of value, the investment would cost between US$640 billion and US$2.7 trillion. International Finance Corporation report suggest emerging market cities require climate related investments in renewable energy, public transport, waste and water to a tune of US$3.1 trillion by 2030. Measures such as cooperation and partnerships between impact investors, sustainable businesses, governments and financial institutions is essential for enhancing the investment for sustainable infrastructure.

1.2 Global Trends in Infrastructure financing

OECD reports [1, 2] suggest that infrastructural investment demands in five key sectors of telecommunications, electricity, surface transport and water were estimated at US$53 trillion by the year 2030. This amounts to approximately US$1.8 trillion per year which is equivalent to 2.5% of world GDP on average. Energy generation will need US$12 trillion and other energy related infrastructure would need an investment of US$6 trillion. Altogether the total investments in infrastructure is estimated to reach US$71 trillion which is about 3.5% of world GDP.

According to Mckinsey report [3], approximately 3.8% of world GDP had been spent on infrastructure during the initial decade of this century. This amounted to an annual amount of US$2400 billion as applied to the 2010 GDP. According to Mckinsey report [4], infrastructure spending has declined from 3.6% of GDP in 1980 to 2.8% by the year 2008 in the developed world. At the same time the infrastructure spending rose from 3.5% to 5.7% in emerging economies during the above period.

In the modern era banks, pension funds, insurance companies, sovereign wealth funds are involved in infrastructure investment due to its attractiveness in terms of long term and stable returns. The global financial crisis of 2008 proved that bond financing as a part of investment portfolios reinforced the concept of infrastructure as a safe haven.

Pwc Global Infrastructure Report 2020 suggest that the global requirement for infrastructure investment is estimated at US$3.9 trillion annually with major requirements from emerging countries. The need for increased infrastructure is propelled by forces such as urbanization, population growth and economic expansion. The urban population is expected to grow from 3.9 billion in 2020 to 6.3 billion by the year 2050. The Asian Development Bank estimates that developing countries have to spend around US$1.7 trillion annually in infrastructure across Asia by 2030 for sustainable economic development. The global population of informal settlements with lack of basic resources such as clean drinking water, sanitation and lighting will be approximately 2 billion by 2030. This constitute 25% of the projected global population with over 80% of affected people located in regions of Southeast Asia, sub-Saharan Africa, Central and South Asia. Governments, multilateral development banks, international financial institutions and other sources of private finance play an important role in infrastructure financing. Multinational development banks are actively seeking private capital through mechanisms such as blended financing. World Bank report suggest that pension funds, sovereign wealth funds, mutual funds and other institutional investors contribute only 0.67% of total global investment in developing countries. The low level of investment is due to various risk factors such as political instability, currency risk, regulatory aspects and tariffs in developing countries. The gap between capital demand and supply particularly in the initial stages of the life cycle of projects in developing countries is widening over a period. Governments and institutions have focused to narrow the gap by providing funding sources for project preparation facilities (PPFs) in the form of platforms to support activities early in a project life cycle and upstream opportunities for project development and investment. Private capital funders are reluctant to invest in greenfield projects on account of budgeting development costs and revenue uncertainties due to lack of an operating history. A positive sign is the growing involvement of institutional investors like pension funds and insurance funds in infrastructural projects with debt and equity financing after the 2008 economic crisis.

A major trend with respect to the financing landscape is the global shift from a "brown" to "green" economy. The financing costs for supporting the UN's Sustainable Development Goals (SDGs) have been estimated at the range of US$5 trillion to US$7 trillion annually through 2030. According to Sustainable Investment Alliance (GSIA) 2019 report, the global sustainable, responsible and impact (SRI) investments amounted to US$30.7 trillion by the year 2018. Europe had the largest proportion with US$14.1 trillion of SRI assets under management followed by the US with US$12 trillion in 2018. According to the Climate Bonds Initiative, the total issuance of green bonds for environmentally friendly projects was valued at US$250 billion in the year 2019.

1.3 Infrastructural Developments in Different Regions

The American Society of Civil Engineers estimate that there exist a deficit of over $4 trillion in investment in infrastructural sectors such as transportation, energy and social infrastructure in US. The focus is on more PPP projects. In Canada the focus is on greater use of private sector for infrastructural development. Australia also focusses on PPP. Australia follows the model of "asset recycling "where the government sells the existing assets and uses the proceeds to build new infrastructure assets. In comparison to other developed countries, Australia 's population is witnessing growth. According to World Bank statistics, the growth rate of Australian population has averaged 1.7% compared to 0.8% in the US, 0.3% in the Euro region and 0.7% in OECD countries. The Australian Bureau of Statistics (ABS) projects that the population will increase from the current 25 million to over 42 million by 2066. This trend will translate into greater demand for infrastructure assets in terms of transport, energy, and telecommunications. Promotion of private investment in infrastructure is a stated policy of successive Australian governments. Sydney Harbour Tunnel was the first PPP in the country which was successfully completed in the year 1992. According to the Bureau of Infrastructure, Transport and Regional Economics (BITRE) of Australia, approximately 197 PPPs and privatizations were completed during the period 1980–2017. Major transportation projects include the AUD17 billion Westconnex and AUD2.9 billion North Connex projects in Sydney and the AUD8.3 billion City & Southwest Metro project. The second Sydney airport valued at AUD5.3 billion is scheduled for completion in the year 2026. Macquarie Infrastructure and Real Assets (MIRA), one of the largest infrastructure fund is active in Australian market for more than 20 years.

The European Commission introduced the "Juncker Plan in the year 2014. It is also known as the "EU Infrastructure Investment Plan". The original plan had estimated investments worth EUR 315 billion. During the economic recession many European nations such as Spain, Portugal and Ireland faced prolonged period of austerity and many nations in the region had made substantial cuts in infrastructure spending. Unlike US and Europe, the Gulf region is developing huge infrastructure assets at a high pace since the region had little infrastructure six decades back. The region has invested heavily to diversify its economy from oil and gas to other sectors. The region is also witnessing growth in population and public infrastructural requirements. The gulf region has invested heavily in infrastructural development projects such as airports, ports, roads and water. Before the economic crisis, Dubai developed economic free zones for developing infrastructural facilities for ports and airports along with major icons such as the Palm and Burj Khalifa. The Port of Jebel Ali developed by DP World serves as a major center facilitating trading activities. UAE has pipeline of projects which are worth over US$300 billion. The Sub Saharan African region's infrastructural development is led by its largest sovereign infrastructure investor and trading partner, China with initiatives such as the Belt and Road Initiative (BRI). According to UN estimates, the sub Saharan population is expected to grow to 2 billion by 2050 and the urbanization rate will be approximately 58% by that time. According to African Development Bank, Africa's infrastructure spending requirement is estimated in the range of US$130 billion to $170 billion annually. These investments are required in sectors of power, transport, telecoms and water infrastructure. China had consolidated its position as a key stakeholder in the sub Saharan's infrastructure growth with investment flows which averaged US$12.6 billion during the period 2012–2017. According to the Infrastructure Consortium for Africa (ICA), sovereign investment flows from France averaged US$2.2 billion over the period. Private participants have started investments in African infrastructure. Investec Asset Management have a strategic partnership agreement with China Africa Development Fund (CADF) for investments worth US$10 billion across PPPs in energy and transportation sectors. Allianz Global Investors have committed investments worth $120 million which are structured as 12-year loan to the Emerging Africa Infrastructure Fund (EAIF).

1.4   Sectoral Trends

To address growing energy demand in the context of environmental concerns, power sector is adopting emerging technologies such as renewable power, distributed generation, smart grids and battery storage. The worldwide battery storage market is expected to more than double from US$6.1 billion in 2018 to US$13.1 billion by 2023. The trend observed is that almost 75% of new global electricity generation capacity in 2019 have used renewable energy sources such as solar and wind. Industrial power users are employing IoT to increase operational efficiency. The modern technological transformation creates huge challenge for the business models of utilities companies. Urban transportation is facing the challenge of technological disruption. To face the demands of increasing urbanization, city planners have moved towards autonomous vehicles (AVs) and electric vehicles (EVs) such as robo-taxis and shuttles. In modern world, the mobility environment is fast changing with micro mobility options such as dockless bikes and scooters and ride sharing options like Uber. The optimal smart mobility option will be centered around a smartphone which can link a journey which span rail and road to last mile personal mobility options such as ebikes or scooters. Travels which span multiple cities can be accessible to users through a single interface. Development of such capabilities require connectivity of physical infrastructure such as rails and roads to operational technology which generates the data by means of sensors and payment systems. Digital infrastructure in form of Wi-Fi and mobile connectivity and IT systems for data management are also key integral part of such a system.[1] Limitations in terms of ground capacity may lead to adoption of more feasible air mobility solutions such as flying Taxis. In this context a major development is the experimental tests carried out by Uber Air, German firms and Airbus to implement piloted flying taxis between airports and sporting venues for Paris 2024 Olympics. In Switzerland, lab samples between local hospitals are delivered through drones. In Iceland, drones are engaged in delivering parcels from online retailers to customers.

Technology is facilitating the improvement of efficiency of project construction and delivery using robotics to automate construction processes. Advanced sensors using 5G networks are facilitating transport infrastructure to collect real time data for creation of digital twins for projects. Construction industry have adopted data-driven technologies such as Building Information Modelling (BIM) and full site data analysis to make reliable budgeting and scheduling. Technological innovations have shortened the life cycles and asset timelines. This changing trend will have immense consequences for contractors and finance providers in terms of shorter term

---

[1] PwC Global infrastructure trends Report 2020.

contracts and a more flexible financing approach. The trend of critical infrastructure assets such as power plants being controlled by cloud based technologies introduces the risk of cyber threats.

The adoption of modern technology into infrastructure projects require changes in policy focus and new financing solutions.

1.5 Infrastructure Financing and Role of Institutional Investors

The financial sector plays a vital role in infrastructure investment. Financial institutions provide short term finances, cash requirements and long term finance for infrastructural projects. Disintermediation and growth of capital markets have fundamentally altered the structure of the financial sector. Institutional investors such as pension funds, insurance companies, mutual funds and sovereign wealth funds have become one of the main sources of long term capital. There has been an increasing mismatch with respect to the amount and time horizon of available capital and demand for long term finance. Banking regulations such as Basel III have negatively affected the ability of banks to provide long term financing. Institutional investors such as pension funds and insurance companies are viewed as alternative source of financing. According to OECD data, pension funds held US\$32.3 trillion assets in the OECD area and US\$0.7 trillion in other jurisdictions. Global financial institutions held assets of over 378.9 trillion US dollars by the year 2018. Pension funds and insurers are major investors in a large number of developed economies with assets representing over 60% of GDP in countries such as Canada, the Netherlands, the United Kingdom and the United States. Institutional investors provide long term capital with investment portfolios consisting of two main asset classes of bonds and equities. Institutional investors have been increasing allocation to alternative assets such as hedge funds, real estate, private equity and infrastructure which includes green infrastructure.

Institutional investors have been increasing allocation to alternative assets such as hedge funds, real estate, private equity and, infrastructure with the focus on green infrastructure. Institutional investors such as pension funds will play a significant role in bridging the infrastructure gap in future.

1.6 Role of Private Sector in Infrastructure Development

Over the decades, public capital investment in infrastructure have declined in OECD countries. The average ratio of capital spent in fixed investment to GDP fell from 4% in 1980 to approximately 3% in 2005. According to OECD estimates, the global infrastructure requirements will be approximately US\$50 trillion by the year 2030. The International Energy Agency estimates requirement to the tune of US\$45 trillion by 2050 for the mitigation of the effects of climate change. Investments in such huge magnitude cannot be financed solely by public finance. Privatization in countries such as UK resulted in a strong regulated asset base for electricity, water, gas, transmission lines and airport businesses for raising private finance through debt and equity. The American Society of Civil Engineers have estimated over a $4 trillion deficit in investment in sectors such as transportation, energy and social infrastructure on account of failing infrastructure and ageing.

The public sector's effectiveness in managing projects had limitations on account of constraints on public finance and failure to deliver efficient investment with misallocation across sectors. Over time, the state changed its role from owner and provider of public services to purchaser and regulator of them. With the decline in government investment in infrastructure, privatization became the key driver. During the period 1990–2013, total privatization of approximately US$900 billion happened in OECD countries with the maximum share accounted by sectors such as utilities, transport and telecommunications. Since 1990s, major countries have increased private sector participation in the financing and implementation of infrastructure projects through "project finance". New business models with public private partnership (PPP) started using project financing techniques thereby enhancing the use of private sector capital and expertise. Governments in advanced, middle income and developing countries are employing PPP models in major infrastructural projects in transport sector. PPP can be categorized into two major categories on the basis of remuneration by tolls levied by the private partner or on the basis of available payments from the government contracting agency. The presence of availability payments signifies lower risk for investors and attract bank loans with insurance and hedging instruments. The tolled facilities require larger equity investments at a higher cost. The role of specialized investment banks and capital market funds is of much significance for availability payment based PPPs which require extensive risk appraisal by investors.

1.7 Private Infrastructure Finance in Europe

The public investment declined from 5% of GDP in the 1970s to 2.5% of GDP in the decade of 2000. Infrastructure investment amounted to around EUR 400 billion in the mid-2000s. Under the framework of private capital spending on infrastructure, project finance contributed 0.33% of EU GDP. Approximately 0.19% of GDP is attributed to the financing of public private partnerships (PPP) and 0.14% to non PPP project finance. This translates to a volume of about EUR 22 billion and EUR 17 billion per annum, respectively. Loan financing constitutes 80% of the capital structure of project finance. Bond financing and equity financing comprises 6% and 14% of the project finance with respect to European region. The focus is more on social infrastructure rather on economic infrastructure. According to European Commission estimates, infrastructure investment needs amounted to an average of EUR 150–200 billion per annum during the period 2010–2020. OECD countries account for more than half of the investments in global telecom, over 40% in the electricity sector, roughly two thirds in the rail & road sectors.

By the end of the twentieth century, UK government initiated the steps of privatization of utilities and promotion of private finance initiatives (PFIs) to develop infrastructure market. Privatization led to the creation of a strong regulated asset base for electricity, water and other utilities. New infrastructure equity players created a new infrastructure sector for long term bond and active bank market.

Private capital is basically provided in two forms-corporate finance which involves operating or service companies operating in infrastructure sectors and project finance which is basically a contractual financing arrangement in infrastructure financing.

1.8 Sources of Infrastructure Financing

1.8.1 Debt Finance

Historically the large majority of project financing debt have been funded by banks. As a result of economic crisis, mismatch exists between the amount and time duration of capital availability for infrastructure projects. As a result of economic crisis, the constraints on bank debt levels have negatively impacted infrastructure markets. The financial crisis had also hampered the working of monolines which focused on insuring bond issuers such as municipal governments against default. Bond issuers basically buy this insurance to upgrade the credit worthiness of their bonds. The decline of monolines have impacted the capital markets for infrastructure.

Bond finance by corporations had been an important source of financing in infrastructure sector. Many firms use the bond market to re-finance existing debt at more attractive rates.

1.8.2 Sources of Capital-Equity

Corporate financing of infrastructural projects in developing nations have picked up momentum in recent years. Transnational companies based in developing countries are increased their investments in infrastructure projects in countries such as Hong Kong, India, UAE, Turkey, Singapore, Russia and Malaysia. On account of high risks, long gestation period and high capital intensity of such projects, these firms use different modes of entry such as sole investors, or via special purpose vehicles or consortiums in cooperation with other investors. This facilitates risk mitigation.

1.9 Alternate Sources of Financing: Institutional Investors

The main exposure of institutional investors like pension funds in infrastructure sector is through listed companies and fixed income instruments. Nowadays infrastructure is recognized as a distinct asset class. Investments in unlisted infrastructure sector is the emerging trend wherein pension funds and other institutional investors invests in less liquid, long term assets such as infrastructure. The suitability of long

1.9 Alternate Sources of Financing: Institutional Investors

term maturity infrastructural assets often matches institutional investors' long term horizons. Infrastructural investments provide attractive benefits to pension funds and insurers in terms of assistance to hedge their liability driven investments through immunization techniques like duration hedging. Infrastructure projects can be considered as long term investments for institutional investors for matching the long duration of pension liabilities. Infrastructure assets linked to inflation can hedge inflation sensitive pension fund liabilities of institutional investors. Institutional investments are attractive for pension funds in terms of profitability and risk and many pension funds have successful experiences. The incentive for pension funds to invest in infrastructural projects is attributed to the low interest rate environment. Infrastructure sector tends to operate like natural, regulated monopolies, or oligopolies with reduced or non-market competition which provides stable asset values for pension funds. Infrastructure projects have greater cash flow stability when projects have matured and offers good risk return trade off.

Pension funds' investments in infrastructure assets are particularly relevant when governments have budgetary limitations and banks are forced to disinvest these assets on account of financial regulation. In this context, countries are introducing regulatory changes to attract increased pension fund investments in infrastructure. A Wharton Study (2017) suggest that on average 72 pension funds across 21 countries invest 5.6% of their assets in infrastructural projects. Europe need to raise EUR 1.5–2 trillion in funds for infrastructure investment by the year 2020. At the same time US will need US$1.7–3 trillion during the above period.

In spite of advantages, investing in infrastructure is a complex process which involves the alignment of different stakeholders' interests such as shareholders, financial institutions, regulators, insurance companies and EPC contractors.

With respect to regulations, the Anglo-Saxon countries like the UK, US, Australia, Canada, Belgium and Netherlands have no quantitative limits on infrastructure investment. Canada promotes direct investment in unlisted infrastructure asset projects and also maintains significant proportion of its infrastructural portfolio abroad. Canada also have one of its most developed project bond markets. Australia have specialized in promotion of specialized financing vehicles managed by infrastructure funds. Large pension funds particularly in Australia and Canada have high allocation of 10–15% among some pension funds.

Another trend observed is the focus of institutional investors on green infrastructure investment. Insurance companies have developed a set of principles for responsible insurance. Many insurance companies have made investments in clean infrastructure projects. By the year 2012, the German insurer Allianz had invested up to EUR 1.5 billion in renewable projects. Allianz made investments in 34 wind farms of 658 MW and 7 solar parks. The UK insurance company Aviva have invested 1.5% of its assets in green infrastructural projects. The investments are done through the Clean Tech fund. Moreover, the company also invests in clean energy projects through its private equity investment vehicles. The asset management subsidiary of Aviva has a European Renewable Energy Fund which invests in solar, biomass, biogas and wind projects. MetLife have commitments to reduce its GHG emissions by 30% from 2019 levels and originate US$20 billion in new green investments by 2030. Earlier MetLife had purchased stake in Texas's largest photovoltaic project. Munich Re had issued subordinated green bond of value amounting to EUR 1.25 billion to finance or refinance sustainable projects related to energy efficiency, clean transportation, green buildings, sustainable water and waste water management. Prudential and its European fund management arm, M&G investments had been investing in infrastructure for over 80 years. Prudential is one of the leading managers of infrastructure assets through holdings in private debt and equity as well as through corporate bonds and public equity investments.

1.10 Superannuation Funds/Insurers

Governments in different regions of world are facilitating financial investors such as superannuation funds and insurers to provide funding for projects. The liabilities of these financial institutions are long term in nature and hence they can naturally match with the long term inflation indexed returns of different infrastructure projects. Superannuation funds are not willing to take construction risks of many infrastructure assets and hence additional structuring through bank guarantees similar to those involved in EIB funded transactions, or debt to equity synthetic transactions become essential. The AMP Capital debt fund has 21 investors which includes pension funds and government entities from countries such as Japan, US, UK, Australia and Hong Kong. The fund has a total investment commitment of EUR 326 million. This fund invests in subordinated debt with tenor in the range of 6–7 years. The target sectors of the fund are regulated utilities, transport and social infrastructure.

IDBI Indian Infrastructure Debt Fund aims to raise US$5 billion in funds to invest in the infrastructure sector in India. The UK government have established the UK Infrastructure Investment Platform to facilitate investment in infrastructure by pension funds. Specialist infrastructure fund managers focus on PPP investment. A new trend observed is the establishment of infrastructure trusts to facilitate the identification, management and investment of major projects. The City of Chicago had set up the US$7 billion Chicago Infrastructure Trust (CIT) to facilitate private sector investment from institutional investors such as pension funds, insurers, endowments, sovereigns and private equity. CIT facilitated the investment of US$1 billion in energy efficiency investments with funds from Citibank, Macquarie, JP Morgan and Ullico.

1.11 Challenges for Infrastructure Investments by Institutional Investors

Large investors only have the leverage to invest directly in infrastructure projects. Collective investment vehicles such as infrastructure funds are faced with problems of high fees. Debt instruments such as bonds for institutional investors to access infrastructure projects are often scarce. Regulatory barriers within the framework of risk based solvency standards have become a constraint for pension funds and insurers to invest in infrastructure and other alternative asset classes. Institutional investors have a preference for brown field type investments which are less risky and more aligned with long term investment horizon. Institutional investors are reluctant to invest in green infrastructure on account of energy and environment regulatory and policy uncertainty and also on account of risks related to new technology related projects. Lack of proper investment vehicles for newer clean technology related projects is another constraint faced by institutional investors.

1.12 Impact of Global Financial Crisis 2008 on Infrastructure Financing

The economic crisis of 2008 led significant trends with respect to infrastructure spending. The governments increased infrastructure spending as a tactic for economic stimulus. Tightened credit markets led to constrained debt financing for infrastructural delivery models both in public and private sector. Governments also found difficult to fund infrastructure projects. Wholesale funding and interbank lending also declined significantly. The Basel III and Solvency II rules required banks to hold higher levels of capital against long term loans. As a result, long term project financing became expensive and less attractive for banks. Infrastructure investment became an integral part of the economic stimulus developed by nations. The European Union had committed $200 billion for infrastructural financing. During the crisis, India committed investments of around $30 billion for infrastructure upgradation. China had made commitments of half of its $585 billion stimulus package towards infrastructure development. Australian government made commitments of $42 billion as part of its Nation Building Stimulus Plan.

The global financial crisis of 2008 provided valuable lessons for the infrastructure finance market. Before the crisis, many infrastructure assets were financed with short term debt. After the crisis many of these assets had to undergo debt restructuring on account of losses on investment. Many infrastructure long term bond holders had to hold on their investment through the crisis and the infrastructure investments turned out to be a safe haven in the midst of crisis. After the crisis new platforms consisting of long term equity and lenders emerged to refinance current assets or fund new assets.

1.13 Impact of Covid 19 on Infrastructure Industry

COVID-19 has introduced new set of challenges for infrastructure industry. The fallout of the crisis will manifest in the form of changes in demand and specific impacts in operational resilience, technology and sustainability. It is important to provide the required infrastructure on an affordable, socially equitable and environmentally sustainable basis. New and emerging technologies will disrupt the way through which capital infrastructural projects are delivered. Covid period with lockdown measures have resulted in dramatic decline in public transport and road infrastructure usage. There are chances that remote working would lead to permanent shift in working patterns with consequential impacts on other industries such as real estates. The potential shift from mass transit to micro form of mobility options could affect future infrastructure planning. The pandemic has severely impacted airline and freight industries. Aviation may have to consider fundamental changes in how airports are designed. Port owners and operators would be compelled to switch to a more localized supply chains. The power sector has also been affected due to lockdown measures. Another lesson learned is the need of operational resilience in the context of fragility of supply chains. On account of heavy reliance on Asian manufacturing, the crisis created scenarios whereby companies had to identify secondary suppliers from local areas as logistics options were closed. The future industry might require deployment of supply chain visibility tools which would provide transparency into capacity constraints at first, second and third tier suppliers. Enhanced use of tools and technologies are required to develop predictive models for proactive scheduling and dynamic planning.

Closure of construction sites is another trend observed on account of COVID-19. Travel restrictions have a profound influence on labor availability. Construction industry is significantly vulnerable to disruptions in onsite operations. This trend might lead to acceleration of new types of project workflows such as modular and offsite production. The process of shifting onsite construction sites into manufacturing environment will require standardized designs, streamlined processes and automated production techniques such as advanced robotics and Internet of Things (IoT).

Technology adoption is the likely solution for the problems of underinvestment in advanced technologies. There is a greater need for technological investment in artificial intelligence and robotics for infrastructure industry. Technologies such as intelligent drones can improve preventive maintenance as the requirement of onsite workers is reduced using this technology. Sustainability issues also affects infrastructure industry. Infrastructure related stimulus must focus on activities which reduce carbon consumption. Pwc Global Infrastructure Report 2020 estimate suggest that 70% increase in future greenhouse gas emissions is expected from future infrastructure. Infrastructure investors have increased their emphasis on environmental, social and governance (ESG) issues and focus on environmentally sustainable assets.

Projects which are financed as PPPs with demand-based contracts—such as airports and toll roads are vulnerable to external shocks on account of long term impact of COVID-19. On account of the impact of COVID-19, investment commitments in the first half of 2020 amounted to US$21.9 billion across 128 projects which reflected a decline of 56% compared to the same period in 2019.[2]

---

[2] https://ppi.worldbank.org/en/ppi

1.14 Megatrends Shaping Infrastructure Industry: A Reflection[3]

Urbanization, rising population and increasing disparity between rural and urban areas have fostered new clusters of urban economies resulting in large infrastructure investments and new challenges with respect to managing overcrowding and congestion. The emerging infrastructure planning will revolve around the needs of megacities and tier 2/3 cities. Ageing workforce population would result in infrastructure workforce shortfall which would delay project completion times.

Stakeholders would pressure on infrastructural companies for greater sustainability practices in the context of increased awareness of Environmental, Social and Governance initiatives. In the context of ecosystem of sharing economy, companies would be under pressure to increase efficiency and productivity.

Ageing and inadequate global infrastructure pose threat to human health and safety and can cost billions in lost productivity. Innovative investments are required for sustainable and more reliable infrastructure networks.

In terms of market demand, emerging economies account for maximum investment in infrastructure. China is the world's leading destination for FDI. The main highlight of China's global development strategy is its infrastructural investment in 152 countries and international organization across the world. One of the current major project is Belt and Road Initiative. Other emerging countries like India are also in the forefront of infrastructure development.

Globally there is an infrastructure financing gap of $15 trillion between projected investment and the amount needed to provide adequate global infrastructure by the year 2040. Higher risks are faced by modern multibillion dollar mega infrastructure projects. Another trend observed is the increased participation of private sector in infrastructure projects.

Globalization and international trade are facilitated by infrastructural development. The global divide in terms of widening gaps in wealth, digital access, education and health makes infrastructural development a complex issue for nations in developing world.

Today's multipolar world is characterized by challenges posed by emerging economies and coalitions against the historical dominance of the G7 states.

Technological trends are also shaping the infrastructure industry. The development of advanced materials such as geo-synthetics, reinforced polymer composites and advanced polymers, nanocellulose, and wood-based composites have led to the design of new and resilient infrastructure. Alternative energy from renewable sources like biofuels, wind, hydro, solar are significant factors affecting infrastructure industry. The rise of internet of things, sensors and smart infrastructure will result in the creation of smart buildings, smart appliances, smart grid, smart packaging and smart logistics. Artificial intelligence techniques and applications have revolutionized the infrastructure industry. The rise of Autonomous Vehicles has

---

[3]Infrastructure Futures The impact of megatrends on the infrastructure industry, Global Infrastructure Hub.

facilitated the emergence of disruptive new mobility models which are based on autonomy, sharing and electrical vehicle. Digitization in terms of Building Information Modelling (BM) have provided new direction for efficient planning, designing and construction of infrastructure.

In terms of sustainability and resilience, ageing and outdated infrastructure impacts the effectiveness of transportation networks, water systems, communication networks and energy grid. Rise of natural disasters, climate change problems and resource scarcity affects infrastructure industry.

The Infrastructure business models will see in future the emergence of national infrastructure champions. In the context of criticality of national security infrastructure, nations will continue to focus on strategic sectors such as energy, water, telecommunications and cyber security.

In the context of new technological innovation, private companies will be the primary supplier of infrastructure assets and services with business models reliant on technology and advanced data analytics. Technology companies will play a leading role in the design and delivery of infrastructure, and control data pools and interfaces.

1.15 Classification of Infrastructure

The American Heritage® Dictionary of the English Language defines infrastructure as "The basic facilities, services, and installations needed for the functioning of a community or society, such as transportation and communications systems, water and power lines, and public institutions including schools, post offices, and prisons." Infrastructure can be segregated along different lines. In terms of physical characteristics, infrastructure include roads, bridges, pipelines and cables. Industrial or economic infrastructure include facilities for transport, energy, water and waste management. Social infrastructure include education, health and security establishments. In terms of economic characteristics, infrastructure can be classified in terms of size, capital intensity, barriers to entry, economies of scale and inelastic demand for services. Investment characteristics of infrastructure projects can be characterized in terms of returns, sensitivity to economic cycles and swings in market, predictability of cash flows, inflation hedging. In terms of regulatory regime, infrastructure projects can be classified in terms of contractual basis or its various variations.

Infrastructure investments can be classified in terms of project stages—greenfield, brownfield, primary, secondary etc. In terms of geographic region, infrastructure investments can be segregated in terms of global, regional, emerging markets, country wise classification. The investment style can be based on core or opportunistic, growth or income style.

Public investment basically includes investment in highways, transportation, power, drainage systems, water systems, education and health care structures. Private investments concentrate on non-residential structures in power, communication, railroads and other structures.

1.16 Listed Infrastructure Equity Financing

Public firms listed on stock exchanges own infrastructure assets and provide infrastructure services. These firms function as operators, contractors and developers of projects. The global infrastructure stock market indices are comprised of 350 infrastructure companies. Approximately 5–6% of the world stock markets are comprised of utilities and economic infrastructure companies. Utilities specifically energy and telecom companies dominate the listed infrastructure indices.

1.17 Infrastructure Funds

Majority of infrastructure funds are equity funds. Infrastructure funds are funds which are investment vehicles as equity partners for large scale projects in economic and social infrastructure. Economic infrastructure includes "clean technology, distribution/storage facilities, environmental services, telecommunications, satellite networks; transportation—aviation/aerospace, bridges, parking lots, railways, roads, sea ports, tunnels, utilities—energy, natural resources, renewable energy, water, waste management". Social infrastructure refers to projects related to national security, education, healthcare and other welfare schemes.

1.18 Infrastructure Investors[4]

Strategic buyers are traditional operators or contractors in the infrastructure sector. Their investment strategy ranges from long term investment to short term "build and sell" strategy. Examples for market players include Abertis, Bombardier, Bouygues, OHL etc. Another class of infrastructure investors are infrastructure funds with PPP allocations. They are basically private or listed equity funds focused on PPP infrastructure investments with long term investment strategy. Examples for this class of infrastructural investors include Amber, AMP Capital, Barclays, Brookfield, Capella, CII, Hastings and HICL Infrastructure company.

1.19 Cofunding in Infrastructure Projects[5]

Under this mechanism, government provide approximately 50% of the total funding at a lower rate of interest. This form of financing with government partnership reduces the cost of funding and more projects can be funded. A classical example is the case of US based Transportation Infrastructure Finance and Innovation Act (TIFIA) loans. The amount of loan provided through this scheme is approximately

---

[4] Alternate Financing for Infrastructure development, Funding Options,2013. Deloitte Report.
[5] Alternate Financing for Infrastructure development, Funding Options,2013. Deloitte Report.

$500 million to $1 billion per year. The cost of loans is roughly equivalent to US Treasury bonds. Such loans fund a maximum of one third of the cost of a transport sector project. Under EIB debt funding provision, the European Investment Bank funds approximately 50% of funding for key infrastructure projects in the European Union at a lower cost. European Governments also facilitate subordinated debt to projects. The project bond 2020 plan had provisions to provide 15% of total funding as subordinated debt to attract institutional investors. Private sector subordinated debt funds are also gaining attraction. For example, Hadrian Wall Capital Fund. UK government had set up the Infrastructure Finance Unit (IFU) to act as a co-lender on major PPP projects. Many Governments also provide a capital contribution through payment of a proportion of the total capital costs or provide an element of work so that the funding requirement for private sector is reduced. This mechanism is extensively used in Europe. Governments also encourage private sector debt funding by providing credit or liquidity support. For example, in Australia Queensland Schools project, the private sector provided all debt during the construction and government took over 70% of the debt after construction completion. Under the Credit Guarantee Finance scheme for PPP projects in UK, the government provided all debt to the project and then received credit guarantees from banks. The French Guarantee of Debt on PPP projects involved setting up of a EUR 10 billion fund to set up guarantee debt on PPP projects with a limit of 80% of total debt for an individual project.

1.20 Alternate Procurement Mechanisms in Infrastructure Projects

In Head contractor set up, the government engages design consultants to design the project and afterwards tenders are called for on a lump sum or schedule of rates once the design is completed. On the behalf of the government, a project manager monitors the construction contract. The head contractor assumes the cost and time risk. In design and construct system, government prepares a design brief with requirements and then calls for tenders on a lump sum or schedule of rates bases to produce design and construct the works. In this case, cost and time risk is passed on to the contractor. In alliance contract, the government and contractor work together to achieve the agreed outcomes of complex projects. The risk associated with the project is assumed by the government.

1.21 Public Private Partnership (PPP): Forms

DBFO is the most popular form of PPP where the private sector is responsible for designing, building, financing, maintaining and operation of the asset. For example, a toll road where the contractor undertakes all operations in return for the tolls collected. DBMO is similar to DBFO with funds being provided by government. DBM is similar to DBMO with private sector responsible for maintenance of the facility and government in charge of operations of the facility. For example, a government hospital, where buildings are built and maintained by the private sector and medical staff are government employees.[6]

1.22 Mega Projects Under PPP

The M11 motorway is the first PPP project in Russia which is financed by the combination of bank debt and infrastructure bonds acquired by the non-state pension funds which included Lukoil–Garant. In 2015, China launched the New Silk Road Initiative by launching a US$28.3 billion PPP fund by Ministry of Finance.

Project finance is the major funding mechanism for infrastructure investment. UK is the leading player in terms of PPP with investments over US$100 billion by 630 Private Finance Initiatives (PFI) during the period 1992–2013. In the scenario of new economic reality of falling oil prices and increased interest rates, oil exporting countries have increased their focus on PPP to fund infrastructure projects. Kuwait and UAE had adopted laws to promote PPP investments.

After the financial crisis due to budgetary constraints, countries have sought greater investment for infrastructure needs for public private partnership. Over the years, PPP models with project finance applications have encompassed greenfield projects in the hard sectors and soft infrastructure projects such as water and sewerage.

1.23 Infrastructure Investment in Gulf

In terms of infrastructure investment, the gulf region has made higher investments in infrastructural projects such as airports, ports, roads, water etc. in comparison with the US and Western Europe. The gulf region is a trading region and one of the milestone in infrastructural projects was the development of the Port of Jebel Ali owned by DP world. Another landmark achievement was the development of Dubai International Airport with annual traffic of 86.4 million passengers in 2019 and has the capacity to handle 3.1 million tons of cargo per year. The infrastructure investment in gulf region is characterized by a range of public private partnerships (PPPs) for long term private financing for capital projects. UAE have pipeline of projects of value of over $300 billion for infrastructure development as part of economic diversification strategy. Saudi Arabia's Vision 2030 Realization Program have planned for infrastructural development projects worth $48 billion in transport and social sectors. Saudi government's strategy is to invest in infrastructural projects covering sectors such as power, water, hydrocarbon, road, rail, seaport and airport sectors. Landmark projects in Saudi include Haramain High Speed Rail which connects Jeddah to Median in 90 min at a speed of up to 330 km/h, King Abdulaziz

---

[6]Alternate Financing for Infrastructure development, Funding Options,2013. Deloitte Report.

International Airport's $4 billion terminal and tallest control tower valued at $3.2 billion. Qatar is expected to invest in projects worth over US$200 billion in infrastructural projects in the next decade. UAE invested $40 billion to develop the first nuclear power plant in Abu Dhabi. In Dubai, the world's largest single site solar park was established to generate up to 200 MW valued at AED1.2 billion. Qatar is involved in building the largest LNG facility in world. UAE have ambitious projects such as the first Hyperloop prototype which would transport passengers from Dubai to Abu Dhabi in just 12 min/1200 km/h. Oil prices have a substantial impact on public spending in countries in GCC region.

1.24 History of Project Finance

The peak wave of project financing took place in the late 1980s and 1990s. The origins of project finance can be traced to the early Greek and Roman times, when the merchants entered into a fenus nauticum (sea loan) with a local lender for risk sharing of a particular voyage. The agreement of fenus nauticum stipulated that the loan would be given to the merchant for goods purchase meant for outward voyage and the loan would be repaid from the sale proceeds of the goods. The agreement was non-recourse in nature as if the ship did not arrive safely at the home port, then the loan was not repayable.

In the early nineteenth century, lenders in the City of London used project financing techniques to finance numerous railway and other projects in South America and India. For example, East India Company used project financing techniques for trade in India. In early 1970s, project finance was used for development of early oil and gas fields in UK continental shelf. British Petroleum made the first major financing in the North Sea by investing £1 billion by means of forward purchase agreement. It was followed by two loans raised by Occidental Petroleum Corporation and International Thompson Organization for investments in North Sea hydrocarbon assets related to the Piper Field. During the late 1970s and early 1980s large volume of project financings transaction was carried out in the oil and gas fields in Danish and Norwegian continental shelf. The decade of 1980s witnessed spurt in growth of project financing in power, infrastructure, transportation and telecommunication sectors in UK.

1.25 Characteristics of Project Finance

Project finance can be described as "the financing of the development or exploitation of a right, natural resource or other asset in which the major part of financing is provided by debt and repaid principally out of the assets being financed and their revenues. According to Finnerty (2006) [5], project financing is defined as "the raising of funds on a limited recourse or nonrecourse basis to finance an economically separable capital investment project in which the providers of the funds look primarily to the cash flows from the project as the source of funds to service their

1.25 Characteristics of Project Finance

loans and provide the return on their equity invested in the project." Project Finance involves the "creation of a legally independent project company which is financed with non-recourse debt and equity from one or more corporations known as the sponsoring firms for the purpose of financing investment in a single purpose capital asset usually with a limited life".

In a typical project structure involving for example an independent power project, the non-recourse debt is provided by lenders through an inter creditor agreement involving bilateral and multilateral credit agencies, export agencies and bank syndicate. The equity part is provided by two or three sponsors through shareholder agreement. Project finance involve the creation of a legally independent entity. The financing is highly leveraged with debt component constituting approximately 70% or above and the rest equity component. Project finance is also known as contractual finance as the structure involves creation of different contracts between different parties. For example, for a power plant, gas input is provided through a supply contract. The power output of the project company is purchased under the purchase contract by the off taker like government. Other ancillary contracts include operations and maintenance contract, construction contract under EPC, labor contract, equipment contract etc. The host government, legal systems, permits, regulations and property rights are all part of the project finance ecosystem. Project finance involve investment in capital asset which is of either stock type or flow type. Stock type of project extract resources such as oil or copper. Flow type of projects involve toll roads, pipelines, telecommunications or power plants. The non-recourse nature of financing in project finance highlight the fact that lenders cannot take over the assets of the sponsors in case of default. They have the rights over the assets of the project company only. The lenders rely on the future cash flow of the project for interest and principle payment. The main security for lenders is the project company's contracts, licenses or ownership of rights. Project finance is a form of off balance sheet financing and is beneficial for a company with respect to credit standing when it raises further funds from financial markets. Table 1.1 gives country wise infrastructural spending as percentage of GDP. Table 1.2 shows the project finance statistics in power sector.

Table 1.1 Global investments on construction and maintenance of infrastructure as share of GDP (2018)

Country	Share
China	5.57%
Georgia	3.06%
Greece	2.47%
Hungary	1.93%
Azerbaijan	1.75%
Bulgaria	1.74%
Australia	1.69%
South Korea	1.65%
Norway	1.43%
Albania	1.32%

Source: https://www.statista.com/statistics/566787/average-yearly-expenditure-on-economic-infrastructure-as-percent-of-gdp-world wide-by-country/

Table 1.2 Project finance transactions in power sector (value in billions of US dollars)

Year	2015	2016	2017	2018	2019
Coal	16.6	13.7	16.3	9.1	6
Gas power	14.3	14.5	14.8	13.5	17.5
Solar	14.9	5.9	12.5	15.2	12.2
Onshore wind	19.7	11.5	15.5	18.1	16.9
Offshore wind	11.6	15.4	7.5	8.9	13
Other renewables	11.6	5.9	5.3	8.1	12.2
Grids and storage	1.4	4.5	4.7	5.9	6.4

Source: ea.org/data-and-statistics/charts/project-finance-transactions-for-power-by-year-of-financial-close-by-technology-2015–2020

1.26 Private Partnership in Infrastructure (PPI) Statistics

The world population is expected to reach 9 billion by 2040. The trend observed is that the Developed economies (OECD) consumed more than 50% of the world's energy resources though having only 20% of the population. The global energy consumption is expected to rise by approximately 35% during the period 2010–2040. Brazil, Russia, India, China account for 40% of the World's GDP. Historically countries have used public money or debt security issued by the states to fund developments. In modern context, the scale of required investment suggest that government financing alone is insufficient and therefore the private sector plays an increasing role in financing critical projects through the use of public private partnership (PPP) models. Private sector firms have historically used project finance for industrial projects such as pipelines, mines and oilfields. During the period 1990s, private firms have financed infrastructure projects such as toll roads, power plants and telecommunication systems.

In the year 2019, private investment in energy, transport, information and communications technology (ICT), water and municipal solid waste infrastructure totaled US$96.7 billion across 409 projects in 62 countries.[7] East Asia and the Pacific (EAP) led by China account for 39% of global investments in infrastructure. Transport sector had the distinction of the largest PPP sector in 2019 with approximately half of the global investments. Among the 150 electricity generation projects, 91% accounted for renewable energy sector. Investment commitments in IDA countries in 2019 amounted to US$8.7 billion across 29 projects in 18 countries. IDA countries are those with gross net income (GNI) per capita below the threshold of US$1175 as defined by World Bank. Table 1.3 highlights the number of PPI projects undertaken and its value.

These five countries accounted for 63% of global PPI investment. In terms of sector trends, the transport sector attracted the maximum investment of US$47.8 billion across 123 projects in year 2019. This investment accounted for half of 2019 global PPI investments. Energy sector received $40.1 billion across 169 projects

---

[7] Private Participation in Infrastructure (PPI), World Bank Annual Report 2019.

Table 1.3 PPI project statistics

Year	No of projects	Value millions of US dollars
2014	389	11,146
2015	385	37,702
2016	353	5430
2017	386	7050
2018	428	3804
2019	409	8637

Source: PPP World Bank Annual Report 2019

Table 1.4 PPI country statistics in 2019

Country	Value in billion US dollars	Number of projects
China	$26.3	142
Brazil	$18.6	33
India	$7.6	34
Vietnam	$4.5	12
Russia	$4.1	13

Source: PPP World Bank Annual Report 2019

Table 1.5 Top mandated lead arrangers (MLA) in 2020

Rank	Company	Total (USDm)	Transactions	Market share (%)
1	Sumitomo Mitsui Financial Group	18,618.66	170	5.18
2	Societe Generale	17,118.96	159	4.77
3	Mitsubishi UFJ Financial Group	17,063.65	158	4.75
4	BNP Paribas	14,427.25	118	4.02
5	Mizuho Financial Group	13,859.64	99	3.86
6	Credit Agricole Group	13,437.37	123	3.74
7	Santander	11,596.91	157	3.23
8	Groupe BPCE	11,515.42	112	3.21
9	ING Group	11,235.39	139	3.13
10	HSBC	8548.03	68	2.38
	Total	359,116.92	1012	38

Source: IJ Global Infrastructure Finance League 2020

which constituted 41% of investment commitments in year 2019. Table 1.4 shows the five country wise statistics for PPI projects.

PPI investments of US$21.9 billion in 128 projects were announced in the first half of 2020 according to PPI World Bank Annual Report.

1.27 Infrastructure Finance League Statistics

Tables 1.5 and 1.6 give the list of top mandated lead arrangers and bond arrangers in the year 2020. In Q3 2020, North America was the leading market in terms of value.

Table 1.6 Top bond arrangers in 2020

Rank	Company	Total (USDm)	Transactions	Market share (%)
1	JP Morgan	45,413.61	205	10.11
2	Citigroup	34,841.93	145	7.76
3	Bank of America	31,651.73	131	7.05
4	Barclays	23,205.98	116	5.17
5	Mitsubishi UFJ Financial Group	20,415.60	131	4.54
6	BNP Paribas	19,436.92	112	4.33
7	Sumitomo Mitsui Financial Group	16,967.43	107	3.78
8	Royal Bank of Canada	15,295.44	105	3.4
9	Mizuho Financial Group	15,067.21	101	3.35
10	Goldman Sachs	14,678.78	80	3.27
	Totals	449,276.51	543	53

Source: IJ Global Infrastructure Finance League 2020

Table 1.7 Top developmental financial institutions (DFIs) Table 1.7 provides the list of top developmental financial institutions

Rank	Company	Total (USDm)	Transactions	Market share (%)
1	Japan Bank for International Cooperation	6496.27	10	12.7
2	China Development Bank	5368.77	7	10.49
3	European Investment Bank	5184.70	27	10.13
4	Export Import Bank of the United States	4700.00	1	9.18
5	China Exim Bank	3172.88	6	6.2
6	Asian Development Bank	2668.65	19	5.22
7	BNDES	2405.75	17	4.7
8	Export Development Canada	2042.64	21	3.99
9	Japan International Cooperation Agency	2013.25	7	3.93
10	Export-Import Bank of Korea	1494.03	8	2.92
	Totals	51,170.44	232	69

Source: IJ Global Infrastructure Finance League 2020

1.28 Flagship Projects in Transportation Sector

Infrastructure projects are characterized by stable cash flows, inflation protected and protected to some extent from financial market cycles. Infrastructure investments are not incremental and full investments are made initially itself. Infrastructural facilities have a service lives of 50 or more years.

Ancient history is witness to landmark projects. During the Roman period, a road network of approximately 8500 km was built throughout Europe. Ancient aqueducts provided water to cities over the centuries. The Chinese built the Great Wall which measured 3640 km and the Grand Canal which measured 1795 km were classic examples of great ancient projects. Dutch had reclaimed 15% of their current territory from sea.

1.29 Suez Canal

The Suez Canal is an artificial sea level waterway in Egypt which connects the Mediterranean Sea to the Red Sea through the Isthmus of Suez and divides Africa and Asia. Suez Canal provide vessels a more direct route between the North Atlantic and North Indian Oceans via the Mediterranean and Red Sea and reduce the travel duration. For example, through Suez Canal, the journey distance from the Arabian Sea to London is reduced by approximately 8900 km.

The construction of a sea level canal started in the year 1859. The Egyptian government which was a part of Ottoman Empire obtained a concession for a canal for over 99 years. The construction of the sea level canal started in the year 1859. Suez Canal had many firsts to its credit. It was perhaps the largest ever private project at the time of its inception. It was also the first joint stock company in Egypt. The equity ownership comprised of 46% ownership by the Egyptian government, 51% by the French Retail investors and 3% by others.[8] The canal was envisaged to represent public interest mission globally with usage open to all nations. The project company raised French Franc 200 million through its initial public offering in the year 1858. The IPO attracted more than 20,000 French retail investors but failed to attract large European institutional investors. The Viceroy representing the Egyptian government had underwritten the remaining number of shares. Compagnie Universelle du Canal de Suez was established to undertake the construction of site access infrastructure which included the foundation of Port Said and entry gate of the canal. On account of adverse geo political problems from Britain and work force issues, the project was delayed by approximately 4 years. The cost escalation for the project was 50%. The total cost for the project amounted to French Franc 415 million including the cost of finance. There was a high level of involvement by the Egyptian treasury in the project.

The Egyptian government undertook expansion of the Suez Canal to widen the Ballah Bypass covering 35 km which was aimed to double the capacity of the Suez Canal from 49 ships to 97 ships per day. This expansion project costed approximately $9 billion and was financed with interest bearing investment certificates issued to Egyptian companies and investors. The project was termed the New Suez Canal.

---

[8]Werner Baer (1956), The promoting of the Suez Canal, the business history review.

1.30 Panama Canal

The Panama Canal is an artificial 82 km waterway in Panama which connects the Atlantic Ocean with the Pacific Ocean. The canal cuts across the Isthmus of Panama and is a conduit for maritime trade. The canal reduces the travelling time for ships between Atlantic and Pacific Ocean. It takes 11.38 h to pass through the Panama Canal. The American Society of Civil Engineers has ranked the Panama Canal as one of the seven wonders of the modern world. The funding pattern of Panama was similar to that of Suez. The project started in year 1880. The canal opened in September 1914. Till 1977, toll payments were paid to US authority. From the year 1977, royalty payments came under the control of Republic of Panama. Approximately 14,000 ships cross the canal every year. In the year 2006, the Panama Canal Authority undertook expansion work estimated at a value of US$5.25 billion.

1.31 Channel Tunnel

The Channel Tunnel also known as the Eurotunnel is a 50.45 km railway tunnel which connects Folkestone, Kent with Coquelles, France beneath the English Channel at the Strait of Dover. It is the only fixed link which connects the island of Great Britain and the European mainland. It is the world's second longest underwater tunnel which is 50-km-long, out of which approximately 38 km is under the sea. The project is of 150 km consisting of two rail tunnels and one service tunnel. The project was completed in 8-year period and employed 13,000 workers.

In March 1986, the Treaty of Canterbury was signed between France and the UK, awarding a concession with a 55-year maturity to design, finance, build and operate a fixed link over the English Channel. The tunnel has the longest underwater section of any tunnel in the world and is the third longest railway tunnel in the world. By 1994, the debts of the company spiraled to 10 billion pounds. The company had to renegotiate its terms with its creditors. The actual volume of passenger and rail traffic was much less than forecasted. The passenger usage was forecasted to 16 million, but was actually 6 million. Eurostar train passengers totaled only 45% of the forecast for the opening year; rail freight traffic reached 40% of the forecast The freight volume was forecasted at 7 million, but actually turned to be just 1.7 million. Cost overruns of 108% for construction led to capital increases several times. Cash shortfalls required debt restructuring. The project was involved in a vicious circle such that it needed to levy heavy access charges to meet its interest payments. In 2006, the court granted the project company protection from insolvency. The company was restructured to form a new company called Groupe Eurotunnel which gave the existing shareholders 13% stake in the firm. A new loan of 2.84 billion pounds and bonds worth 1.275 billion pounds were initiated as a part of restructuring. The reorganization plan enabled the company to reduce its debt from 6 billion pounds to 2.8 billion pounds.

1.32 Belt and Road Initiative

The Belt and Road Initiative (BRI) is a global infrastructural development initiative by Chinese government in 70 countries and international organizations. Belt or the Silk Road Economic Belt refers to the proposed overland routes for road and rail transportation through landlocked central Asian region and historical trade routes of Western regions. The project has a target completion date of 2049. The project is aimed to accelerate the economic growth across the Asia Pacific, Africa and Central and Eastern Europe. It is estimated that the project on completion would affect more than 60% of the world's population and approximately 35% of the global economy. Approximately 40% of the total world trade would be accounted by the Silk Road project. The Asian Infrastructure Investment Bank was established to fund the project. The bank has an authorized capital of $100 billion with China being the single largest stakeholder with 26.63% of voting rights. China had announced over US$160 billion of investment for planning or constructions related to the Belt initiative.

1.33 Resund Bridge

The Resund Bridge is a combined railway and motorway bridge across the resund strait between Sweden and Denmark. The Resund Bridge is a 16 km link which services both highway and railroad traffic across the neck of the Baltic Sea called resund channel between Copenhagen, Denmark and Sweden. It is the longest combined road and rail bridge in Europe. The link consists of a 4 km immersed tunnel, an 8 km, two deck bridge and a 4 km artificial island. The project was completed in July 2000—3 months ahead of schedule. The cost overrun was 27% due to changes in design on account of enhanced environmental and safety standards. In the first full year of operation, the average daily traffic was 8100 road vehicles and 13,400 rail passengers. The bridge covers half the distance between Sweden and the Danish island of Amager. The project was carried out by the joint venture of Hochtief Skanska, Hojgaard & Schultz and Monberg & Thorsen and completed by August 1999.

1.34 Vasco da Gama Bridge (Portugal)

The Vasco da Gama bridge is a cable stayed bridge flanked by viaducts which spans the Tagus river in Portugal. It is the longest bridge in the European Union with a total of 12.3 km. The bridge is served by 4.8 km of dedicated access roads. The construction of the bridge began on February 1995 and the project was completed on schedule by March 1998. The project was executed by the consortium Lusoponte in the form of PPP. For maintaining the financial future of the project, Lusoponte was granted the monopoly on every potential future road link across the Tagus within a radius of 25 km around the bridge. One of the special feature of the concession period of the project was that it would mature after 33 years or once 2.25 billion vehicle trips were made on two bridges combined whichever first occurs and ownership is reverted back to the government. The project also faced opposition from environmental lobbyists and design modifications were made to allay concerns of wetland and bird preservation issues. Mota-Engil and Autostrade are the major shareholders of the project. In the year 2008, Macquarie sold its stake in the project. Vinci, Mota-Engil and Autostrade are now the major shareholders.

References

1. OECD (2006), Infrastructure to 2030: Telecom, Land Transport, Water and Electricity.
2. OECD (2007), Infrastructure to 2030, Volume 2: Mapping Policy for Electricity, Water and Transport.
3. McKinsey (2013), Infrastructure productivity: How to save $1 trillion a year. McKinsey Global Institute, January 2013.
4. McKinsey (2010), Farewell to cheap capital? The implications of long-term shifts in global investment and saving. McKinsey Global Institute, December 2010.
5. Finnerty John, Project Financing, Asset based financing engineering, second edition, John Wiley & Sons.

Further Reading

Emerging trends in infrastructure, KPMG; kpmg.com/emerging trends. 2018.
Alonso, J., Bjeletic, J., Herrera, C., Hormazabal, S., Ordóñez, I., Romero, C., Tuesta, D. and Ugarte, A. (2009). 'Projections of the Impact of Pension Funds on Investment in Infrastructure and Growth in Latin America,' BBVA Research Working Papers No. 1002. Madrid. Spain: BBVA
Della Croce, R. and J. Yermo (2013), "Institutional Investors and Infrastructure Financing", OECD Working Papers on Finance, Insurance and Private Pensions, No. 36, OECD Publishing. https://doi.org/10.1787/5k3wh99xgc33-en
Javier Alonso, Alfonso Arellano, and David Tuesta, Pension Fund Investment in Infrastructure and Global Financial Regulation, PRC WP2015-22 Pension Research Council Working Paper Pension Research Council, Aug 2015.
Kaminker, C. and F. Stewart (2012), "The Role of Institutional Investors in Financing Clean Energy", OECD Working Papers on Finance, Insurance and Private Pensions, No. 23, OECD Publishing, Paris
OECD (2011), Pension Fund Investment in Infrastructure: a Survey.
Preqin, Infrastructure Spotlight. (Various dates)
Välilä, T., Kozluk, T. and Mehrotra, A. (2005). "Roads on a downhill? Trends in EU infrastructure investment". EIB Papers, (10:1), pp. 19–38
Georg Inderst, Inderst Advisory, Private Infrastructure Finance and Investment in Europe, EIB Working Papers 2013/02
Alternate Financing for Infrastructure development, Funding Options, 2013. Deloitte Report
Global Infrastructure Trends, Pwc Report 2020
PwC, 23rd Annual Global CEO Survey: Navigating the rising tide of uncertainty, 2020: https://www.pwc.com/gx/en/ceo-agenda/ceosurvey/2020.html.
PwC and Global Infrastructure Facility, Increasing private sector investment into sustainable city infrastructure, January 2020: https://www.pwc.com/gx/en/industries/assets/pwc-increasing-private-sector-investment-intosustainable-city-infrastructure.pdf

References

United Nations Department of Economic and Social Affairs, The Sustainable Development Goals Report, "Goal 11: Sustainable Cities and Communities," 2019: https://unstats.un.org/sdgs/report/2019/goal-11. 12. Ibid., and Inter-American Development Bank, "Investing in Safe Sanitation in Informal Settings,"

Nora Manthey, "Paris may offer flying cabs by Airbus at 2024 Olympics," electrive.com, 25 June 2019: https://www.electrive.com/2019/06/25/paris-may-offer-flying-cabs-by-airbus-at-2024-olympics

Global Infrastructure Outlook 2017, Global Infrastructure Hub, Oxford Economics.

PwC and Oxford Economics, Capital project and infrastructure spending outlook: Agile strategies for changing markets (2016).

New Suez Canal project proposed by Egypt to boost trade. caironews.net. Retrieved 7 August 2014

Bernhard Simon: Can the new silk road compete with the maritime silk road?, The Maritime Executive, 1 January 2020

Fitch Rating, Assessing Infrastructure and Project Finance An Investor's Guide: Updated, Infrastructure Reference Guide, Pages 320.

Infrastructure Financing Instruments

In early period infrastructure investments were financed with government funds. Over a period of time, public deficits, increased public debt to GDP ratios, budgetary pressures compelled governments to reduce the level of public funds which were allotted to infrastructure. Banks were constrained to reduce infrastructure financing on account of steps taken to strengthen prudential regulation in the banking sectors. After the economic crisis, banks were faced with situation to take initiatives to repair bank balance sheets and build capital and liquidity buffers. In this context the role of alternative sources of financing to support infrastructure development by institutional investors is of paramount significance. The long term nature of the liabilities for many types of institutional investors and their need for suitable long term assets is strategically significant for infrastructural investment.

It is observed that institutional investors currently allocate only a small fraction of their investment to infrastructure assets. Traditionally the investments were made in infrastructure sector by institutional investors through listed companies and fixed income instruments.

Financing of infrastructure involve different financial structures and instruments. Capital instruments like stocks and bonds are market based instruments with well-established regulatory frameworks. Banks were the traditional providers of infrastructural loans. The proper securitization of bank loans facilitates lending and diversification of risks along with the development of transparent capital market instruments.

It has to be noted that only large investors have the capacity to invest directly in infrastructure projects. Smaller pension funds have the capability to invest in infrastructure projects through pooled investment vehicles which are characterized by high fees, excessive leverage and mismatches between asset life and fund vehicle.

2.1 Challenges of Infrastructure Financing[1]

Infrastructure funding requires high upfront costs with long asset life requiring substantial financing. It is also characterized by lack of liquidity. Infrastructure projects are highly risky due to the costs incurred during the predevelopment and construction stage. Infrastructure projects may not generate positive cash flows during the early phases of the project. Stable cash flows result only when the project enters the operational phase. Infrastructure assets sometimes do not generate cash flows at all when users do not pay for services and government supports the creation of investment value for such projects.

Infrastructure projects comprised of natural monopolies such as national highways or water supply can generate social benefits. The costs of such infrastructure projects cannot be recovered from direct payoffs. The indirect externalities in the form of social benefits will facilitate the economic development. It is difficult to quantify such social cost benefits.

Infrastructural projects are characterized by heterogeneity, complexity and have numerous contractual obligations with different stakeholders along with complex legal arrangements. Legal arrangements are necessary for equitable distribution of returns and risk sharing among the different stakeholders. Infrastructure investments are characterized by less liquidity.

Infrastructure projects tend to be lacking transparency due to opaque and diverse structures. The risk structures cannot be properly assessed by investors due to the lack of information. These characteristics of infrastructure projects make the process of infrastructure financing risky.

2.2 Financing Instruments and Channels

Corporate finance is the most dominant channel in private infrastructure finance. Firms listed on public exchanges take upon different roles such as owners of infrastructure assets, providers of infrastructure services and investors in infrastructure projects.

On account of budgetary constraints, the financing of infrastructure by public funding is found to have declined over a period of time. Project finance have emerged as the financing solution for infrastructure in modern times. Project finance have become the popular financing method to attract private capital for investment projects characterized by highly specificity with low re-deployable value and high intensity of capital.

Current trends indicate the development of co-investment platforms to support institutional investors' capital in project finance. These co-investment platforms pool investor capital and invest directly in infrastructure projects avoiding intermediary functionaries like investment banker or other banks. Large funds align directly with

---

[1]Infrastructure Financing Instruments and Incentives, 2015 OECD Report.

2.2 Financing Instruments and Channels

Table 2.1 Taxonomy of instruments and vehicles for infrastructural financing

Modes		Infrastructure financing instruments		Market vehicles
Asset category	Instrument	Infrastructure project	Corporate balance sheet/Other entities	Capital pool
Fixed income	Bonds	Project bonds Municipal, Sub sovereign bonds Green bonds, Sukuk	Corporate bonds Green bonds Subordinated bonds	Bond indices, bond funds, ETFs
	Loans	Direct/Co-investment lending to infrastructure project, syndicated project loans	Direct/Co-investment lending to infrastructure corporate	Debt funds (GPs)
			Syndicated loans, securitized loans (ABS), CLOs	Loan indices, loan funds
Mixed	Hybrid	Subordinated loans/Bonds, mezzanine finance	Subordinated bonds, convertible bonds, preferred stock	Mezzanine debt funds (GPs), hybrid debt funds
Equity	Listed	YieldCos	Listed infrastructure and utilities stocks, closed end funds, REITs, IITs MLPs	Listed infrastructure equity funds, indices, trusts, ETFs
	Unlisted	Direct/Co-investment in infrastructure project equity, PPP	Direct/Co-investment in infrastructure corporate equity	Unlisted infrastructure funds

Source: OECD [1], Infrastructure Financing Instruments and Incentives, https://www.oecd.org/finance/private-pensions/Infrastructure-Financing-Instruments-and-Incentives.pdf

infrastructure investments. Table 2.1 provides a framework for infrastructural financing.

Loans and bonds comprise the largest component with respect to sources of infrastructure finance. Debt instruments can be structured with maturities that match the life of long term assets. Debt instruments can take different forms such as direct loans held on balance sheets of financial institutions; private placement debt or public markets through the channels of corporate and government bonds.

Debt instruments can be tailored to meet specific demands of certain investors known as client effect. Using infrastructural financing, pension and insurance funds can hedge their long term liabilities with long term fixed income instruments.

Hybrid instruments such as mezzanine finance have characteristics of debt instruments with equity like participation. Equity finance play an important role in infrastructure financing as capital providers to start a project or for refinancing needs. Listed shares represent indirect stakeholder rights in corporations and projects. Unlisted shares often confer direct ownership, control and operation of firms.

2.3 Infrastructure Project Finance

Project finance have different characteristics compared to corporate finance. Financing is basically recourse in nature with lenders providing loans on the basis of the cash flow generation capacity of the project. Project finance is characterized by risk sharing structures among various project partners through contractual obligations for managing and controlling risks. The financial instruments in project finance debt component include project bonds, sub sovereign issues in bond markets, loans and direct lending in nonpublic markets. The equity component comprises of listed entities such as yieldcos in public equity markets and direct/co-investments in project equity. The usage of Public Private Partnerships (PPP) contracts are found in project finance which has the characteristics of major legal structure. Project debt finance is highly leveraged and accounts for 70–90% of the total capitalization of infrastructure projects. There are infrastructural projects in which the debt financing accounts for 100%. For example, projects such as Second Severn and Skye Bridge crossings in the U.K. [2]. In such projects, the responsibility of operations of the asset lies with the lender. In infrastructural debt financing, features of instruments include tranches of issues, collateralization, covenants and credit enhancement tools.

Project finance debt are issued basically in local currency to hedge exchange rate fluctuations between project revenues and financing flow. Cash flows can also be hedged through the use of currency derivatives thereby facilitating multi-currency financing structures.

Infrastructural debt can be segregated in terms of the type of the project. In greenfield projects, the debt financing includes project loans in greater proportion, project bonds, mezzanine or subordinated debt issues.

In brown field projects, institutional investors invest in long term bonds issued by the infrastructural company.

2.4 Project Mezzanine Finance

Subordinated debt and mezzanine tranches provide credit support for senior notes. Development banks, commercial banks or project SPVs can issue subordinated debt in the market or as private placements. The different tranches in the form of subordinated or senior debt tranche creates different risk/return profiles for investors. Mezzanine debt offers higher yields and can be offered in combination with equity participation rights. Such features are attractive to institutional investors such as pension funds.

2.5 Project Equity Finance

Project finance is also known as contractual finance. In project finance risk sharing and control initiatives are basically determined through contracts such as concessions, long term leases and public private partnerships. Project sponsors initiate projects by contributing equity to a Special Purpose Vehicle. Project sponsors also act as bidders for public sector projects with PPP structures. Equity basically constitute 10–30% of a project's capital investment. In periods of credit crisis, equity sponsors are required to bring in additional funds. Equity sponsors by lowering their equity proportion can improve their return on investment. Equity financing is a vital source of financing for projects with high risk return profile where securing debt finance is challenging for projects with high risks and unstable cash flows.

2.6 Corporate Balance Sheet Finance

This is the traditional form of nonpublic infrastructure financing. Infrastructural firms issue shares in the primary capital market or borrow funds through capital market to finance projects. Retail and institutional investors purchase the shares of infrastructure firms directly from market or asset managers helps these investors for portfolio selection.

Corporate finance debt instruments include straight corporate bonds, subordinated bonds, convertible bonds etc. Firms can also access funds from banks through syndicated loan markets. The process of securitization facilitates firms to pool individual small loans and sell then on bond market as securities. Firms can raise equity and debt financing through private placements or with the services of institutional investors. The greatest advantage of debt finance involves the interest tax shield in different regions of the world. The treatment of interest payments before tax expense lowers the after tax cost of debt for infrastructural debt financing.

2.7 Hybrid Instruments

Hybrid Instruments possess both debt and equity characteristics. Convertible bonds are hybrid instruments. Subordinated debt and preferred stock also are hybrid instruments.

2.8 Equity Instruments

Equity finance consists of listed public equity and unlisted private equity. Public equity is traded on listed stock exchanges. Private equity investors provide capital to unlisted firms. Public capital equity investors are not involved in the management of the company. There is separation of ownership from management. Private equity capital providers actively participate in the management of the assets of the firms. Close-ended funds, MLPs, REITs also invest directly in infrastructure assets.

2.9 Market Vehicles

Market Vehicles facilitate the pooling of capital meant for infrastructure finance in a diversified portfolio of securities, loans or private investments Market vehicles include public market funds such as mutual funds, index funds, Exchange traded funds. Retail investors and institutions can access securities through these market vehicles. Index funds which include infrastructure firms also facilitate active and passive portfolio management in listed infrastructure companies. General partnerships (GPs) are private market funds which focuses on institutional investment market.

2.10 Bond Market Debt Instruments

Bond debt market instruments can basically be classified into government and corporate bond market.

Public bond market offers instruments such as government bonds, municipal bonds and sub sovereign bonds. Bond issues to finance the construction and operation of an infrastructure asset are sponsored by federal governments, local governments and government agencies and multilateral banks. Sub sovereign agencies like mortgage institutions have the backing of sovereign entities. Government finance is the major traditional source of funding for infrastructure. In terms of taxonomy, Government bonds can be classified into general obligations (GOs) and revenue bonds. General obligation bonds are backed by the taxing authority of the government whose performance is related to the fiscal creditworthiness of the borrower. The revenue bonds issued by government or municipal agencies are market based instruments issued to finance infrastructure projects and the cash flow to investors are primarily through the cash flows from the bonds. Revenue bonds are sold directly to investors through the fixed income markets. These bonds offer fixed or floating coupon, have long term maturities and rated by credit rating agencies. Institutional and retail investment grade bond portfolios comprise of core investments in government and agency bonds. Mutual funds, ETFs and indices invest in core investment grade bonds related to infrastructure assets. The tax savings on issuance of municipal bonds in US has contributed to the growth of this market. On account of its tax saving nature, these municipal bond issued have strong demand from households for tax saving purposes, commercial banks and insurance companies.

Qualified Public Infrastructure bonds (QPIBs) are new innovation in the infrastructure bond market of United States. During January 2015, US government introduced this innovative class of municipal bond with tax exemption to control private investment in infrastructure. QPIBs were introduced to provide the benefits of municipal bond finance to PPP involved in infrastructure projects.

2.11 Debt Instruments: Syndicated Loans and Bank Loans

Syndicated loans are pooled loans created by commercial or development banks. They are sold directly to investors through syndicated loan markets. Large institutional investors participate in syndicated loans through co-investment arrangements.

Banks underwrite loans for infrastructure projects and service the loans through maturity. The modern trend observed is that loans are originated by a lead underwriting bank or consortium of banks. A club deal refers to a mechanism in which several banks form a syndicate to structure the loan.

In syndication, the lead manager invites only creditworthy banks who have the capability to meet the obligations in terms of magnitude of the loan. The loans are priced at a certain spread over the reference rate of LIBOR or other reference rate such as SIBOR. The common options are 6 months or a 3-month option. Usually euro credit loans are denominated in US dollars. However, borrowers also are given a multicurrency option. Syndication loans are subject to different fees. A management fee also known as syndication fee is the front end fee paid by the borrower to lead manager. Management fee is a onetime payment which is payable upon either loan signing or first drawn down. The fee apportioned by the lead managers to the participating banks of the syndicate is termed Co manager fee. Participation fee is the fee apportioned by the lead managers to the participating banks of the syndicate. "Share of the Pool" refers to the residue of management fee which is shared by lead managers in proportion to their participation. The administrative agent of the syndicated loan receives agency fees for services rendered as agent bank. Basically it is the fees which covers the cost of administering the loans. Agent is normally the principal or lead manager of the syndication which provides the loan. In European region, the agent bank undertakes supervisory role to monitor the borrower's compliance with respect to the terms of loans. The role also includes monitoring the credit position of the borrower in terms of evaluation of borrower's current financial condition and compliance with financial covenants in terms of financial parameters for leverage, working capital etc. According to Reuters, the global syndicated lending totaled US$ 2.5 trillion during the first 9 months during the year 2020. In 2019, the total corporate lending exceeded $2.1 trillion.

Project finance loans can be accessed during the different stages of a project like construction phase or operating phase. There is flexibility to adjust the repayment terms of the loan or coupon payments during the course of the loan's life time. Interest rates on project finance loans can be either fixed or floating tied to benchmark reference rates such as LIBOR, SIBOR or EURIBOR. Short term maturities for project finance loans have range of 7–12 years and long term maturities have range of 20–30 years. Bank loans are senior debt instruments with the lowest level of risk on the project finance debt scale. It is largely secured by sufficient collateral. After the economic crisis of 2008–2009, leveraged loans became a popular credit investment among financial institutions due to liquidity.

2.12 Corporate Bonds

Corporate bonds are issued by corporates in public markets or placed privately. Corporate firms such as publicly traded infrastructure companies and utilities are the primary issues of corporate bonds. Corporate bond issues have covenant structure and indentures. These bonds can be divided into fixed bonds or floating rate bonds based on the nature of coupon payments. Bonds are rated by credit rating agencies and the issues are governed by the regulations of security exchange commissions. Major bond indexes are comprised of corporate bonds. Investment products such as index funds, actively managed and ETFs consists of portfolios in bond market. Investment banks act as underwriters for these issues.

2.13 Euro Marketable Securities

The Euro bond market took a center stage with respect to project financing since the 1960s. The first Eurobond issue was floated in the year 1963 by Autostrade, the Italian government highway authority. The Eurodollar loans were generally large in size with longer maturity period. The interest rates were basically floating rates tied to LIBOR or the prime rate. The absence of reserve requirements and interest rate ceilings facilitated the development of Eurodollar market.

Euro commercial paper is a short term debt instrument which is used by companies and financial institutions in any major currency outside the country of domicile of the issuer to investors around the world. These promissory notes usually have maturities less than 1 year. These instruments are sold on a discounted basis with no coupon payments. Institutional investors invest their short term cash surpluses in euro commercial papers. Through euro commercial papers, issuers can raise sources of finances at low costs which are sometimes below LIBOR.

Euro notes are short term euro commercial papers which are guaranteed by long term guarantee facilities provided by rated institutions such as note issuance facility (NIF) or revolving underwriting facility (RUF). Guarantee support of credible financial institutions are required for these issuers to access the euro commercial paper market. Note issuance facility are provided by a group of banks with condition such as that if the issuer is not able to sell euro notes of certain amount at a certain interest rate involving LIBOR for a certain period of time, then the banks will guarantee to purchase the unsold portion of the euro notes. Note Issuance facility is a purchase guarantee or back up credit guarantee provided by group of banks to the user.

Eurobonds are medium to long term marketable debt securities which are structured and sold in major currency outside the country of domicile of the issuer to investors in different parts of the world. These bonds are structured in an unregulated environment outside the regulatory jurisdiction of national governments. The Eurobonds are issued in large amounts, generally between $100 and $500 million. These bonds are typically underwritten by a syndicate of international banks. Eurobonds have maturity of 15 years for fixed rate euro bonds and 30 years for variable rate euro bonds. Eurobonds are redeemable in full at maturity. There are different types of Eurobonds like convertible bonds, equity warrant bonds, zero coupon bonds and indexed linked bonds. Convertible bonds can be converted into the equity of the issuing firm at the option of the bond holder. The price of the conversion would normally be at a premium to the market price of the equity at the time of the provision. The investor can exercise the conversion option at one specified future date or within a range of dates. Convertible bonds usually pay a coupon which is lower than the coupon rate of a straight bond without the conversion feature. Exchangeable bonds are bonds which can be exchanged into shares of the issuer firm's subsidiary or affiliated company at a pre-determined exchange price on a particular date. Government agencies which face regulatory constraints for dilution of their share ownership often issue exchangeable bonds. Equity warrant bonds have warrant features which grant the holder the option to purchase equity in the issuer. The exercise of equity warrants increases the total equity capital of the issuer. Zero coupon bonds are discounted bonds with no coupon payment. These bonds pay an interest income which is equal to the difference between the discounted price at which the bonds are issued and the full face value price at which bonds are redeemed on maturity. Indexed linked bonds' coupon or redemption value or both are linked to a stock market index or price index. Indexed linked bonds are used as a part of hedging strategy in financial markets.

2.14 Other Innovative Bonds

In commodity linked bonds, the coupon, redemption value or both are linked to a commodity price or index. In a scenario in which the commodity price rise above a certain strike price per unit of commodity, the redemption value of the issue as well as the coupon increases and thus investors will have increased wealth. The coupon on commodity linked bonds are generally lower as investors can expect to benefit from the future increases of commodity prices. Debt warrant bonds have warrant features which grant the holder the option to purchase from the issuer additional bonds with the same coupon at a particular period. For example, a debt warrant bond with coupon rate of 8% allows the bond investor to acquire from the issuer a certain amount of additional bonds with the same coupon. The warrant can be traded at a premium if the interest rate drops below the coupon.

Liquid Yield Options Notes (LYONS) are zero coupon bonds which have option features to convert into the stock of the issuer company at a pre-determined conversion price during the redemption period. Currency linked bonds are bonds wherein the coupon and redemption payment are in different currency compared to the currency in which the bonds were originally issued. The currency linked bonds will be issued in a currency which is preferred by the issuer, but the coupon and redemption would be in terms of currency preferred by the investor. Suppose a French company issues euro currency linked bonds for financing projects. If dollar interest rates are lower than euro, the euro currency linked bonds can offer interest and principal payments to investors in dollars. In dual currency bonds, the currency of issue and coupon payments will be the same, but the redemption payments will be in another currency.

Global bonds are bonds which are simultaneously introduced in different global markets. These bonds have features of both foreign and Eurobonds. The World bank pioneered the first global bond issue in the year 1989. Foreign bonds are bonds issued in a domestic capital market by nonresident issuers. Examples of foreign bonds include Yankee bonds, Samurai bonds, Shogun and Dragon bonds. Yankee bond is a foreign bond denominated in US dollars issued by any foreign government or company and traded in US markets. Samurai bond is a yen denominated foreign bond issued in Japan by non-Japanese companies which are subject to Japanese regulations.

Euro medium term notes are non-callable unsecured senior debt securities with fixed rate coupon. Floating rate notes (FRNs) are floating rate Eurobonds. FRNs are basically classified into Perpetual FRNs, Fake Perpetual FRNs and Reverse (Inverse) FRNs. In Perpetual FRNs, the principal never matures. The perpetual coupon payments are periodically revised by reference to standard base rates such as LIBOR. Fake Perpetual FRNs have call option features granted in favor of the issuer. In Reverse FRNs, the coupon rate moves inversely to the changes in the market interest rate.

FRNs are also classified as Collared FRNs, Step up Recovery FRNs (SURF), Range (Corridor) FRNs and Ratchet FRNs.

Collared FRNs are known as mini max FRNs. Collared FRNs contain maximum (cap) and minimum (floor) bands between which coupons could fluctuate based on a pre-determined reference rate. In SURF, the coupon payments are linked to yield on comparable bonds rather than standard reference rates such as LIBOR. In Range FRNs, the coupon payment calculation is based on the number of days during the preceding interest period in which a reference rate fluctuated within a pre-defined corridor or range. The coupon payments in Ratchet FRNs never fall below the level of the preceding payments.

2.15 Project Bonds

Standalone infrastructure projects can be financed by standardized instruments such as project bonds. Project bonds can be issued in public markets as well as privately placed. Project bonds are issued commonly for brownfield projects with projects worth in excess of US dollar 100 million. The project company can issue project bonds which are either straight bonds or secured through credit enhancement techniques like monoline insurances. Project bonds are basically used during the operational phase of the project. Public issue of bonds is subject to different regulatory requirements. Deferred bond structures termed as forward purchase bonds can also be issued. Some of project bonds' unique characteristics makes it more attractive to institutional investors than banks. Large bond issues being standardized capital market instruments possess greater liquidity characteristics and hence cost of funding can be lower compared to syndicated loans. These large size bond issues have potential to become constituent of bond indices and hence more demand from passive investors. Project bonds have longer maturity tenors compared to syndicated loans. The Touwsrivier solar project bond issued in South Africa is an example of use of project bonds to infrastructure projects. This green bond was issued to finance the construction of a 44 MWp concentrated Photovoltaic plant. The bond was issued with a 15-year maturity with 11 per coupon. The innovative feature of the bond was its amortizing repayment structure.

2.16 Green Bonds

Green bonds are corporate bonds, project bonds, and sub-sovereign bonds that finance investment in green infrastructure assets such as clean energy. Green bonds fund projects which have positive environmental and/or climate benefits. Green bonds can be issued by development financial institutions, corporations, banks and Special Purpose Vehicles of project companies. The standardization of green bond market is being promoted by initiatives such as Climate Bond Standard and Green Bond Principles. The relevance of green bonds in infrastructure investments is emphasized in the context of adoption of ESG criteria for the investment management process. Barclays introduced the Barclays/MSCI Green Bond Index in the year 2014. Introduction of such indices facilitate in developing liquidity for the green bond issues. In the year 2018, Green bond issuance amounted to US dollars 167.3 billion. In the year 2007, European Investment Bank (EIB) and World Bank undertook AAA rated green issue. During March 2013, IFC had $ 1 billion green bond issue. Green bonds were issued by corporates such as SNCF, Apple, ICBC and Credit Agricole. The first Green municipal bond issue in USA was made by the State of Massachusetts. Tesla Energy issued the first solar asset backed security in the year 2013. Green bonds can be classified into different categories. The "use of proceeds" bond earmarked for green projects have recourse to the issuer. The "use of proceeds" revenue bond or ABS refinances green projects and the debt recourse is basically through revenue streams from the issuers. Securitization (ABS) refinance portfolios of green projects.

Green bonds are issued to finance environmental or climate related investment. Through green bonds, institutional investors invest in renewable energy in capital markets. Green asset-backed securities are securities issued out of an SPV holding a pool of assets. The construction of 550 MW Topaz solar farm was financed by USD 850 million project bond issued by MidAmerican Energy which was the holding company of the utility Pacific Gas & Electric. In 2015, half of the USD 41.8 billion proceeds labelled green bonds went to renewable energy projects. The Project Bond Credit Enhancement Facility of EIB aims to support trans-European networks in the fields of transport and energy.

2.17 Islamic or Sukuk Bonds

A Sukuk is a sharia complaint bond like instrument used in Islamic finance. It involves direct asset ownership interest. Sukuk complies with Islamic religious law known as Sharia. The issuer of a sukuk sells an investor group a certificate and then uses the proceeds to purchase an asset in which the investor group has direct partial ownership interest. Sukuk represent aggregate and undivided shares of ownership in a tangible asset since it is associated with a specific project or investment activity. The asset backed characteristics of Islamic financial instruments like sukuk is suited for infrastructure projects. Sukuk can be categorized to include multiple structures such as project finance sukuk, asset backed sukuk, sale/lease back structures or rent/income pass-through. The most common type of sukuk comes in the form of a trust certificate. The Islamic Development Bank has facilitated the development of sukuks. Unlike conventional bonds which pay out interest to bond investors, sukuk transfer the profits or losses from the underlying asset to sukuk investors.

2.18 Securitization and Asset Backed Securities

The process of securitization involves pooling of infrastructure loans and issuing of securities in tranches based on different levels of credit and prepayment risk. These assets backed securities which are backed by infrastructure loans are sold to investors in different parts of world directly through the capital markets. In securitization, the bank places a pool of infrastructural loans in Special Purpose Vehicle (SPV). The notes issued by the SPV are rated by agencies and sold to investors in capital market. The process of securitization facilitates banks to transform long term infrastructure loans into cash. Banks also charge a fee for the origination of the ABS. Securitization enables the transformation of a pool of illiquid infrastructure loans into tradable securities.

2.19 Debt Funds

Debt funds raise sources of finance from limited partners related to infrastructure debt instruments. By means of debt funds, institutional investors can lend directly to infrastructural projects. In a typical debt fund model, an institutional investor provides fund to a resource fund represented by an asset manager whose function involve selection and monitoring of investments as a delegated agent for investors. The manager usually participates in bank syndications, club deals or lend directly to infrastructure projects.

2.20 Direct Lending and Co Investment Platforms

Modern infrastructure finance includes mechanisms like direct lending and co investment platforms. Large investors lend directly to infrastructure projects. In this model, the lead underwriter such as a pension fund or insurance company organizes a syndicate and retains a pre-agreed percentage of each loan in its loan portfolio. The sub underwriters such as banks also participate in the deal. This type of lending mechanism can be used for both greenfield and brownfield investments.

2.21 Mezzanine Funds

Mezzanine loans are subordinate tranches of debt which are used as credit enhancement tools for senior debt tranches in project finance. This type of subordinated loans and bonds offer higher yields than senior securities and can be privately placed in project finance. Subordinated debt tranches are known as junior tranches. Multilateral development institutions provide internal credit support for project finance through debt or mezzanine tranches. Institutional investors such as pension funds and insurance funds invest in mezzanine debt instruments. General partners' sources funds from limited partners and invest in mezzanine debt instruments. The usage of mezzanine capital assumes significance when there are limitations for the issue of high quality debt. Mezzanine debt offers attractive yields on shorter to medium term issuance and is suited for private equity type structures which are designed for institutional investors. Institutional and retail investors invest in subordinated debt issues for higher yields.

2.22 Convertible Bonds and Preferred Equity

Infrastructure companies issue convertible bonds which are junior bond issues that have embedded call options on the price of shares. The cost of convertible bonds is less for companies since the investors are ready to accept a lower coupon rate for future equity participation. Green technology firms such as solar panel manufacturers use convertible bonds as instruments for raising funds for projects.

Preferred shares are also hybrid instruments which have the characteristics of common shares and debt. Preference shareholders receive fixed dividend payments unlike common shares.

2.23 Listed Infrastructure Firms

Public infrastructure firms raise funds through issue of shares in equity markets through stock exchanges. Infrastructure firms such as utilities, transportation, heavy construction, airports raise funds through IPO listing. By the year 2007, infrastructure companies accounted for 5–6% of global stock markets. Major indexes offer specialist infrastructure indices. MSCI World Infrastructure Index is the broadest infrastructure index which tracks 145 companies in advanced countries. The S&P Global Infrastructure Index comprises of 75 firms in the infrastructure sector with weightage of 40% each in transportation and utilities and 20% from energy sector. The S&P Emerging Markets Infrastructure Index represents the thirty largest publically listed emerging market companies in the global infrastructure industry with weightage of 20%, 40% and 40% for energy, transportation and utilities sector. The Macquarie Global Infrastructure Index (MGII) which was introduced by Macquarie and FTSE in the year 2005 represent infrastructural sectors such as water, transport services, pipelines, gas distribution, electricity and telecommunications hardware. The MGII index have 80% weightage in utilities sector. The Dow Jones Brookfield Infrastructure Index was established in year 2008. Investment products related to mutual funds, index funds and ETFs which track benchmarked infrastructure indices facilitate investors to make targeted allocations in infrastructure sector.

2.24 Listed Infrastructure Funds

Retail investors can directly invest in infrastructure assets through listed infrastructure funds. These funds raise capital from securities market through IPO or raising funds through private placement. Listed infrastructure funds may be closed or open ended funds or investment trusts. Listed infrastructure funds can invest in listed project companies or in unlisted project companies. The Macquarie Infrastructure company is a listed closed ended fund which invests in airports, storage, transportation, gas production and distribution and contracted energy.

2.25 Yieldcos

Yieldcos can be categorized as equity instruments which are special power projects which consists of multiyear power purchase agreements for power generation. Yieldcos are particularly structured for spun off power plants or other utility projects. Yieldcos are established as new subsidiary for a parent company and listed usually through an IPO. Yieldcos provide attractive returns in form of income and dividends to investors through long term contracts. The establishment of yieldcos are noted in renewable energy projects such as solar and wind generation. Yieldcos are the emerging trend in renewable energy finance. Global Yieldco Index is the market weighted index of global yieldco market.

Yieldco structure is a viable option for energy utilities. Yieldco structures are created by spinning off operative assets from a company to finance and implement new projects. Equity based Yieldco structures are used by institutional investors to make investment in renewable energy sectors. In a typical Yieldco structure, an entity transfers its operative renewable energy assets into a new company which has the Yieldco structure. The new entity is listed and new equity is raised through an IPO issue. The parent company have a significant minority ownership in the Yieldco.

Through Yieldcos, institutional investors can access a portfolio of renewable energy projects. The renewable energy assets in the Yieldcos typically have long term, fixed price and inflation-indexed cash flows. Yieldco investors are not exposed to construction risk since the project developer manages the construction risk.

2.26 Specialized Equity Instruments

Master Limited Partnerships (MLPs) are structured as partnerships to avoid double taxation. These structured partnerships combine the tax benefits of limited partnerships with the benefits of being listed on an exchange. MLPs are structured in businesses in oil and gas and natural resources. REITs are special trusts which invest directly in properties with shares listed on stock exchanges. The trust managers are responsible for the operations and management of the specific assets held in the trust. MLP based mutual funds and ETFs were introduced in the year 2010. Infrastructure Investment Trusts (IITs) have similar characteristics like REITs.

2.27 Direct Equity Investment in Unlisted Firms and Co Investment Platforms

Institutional investors such as pension funds and insurance companies directly invest in project finance firms through acquisition of equity stake in the firms. These financial institutions source assets, undertake due diligence, finance and manage the operations of the firm. The investment horizon of such investments are long term in nature. Co-investment platforms are established by institutional investors to circumvent the high fees charged by financial intermediaries in infrastructure funds. Co-investment platforms are established by large pension funds and sovereign wealth funds for investment in infrastructure funds. The co investment platform offers network opportunities for these financial institutions in terms of asset management for deals and higher returns and access to deal flow. One of the classical example for co investment alliance platform is the Global Strategic Investment Alliance (GSIA) established by the Ontario Municipal Employees Retirement System (OMERS) in the year 2012. The investment alliance have targeted investment in infrastructure assets with a value of USD 2 billion in sectors such as airports, railways, ports, power generation & distribution and gas pipelines in regions of North America and Europe. In the year 2012, Mitsubishi Corporation (MC) established co investment alliance with Japanese financial institutions such as Pension Fund Association, Japanese Bank of International Cooperation and Mizuho Corporate Bank. In the year 2014, OMERS established co investment platform with Japan's Government Pension Investment Fund and Development Bank of Japan with capital commitments of USD 11.25 billion.

Institutional investors take the role of Limited Partners (LP) in unlisted infrastructure funds which are generally managed by General Partner (GP). The General Partner is responsible for raising capital commitments for the fund on behalf of LPs.

Banks are the major source of financiers for projects particularly in the early stages of infrastructure projects. Debt holders like banks serve an important role in monitoring the project. Bank loans are sufficiently flexible as infrastructure projects need a gradual disbursement of funds. Banks are constrained as their short term liabilities are not well placed to hold long term assets on their balance sheet for extended period of time. Bonds are suitable instruments for infrastructure financing of institutional investors such as pension funds and insurance companies on account of their long term liability characteristics. Development banks and export credit agencies play a significant role in infrastructure financing in both developed and developing markets through the use of financial instruments such as guarantees and mezzanine capital.

Infrastructure investments involve major complex legal and financial arrangements. The direct payoffs of infrastructure projects to an owner may not cover its costs but the indirect externalities in the form of infrastructure services provide benefits to a wide range of sectors. The initial phase of an infrastructure project is subject to high risks and cash flow generation for infrastructure investments take place after long period. On account of cash flow characteristics, high risks and illiquidity, private investments are not feasible as financing sources for the initial phase of the projects. In the planning phase of the project, Special purpose vehicle (SPV) are designed to attract private finance for the project. The degree of involvement of private sector in an infrastructure project is determined by the contractual arrangements which takes forms ranging from simple management contracts to partial or full private ownership. PPPs are complex long term contracts which are relevant when private partners have significant expertise and capacity for innovation. Equity and loan financing are major forms of financing in the construction phase. New groups of direct equity investors such as insurance or private equity funds have invested in unlisted infrastructure equity funds. Syndicated loans are suited for debt financing of mega projects. The role of credit guarantees is vital in project financing. Credit insurance is provided by different multilateral agencies. Monoline insurers which were the main provider of credit insurance in infrastructure projects are no longer providing credit insurance to infrastructure projects.

2.28 Leasing

Leasing as a form of finance is applicable for projects which involve heavy capital goods. Lease finance is applied on assets such as ships, aircraft and satellites. Leasing is popular in power project financings. Sponsors can gain accounting earnings and tax benefits through lease finance. On account of long useful lives and operating characteristics, lease financing is used for power plant projects. The two types of leases applied in project finance are tax or true leases and financing or synthetic leases. In leveraged or financial lease, the owners contribute only a minority portion of financing for the equipment. In other words, under a leveraged lease, the lessor only contributes part of the price of equipment and thus leverages or gears up the depreciation benefits. The lessor obtains the tax advantages of depreciation. The owners who are called equity participants obtain the benefit of leveraging but without the liability for repayment of loan.

2.29 Standardized Contracts

Standardized contracts are used to establish ownership structures in purchasing power agreements (PPA) in projects. For example, the standardized elements of a PPA in energy projects involve features such as energy purchase agreements and rates, grid interconnection and transmission responsibilities; agreement assignment and aspects such as adverse regulatory or tax changes. The National Renewable Energy Laboratory (NREL) has developed a standardized residential lease and commercial PPA contracts via the Solar Access to Public Capital Working Group which represent 440 organizations.

2.30 Aggregation

On account of transaction costs involved, banks prefer larger deals. Institutional investors such as pension funds and insurance companies require benchmark size deals of more than USD 300 million for funding purposes. Asset aggregation in distinct structures permits the creation of various individual tranches thereby attracting a potential pool of capital providers. The aggregation of smaller scale projects would scale up investment volume and reduce due diligence costs per project for institutional investors. Small or medium energy based projects can improve their access to financing sources and investors through the process of aggregation.

2.31 Securitization

Asset securitization allows project sponsors to issue individual securities with a variety of ratings, risks and returns to different investors. In this process of securitization, assets with similar characteristics are grouped together and sold to a separate entity such as Special Purpose Vehicle (SPV) which are sold to investors in financial markets. In the process of securitization, the principal and interest payments are paid to the senior tranche. The remaining funds are then given to the lower tranche. Dutch impact investor Oikocredit International, New York-based merchant bank Persistent Energy Capital and London-based developer BBOXX are involved in securitization of residential solar panels in Kenya and Rwanda.

2.32 Public Finance and Its Role in Infrastructural Development

Public finance plays a critical role in infrastructural development particularly in reference to renewable energy investment. Public financial institutions provide public sources of funds to infrastructure projects in both public and private sectors. The public financial institutions can be classified into International financial institutions, Developmental Financial Institutions (DFIs), Local financial institution, export credit agencies and climate finance institutions. International financial institutions consist of global and regional multilateral development banks such as the World Bank Group, the Asian Development Bank (ADB), the European Investment Bank (EIB), the European Bank for Reconstruction and Development (EBRD), the African Development Bank (AfDB), the Islamic Development Bank. Other regional financial institutions include the Inter-American Development Bank, the Asian Infrastructure Investment Bank and the New Development Bank. These institutions are involved in providing sources of funds for financing and risk mitigation instruments. The sources of capital for these institutions are provided by multiple government donors. Developmental financial institutions also include international financial institutions. Developmental financial institutions provide bilateral finance for projects from a developed country to several developing countries. Examples for DFIs include French Development Agency, the German Development Bank and the Japanese International Cooperation Agency, Brazilian Development Bank.

Export credit agencies are established by government to provide assistance to firms for export of goods and services which are sourced from the country. Climate finance institutions provide public funds from developed nations to climate relevant projects in developing nations. Examples for institutions which provide green funds for renewable energy deployment are the Global Environment Facility (GEF), the Climate Investment Funds (CIFs) and the Green Climate Fund (GCF).

2.33 Export Credit Agencies

Export credit agencies provide assistance in different forms like political risk insurance, commercial risk insurance, interest rate support and direct lending. Export Credits Guarantee Department (ECGD) of UK is the oldest ECGD established in the year 1919. The Export Import Bank of the United States (US EXIM) was established in 1934 to facilitate financing of US exports. US EXIM supports Boeing aircraft sales throughout the world. The export credit agencies of Germany, France, Italy, Japan and Canada are HERMES, COFACE, SACE, JBIC and EDC.

ECAs provide political risk insurance for a project which might not be feasible in insurance market. The repayment periods of ECA are usually longer than those provided by commercial banks. When a loan is guaranteed by ECA, the lending bank categorizes the risk of the loan as sovereign credit risk. The credit risk is applicable to the host government of the ECA. This facilitates the bank to charge lower interest rates. The long repayment periods of ECAs which are usually more than 10 years increase the debt capacity of the project. For ECA financing, the maximum term of financing is subject to a maximum average weighted life of 5.25 years from the start point of the credit. The project company have the total flexibility in arriving at the repayment profile and maximum repayment term for an ECA loan. The average weighted life of an export loan can be extended to a maximum 7.25 years provided two conditions are satisfied. The first condition is that the first repayment of principal due is within 2 years of the initiation of the credit for the project. The second condition is that the final repayment is due within 14 years of the starting point of credit. ECA provides political risk insurance in the context of default by a project company on account of political event. Under general standards the risks covered include expropriation, foreign exchange restrictions and actions by government which breaches specific undertakings. Under commercial risk insurance, the ECA guarantees the whole or a portion of the repayment of principal and payment of interest on a loan made available by the banks to the project company. In the context of changing nature of infrastructural project financing, ECAs have put more focus on analyzing project risk and evaluation of the economics of the projects. ECAs have a specialist project finance department to evaluate projects. Now ECAs cover both political and commercial risks during the construction phase of a project.

2.34 World Bank Group

World Bank Group is a unique global partnership with five institutions working for sustainable solutions aimed at eradication of poverty and development of the countries. The major arms of the World Bank Group consist of the International Bank for Reconstruction and Development (IBRD), the International Finance Corporation (IFC), the International Development Association (IDA), the Multilateral Investment Guarantee Agency (MIGA) and the International Centre for Settlement of Investment Disputes (ICSID). The World Bank basically lends to sovereign states and government agencies. The Group also provides guarantees to commercial lenders for public and private sector projects. IBRD is the lending arm of the World Bank Group which offers loans to middle income developing countries. IBRD is the largest development bank in the world owned by 189 member countries. It provides loans, guarantees, risk management products and advisory services to middle income and credit worth low income countries. IBRD finances investments across all sectors and provides technical support at each stage of a project. IBRD also provides expertise with respect to global knowledge transfer and technical assistance. IBRD provides advisory services in public debt and asset management to governments, sector institutions and other organizations to protect and expand financial resources. IBRD also lends to creditworthy poorer countries that are also eligible for IDA support. The major source of funds for IBRD is the World's financial markets. IBRD was able to provide more than $500 billion in loans to alleviate poverty around the world since 1946. The shareholder governments had paid approximately $14 billion in capital. IBRD has maintained a triple A rating since 1959. This high credit rating facilitates the bank to borrow at low cost and offer middle income developing countries access to capital on favorable terms. IBRD plays a critical role in development of sustainable renewable energy resources. For example, World bank have partnered with largest bank, State Bank of India for the market for rooftop solar project. India aims to achieve the target of generation of 100 GW of solar energy by 2022.

IFC is the largest global development institution which focuses on the private sector in developing countries. IFC is the multilateral source of loan and equity financing arm of the World Bank which provides funds for projects in the developing world. Since the year 1956, IFC has leveraged US $2.6 billion in capital to deliver more than US $285 billion in financing for businesses in developing countries. IFC facilitates the development of private sectors in developing countries in different ways such as investing in companies through loans, equity investments, debt securities and guarantees; mobilizing capital from lenders and investors through loan participation and parallel loans and advising businesses and governments to encourage private investment. IFC had long term investment commitments of $22 billion in the fiscal year 2020.

The International Development Agency is the concessional lending arm of the World Bank Group which provide soft loans to low income countries. IDA provides support to the world's poorest countries. IDA is sponsored by 173 shareholder nations which aims to reduce poverty by providing zero to low interest loans (called credits) and grants for programs which are aimed to facilitate economic growth, reduce inequalities and improve people's living conditions. IDA is the largest funding source for the 74 poorest countries in the world. The repayments are structured over 30–40 years which also include a 5–10-year grace period. In addition to concessional loans and grants, IDA provides debt relief programs such as Heavily Indebted Poor Countries (HIPC) Initiative and the Multilateral Debt Relief Initiative (MDRI). In 2020, IDA made commitments worth $30.48 billion. Multilateral Investment Guarantee Agency (MIGA) promote cross border investment in developing countries by providing guarantees such as political risk insurance and credit enhancement to investors and lenders. The guarantees provided by MIGA help investors to access funds with improved financial terms and conditions. MIGA help investors by insuring projects against losses related to currency inconvertibility and transfer restriction, expropriation, war, terrorism, breach of contract and non-honoring of financial obligations. For example, during October 2020, MIGA issued a guarantee of US $ 5.7 million to Korea Land & Housing Corporation of the Republic of Korea (LH) covering its equity investment to the Korea-Myanmar Industrial Complex Development Co Ltd (KDC) for a period of up to 15 years. The MIGA guarantees provide protection to LH against the risks of currency inconvertibility and transfer restriction, war and civil disturbance and breach of contract. MIGA Guarantee facility under IDA Private sector window would be used to share the exposure risk. The project consists of development, financing, construction and operation of Zone A, the first phase of the Korea–Myanmar Industrial complex located in Nyaung Hnit Pin.

ICSID is the world's leading institution of the World Bank Group which is devoted to international investment dispute settlement. Countries have acknowledged ICSID as a forum for investor–State dispute settlement in most international investment treaties and in numerous investment laws and contracts. ICSID was established in the year 1966 by the Convention on the Settlement of Investment Disputes between States and Nationals of other States.

2.35 European Bank for Reconstruction and Development (EBRD)

EBRD was established in the year 1991 for the development of the regions of Central and Eastern Europe. Over a period of time, the bank had invested over 150 billion euros in over 6000 projects. The bank has expertise in areas such as banking system reforms, liberalization of prices, privatization and creation of proper legal frameworks for property rights. EBRD financing for private sector generally ranges from $5 million to $250 million in the form of loans or equity. The average investment amount is $25 million. The loans are structured based on each loan currency and interest rate formula. The loan may be secured by a borrower's assets and/or it may be converted into shares or be equity linked. Bank offers both fixed and floating interest rate loans. The debt given can be in the form of senior, subordinated, mezzanine or convertible debt. The maximum duration of the debt is up to 15 years. With respect to fees and charges, a margin is added to the base rate. The margin is a combination of country risk and project specific risk. The bank may also charge front end commission, commitment fee and prepayment or late payment fees. The equity investments made by EBRD range from 2 million euros to 100 million euros in private sector projects. EBRD invest in minority equity positions. EBRD also invests in private equity funds which are focused on a specific region, country or industry sector. EBRD also have an Equity Participation Fund to attract funds from global institutional investors for direct equity investments in the private sector.

2.36 European Investment Bank (EIB)

EIB was established in the year 1958. The bank has made investments worth over a trillion euros since its establishment. EIB focuses on the development of European Union and support its policies in over 140 countries globally. EIB offers innovative solutions to promote sustainable growth, human rights and reduce poverty and inequality in developing world. During the past 10 years, the EIB financed 78 billion euros worth of projects outside the European Union of which 26.6 billion euros was accounted by the African subcontinent. Loans to public sector is normally given to finance a single large investment programme of 25 million euros. EIB provides project finance to private sector in the form of debt and hybrid debt structures. EIB also provides intermediated loans for SMEs and mid-cap firms. The development bank provides equity financing primarily investing or co-investing along with funds focused on infrastructure, environment, small and medium sized enterprises. The bank also facilitates quasi financing to support innovative companies. EIB offers a variety of guarantee instruments to cover risks in projects. EIB offers a range of advisory services during different stages of a project. Approximately 90% of the funding by EIB goes to EU member states.

2.37 Asian Development Bank (ADB)

ADB is a regional development bank established in the year 1966 and headquartered in Manila, Philippines. ADB's strategic vision is for the development of a sustainable Asia and Pacific. ADB provides loans, technical assistance, grants and equity investments to its member states for the promotion of social and economic development. ADB also facilitates policy dialogues, provides advisory services and mobilizes financial resources through co financing activities. ADB have 49 member states from Asia and Pacific region representing the United Nations Economic and Social Commission for Asia and Pacific and rest 19 from outside the region. Eighty percent of ADB's loans is distributed in five sectors comprising education, environment, climate change, disaster risk management, finance sector, infrastructure and regional cooperation and integration. ADB offers hard loans on commercial terms to middle income countries in Asia and soft loans with lower interest rates to poorer nations in the region. ADB provides direct financial assistance in the form of debt, equity and mezzanine finance to companies with projects of social significance.

2.38 African Development Bank (AfDB)

AfDB was established to promote sustainable economic development in its regional member countries. The bank mobilizes and allocate resources for investment in member countries. The bank was established in the year 1964. The constituent institutions of AfDB are the African Development Bank (ADB), The African Development Fund (ADF) and the Nigeria Trust Fund (NTF). The shareholders consist of 54 African countries and 27 non-African countries. The AfDB sources finances from capital markets for on-lending to its regional member countries. The development assistance provided by the bank has been channeled through various conventional instruments like project loans, lines of credit and technical assistance. After the initiation of structural reforms in mid 1980s, the instruments of structural adjustment loans and sectoral adjustment loans are being used as modes of financing.

2.39 Inter-American Development Bank (IDB)

IDB provide financial and technical support for countries in Latin America and Caribbean region for reduction of poverty and inequality. The bank provide loans, grants and technical assistance for regional development, social inclusion and equality, productivity and innovation across Latin America and the Caribbean region. The approved lending by the bank in year 2019 amounted to US $11.3 billion. IDB clients include central governments, provinces, municipalities and NGOs. IDB has three lending categories based on the development purpose, eligibility and disbursement requirements of the loan. Investment lending is provided to IDB borrowing member countries to finance goods, works and services to promote social and economic development. Policy based lending facilitate the bank's borrowing member countries with accessibility to liquid (fungible) funding to support policy reforms and/or institutional changes in a particular sector or subsector. Special development lending supports borrowing countries to face macroeconomic crisis The IDB does not make direct equity investments itself, but the IDB group members—Multilateral Investment Fund (MIF) and the IDB Invest make investments in private sector businesses. MIF invests in equity funds and microfinance institutions. IDB Invest make investments in small and medium size private projects either directly or through equity funds. IDB Invest makes equity investments of up to 33% of a company's capital. IDB also guarantee loans made by private financial sources in public sector projects. IDB offers two types of guarantees in investment lending. Partial credit guarantees are designed to help government institutions to access new sources of long term debt financing and covers risks that affect their repayment. Political risk guarantees by IDB covers the risk of non-compliance of contractual conditions agreed between public or sovereign entity and private institution such as bank or investment partner.

2.40 Common Wealth Development Corporation (CDC)

CDC provides flexible capital to support private sector growth and innovation. CDC is the world's first impact investor with over 70 years of experience in supporting the sustainable long term growth of businesses in Africa and South Asia. The company had made investments in over 1200 businesses in emerging countries with total net assets of £6.5 billion and a portfolio of £4.7 billion. CDC is entirely owned by the UK government. The only shareholder is the Foreign, Common Wealth Development Office. CDC focus on economic growth of less developed or fragile markets in Africa and South Asia.

CDC provide finances in the form of direct equity, intermediated equity and debt. Equity investments are made in priority sectors such as financial services, infrastructure, health, manufacturing, food and agriculture, construction and real estate. The equity investments are in the range of US $ 10 million–$150 million. Debt finance is provided through project finance, corporate lending, trade finance and lending to financial institutions. Project finance is provided to sectors such as power, transport and telecommunications. CDC also provides Tier 2 capital to financial institutions within the range of US $ 20 million–$100 million.

References

1. Financing Instruments and Channels: Infrastructure financing instruments and incentives. © OECD 2015
2. Sawant, R.J. (2010), "Emerging Market Infrastructure Project Bonds: Their Risks and Returns", The Journal of Structured Finance, 15, 4, pp. 75–83

Further Reading

Della Croce, R. and J. Yermo (2013), "Institutional Investors and Infrastructure Financing", OECD Working Papers on Finance, Insurance and Private Pensions, No. 36, OECD Publishing, Paris. DOI: https://doi.org/10.1787/5k3wh99xgc33-en

Della Croce, R. and Sharma, R. (2014), "Pooling of Institutional Investors Capital, Selected Case Studies in Unlisted Equity Infrastructure", OECD, Paris, http://www.oecd.org/finance/OECD-Pooling-Institutional-Investors-Capital-UnlistedEquity-Infrastructure.pdf

Deloitte, "Project Bonds: An Alternative Source of Financing Infrastructure Projects" report on Project Bonds: An Alternative Source of Financing Infrastructure Projects", http://www2.deloitte.com/za/en/pages/

FTSE (2007, 2015) FTSE Macquarie Global Infrastructure Index Fact Sheet.

Gatti, S. (2012a), Project Finance in Theory and Practice, II Edition, Academic Press, San Diego

Gatti, S. (2014), "Private Financing and Government Support to Promote Long-term Investments in Infrastructure", OECD Publishing, Paris

Weber, B. and Alfen, H. W. (2010), Infrastructure as an Asset Class: Investment Strategies, Project Finance and PPP, Wiley, Chichester.

https://www.climatebonds.net/market/explaining-green-bonds

Torsten Ehlers, Understanding the challenges for infrastructure finance Prospects for new sources of private sector finance, Bank for International Settlements 2014

IRENA (2016), 'Unlocking Renewable Energy Investment: The Role of Risk Mitigation and Structured Finance,' IRENA, Abu Dhabi ISBN 978-92-95111-92-9 (PDF)

Dentons, A guide to project finance

Climate Bonds Initiative and HSBC (2015), Bonds and Climate Change The State of the Market in 2015, Climate Bonds Initiative and HSBC.

Hirtenstein, A. (2016), African Sunshine Can Now Be Bought and Sold on the Bond Market, Bloomberg Business, www.bloomberg.com/news/articles/2016-01-12/african-sunshine-can-now-be-bought-and-sold-onthe-bond-market.

Kidney, S. and P. Oliver (2014), Greening China's Financial Markets Growing a Green Bonds Market in China: Reducing costs and increasing capacity for green investment while promoting greater transparency and stability in financial markets, International Institute for Sustainable Development (IISD).

NREL (National Renewable Energy Laboratory) (2015), Solar Securitization and the Solar Access to Public Capital (SAPC) Working Group, Renewable Energy Project Finance, financere.nrel.gov/finance/content/solarsecuritization-and-solar-access-public-capital-sapc-working-group

NREL (2012), MidAmerican Takes Solar Out to Wall Street, Renewable Energy Project Finance, financere.nrel.gov/finance/content/midamericansolar-thin-film-utility-scale-project-Topaz-550-MW-megawatt-bond financing

Risks Inherent in Project Finance and Its Mitigation

The critical element of project financing is the identification of all risk elements and the process of apportionment of these risks among different stakeholders involved in the project. It is very pertinent for the sponsors to identify and monitor these risks and pass on the risk to parties who will be able to manage and monitor these risks effectively than the sponsor. For lenders, it is very important to understand that there are no regulatory constraints imposed by authorities which would regulate their activities. For projects with higher risk intensity, lenders are expected to receive higher rewards in terms of interest and fees from the project. Risk analysis is required to be undertaken at the early stage of the project. In terms of a general condition, risks should be assumed by the party who is in the best position to manage and control the risk. For example, in a construction project, the main contractor is best suited to manage the risk of cost overruns or delay on a construction project. In a power project, the government or off taker will be able to manage risks associated with electricity supply issues or grid failure.

Infrastructure investment faces complex risk on account of the nature of investment. PPP highlights the type and magnitude of risks as well as the risk mitigants adopted. The debt financing to project companies are basically non-recourse in nature and in the case of default, the recovery of loans depends on the collateral value of project assets. Economic losses for infrastructure players can result either through a reduction of expected cash flows or through the default of project counterparty to meet obligations. Effective risk mitigants reduces the uncertainty and potential severity of losses. A government guarantee might not lead to reduction of the probability of default, but the exposure to losses is reduced by either complete or partial compensation. Insurance covers losses though it does not reduce the risk of happening of an event. Revenue grants reduces the project risk by reduction of potential losses to equity shareholders. Risk management process aims to identify the strategies to mitigate the impact of risks on project cash flows. Internal risk procedures have a significant role to minimize the effects of risk on infrastructure. The degree of risks varies across the life of the project. During the project development and construction phase, risk is perceived to be higher. Sovereign risks in infrastructure finance can be mitigated through the use of credit default swaps on traded government issued debt instruments.

National governments can create a conducive institutional environment to mitigate political and regulatory risk by making credit commitments for honoring the terms of agreements and developing guidance plans on mitigation of construction costs. Government's long term commitment for infrastructural development can be strengthened through promotion of PPP initiatives. Establishment and implementation of clear policies with respect to permits, taxation, litigation are effective in controlling political and regulatory risks. Bilateral investment treaties and protection agreements provide international law protection to sponsors of major projects.

Political risks such as changes in taxation and legal environment are subjective in nature and hard to quantify in terms of its impact on the success of the project. The first step in risk management involves development of well-designed internal risk procedures to control the risk. Monitoring project progress and asset performance facilitate managing risks internally. Risk transfer is a key risk management strategy employed in project finance through instruments such as non-financial contracts. Key contracts such as supply, purchase, EPC and O&M agreements can be used as risk mitigation techniques. In such contracts the counterparty will be responsible for the effects of risk occurrence on project cash flows.

3.1 Types of Risk

3.1.1 Construction Risk

This risk is also known as completion risk. Completion risk is a major risk involved in infrastructure project. Completion risk involve aspects such as timely completion of project, budgetary constraints, performance criteria and appropriate specifications. The concern areas for lenders would be in terms of type of contract, completion, bonding requirement and supervision. Lenders prefer construction contracts being a "turnkey" contract arrangements rather than a series of consultants and contractors. Lenders prefer fixed price lump sum contracts and assumes that the cost overruns are the responsibility of the contractor. The lenders also expect a fixed date for completion and in case of delays, there ought to have provisions for liquidated damages which are sufficient to cover the project's costs of servicing the loans and operating costs during the period of delay. Lenders also expects to have appropriate performance and defects liability bonding in place with acceptable credit ratings from institutions. Performance guarantees in the range of 10 to 20 percent of the contract price are common. The supervision of the construction works is carried by the personnel of the lenders.

3.1.2 Political and Regulatory Risk

Political and regulatory risk can be described as risk which occurs due to changes of laws, regulation or concession contracts with respect to operations of firms during the life of the project. It is characterized by different forms such as unilateral contract variation, specific regulatory changes, forced changes in ownership or control, sweeping tax changes or outright expropriation. The extreme form of political risk is expropriation risk. Political risk arises from changes in policies of governments with respect to specific sectors. It is very difficult to quantify political risks as they are highly subjective in nature.

Political and regulatory risk for a project can be highlighted in terms of procurement of permits for purchase of land, construction and environmental activities. Political and regulatory risk also rises in terms of cancellation of permits, contract renegotiation, changes in tariff regulation and contract duration. For decommissioning of projects, risk arises on account of disposal of asset at the end of the contract agreement or useful life of the asset. The enforceability of contracts related to leases, concessions and other contracted payment schemes can also face political and regulatory risk. Changes in taxation can be attributed to political and regulatory risk. Issues of currency convertibility related to repayment of foreign debt or repatriation of dividends and principal are also part of regulatory and political risk. Opposition to large public infrastructure projects on account of social acceptance may affect the different phases of a project.

The relevance of political risk is more for projects in power generation, transport or other infrastructure related to extraction of minerals since such projects may require governmental concessions, licenses or permits in place.

Political risks for mega projects can be summarized in terms of

- Expropriation or nationalization of project assets which includes the shares of the project company.
- Non grant of consent or permit which are essential to start, complete or commission the operation of the project.
- Imposition of increased taxes and tariffs or withdrawal of tax holidays and/or concessions.
- Imposition of exchange controls restricting transfer of funds
- Changes in law which adversely increases the project sponsors obligations
- Imposition of new safety, health or environmental standards.
- Political strikes and acts of terrorism.

Political risks in projects can be reduced through a number of methods. Project sponsors can aim to get government assurances with respect to specific political risks such as nationalization, inconvertibility and changes in law and taxes. Guarantees and assurances are protective mechanism whereby the project sponsor have a contractual basis for political risk mitigation. Project sponsors can also involve influential and powerful organizations from the host country such as major corporations, banks and financial institutions as either investors or lenders for the project. An effective way to reduce political risk is to link the outcome of the project to different international economic interests since any adverse action by the state will face opposition from international community. Project sponsors can rope in export credit agencies like EXIM bank of the country or involve local developmental institutions to manage political risks. A guarantee facility or financing arrangement from such export credit agencies are effective ways to mitigate political risks. Insurance from national export credit agencies such as ECGD, COFACE in France, HERMES in Germany can be used to mitigate political risks. Export credit agencies offer guarantees, direct loans and interest subsidies. Normally these are provided in relation to exports of goods and/or services by a supplier to the project. The central bank of host country can guarantee the availability of hard currency for export of products related to the project. The involvement of multilateral or bilateral global financial institutions can be used for effective political risk mitigation. Involvement of World Bank, Asian Development banks and other bilateral agencies can provide a protective political shield against the host country's adverse actions. Any adverse action by host country against the project have the scope of inviting reaction from such agencies in terms of future financial support from these organizations for the host country's development projects.

3.1.3 Policy or Regulatory Risk

These risks are associated with changes in legal or regulatory policies which have an adverse impact on project development or implementation.

3.1.4 Macroeconomic or Business Risks

Exchange rate risk, liquidity risk, refinancing risk, inflation, interest rate risk is part of macroeconomic risks. Projects face exchange rate risks when revenues and liabilities are in different currencies. The default of any provisions in project agreement by parties involved such as government, suppliers, lenders and insurers is an example of business risks involved in project. Constraints with respect to prefunding for feasibility studies makes raising funds a difficult task for the project. Liquidity risk arises when there are constraints in cash flow to service debt or any other related payments. Refinancing risk is the inability to refinance loans at maturity due to unfavorable performance or market conditions.

3.1.5 Currency Risk

It is the risks on account of volatile foreign exchange rates which would adversely impact the value of investments. This is basically due to the mismatch between the assets (revenues) and liabilities (debt financing).

3.1.6 Liquidity Risks

Liquidity risks arises on account of possibility of operational liquidity issues which arises due to revenue shortfalls or mismatches between the timing of cash receipts and payments.

3.1.7 Technical Risk

Technical risk might arise due to obsolescence. New technological processes may face technological risk. Force majeure causes physical damage or economic losses on account of natural disasters, strikes and war. Force majeure affects the proper delivery, operation and termination of projects. ESG guidelines advocates analyzing the environmental risks of projects through environmental impact studies on the project. These studies can quantify the exposure to environmental risk and establish compliance in terms of current laws. Technical risks involve in project construction and technology. Technical risks vary significantly by the type of the project. Technical risk is not high for conventional projects.

3.1.8 Completion Risk

Completion risk covers the risks in the construction, commissioning and ramp up phases of project. Completion risk can be attributed to non-completion on time, budget constraints and performance standards. The sensitivity of completion risk depends on factors such as changes in attributes, ease of contractor replacement, contractual terms, credit enhancement. Projects which have a sizeable portion of revenue that depend on completion of construction work are exposed to completion risk.

3.1.9 Operation Risk

Operation risk is the risk that the project will suffer a reduction in availability, productivity or output. In other perspective, the project might suffer operating, maintenance or life cycle costs which are higher than projected. Operation risk sensitivities depend on factors such as productivity, operations and maintenance costs and life cycle factors. With respect to operating risk, lenders will be concerned with the proven track record of the operator and operating costs.

3.1.10 Market Risk

Market risk consists of principal elements of demand for the project's products and the price at which the products can be sold to service the project debt. Long term off take contracts are used to cover the market risks. For example, in a power project, a power purchase agreement between the local state energy authority may be entered into with a pricing mechanism designed to cover the operating costs of the project company as well as its debt servicing requirements. This mechanism is termed capacity charge or availability charge. In the absence of a guaranteed offtake arrangement, the lender will be concerned about the ready market for the project's product. In oil based projects, the market risk is basically the price risk rather than purchaser risk since there exist an international spot market for oil. Gas is not traded on spot basis due to its characteristics of handling difficulties and transportation problems. In such cases, lenders will insist on long term gas offtake contracts. Project financiers can manage market risk using take-or-pay contracts. In take –or–pay contract, an agreement is entered between the project company and the buyer such that the buyer agrees to take delivery of a minimum amount of products of the project over a stipulated period of time and is obliged to pay for those products whether or not it actually takes the delivery of the products. Such contracts contain "hell or high water" clauses which stipulates that obligation of the buyer to pay for the products even in the scenario of any default by the project company or otherwise. Buyers are ensured of supply of the product at a price which otherwise may not be available to them. Take-or-pay contract in fact is an effective virtual financial guarantee of the loan during the operating period.

3.1.11 Reserve/Production Risk

This type of risk is predominantly found in hydrocarbons and minerals projects. Lenders will analyze the geology and structure of hydrocarbon reservoir in terms of industry wide classifications such as proven reserves. On the basis of estimation of such probable reserves, lenders would determine the amount of financing. Lenders will analyze the extent of difficulty in extracting those reserves when a new technology or drilling is involved.

3.1.12 Supply Risk

Some projects require that a resource or product is available for operation. Supply risk arises when the resource or product are not available in sufficient quantities and/or at prices which allow the project to operate as estimated. In projects which involve the extraction of a resource or commodity, the assessment of supply risk involves the determination of the sufficiency of reserves and cost of extraction of the commodity. Supply risk can be mitigated by long term supply contracts which can fix the volume and/or price at which the resource or product is supplied.

3.1.13 Technology Risk

This risk refers to risks associated with use of nascent technology or unskilled labor deployed for using it.

3.1.14 Revenue Risk

The revenues of a project are driven by factors such as the availability, price and volume of output. Revenue risk arises when the output or service is not properly provided or the project's operating expenses is not met by the revenue generated due to low price or low demand scenario. The revenues are provided by off takers such as government, utility companies, airlines or shipping firms. Projects which have fully contracted revenues such as availability based concessions and energy facilities with tolling agreements are subject to less demand risk. Revenue risks can be related to performance against contract terms such as throughput, availability, efficiency cost risk and counterparty risks associated with the off taker. Some projects such as toll road projects or merchant facilities based power projects without any contractual support are exposed to greater demand risks. Revenue risk sensitivities depend on factors such as counterparty credit quality, demand for output, diversity for output, price elasticity of demand and pricing structure. In airline industry, the revenues are directly related to the volume of traffic. In other words, the substantial portion of airport revenue is ultimately driven by underlying passenger demand.

3.1.15 Obsolescence Risk

Obsolescence risk arises due to competing innovation or demand shift. Projects with fully contracted structures such as power purchase agreements are less exposed to obsolescence risks.

3.1.16 Industry Risks

Industry risks can be viewed in the context of current industry sector outlook in terms of relative competitive position and overall demand and supply conditions.

3.1.17 Force Majeure or Event Risks

These risks are beyond the control of the firm. Event risks arises from natural hazards such as floods, earthquakes, hurricanes, tornadoes and mechanical malfunctions on account of human error. Examples include industrial accidents and explosions. Comprehensive insurance is typically used to cover these risks.

3.1.18 Counter Party Risk

This refers to credit and default risk by a counterparty in a financial transaction. For example, in a renewable energy investment, it is related to the risk of default by power off taker. It is the risk that any counterparty with whom the project company contracts might default the provisions of the contract. The counterparty could be a contractor, bank, purchaser of the product or an insurer. The litigation process as a result of this risk will be time consuming and expensive.

3.1.19 Legal and Structural Risks

Legal risk refers to the risks in which the laws in the host jurisdiction will be interpreted. The laws related to security arrangements is the focus of this kind of risks. Structural risks refer to risks in which all components of a complex project are structured which involves legal advisers and other experts. Typically, complex contractual deals consist of many interlocking documents running into thousands of pages and there is probability of errors and oversights.

3.1.20 Refinancing Risk

Refinancing risk arises on account of the inability of the borrower to refinance the outstanding loan midway through the life of project. This happens due to inadequate loan terms wherein the maturity of the loan is mismatched with the lifetime of the asset.

3.1.21 Resource Risk

It is the risk associated with uncertainties with respect to availability, future price and/or supply of resources for the project. For example, resource risk exists in a renewable energy projects such as geothermal projects. Table 3.1 provides a framework for risk classification related to infrastructure assets. Table 3.2 discusses the financial risk mitigants and incentives for infrastructure finance.

3.2 Risk Mitigation

Risk spreading is critical for project financing since they provide the legal basis for transferring critical project risks to various stakeholders. These stakeholders include the off taker, the suppliers, the constructor, government and the operator [2]. National governments provide credit support for projects of national importance based on economic, political and social factors. Sponsors secure different forms of credit enhancement such as insurance, hedging and third party guarantees. Sponsors also

Table 3.1 Classification of risks linked to infrastructure assets

Risk types	Development Phase	Construction Phase	Operation Phase	Termination Phase
Political and regulatory	Environmental review	Cancellation of permits	Change in tariff regulation	Contract duration
	Rise in preconstruction costs (longer permitting process)	Contract renegotiation		Decommission
				Asset transfer
			Currency convertibility	
	Change in taxation Enforceability of contracts, collateral and security			
	Social acceptance			
	Change in regulatory or legal environment			
	Enforceability of contracts, collateral and security			
Macroeconomic & business	Prefunding	Default of counterparty		
	Financing availability	Refinancing risk		
		Liquidity		
		Volatility of demand/market risk		
	Inflation			
	Real interest rates			
	Exchange rate fluctuation			
Technical	Governance and management of project			Termination value different from expected
	Environmental			
	Project feasibility	Construction delays and cost overruns	Qualitative deficit of the physical structure/service	
	Archaeological			
	Technology and obsolescence			
	Force majeure			

Source: OECD [1], Infrastructure Financing Instruments and Incentives, https://www.oecd.org/finance/private-pensions/Infrastructure-Financing-Instruments-and-Incentives.pdf

bring in additional equity contributions on account of occurrence of certain specified events. Risk spreading instruments in project financing include different kinds of guarantees, long term undertakings and other credit enhancement mechanisms. Direct, limited, indirect, implied or contingent guarantees from sponsors also form credit support for projects. Credit support can also take the form of advanced payments, production payments, commercial guarantees, government assurances and liquidated damages. Risk mitigation in infrastructural projects particularly in renewable energy projects is vital on account of its high upfront capital requirement [3].

3.3 Financial Risk Mitigation Instruments-Guarantees

Guarantees are issued by governments and financial institutions to address political, policy, credit and currency risks. Guarantees are efficient risk mitigation techniques for leveraging private investment with limited public capital. At the same time, probability of potential moral hazard exists as the guarantee may facilitate the buyer with counterproductive incentive to engage in riskier behavior.

Table 3.2 Financial risk mitigants and incentives for infrastructure finance

Type of measure	Instrument
1. Guarantees, realized directly by Government or by its own controlled agency or development bank	1. Minimum payment, paid by contracting authority
	2. Guarantee in case of default
	3. Guarantee in case of refinancing
	4. Exchange rate guarantees
2. Insurance (private sector)	1. Wrap insurance, technology guarantees, warranties, commercial and political risk insurance
3. Hedging (private sector)	1. Derivatives contracts such as swaps, forwards, options etc
4. Contract design, paid by contracting authority	1. Availability payment mechanisms
	2. Offtake contracts
5. Provision of capital, realized directly by Government or by its own controlled agency or development bank	1. Subordinated (junior) debt
	2. Debt: 2.1 at market condition 2.2 at lower interest rate
	3. Equity: 3.1 at market conditions 3.2 at more advantageous conditions
6. Grants, generally delivered by contracting authority, even if some dedicated fund at national level may exists. Tax incentives can be delivered by national or local authorities	1. Lump sum capital grant
	2. Revenue grant: 2.1 Periodic fixed amount (mitigating the demand risk) 2.2 Revenue integration (it leaves the demand risk on the private player)
	3. Grant on debt interests
	4. Favorable taxation schemes for SPV
	5. Favorable taxation schemes for equity investors

Source: OECD [1], Infrastructure Financing Instruments and Incentives, https://www.oecd.org/finance/private-pensions/Infrastructure-Financing-Instruments-and-Incentives.pdf

Research have suggested that enhanced use of guarantees would attract approximately USD 100–165 billion of additional private sector investment in sustainable infrastructure over the next one and half decades [4].

3.4 Direct Guarantees

In a direct guarantee, a guarantor is obligated to perform all the payment obligations of a borrower in case of default of payment by the borrower. Through debt finance guarantee, a sponsor or third party guarantor can secure finance for a project without borrowing the funds directly and thus the direct liability is not shown on its balance sheet. A direct guarantee is basically disclosed as a footnote in the guarantor's financial statement.

3.5 Different Forms of Guarantees

Limited guarantee refers to a guarantee that can be limited in amount, term, scope or combination of them. One of the common guarantee limited in amount which is used in project finance is the cost overrun guarantee. In a cost overrun guarantee, the sponsors provide additional funds at appropriate times to fund the projects during cost overruns. The sources of finances are raised through additional capital, subordinated loans or through hybrid means. Deficiency guarantees cover the lenders' losses in terms of lost interest, unpaid principal amount and unrecoverable expenses. A fully implemented deficiency guarantee along with other credit enhancement tools can provide lenders the same degree of protection similar to a full direct guarantee. Completion guarantee is an example for guarantees limited in time. It is limited in time due to the reason of its expiration on the completion date. A completion guarantee includes both performance and payment guarantee. Contingent guarantees are guarantees limited in scope. In contingent guarantee, the lenders stipulate that guarantee provider undertakes to guarantee debt financing upon occurrence of specific contingencies. Contingent guarantees cover risks such as residual force majeure and political risks. Completion guarantees are expected from shareholders or sponsors of the project by lenders with respect to completion of the project by the stated date. The project is expected to demonstrate the required performance criteria. Minimum demand guarantee stipulates guarantee of a minimum demand of the project output so that minimum cash flow is realized for the project. This type of guarantee is used in toll road projects where a certain minimum traffic flow guarantee from the government is necessary for the viability of the project. Implied guarantees imply that the guarantors will support a project in times of difficulties. The specific feature of indirect guarantees is the presence of certain credit enhancement mechanism to shift specific operating risks to project participants.

3.6 Management Agreements

Management agreements specify the technical assistance, manpower requirements to be available for the completion of the project. These services will have to be provided by the sponsors.

3.7 Equity Contribution Agreements

These agreements specify the additional equity to be provided to the project work.

3.8 Collateral Warranties

Collateral warranties are entered between lenders and professional service firms such as architects, surveyors employed by project company to provide advice and services to the project company. Through collateral warranties, lenders will have enforceable right of recovery against the professional firms to cover the losses incurred by lenders on account of the acts or omissions of the professional service firms.

3.9 Direct Agreements

Direct agreements refer to important commercial agreements which project company enters with third parties. The aim of direct agreement is to protect lenders against the probability of loss of their investment in the event of default by project company based on the key contracts which it had entered with different parties. The key contracts include concession agreement, construction agreement, long term supply contract and off take contract. The EPC contractor, O&M contractor, off taker, input supplier, host government and other stakeholders are required to sign the direct agreement with the lender of the project. Through direct agreement, the security interests of the lenders in the underlying project contracts are acknowledged. No amendments to the direct agreement can be made without the lenders' consent. The lenders can appoint a nominee to undertake the project company's rights.

3.10 Government Support Agreement

It is also known by different names such as coordination or cooperation agreement. In many countries, there is no need for government support agreement as the general law of the country safeguards the interest of the project in the host country. The agreement sets the general framework for the project and provides guarantees of non-discrimination for the construction and operation of the project on an exclusive basis. The project company may be given the right to use the project site through a lease agreement. Under the agreement, the host government may exempt the project company from obtaining permits for import of equipment. Host government guarantees is provided for provisions of utilities such as road, rail, water, power and telecommunication facilities for the proper functioning of the project. Government support agreement also include features such as the principle of non-discrimination like no change of law that will have a material adverse effect on the project in terms of changes to specifications of the project. Host government support agreement also provide guarantees for availability of foreign exchange to the project company to service its debt obligations to the project lenders. Such support systems are critical when the revenues from project are in local currency and debt payments are in terms of a foreign currency. Government support agreement also stipulates no expropriation or nationalization without full compensation to the project company. The agreement may also deal with taxation levels for the project company in terms of principle of nondiscrimination. The agreement covers guarantee with respect to consents and permits for the effective implementation of the project work. Early projects such as North Sea oil and gas financing undertakings had entered into government support agreement with UK government.

3.11 Comfort Letters

Comfort letters are provided by host government or shareholders of the project company to the project company. The host government or the shareholder may be constrained to provide legally binding commitment and hence provide comfort letters which contain obligations which are enforceable in the courts.

3.12 Public Sector Guarantees

Guarantees can be classified into revenue guarantees and credit guarantees. Credit guarantees are offered by governments or multilateral development institutions on debt instruments and exports. A minimum revenue guarantee (MRG) are offered for commercially viable projects with uncertainty in future revenue generation. MRG covers the amount of revenue which is necessary to cover debt payments. MRG are used for transportation projects such as toll roads on account of uncertainty in traffic estimates. In the year 2009, Indonesia established the Indonesian Infrastructure Guarantee Fund to back MRG guarantees. The important characteristics of guarantees on debt is that public funding will be provided to service debt held by third party investors in a scenario in which the project is not able to generate enough revenues to cover the interest or principal payment. Full credit guarantees cover the entire amount of debt service in the event of default. Full credit guarantees are also known as wrap guarantee. Wrap guarantee can also be structured to cover specific tranches of debt. First loss coverage guarantee provided by US's SIB, TIFIA etc. provide credit support for senior tranches. US State Infrastructure Banks (SIB) facilitate financing support to projects through loan guarantees, bond insurance and standby letters of credit. The US Transportation Infrastructure Finance and Innovation Act (TIFIA) provides direct federal loans or guarantees on projects up to 33% of project cost. Partial credit guarantees (PCG) aims to cover a part of certain predetermined portion of debt or particular instruments related to the capital structure of a special purpose vehicle. This type of guarantees is also known as pari-passu guarantees in which private lenders and public sector guarantors share in credit losses to the extent of the amount guaranteed. Export credit guarantees cover risks linked to the export of goods and services and are provided by export credit agencies. Export credit guarantees may cover a part of both political and commercial risk. Guarantees are issued by multilateral and bilateral institutions, national government and development banks. Institutions such as Overseas Private Investment Corporation (OPIC) provides both political risk insurance and loan guarantees. Guarantee mechanism take different forms such as direct commitments from public budget or establishment of a separate guarantee fund. The public guarantee lowers the cost of credit since the guarantee reduces the repayment risk.

3.13 Government Guarantee

Basically, government guarantee is issued by the treasury or ministry of finance for projects in developing countries. In many cases, the commercial lenders require government guarantee due to the lack of confidence about the project's financial viability without government backing. In some cases, governments are constrained to provide a letter of comfort on account of public sector financial constraints or IMF obligations. For some government backed PPA, additional guarantee letter is not provided.

3.14 Alternatives to Government Guarantees

In a national bank guarantee, the central bank or state level public financial institution may guarantee a project instead of the government department like Ministry of Finance. In countries such as Argentina and Spain, reciprocal guarantee partnerships are set up by federal or provincial government banks along with a liquid fund for collateral purposes. Corporate guarantee fund or trust with good credit rating and solvency standards can be considered as alternatives to government guarantees.

3.15 Private Sector Guarantees and Insurance

Risk mitigation can be achieved through letters of credit, guarantees and insurance contracts in private sector. Revenue guarantees for business risks, credit guarantees on debt instruments and insurance against political and regulatory risks are also prevalent in private sector. In renewable energy sectors private insurance guarantees covers construction and operational risks.

3.16 Project Insurance

From lender's viewpoint insurances are integral and critical element of the overall security package for a project. Different parties will be responsible for insurances for the project during the different life stages of the project. For example, during the construction period, the principal insurance cover will be arranged by the contractor through a Contractor's All Risks policy. In some cases, sponsors delegate insurance arrangement to individual project firms to arrange on a project by project basis instead of centralization of all insurance arrangements. Insurance related to project finance are classified into commercial insurance and political insurance. Political insurance is provided by export credit agencies, bilateral and multilateral financial institutions and development financial institutions. Commercial insurance is provided for all kinds of casualty risks. Commercial insurance covers the construction and operation phases of a project. Commercial insurance covers the construction, testing and commissioning phase of the project. Insurance program for construction phase covers all risk insurance known as builder's risk; delay in startup insurance, marine cargo insurance and third party liability insurance. Project insurance in construction phase covers physical damage to project facilities; assets; transit insurance; workmen compensation, environmental liability insurance etc. Similar insurance covers are also provided during the operating phase of projects. All or a significant part of an insurance policy is reinsured with other insurers. Reinsurance with offshore insurers is expected by both lenders and local insurers.

3.17 Political Risk Insurance

Political risk insurance is of much significance particularly for projects undertaken in countries with weak political system or inadequate laws. Political risk insurance is provided by public financial institutions. Multilateral Investment Guarantee Agency (MIGA) of World Bank Group is the largest provider of political risk insurance in terms of volume. MIGA provide political risk insurance for events such as war, terrorism and civil disturbance; Currency inconvertibility; breach of contract; expropriation and non-honoring of commitments towards financial obligations. Political risk insurance covers losses from revolution, insurrection and sabotage. Losses due to currency inconvertibility and transfer restrictions arises when investor is constrained to convert local currency into hard currency due to government actions. Breach of contract results in losses due to breach or repudiation of a contract related to a project by a government organization. The coverage of breach of contract in a PPA involves arbitration. Expropriation results in losses and reduction in investors' ownership or control over an asset through government action such as outright nationalization or confiscation. Creeping expropriation refers to a series of acts over time which lead to expropriation. Losses are realized when state owned enterprises default on financial payment obligations such as guarantees of loan repayment or equity injection. Political risk insurance is also used to mitigate policy and power off taker risks. US based development financial institution (DFI) offers protection against power off taker risks for renewable energy investments. Such insurances become applicable when government owned utility firms breaches the purchasing agreement by changing policies without negotiations. Governments in different markets assume the role of off takers through state owned utilities and are involved in implementing policies for revenue generation through feed –in-tariffs and tax credits. The use of political risk instruments can attract private capital for projects. The government related risks in the 250 megawatt Bujagali hydropower project in Uganda was covered by MIGA political risk insurance through breach of contract coverage for up to 90 percent of the equity investment. On account of this attractive feature, Bujagali project was able to attract higher level of private investment [5].

3.18 Partial Risk Guarantee

Partial risk guarantee can be used to mitigate policy and regulatory risks. World Bank introduced this type of guarantee to cover political risks for project with longer duration. This instrument ensures government's obligation to compensate for loss of regulated revenues which results from defined regulatory risks. Partial risk guarantees are used for covering transmission line and grid interconnection risk which are owned by government organizations. African Development Bank issued its first ever partial risk guarantee through the African Development Fund for the largest wind project in Africa, the Lake Turkana project [6]. The project involved the construction of a 310 MW wind farm which comprised of 365 turbines of 850 KW capacity. The bank deposited EUR 20 million into an escrow account of EUR 90 million for the project. This scheme covered the off taker's PPA payment obligation for the first six months. Kenyan government provided EUR 70 million and issued a letter of support to cover political risk [7]. The partial risk guarantee covered the delay risk for the construction of a 428 kilometer publicly owned transmission line between substations which was required to connect the project to the national grid [8].

3.19 Partial Credit Guarantee

Partial credit guarantee is used to cover part of the debt service default by the borrower for a specific period of debt term. This type of credit guarantees is used to cover currency transfer and convertibility risks in renewable energy projects. IFC have a partial credit guarantee which is aimed to mitigate currency risk and provide guarantee for the debt portion of financing during a specified period. Partial credit guarantees can be used in small and medium sized renewable energy companies. The US department of Energy loan guarantee scheme supports the promotion of new projects involving nascent technologies through partial credit guarantee programs. Partial credit guarantees are often used to reduce power off taker risk in developing countries. Partial credit guarantee structure was used to mitigate power off taker risk in Kalangala Infrastructure Services project in Uganda. This project was envisaged to provide a range of infrastructure services like improved access to water, transportation and solar energy [9]. This partial credit guarantee provide cover to both commercial banks and institutional lenders thereby facilitating private sector investment in the project.

3.20 Export Credit Guarantee

Export credit guarantees cover default on any debt service of private exporters or their lenders. Export credit guarantees offers a comprehensive risk coverage for mitigating technology risks for projects and equipment manufacturers without a proven track record. Export credit guarantees also facilitate access to affordable project finance with long term tenors. Under OECD arrangement, export credit agencies offer longer credit repayment periods for renewable energy projects. The longer tenor enables more flexibility in cash flow and reduce the repayment risk to borrowers.

3.21 Currency Risk Mitigation Instruments: Derivative Contracts

Currency risk arises when the inflows are in one currency and outflows (loan) repayments are in another currency. A mismatch between financing currency (hard currency) and revenue currency would lead to debt repayment issues. It is often observed transnational project developers often insulate from currency risk by dealing with hard currency. On account of high costs involved in currency hedging instruments, other options such as currency risk guarantee fund or local currency lending instruments are often used in energy projects.

The technique of taking an offsetting position on a security involving selling or buying is called hedging. This technique is used to mitigate market and commercial risks. Hedging instruments such as forward contracts and swaps are used to address currency mismatch in projects.

Derivative contracts are used for hedging purposes in project finance. Derivative contracts are used to hedge interest rate exposures. Currency derivatives such as forwards, futures and swaps are used for hedging currency exposures in project finance. Derivative contracts are used to hedge market exchange rate fluctuations and hedge convertibility risks.

3.22 Currency Risk Guarantee Fund

This type of guarantee fund covers the differences in exchange rate values between local and hard currencies over a longer term period. The solar development plan proposed by Government of India aims to support solar development through currency risk guarantee fund. In this scheme, the distribution firms would quote their price for solar energy in hard currency (USD) by entering into 25 year contracts and charge customers in Indian rupees [6].

3.23 Local Currency Lending

Currency mismatch can be addressed through local currency financing. Developmental financial institutions can provide local currency lending by establishing capital in funds. For example, TCX Currency Fund offers local currency lending in 40 developing markets [10]. GuarantCo which is sponsored by governments of the UK, Sweden, Switzerland and Netherlands facilitates local currency loans for projects in emerging markets. GuarantCo provides flexible guarantees over local currency loans to support projects and companies in raising debt financing in emerging markets. GuarantCo provides partial credit and partial risk guarantees, first loss guarantees, tenor extension or liquidity guarantees [11, 12].

The 25.5 MW Cabeólica wind farm project was the first commercial-scale wind farm in sub-Saharan Africa. To address the currency risk, the PPA envisaged transactions denominated in local currency but pegged to the Euro. A clause was included to adjust the payment currency in the extreme scenario that the local currency should be disconnected from the Euro at any point during the life time of the PPA which was 20-year period.

3.24 Liquidity Risk mitigation Instruments-Internal Techniques

Liquidity risk arises when projects are affected by liquidity constraints or when there is a mismatch between the timings of cash receipts and payments. Liquidity risk mitigation instruments are used to provide short term cash flow to a project. These instruments are used internally within a project structure or externally alongside the special purpose vehicle (SPV). Internal liquidity facilities are used to support payments to bridge short term cash flow problems [13]. Internal liquidity facilities such as debt service reserve accounts can be used to provide funding for a limited period of time during cash flow crisis. Excess spread account can be created to accumulate cash flow above that is required for debt service in a separate account. The process of over collateralization provides additional assets in which the SPV can draw on to supplement the cash available for debt service. When the amount of collateral is more than which is required for securing financing, the project company can have bond issuance. This process of over collateralization provides additional assets which the SPV can draw on to supplement the cash flow available for debt service. In 2013, Solar City issued its first asset backed securities and approximately 62 per cent of the value of the underlying assets (solar PVs) was held as over collateralization. During the project development phase, contingent equity protects lenders from cost overruns. Contingent equity tranches were used for renewable energy projects such as Sarulla geothermal and Walney off shore wind farm projects.

3.25 Liquidity Risk Mitigation Instruments: External Liquidity Techniques

The additional risk on account of cash flow shortfall is adjusted using liquidity premium. This liquidity premium is added to the financing cost thereby increasing the cost of capital for the project. External liquidity facilities can loosen liquidity constraints for power off takers. It has to be noted that most off takers have to provide full cash collateral to back their letters of credit. Liquidity facility can provide short term letter of credit or credit line without the additional cash requirements from utilities. Regional Liquidity Support Facility (RLSF) is offered to projects implemented in five countries by German development bank in collaboration with African Trade Insurance Agency and IRENA. The program is aimed at renewable IPPs in the region [14].

3.26 Liquidity Guarantee

Liquidity guarantee aims to help project developers to overcome liquidity and refinancing risk. Multilateral financial institutions use liquidity guarantees to lengthen the maturities of local currency finance. World Bank used liquidity guarantee facility for the West Nile Rural Electrification Project in Uganda. In Uganda, the regulation stipulates maximum loan tenor to eight years. To circumvent this regulation for a longer term loan, World Bank structured two separate senior loans for local banks to provide financing for the project. The tenure of the first loan was eight years and would expire when a bullet repayment of outstanding principal was made. The funding for repayment was made from a new seven-year loan thereby extending the repayment period to 15 years. The fees and margin payable for banks were designed to incentivize the financing for the extended period.

3.27 Put Options

Put options can be used to mitigate renewable energy investment refinancing risk. Multilateral financial institutions provide a put option to local commercial bank lenders to facilitate long term lending for borrowers. Put options were used by World Bank for Leyte geothermal project in Philippines [15].

3.28 Resource Risk Mitigation

Governments support risk mitigation with respect to resource risk through distribution of grants and guarantees to eligible exploration projects. Dedicated guarantee instruments can manage specific challenges of energy project development.

3.29 Grants

Grants can aid in renewable energy development. For example, Geothermal Risk Mitigation Facility established by the African Union Commission, the German Federal Ministry for Economic Cooperation and Development in collaboration with EU-Africa Infrastructure Trust Fund provides grants for surface studies and exploration drilling in energy projects [16, 17].

3.29.1 Convertible Grants

Financial institutions and government agencies provide convertible grants for mitigating resource risk in geothermal exploration drilling process. For example, the Geothermal Development Facility in Latin America established by the consortium of EU, Germany and development banks had allocated funds of USD 75 million as convertible grants with additional commitments of USD 1 billion. These grants provide a safety cushion for projects as a buffer against unsuccessful drills [15].

3.29.2 Guarantee Funds

This funds provide a safety net for developers of energy project in the scenario of unsuccessful drilling results. The Inter-American Development bank established a geothermal financing and risk transfer scheme with funds of USD 85 million to provide loan guarantees for drilling and production phase for projects. Ministry of Finance, Indonesia had also set up USD 300 million geothermal guarantee fund to mitigate resource risk [18, 19].

3.29.3 Exploration Insurance

Exploration insurance through public private partnership facilitate private insurers and government to share the risk in energy projects. Munich Re had implemented an insurance product for exploration risk in Turkey.

3.29.4 Portfolio Guarantees

Portfolio guarantees cover a proportion of the losses on a group of projects in order to diversify exploration risks across different geothermal projects. Munich Re have provided portfolio guarantees for eight drillings to cover exploration risks.

3.29.5 Advance Payment Contracts

An off taker purchases the future production in advance from the project company at a price which will be equal to the present value of the future cash flows.

3.30 Availability Payments

Availability payments are commonly used by the state in infrastructure sector projects. The contracting authority usually pays the counterparty for providing the facilities. Availability payments are used in social infrastructure sector and public transportation projects such as roads, railways, bridges etc. The concept of shadow toll is conceived in the context that user does not pay directly for the usage of the facility, but the facilitator receives payment from the public authority on the basis of usage volume. This form of shadow toll is used in transport sector.

3.30.1 Offtake Contracts

In offtake contracts, project company in sectors such as power supply output to the contracting authority at a pre-agreed price thereby reducing future revenue uncertainties. Offtake contracts aid in locking in an agreed upon rate with regulators. Offtake contracts facilitate in lowering cash flow volatility and enhances the credit rating of the project.

3.30.2 Capital Financing

Project risk mitigation strategies also involve provisions of equity or debt investments by government agencies and multilateral development institutions. Subsidies offered can reduce financing costs and free up capital for other commitments. Under the TIFIA program, low cost loans based on treasury rates are offered to eligible transportation projects in US [12].

3.30.3 Grants and Taxation

A grant is a payment made by the contracting authority to the executioner of the project. Grants are paid out at any time of the project life cycle. A grant can reduce or offset the objective risks in project finance. Tax incentives such as reduction or suspension of property tax or extension of tax breaks on investment revenues can result in providing subsidy benefits for the life of the projects.

3.30.4 Designing Security Arrangements for Projects

Security is a critical element in project financing. Lenders have no recourse to the assets of the sponsors of the project. The lenders primarily look at the potential of future cash flows generated by the project for repayment of loans taken by the project company. Hence it is paramount for lenders to put in place adequate security to cover their risks in the project. If the project company is a Special Purpose Vehicle (SPV), then the lenders will control the assets of the project company. If the project company is not a SPV, then the assets will be ring fenced in the context that the lenders activities will be limited to the process of enforcing their security against the project assets only. This principle of ring fencing of individual projects is of much significance to sponsors, project companies and lenders.

3.31 Completion Agreement

The features of completion agreement will depend on factors such as type and magnitude of project risks, the financial strength and profitability of the project. The security arrangement related to completion involve an obligation to complete the project on time or else repay the debt amount. Lenders require an unconditional undertaking from sponsors to provide additional funds needed to complete the project according to design specifications. Completion agreement is defined in terms of the commercial completion when all elements of the project are completed. Specifically, it refers to the condition in which the project has sustained a certain level of operations over a specified period of time.

3.32 Concession Agreement

Concession agreement is an important part of the security structure. It basically bestows the right to the project company to build, use and operate the project. In the absence of concession agreement, the value of security over any fixed assets like plant and machinery is likely to be very limited. In Build -Operate –Transfer projects, the concession agreement is the main contractual agreement in which the project company is entrusted with the right to explore, exploit, develop the concession or other relevant rights to the project. A concession agreement is a contract between project company and a public sector entity to provide service through the project. Examples of concession agreement include contracts for construction and operation of toll roads, bridges and tunnels. Concession agreements also covers transportation system such as railways or metros; water and sewage systems; ports and airports. Concession agreements can be classified into service contracts and toll contracts. In service contracts, the service is provided to a contracting body but the usage risk tends to remain with the contracting authority. In toll contracts, the concession agreement gives the right to collect tolls of fares from the public. Toll contracts are widely used in infrastructural projects for construction of roads, bridges, tunnels and railways. The concession agreement covers the obligation of the project company to complete the project within the agreed upon date. The contracting authority is entitled to provide the required land and rights under the concession agreement. The ownership of the project facilities will remain with the public sector. The concession would be granted for a fixed period of time. Usually a maximum toll or fare is set with indexation for inflation. The project company will have to pay penalties for failure to maintain safety standards.

3.33 Construction Agreement

Construction agreement which is an important part of the lender's security is one of the key contracts entered for the construction period. Normally the lenders seek a direct agreement with the contractor. Turnkey contract is the most common form of construction contract in which a single general contractor assumes all risk of on time completion of project within the guaranteed performance standards. In a typical turnkey contract, the sponsor specifies overall performance and reliability standards for the plant and the complete responsibility to design, construct, supply, install, test and commission the plant within the framework of specified requirement is entrusted to the turnkey contractor. In a scenario wherein there is no turnkey contractor, then lenders will implement separate security interests over all of the construction related agreements. The EPC contract sets out the design, technical specification and performance criteria for the project. EPC contractor has the responsibility to employ or pay any subcontractors or equipment suppliers involved in the project. In principle the EPC contract is fixed and payment is normally made in stages with pre agreed milestones based on completion of major stages of the work.

3.34 Operating and Maintenance Agreements

Once the project is commissioned, the role of an experienced and skilful operator is critical for the overall success of the project. The salient feature of operating and maintenance agreement (O&M) will involve the allocation of risk of operation and maintenance of the working of project to the operator. In this process, the project company and lenders pass on the risk of operations and maintenance to the operator. The O&M agreement envisages that the project is operated to maximize the revenue earning capacity of the projects. Another focus of the agreement is to ensure that the facilities are operated and maintained at standard levels within the budgetary constraints as agreed upon with project company and lenders. There are three basic structures for an operating and maintenance agreement. In the fixed price structure, the operator is paid a fixed price for operating the project. When cost overrun occurs based on operating budget, the operator will bear the risk. When cost savings result, the operator will earn higher profits. As the operator is bearing the risk, fixed price contracts are designed to be more expensive in nature. In cost plus structure, the project company will pay the operator an agreed fixed fee along with the costs incurred by the operator for the operation of the project. Under this scheme, the operator will transfer the costs involved in operating the project to the project company and the fixed fee is the profit for the operator. In this structure the project company assumes the risk of enhanced operating costs. In this structure the project company is entitled to get the right to terminate the contract at a short notice if the operator fails to operate the project efficiently according to stated standards. In incentive or penalty structure the operator's remuneration is tied to the strict performance targets such that in instances where the operator achieves the stated targets, the operator will receive bonus for performance. Conversely if the operator fails to achieve the agreed performance targets, penalties in the form of reduced compensation will be imposed. The maximum level of bonuses or penalties will be specified in the contract. Basically lenders prefer incentive/penalty structure form of contract, as it insulates the project company from operating risks to a greater extent and enable the project to operate efficiently within the budgetary constraints. The major responsibilities of O&M contract include securing operating permits, ordering and handling input supplies, keeping operating costs within budget limits, scheduling and carrying out routine inspections and maintenance. Normally a range of 5%–10% of each contract payment is retained by the project company until the satisfactory final completion of the project. EPC contractor is usually required to provide a bond for approximately 15 percent of the contract value. EPC contractor normally provides warranties against failure of equipment known as maintenance bond for a specified period of time [20].

3.35 Performance Bonds

Performance bonds are also known as parent company guarantee. If the contractor has to submit performance bonds from bank or insurance company or a parent company guarantee for a construction agreement, then it would offer additional security for the lenders. Performance bonds or guarantee are commonly valued in the range of 10–20 percent of the total contract price. Such bonds provided by banks or insurance companies are payable on demand and are not subject to proof of default or breach by the contractor.

3.36 Fuel Supply Agreement

The project company along with off take contract often enters into an input supply contract which matches the general terms of the offtake contract like the duration of the contract. Otherwise the input supply contract matches at least the term of debt. The fuel supply agreement covers the technical specification of the input supplies. The supply could be variable or fixed. Sometimes the input supplier dedicates the entire output from its plant to the project company. In cases wherein the input supplier has to build a pipeline to the project site, then the project company would be required to pay a capacity payment to cover the cost of construction of the pipeline. For operations, many projects require fuel supply agreement for uninterrupted supply of fuel such as coal and oil. Lenders also prefer the project company to enter into a contract to secure reliable source of fuel for the entire period covering the project. The biggest advantage for the project company is that the fuel supply agreement with supplier on a long term basis provides the fuel on a pre-determined price structure. Otherwise the project company will be compelled to purchase fuel from spot market thereby exposing to fuel supply and price risks. Fuel supply agreements exist in two forms. Under pay or take contract, the project company is obliged to take delivery of an agreed volume of fuel at an agreed price over a specified period. Even if the project company do not take the delivery of the agreed level of fuel, the payment must be made according to the provisions in the contract. The fuel supplier is obligated to supply the agreed level of fuel at the stipulated price. Under the sole supplier contract, the project company enters into a contract with a single supplier to purchase the project's entire fuel requirement from that supplier. In sole supplier contract, it is not necessary to specify the actual amount of fuel requirement and the price to be paid for it. The project company will pay for the fuel it actually buys. Lenders prefer take or pay contracts since the contract commits a secure source of supply at a pre-determined price for the project.

3.37 Sales/Offtake Agreement

A long term sales contract entitles sales on arm's length terms with the price in reference to market prices. Pass through agreements and Take or pay agreement are the two major types of sales agreement. Pass through agreement is a common structure for power projects. In pass through agreements, the charges are calculated on a pass through basis and are calculated by reference to the costs incurred by the project company. The costs transferred to the buyer might include the whole or any part of the costs of purchasing fuel, principal and interest payment to lenders and operating and maintenance costs. In take or pay agreement, the buyer pays for the supplies of the project company's product even if the buyer does not require the product. In gas sector, long term off take contracts are common.

3.37.1 Throughput Agreement

Throughput agreement are found in oil and gas pipeline projects wherein the user of the pipeline agrees to carry a certain minimum quantity of the product through the pipeline and is obliged to pay for the use of such pipeline even if it doesn't use the pipeline.

3.37.2 Take if Needed Contracts

The purchasers in long term sales and purchase agreement has the right to decide if or not to take the output from the project based on the needs.

3.37.3 Put or Pay Contracts

These are long term contractual obligations of the seller or supplier to unconditionally deliver a particular supply to a project at a fixed, escalated, variable or maximum price. Put or pay contracts are used by project company to meet the production costs and delivery targets as specified under the off take contracts.

References

1. OECD REPORT 2015, Infrastructure Financing Instrument and Risk Incentives.
2. Gatti, S. (2014), "Private Financing and Government Support to Promote Long-term Investments in Infrastructure", OECD Publishing, Paris.
3. The Inter-American Dialogue (2015), Is Latin America a Good Fit for Geothermal Energy?, Latin America Advisor.
4. Bielenberg et al. (2016), Financing change: How to mobilize private sector financing for sustainable infrastructure. McKinsey Center for Business and Environment.
5. Frisari, G. and V. Micale (2015), Risk Mitigation Instruments for Renewable Energy in Developing Countries: A Case Study on Hydropower in Africa. Climate Policy Initiative.
6. Clean Energy Pipeline (2015), Clean Energy Africa Finance Guide 2015 Edition, Clean Energy Pipeline
7. Unlocking renewable energy investment: The role of risk mitigation and structured finance, Copyright © IRENA 2016.
8. AfDB (2013), AfDB Approves First Partial Risk Guarantee for Renewable Energy Project, African Development Bank, www.afdb.org/en/news-andevents/article/first-adf-partial-risk-guarantee-approved-in-kenya-forlargest-african-wind-power-project-12324
9. Gatti, S. and Della Croce, R. (2015). "International trends in infrastructure finance", in Caselli S., Corbetta G., Vecchi V. (2015), Public Private Partnership for infrastructure and business development, Palgrave Macmillan, New York.
10. TCX Fund (2013), Local Currency Matters, TCX Fund, www.tcxfund.com/sites/default/files/attachments/160113_tcx_overview_global_english_ master.pdf
11. GuarantCo (2016), About GuarantCo, GuarantCo, www.guarantco.com/about-us (accessed April 2021).
12. White House Factsheet: Increasing Investment in U.S. Roads, Ports, Drinking Water Systems Through Innovative Financing
13. Yescombe, E.R. (2014), Principles of Project Finance, Elsevier
14. Matsukawa, T. and O. Habeck (2007), Review of Risk Mitigation Instruments for Infrastructure Financing and Recent Trends and Developments (Trends and policy options No. 4), The World Bank Public-Private Infrastructure Advisory Facility (PPIAF), Washington, D.C., USA.
15. Wang et al. (2013), Unlocking Commercial Financing for Clean Energy in East Asia (No. 81112), Directions in Development Energy and Mining, World Bank, Washington D.C., USA
16. Schwartz, J. Z., Ruiz-Nuñez, F., & Chelsky, J. (2014). „Closing the Infrastructure Finance Gap: Addressing Risk". Financial Flows Infrastructure Financing, 141.
17. Qbic (2015), Mitigating risks in geothermal development, Workshop on Financing Geothermal Development in the Andes, 23 September, Bogota, Colombia
18. Farooquee, A. and G. Shrimali (2016), Driving Foreign Investment to Renewable Energy in India: A Payment Security Mechanism to Address Off-Taker Risk (Technical Paper), Climate Policy Initiative
19. KfW (2015), Geothermal Development Facility (GDF): the First MultiDonor Climate Initiative to Promote Geothermal Energy in Latin America, KfW.
20. ME Project finance guide, A guide to project finance. Dentons/dentons.com.

Structuring and Implementation of the Project

A typical structure for project finance is a special purpose vehicle (SPV) structure. The Special Purpose Vehicle is structured in the form of contractual agreements with different stakeholders. There will be shareholder agreement and loan agreement, offtake contracts, direct agreements and security agreements with different parties. Sponsors choose project finance with non-recourse provisions basically to insulate themselves from risk of failure of project which would have an effect on their debt repayment capacity. Structuring the project vehicle can take different forms like joint venture, partnership, limited partnership or limited company structure. Joint venture is a common form of project financing vehicle observed in oil and gas projects. Joint Ventures and limited company structure are the most common form of project financing structures used. A joint venture is a contractual arrangement between different companies to engage in a business activity. The joint venture partners will bring in their expertise to the project along with funds for the project costs. One of the partner may have the overall responsibility to manage or operate the project. Partnerships are similar to joint ventures Limited partners provide project capital for a project. In a special purpose vehicle structure, the SPV is established exclusively for the purpose of the project. The terms on which the SPV is structured would be set out in the shareholder's agreement. The joint venture or the SPV established depend on a number of legal, tax, accounting and regulatory issues. The lenders to the SPV will have no recourse to the sponsors other than guarantees given by the sponsors. In real sense, the sponsors exposure to the project is limited to the value of the equity or subordinated debt which they had contributed to the project. Project finance is also known as off balance sheet financing. The sponsors don't show the liabilities in the balance sheet, instead it appears in the footnote. The use of joint venture can result in significant tax advantages in some jurisdictions. The form of special purpose vehicle would be attractive when different sponsors require to fund their investment in the project in different ways. The sponsors have multiple functions with different aspects such as specifying technical aspects, negotiating with lenders, suppliers and off takers, making arrangements for consents and permits. Sponsors will also have to carry out tasks such as appointment of financial, technical, insurance, environmental and legal advisers to the project.

In Undivided joint interest structure, all assets of the project are owned by participants as tenants in common and ownership interests relate collectively to all property. The co-owners appoint an operator to manage the project. In corporation structure, a new corporation is formed to construct, own and operate the project. In corporation structure, the sponsors of the project raise the funds through the sponsors equity contributions and debt securities issued by the corporation. The debt securities issued may be mortgage bonds or debentures. The corporation form can also be used to issue other forms of debt securities such as second mortgage, unsecured or subordinated debt, preferred stock or convertible securities. The partnership form of organization is used for structuring joint venture projects. The project sponsor can become the partner in the partnership either directly or through a subsidiary. The partnership hires its personnel for operations and provides a management structure for the functioning of the partnership. Master Limited partnership (MLP) is a form of publicly traded limited partnership. MLP structure exist in industries such as oil and gas and other natural resource extraction. The owners enjoy limited liability and qualify for partnership tax treatment. MLPs were free of double taxation and are publicly traded.

4.1 Stakeholders in Project Financing

Borrower or Project Company will be the company, partnership or the joint venture. According to certain legal regulations in certain jurisdiction, it is mandatory for the holder of the license be a company incorporated in that particular country. The project company will be the borrower of the project finance. The project sponsor or the shareholder has the responsibility of bringing together different stakeholders and obtaining the necessary permits and consents for the project during the construction, operation and maintenance stages. Third party equity investors also invest in the project. Their role is primarily passive in nature and investment is basically to earn returns rather than providing services to the project in terms of construction or operating activities. Banks play a crucial role in project finance through the process of loan syndication in the project. The lead bank will be the main underwriter of the project and provides the necessary funding along with the other group of banks selected for syndication purposes. These banks share the fees for the syndication. One of the lending bank act as a facility agent to administer the loan on behalf of the syndication group. The technical bank will evaluate the technical aspects of the project on the behalf of the syndicate group. The insurance bank will be responsible for negotiations in connection with the project insurances on behalf of the lenders. It will liaise with an insurance adviser on behalf of the lenders for the project. The insurance bank has the responsibility of the completion and documentation of project insurances. The lender bank which will process the project cash flows is known as the account bank. Disbursements are processed through disbursement account and project receipts are received through proceeds account. Multilateral development banks play a vital role in project finance. These financial institutions like World bank, IFC, European Bank for Reconstruction and Development (EBRD) provides international commercial banks guarantees against a multitude of political risks which the project might encounter. Export credit agencies also play a significant role in the financing of infrastructure projects in emerging countries. These agencies provide subsidized finance to the exporter or to importers through buyer credits. In an infrastructure project on turnkey model basis, the construction company is given the full responsibility to design, procure, construct and commission the project facility by the project company. The operator is responsible for the day to day operation and maintenance of the project in accordance with pre agreed parameters and guidelines as specified by the operations and maintenance contract agreement. Experts are the expert consultancies and professional firms who provide advice to lenders with respect to technical aspects of the project. Host government is also an important stakeholder in major projects. Suppliers are companies which supply essential goods and services in connection with a project. For example, the fuel supplier is a key stakeholder in a power project. Purchasers generally purchase the output of the project. Usually off take contracts are signed in advance with the purchaser to purchase the project's output on a long term basis. For example, there may be a long term gas offtake contract with a government gas off taker. In a power project, the off taker may be a national energy company. The host government supports the project by facilitating issuance or permits and consents. The host government may also become the purchaser or off taker of products. The host government may provide a protective environment for the project to function through agreements such as government support agreements. Insurers provide cover against loss due to major casualties affecting the project. In oil industry sector, big companies have set up their own offshore captive insurance companies.

4.2 Project Documents

The financing documents in a project can be categorized into shareholder/sponsor agreements, loan and security documents and other project documents. Predevelopment agreements are entered into by project sponsors to undertake feasibility study with respect to a project. The project sponsors enter into shareholder agreement and establish special purpose vehicle for the project. The agreement specifies the features such as share capital investment, funding of project company, voting requirements, resolution of disputes and management of special purpose vehicle. Joint venture agreement also contains many of the above stated features. The sponsors may also enter into a support agreement with project company and lenders which basically deals with commitments on the part of the sponsors towards lenders and project company. Sponsors give completion guarantees and undertakes to provide management and technical assistance. Project loan agreement is basically a syndicated loan agreement entered between borrower, the project lenders and the facility agent. The project loan agreement will additionally specify the provisions relate to representations, covenants and events of default.

The agreement will contain the usual provisions relating to representations, covenants and events of default found in other syndicated loan agreements but expanded to cover the project, project documents and related matters.

4.3 Build Operate Transfer Model

Different projects have been structured and financed on the basis of BOT model. The model of DBFO stands for design, build, finance and operate structure. BOT model refers to build, operate and transfer. DBOT signifies design, build, operate and transfer structure. FBOOT structure refers to finance, build, own, operate and transfer model. BOD model refers to model of build, operate and deliver. BOO concept is based on build, own and operate. BOOST model is based on themes of build, own, operate, subsidize and transfer. BOL is based on the concept of build, operate and lease. BRT is based on model of build, rent and transfer.

BOT and BOO refer to structures which utilize private investment to undertake public sector infrastructure projects. In these systems, a project would be designed, financed, built and operated by a private entity under the terms and conditions of a concession or license granted by the appropriate agency representing the government. BOOT form represent an intermediate degree of privatization since the ownership of the facility is transferred to the private sector for a limited period of time. In projects such as toll roads, toll bridges, railways which uses BOT structure, governments are reluctant to transfer ownership of transport networks to private sector. However, power generation projects may be privatized by BOT, BOOT or BOO structures.

4.4 Forward Purchase Model

In this structure, the project lenders would facilitate an "Advance Payment Facility" for the purchase of products generated by the project. The project company would use the proceeds of the advance payment for the construction and development of the project. Following the delivery of the products, the lenders will sell the product on the market or sell them to the project company and receive the proceeds. There will be an indemnity by the lenders for any loss or liability which the lenders might suffer on account of taking the products. A production payment structure is often used to gain significant tax advantages. Under this structure, the lenders acquire a production ownership in a project. The lenders would be entitled to an agreed share of the project's production which is proportionate to the production payment which the lenders have received.

4.5 Borrowing Base Model

Borrowing base model is used in financing of oil and gas assets. Borrowers are entitled to drawn funds for financing of projects in such a way that the cover ratios are satisfied. For risk coverage, the lender would take the security of all assets based on the borrowing base formulae.

4.5.1 Issues in Project Finance Loan Documentation

Project lenders use financial cover ratios in evaluating the performance of the project. Basically two ratios are used to evaluate the performance of the project. Annual debt service cover ratio tests the ability of the project's cash flow to cover debt service in a particular year. Loan life cover ratio and project life cover ratio test the ability of a project's cash flow over respectively the loan life and the project life to repay the loan. The cover ratios are often used as a tool for pricing of the loan. The model for estimation of cover ratios are based on different assumptions which affect the underlying fundamentals of the project. The sensitivity of factors such as changes in interest rates, exchange rates, operating costs, cost overruns and changes in tax rates and delay in completion are considered in the model for estimation of these ratios.

4.6 Completion Issues

The completion issues in infrastructure projects centers around aspects such as the confirmation that the project is physically complete and the project had met the required performance criteria. The project can demonstrate the ability to operate reliably as represented by the project company over the term of the loan.

Further Reading

ME Project Finance guide.www.dentons.com

Case 1: The Chuo Shinkansen Project, Japan

The Chuo Shinkansen project is a major transportation project in Japan. The Chu Shinkansen project also known as Tokaido Shinkansen Bypass is a new rail line being constructed in phases based on the Japanese Superconducting Magnetic Levitation (Maglev) system. The Japanese maglev line is expected to connect Tokyo and Nagoya city in 40 min. The initial project was designed to cover Shinagawa Station in Tokyo and Nogoya Station along with the construction of stations in Sagamihara, Kofu, Iida and Nakatsugawa. The maximum speed of the maglev project was designed to be 500 km/h. Approximately 90 percent of the 286 kilometer travel to Nagoya will be through tunnels. The Japanese government funded maglev project initiated in the seventies was supported by Japan Airlines and the Japanese National Railways. The project is aimed to use the Shinkansen high speed train lines to cover all of Japan through Japan Railways (JR) network. The most popular line is the Tokaido Shinkansen that connects Tokyo with Osaka.

Based on the superconducting Maglev (SCMAGLEV) technology, the new line will first connect Toyko to Nagoya, the capital of Japan's Aichi Prefecture in under 40 min. On completion the Chuo Shinkansen is expected to connect Toyko to Osaka in approximately 67 min at a maximum period of 314 mph (505 km/h). Initially the 18.4 kilometer test track in Yamanashi Prefecture was created and high speeds of 500 km/h. were achieved on the test track for the development of the Chuo Shinkansen line. In 2013, the track was extended along the planned route. The project is expected to reduce the travel time between Tokyo and Nagoya by approximately 50 percent. The new line under phase 1 which started work in the year 2015 is expected to be operational by 2027.The investment in phase 1 is estimated to be JPY 5.5 trillion ($52 billion) approximately. The confirmed stations along the Toyko-Nagoya line are Hashimoto in Kanagawa Prefecture; Kofu in Yamanashi Prefecture; Iida City in Nagano Prefecture and Nakatsugawa in Gifu Prefecture. The maglev station at Shinagawa will consist of four tracks and two platforms. This station is being built beneath the existing Shinkansen station and would take an estimated 10 years for full completion. The project involves the

Table 5.1 Timeline for the new project

Period	Milestones
1990–2009	The topographical and geological studies were commenced and completed during this period
2008–2009	Consultation phase was performed
2011	Japanese Railway Central was given ownership
2013	Draft Environmental Impact statement for phase 1 was published
2014	Construction implementation plan was given approved by the Ministry of Land, Infrastructure, Transport and Tourism. Construction of two stations under phase I commenced
2015	Construction work of Southern Alps Tunnel in Yamanashi Prefecture started
2016	Construction of underground Shinagawa Station was commenced
2017	Work on underground route to Central Tokyo was initiated

construction of a 25 kilometer tunnel under the Southern Japanese Alps which is stated to be the deepest tunnel in Japan.

The Phase 1 will include the construction of a 285.6 km superconductive maglev line which consists of 256.6 km of tunnels, 23.6 km of viaduct, 11.3 km of bridges and 4.1 km of rail beds. The specific features of the route include a minimum curve radius of 1000 meter and a maximum grade of 40 percent. The distance between the track centers will be more than 5.8 meter.

The designed trainsets are known as linear motor care in Japan. The construction of the line started in the year 2014 and is expected to cost over Yen 9 trillion. The plan was designed to begin commercial service between Tokyo and Nagoya in the year 2027. The work in the Nagoya-Osaka section is expected to be completed by the year 2045. The project faced some risk issues when Shizuoka Prefecture denied permission for construction work in one portion of the route during June 2020. The government of Japan had plans to reduce the time line of construction of the Osaka section by eight years thereby aiming to complete the project by 2037. After the inauguration of the Tokaido Shinkansen between Tokyo and Osaka in the year 1964, the Japanese Railway focused on the development of faster Maglev technology. A test track for Maglev research and development initiative was developed in Miyazaki Prefecture during the year 1970. The Japanese Railway Central started offering public train rides at 500 km/hour on the Yamanashi test tract via a lottery selection method in the year 2014. The train journey created world record in terms of the fastest manned train on the track.

The Osaka extension of Chuo Shinkansen which was expected to be completed by 2045 is now advanced for completion by the year 2037 as the government had secured extra funding for the project.

The project currently focusses on environmental assessment to ensure that the track is close to a straight line to maximize the maglev's capabilities. A short underground route to central Tokyo was initiated in the year 2017. Tokyo station will be the terminus for all of the Shinkansen high-speed lines in the Japanese capital

Table 5.2 Details of the plan

Route between Kofu and Nakatsugawa	Distance from Tokyo (Km)		Construction costs(JPY) from Tokyo		Shortest journey time from Tokyo	
	To Nogoya	To Osaka	To Nagoya	To Osaka	To Nagoya	To Osaka
Under the Japanese Alps and Iida City	286	438	5.10 trillion	8.44 trillion	40 minutes	67 minutes

route. Table 5.1 shows the major milestones for the project. Table 5.2 gives some significant details about the project.

Long distance running tests are currently conducted on the Yamanashi Maglev test line for the Chuo Shinkansen project by deploying new Series L0 Maglev trainsets. Maglev trainset in the Series LO for the Chuo Shinkansen project recorded top speed of 603 km/hr. and covered maximum daily travelling distance of 4064 km during April 2015. JR Central had ordered for 14 series LO Maglev trains to serve as the rolling stock for the route. The route passes through sparsely populated areas in the Akaishi mountain regions. The route has a minimum curve radius of 8000 meter. The planned route between Nagoya and Osaka included a stop in Nara.

Initially there were three plans. In 2009, JR Central selected the shortest plan C which consisted of long tunnels under the Japanese Alps. During October 2014, the Japanese Ministry of Land, Infrastructure, Transport and Tourism approved plan C for construction. The station in Nagoya was completed in the year 2016. Japanese Railways initially planned to raise funds for the construction of the project using its own funds and without government assistance. In 2007, the initial cost which was estimated at 5.1 trillion yen escalated to over 9 trillion by the year 2011.The huge expense for the project was basically due to the cost incurred for the construction of a tunnel which accounted for approximately 86 percent of the initial section from Tokyo to Nagova. The tunnel was characterized with deep underground depth of approximately 40 meter at some sections which covered about 100 km in the regions of Tokyo, Nagoya and Osaka areas. The construction of the Tokyo-Nagoya segment and the Nagoya-Osaka segment kept the total debt around 5 trillion yen for the Japanese Central Railway. The 7-kilometer-long tunnel in Yamanashi and Shizuoka prefectures are expected to be completed by the year 2025.The 25 km along tunnel in the Southern Alps area commenced on December 2015. With respect to pricing, Japanese Railways Central estimates that Chuo Shinkansen fares will be more expensive than Tokaido Shinkansen fares. On account of reduction of the travel distance between cities, the cost savings is expected to range between 5 and 17 trillion yen during the first fifty years of operations of the Chuo Shinkansen project. The original construction schedule for the Tokyo-Nagoya segment which was supposed to be completed by 2045 was advanced to the year 2037 on account of receipt of loan from the government. It is estimated that approximately 90 percent of the 286 kilometer line to Nagoya will consist of tunnels with a minimum curve radius of 8000 meters and a maximum grade of 4 percent.

The project will employ the SCMagley technology which is a magnetic levitation train system developed by Japan Railway Central. The levitating force will generate superconducting magnets on the trains and coils on the track. The absence of wheel friction facilitates normal operations at over 500 km per hour. The superconducting coils uses the Niobium titanium alloy which is cooled to a temperature of $-269\,°C$. The energy consumption of the Maglev train is estimated at 90–100 Wh (seat km) with normal operating speed.

In the year 2021, the Central Japan Railway company revised the total construction cost for the Chuo Shinkansen section between Shinagawa and Nagoya. The forecast of the construction cost increased by approximately 1.5 trillion yen to 7.04 trillion yen. This included the cost of the rolling stock and excluded the expenses spend on the Yamanashi Maglev line. The capital investments will amount to 220 billion yen per year in and after FY 2028. The interest rate on financing was 3%. The construction cost was estimated to increase by over 500 billion yen due to geological uncertainties and severity of construction constraints. The earthquake counter measures were estimated to increase the costs by over 600 billion yen. The process of securing utilization sites of excavated soil resulted in increased costs of over 300 billion yen. Transportation and receiving costs are expected to increase for soil excavated from mountain tunnels due to proper utilization of sites.

Further Reading

1. https://en.wikipedia.org/wiki/Ch%C5%AB%C5%8D_Shinkansen
2. https://www.jrailpass.com/blog/chuo-shinkansen-maglev
3. https://www.railway-technology.com/projects/chuo-shinkansen-maglev-line/
4. *2010-10-21. Archived from* the original *on 2010-10-24*. Retrieved 2010-10-26.
5. Kyodo News, "JR Tokai to list sites for maglev stations in June", The Japan Times, 2 June 2011, p. 9.
6. JR Central starts construction on Chuo maglev". *International Railway Journal.* .
7. Planned start of maglev trains brings construction boom, concern in Nagoya". *The Asahi Shimbun. 29*
8. https://global.jr-central.co.jp/en/

Case 2: Developing the World's Largest Passenger Aircraft-Airbus A3XX

Airbus is an established leader in the global aerospace sector whose cutting edge products and services span the commercial aircraft, helicopter, defense, security and space segments. Airbus is the largest aeronautics and space company in Europe and is a worldwide leader with presence in 180 locations and have relationship with 12,000 direct suppliers. By December 2019, Airbus has delivered 12,626 aircrafts to airlines worldwide. It has also delivered 12,000 helicopters to 3000 customers globally. Airbus is a major global innovator with R&D investments over 3 billion dollars. Airbus holds 37,000 patents globally. Airbus's commercial aircraft family consists of the A220, the purpose built for the 100–150 seat commercial air transport market; the single aisle A320, the bestselling wide body long range A330 Family, the next generation A350XWB Family and the double deck A38.

Airbus's civil portfolio consists of the twin engine H145 and H1 60. The NH90 multi role helicopter of Airbus is used for tactical transport and naval applications. Airbus have a strong market position in transport, mission and compact aircraft and services with the flagship products consisting of A400M airlifter, the A330MRTT and the Eurofighter Typhoon combat aircraft. Airbus is also a specialist in cybersecurity and protect critical infrastructures from threats. Airbus is a leading manufacturer of Earth observation, navigation, science and telecommunications satellites.

Airbus was always known for innovative design and technology. Airbus has employed pioneering models with varying range and capacity combinations from the time of introduction of its first fleet A300. Airbus has employed "flyby-wire" technology that substituted computerized control for mechanical linkages between the pilot and aircraft's control surfaces. This technology combined with a common cockpit design facilitated "cross crew qualification (CCQ) whereby pilots were certified to fly similar aircraft. In other words, it was possible for the pilots to fly and maintain certifications in several planes which included the A3XX, A340 and A330. This flexibility to schedule flight crews interchangeably on various models led to better pilot utilization and lower training costs. By the year 1999, Airbus had received over half of the total large aircraft orders. It has to be noted that though

Airbus had gained market share, Airbus did not have a product to compete with Boeing's 747 in the VLA market.

During 1999, the world commercial jet fleet comprised of 12,000 passenger and 1600 cargo planes which were operated by more than 400 scheduled passenger and cargo airlines. Large aircrafts characterized with capacity of 70 or more seats accounted for more than 90 percent of deliveries. Very large aircraft (VLA) are the largest category of aircrafts with capacity of 400 passenger seats or which carry more than 80 tons of freight. The manufacture of large aircrafts was the monopoly of Boeing Company and Airbus Industrie.

In June 1994, Airbus announced its plan to develop its own Very Large Aircraft (VLA) which was designated as A3XX. The marketing plan was initiated in June 2000 with initial 22 firm orders and Airbus expected to get 40 to 50 orders before the industrial launch.

In the year 2000, Airbus sales force team got authorization from the Board to take firm offers for the A3XX project. The list price for A3XX was $216 million and the cost of development was estimated to be $13 billion. Airbus expected to secure 50 firm orders from five major airlines.

The Airbus A380 is the world's largest passenger aircraft build by Airbus. The full length double deck aircraft termed superjumbo have a typical seating capacity of 525 with certification up to 853 passengers. Airbus A380 is powered by four Engine Alliance GP7200 or Rolls-Royce Trent 900 turbofans with a range of 14,800 km. In total Airbus had received 251 firm orders and had delivered 246 aircrafts. Emirates airlines was the biggest customer with orders of 123 aircrafts of which 118 were delivered. Airbus launched the $10.7 billion A380 programme in the year 2000. The first prototype was unveiled in Toulouse on 18th January 2005. There was a two-year delay due to electrical wiring problems and development costs escalated to euro 18 billion. In 2006, Airbus received its type certificate from the European Aviation Safety Agency (EASA) and the US Federal Aviation Administration (FAA).

There was uncertainty with respect to the long term demand for A3XX. Based on the projections, management of Airbus estimated that they needed to sell 250 aircraft for breakeven and could sell over 750 aircrafts over the next 20 years. With respect to the demand for very large aircraft market, Boeing and Airbus had estimated different views on the size of the very large aircraft market. Very Large Aircraft (VLA) market includes large aircraft with seating capacity for 500 or more passengers or which carry more than 80 tons of freight. Airbus predicted that the demand would exceed 1500 planes over the period 2000–2020 with sales of over $350 billion. Boeing predicted that the demand for VLA market would be approximately 330 passenger aircraft and 270 cargo planes during the above period. Boeing's view on VLA market was based on the vision of "fragmentation" in which the creation of new point to point routes will satisfy the demand. Airbus's forecast on VLA was based on the "hub to hub" travel at congested airports. The size of the VLA market and Airbus's likely share were the major sources of uncertainty. In hub and spoke operations airlines seek to collect travelers from different cities at a central collecting point or hub in order to fill large planes for flight to international destinations. Airbus envisioned that the future of flying would be based on the 'hub and spoke' model with passengers travelling between major airports and using connecting flights to reach final destination. Point to point focus on non-stop flights between cities through mid-sized body planes.

6.1 Reflections on Airbus A3XX

Boeing and Airbus initially collaborated on feasibility studies for developing a jumbo jet for the VLA market. In 1995 Boeing withdraw from the project citing cost factors and uncertainty in demand. In comparison to Boeing's 747, A3XX had more space per seat and wider aisles. A3XX had superior safety features since it was a four engine plane compared to two engine plane like Boeing 777. A3XX had the same fly by wire technology, flight deck design and performance characteristics similar to other planes in the Airbus family. Airbus believed that synergy in terms of increased capacity and reduced costs would compensate for the higher price in terms of economics of the project. An analysis revealed that the operating cost per flight would be 12 per cent more than the 747 cost, but on account of 35 per cent greater capacity, space volume would increase by approximately 25 percent. Another estimate suggested that A3XX needed only 323 passengers to break even compared to 290 for the 747. The major challenges were in the form of noise, emissions, turnaround time, taxiway movement and evacuation. Airbus has forecasted demand for 14,661 new passenger aircraft and 703 new air freighters over the twenty-year period of 2000–2019. The analysis by Airbus forecasted demand for 727 new aircraft which have seating capacity in the range of 400–500 seats and 1550 new aircraft which seats 500 or more passengers. Boeing believed that VLA market is a much smaller market. Boeing revealed that the demand for VLA flights are only 330 aircrafts. Further, Boeing believed that most of the demand for the larger planes would not materialize for at least 10 years from the year counted from 2000. The cost of the project was estimated to be $13 billion. The cost per plane was estimated to be $216 million. The project life was estimated to be 30 to 50 years. It was estimated that it would take at least five years for the first delivery.

Major structural sections of the A380 are built in France, Germany, Spain, and the United Kingdom. The major suppliers of A380 components are Rolls Royce, Safran, United Technologies and General Electric. The planes are assembled in Jean-Luc Lagardere Plant assembly hall in Toulouse. Airbus had designed for the production and supply chain facilities to streamline the production at a rate of four A380s per month. The cabin wiring system was complex with 98,000 wires and 40,000 connectors. The initial production time line witnessed delay of two years. The A3XX design which converged on a double decker layout provided more passenger volume than traditional single deck design.

6.2 Financing the Project

The cost of development included approximately $13 billion which consisted of $11 billion for research and development ($10 billion to develop two passenger versions and $1 billion for the development of the cargo version); $1 billion was accounted for property, plant and equipment and $1 billion for working capital. The sources of financing were $3.5 billion from risk sharing partners (RSPs) or vendors; $3.6 billion of launch aid from the partner governments of UK and France; $5.9 billion from Airbus partners in proportion to their partnership interests. The risk sharing partners agreed to bear the cost of development under the condition to become the exclusive suppliers for the A3XX. Airbus had entered into agreements with nine risk sharing partners. According to the agreement, the partners were to be paid on a per plane basis. Table 6.1 highlights the expenditures incurred for the development of AirbusA3XX.

By 2016, the A380 development costs escalated to $25 billion for 15-year period. The national governments of Germany, France and UK provided loans amounting 3.5 billion euros and refundable advances which amounted to 5.9 billion euros. In 2018, Airbus revised its deal with the governments to save $1.4 billion on restructured terms and lowered the production rate from eight in 2019 to six per year. In 2018, a WTO ruling stated that A380 received improper subsidies through $9 billion of launch aids.

6.3 Project Features

For Airbus, A3XX was the natural extension of the Airbus "fly by wire family of jets and it would fill the gap for the segment which the company didn't serve. The Airbus forecasted attractive financial returns for the project. The project estimated sales of approximately $11 billion during the period 2006–2020. The forecast suggested that approximately 50 planes per year (750 planes for 15-year period) could be sold with price tag of $216 million per plane. Airbus also estimated that it needed only 250 planes to breakeven on an undiscounted cash flow basis. On an operating margin of 20 percent, the project aimed to generate $2.2 billion in operating profit. By entering into the VLA segment, Airbus aimed to compete with Boeing for monopoly position in the VLA market segment. The project received support from

Table 6.1 Development expenditure in million US dollars

Investment	2001	2002	2003	2004	2005	2006	2007	2008	Total
R&D Expenditure	1100	2200	2200	2200	1320	880	660	440	1100
Capital Expenditures	0	250	350	350	50	0	0	0	1000
Working Capital	0	150	300	300	200	50	0	0	1000
Total	1100	2600	2850	2850	1570	930	660	440	1300

Source: Dresdner Kleinwort Benson, Aerospace and Defense Report, 2008

governments of France and United Kingdom. French government had placed orders for 10 A3XX before the industrial launch and British government had made commitments of $835 million of launch aid. Before the launch, Airbus received customer support in terms of 22 firm orders and another 115 potential orders were in the pipeline.

6.4 Risks Involved in the Project

There were lot of uncertainties with respect to the demand for the VLA segment. Though both Boeing and Airbus projected the annual growth rate of air transportation industry in the range of 4.8–4.9%, they held divergent views with respect to the size of very large market. There were doubts about the projections on VLA market by Airbus. Many aircraft manufacturers went bankrupt following failed launches. For example, Boeing went bankrupt when initially it launched the 747. During the scenario surrounding the project decision, Airbus had taken more than 50 percent of existing aircraft orders and in fact was taking an enormous gamble through this initiative. An aggressive response may pose greater challenge with respect to the success of project for Airbus. An analysis revealed that the initial orders came from interested parties. It was observed that airlines rarely order more than four to five years in advance and hence Airbus was expected to get not more than 50–100 orders before the industrial launch. The conversion rates of the extent to which specific aircraft would migrate to the VLA segment depends on how the industry travel evolves over time. Based on the Airbus management estimation of sales of 750 planes during 15-year period, it is expected that Airbus could capture half of the VLA market. The leading airline industry journal Airline Monitor forecasted demand for 515 A3XX aircraft over the period 2000–2020.

It was important that Airbus had to actively participate in the commercial aviation industry to become the dominant competitor. With over $700 million spent by the year 2000 on market research and product design, the A3XX is the most researched product launch in history.

A3XX offered is a vastly superior plane compared to 747 of Boeing. It offers more space with respect to larger aisles, seats and amenities. From the airline's perspective, A3XX provides better economics and can be easily integrated with the fly by wire family. It can have better pilot utilization in terms of less training and more flying time.

6.5 Risk Mitigation Strategy

Airbus had selected an organizational and financial structure to mitigate the risks involved in the project. The ownership was in the form of joint venture which contain the element of risk sharing and no single shareholder was exposed to the full financial risk of the project venture. Airbus raised $7.2 billion in the form of government launch and risk sharing capital. The $3.6 billion launch aid was similar to non-recourse loan. In this case, the repayment was contingent upon plane sales. The launch aid also ensured government support in the form of plane purchases or political support for the project. Airbus also raised $3.5 billion from risk sharing partners. The use of external capital reduced Airbus's share of total development cost from 100% to 45%.

6.6 Delivery

The first delivery of the aircraft was made to Singapore Airlines during October 2007. The production of Airbus A380 had peaked 2012–2014 at a rate of 30 per year during the period. The second airplane was received by Emirates in the year 2008 and services started between Dubai and New York. Qantas Airlines started flights between Melbourne and Los Angeles. Air France received its first A380 in 2009 and Lufthansa in the year 2010. The 100th A380 was delivered to Malaysia Airlines in the year 2013.

6.7 Challenges for A3XX

Airbus had positioned A3XX as a luxury plane with some carriers having amenities such as showers, lounges, duty free shops as well as bars on both the decks of the A380. A3XX was the first flight to have two full decks. Most airlines preferred smaller aircraft which were economical to operate. In 2019, Airbus announced that A380 production would end in the year 2021 after Emirates Airlines reduced its orders and decided to buy A350 and A330neo. In 2019, Emirates cut its orders by 39 planes. Emirates serves 50 global destinations with A380s Australia based Qantas had cancelled plans to buy A3XX and Virgin Atlantic also cancelled its orders in the year 2018. In 2019 Lufthansa had retired six of its 14 A380s due to lack of profits. In the same year Qatar Airways announced a switch from A380 to Boeing 777X from the year 2024 onwards.

It was estimated that Airbus would require over $90 million in profit from the sale of each aircraft to cover the estimated $25 billion development cost. The $445 million price tag for A380XX was not adequate to cover the production cost which necessitated the shutdown of production in an economic sense. The commercial viability of A3XX in terms of its large capacity was not achieved as the principle of hub and spoke system advocated by Airbus was not feasible in the changing air transport industry scenario which witnessed a fundamental transition from point to point system wherein customers get to their destination in one flight instead of more number of destinations. The closure of the A380 program is expected to result in a loss of 3500 European jobs.

Airbus's the World's largest passenger aircraft progamme was often described as a "hotel in the sky". The A380 was basically pitched at the fast growing Asia and Middle East markets where airlines focused on flying more people per flight. On account of rising fuel prices and environmental concerns, airlines opted for smaller

Table 6.2 Airlines with A3XX

SL	Airlines	No of A380s
1	Emirates	109
2	Singapore Airlines	24
3	Lufthansa	14
4	Qantas	12
5	British Airways	12
6	Qatar Airways	10
7	Korean Air	10
8	Etihad Airways	10
9	Air France	10
10	Thai Airways	6
11	Malaysia Airlines	6
12	Asiana Airlines	6
13	China Southern Airlines	5

Source: Airbus

planes produced by both Boeing and Airbus. Boeing was expected to introduce new family of 777s deliveries with fewer seats and more payload in the year 2020. A total of 57 firm orders for A3XX were cancelled by different airlines like Emirates, Virgin Atlantic and Lufthansa since the year 2005. Moreover the envisaged cargo version of the plane never materialized.

The Airbus A380 which was supposed to represent the future of flying is being discontinued after 12 years of service. A380 was never able to match the success of the 747. The global financial crisis had started affecting the operators and customers in the year 2008 when A380 took the first flight in the year 2007. Boeing introduced the smaller and sleeker Dreamliner 787 aircraft which could cover the same distance as Airbus's jumbo based on two fewer engines. An aircraft which was smaller and quicker to refill had a far more appealing offer. The fastest growing markets for aviation are in the developing world and focusses on models of smaller lower cost fuel efficient single aisle aircraft.

On a comparative basis, Airline found it feasible to fly two 777s on a typical long haul route at a lower total cost than flying one A380. For the functioning of A380, airports had to be refitted to accommodate the jumbo jet and runways had to be strengthened to cope with its weight and terminals had to be adjusted to ease potential passenger congestion issues due to A380's capacity. Table 6.2 list airlines which purchased A3XX. Table 6.3 gives the details on A380 order and delivery statistics during the period 2001–2020.

Table 6.3 Airbus A380 orders and delivery statistics

Year	Net orders	Deliveries
2001	78	
2002	–	
2003	34	
2004	10	
2005	10	
2006	24	
2007	33	1
2008	9	12
2009	4	10
2010	32	18
2011	19	26
2012	9	30
2013	42	25
2014	13	30
2015	2	27
2016	–	28
2017	−2	15
2018	4	12
2019	−74	8
2020		4
Total	251	246

Source: Airbus

Further Reading

1. https://en.wikipedia.org/wiki/Airbus_A380
2. Esty, B, C and P. Ghemawat, 2001., Airbus vs Boeing in superjumbos: Credibility and preemption, Harvard Business School mime, August.
3. Airbus Industrie, Global Market forecast, 2000, http//www.airbus.com
4. The Boeing Company, Current Market Outlook, 2000, http://www.boeing.com/commercial/cmo
5. Airbus Industrie: http://www.airbus.com
6. The Boeing Company: http://www.boeing.com
7. The Airline Monitor: http://www.airlinecapital.com/
8. https://www.airbus.com/aircraft.html
9. Benjamin Esty, Airbus A3XX: Developing the World's Largest Commercial Jet(A), HBS Case 9-201-028, April 26, 2004.
10. J Cole, Airbus prepares to 'Bet the Company' as It builds a huge new jet', The Wall Street Journal, Nov 3 1999 p.A1
11. K West," Boeing May Quit Large Jet Venture Timing and Market Don't Appear Right." Seattle Post Intelligence, July 8, 1995,p.A1.
12. Boeing, 2000 Current Market Outlook, p. 34
13. Airbus,"First Quarter 2000 Briefing, p 12.
14. US Questions UK's Big Loans to British Aerospace for Airbus jet, The Wall Street Journal, March 14 2000 p. A 27.
15. Airbus bets the company, The Economist March 18 2000, p. 24.

Further Reading

16. Daniel Thomas, BBC News, Why did Airbus A380 fail? Feb 14, 2019. https://www.bbc.com/news/business-47225789#:~t.
17. Dan Reed, The Plane that never should have been built: The A380 was designed for failure, https://www.forbes.com/sites/danielreed/2019/02/15/
18. Michael Newell, Why the Airbus A380 failed to take off, https://www.theneweconomy.com/strategy/why-the-airbus-a380-failed-to-take-off/June
19. O'Hare, Maureen (18 March 2021). "The final Airbus A380 superjumbo makes its first flight". CNN. Retrieved 19 March 2021.
20. "Aviation giants have Super-jumbo task". Orlando Sentinel. 27 November 1994. Retrieved 30 December 2011.
21. Karl West (28 December 2014). "Airbus's Flagship Plane May Be Too Big To Be Profitable". The Guardian. Business Insider.
22. Bloomberg (13 December 2004). "Airbus Says Its A380 Jet Is Over Budget". The New York Times.
23. Jens Flottau (5 June 2017). "Airbus confirms more A380 production cuts". Aviation Week Network.

Case 3: South North Water Transfer Project China

South North Water Transfer (The SNWT) megaproject is often described as combination of "four horizontals and three verticals" which connects the basins of the Yangtze, Yellow, Huaihe and Hai rivers through the canals of the Eastern, Middle and Western Route. The SNWT project is the most expensive and expansive Chinese infrastructure project and the construction began in the year 2002. The project brought fundamental changes to the hydrology and ecology of the Yellow and Yangtze river systems. Approximately 17 billion cubic meters of water would be diverted per year to meet the water shortages in the Northern region by the year 2050.

SNWT project in China took 50 years from conception to commencement and is planned for completion in the year 2050. The project involves diversion of 44.8 billion cubic meters of water annually from southern rivers to the dry northern region of China. The project involves the linkage of China's four main rivers—the Yangtze, Yellow River, Huaihe and Haihe. The project is expected to cost $62 billion.

SNWT project is the largest of its kind in the world and is expected to benefit over 100 million people over a period of time. The distribution of water resources is extremely uneven between the South and North. The project consists of three lines-western, central and eastern. The areas covered by the project account for one third of China's GDP. The $62 billion scheme initiated in year 2002 was designed to divert 12 trillion gallons of water over more than 1000 km. It is one of the most ambitious and expensive water transfer projects in the world. The project was aimed to reduce water insecurity in the north region and support economic development. The project facilitates improved irrigation and food security. The health benefits would result from improved water quality. Industry would benefit from improved water supply.

The middle route which starts from the Danjiangkou reservoir in central China's Hubei province and covers Henan and Hebei before reaching Beijing and Tianjin. The project was designed to take water from China's longest river, the Yangtze through eastern, middle and western routes to feed the dry areas in the northern region. The middle route was the most attractive part of the project as this route delivers water to the Chinese capital. More than 70 per cent of tap water in Beijing's major urban areas is provided from the Danjiangou reservoir. The project benefits over 12 million residents which constitute nearly half of the city's total population. Beijing's annual water consumption is estimated to be about 3.6 billion cubic meters. The local supplies provide 2.1 billion cubic meters. The shortfall gap of 1.5 billion cubic meters every year was met through groundwater extraction. The SNWT project has replenished the water resources for the city and ensured security of water supply. After the project implementation, the city's per capita water resources increased from 100 cubic meters to 150 cubic meters. The average depth of underground water in Beijing increased by 2.88 meters after the diversion of water flow into Beijing.

Northern China had been the epicenter of industry and agriculture. Historically the overexploitation of groundwater for urban and industrial development led to severe water shortages in Northern China. Additionally, land subsidence and frequent sandstorms had been linked to the excessive use of groundwater. Late chairman Mao Zedong proposed the idea of the diversion project in the year 1952. The ambitious project was expected to ease water shortages in the cities of Beijing and Tianjin and the northern provinces of Hebei, Henan and Shandong. The project was approved by the State Council during August 2002 and the construction on the central route commenced in year 2003.

The unofficial proposal also includes a canal linking Shumatan point in Tibet with Tianjin and another plan to divert water to Xinjiang. These new proposals would additionally feed China's north region with water from transnational rivers such as Yarlung Tsangpo, the Nu and the Lancang. The Tibet-Tianji canal would realize the diversion of 200 billion cubic meters of water which is the equivalent of four Yellow rivers being diverted from the Yarlung Tsangpo to the Yellow river. The Red Flag River scheme proposed in the year 2017 would cover 6188 km and is expected to divert 60 billion cubic metres of water which is more than the annual flow of the Yellow river.

7.1 Project Highlights in Different Routes

The eastern route facilitated the supply to regions of Shandong Province and the northern part of Jiangsu. The route linked Shandong with the Yangtze River and brought water north to the Huang Huai Plain through the Beijing-Hangzhou Grand Canal. The diversion from a major branch of Yangtze River near Yangzhou city diverted the water along the existing river channels to the Weishan mountains of Shandong before crossing the Yellow River through a tunnel and flowing to Tianjin. The first stage of diversion was over 1155 km long and involved the construction of 23 pumping station with the installed capacity of 453.7 MW. This stage of project also included nearly 9 km of tunnels from the outlet of Dongping Lake to the inlet of the Weilin Canal. This stage of project also included a 634-meter-long siphon section along with two 9.3-meter diameter horizontal tunnels of 70 meter under the Huanghe river bed.

The central route which covered 1267 km in length was initiated in the year 2003. The central route collected water from the Danjiankou reservoir on the Han River through canals near the west edge of the Huanghuaihai Plain and facilitated the flow of water through the Henan and Hebei provinces to Beijing. The project also included the construction of two tunnels of 8.5-meter internal diameter which was 7 km long.

The work on the western route was initiated during the year 2010 and involved work on the Qinghai Tibet Plateau which was 3000–5000 meter above the sea level. The project when completed in the year 2050 will bring brought 4 billion cubic meters of water from the three tributaries of the Yangtze—the Tongtian Yalong and Dadu rivers.

It was estimated that an additional 4.5 billion cubic meters of water will be required by 2030 to maintain economic growth in this region.

7.2 Financing the Project

The development costs for the eastern and central routes is estimated to be $37.44 billion. The allocation for the south to north water diversion project is expected to be $7.9 billion (53.87 billion yuan). Out of the 53.87 billion yuan, the central government had budgeted 15.42 billion yuan. In terms of contribution as special funds in treasury bonds, the central government accounts for 10.65 billion yuan and local government will fund approximately 7.99 billion yuan. Loans will account for approximately 19.81 billion yuan for the project. The construction costs have increased due to inflation, changes in the national policy and investment structures of the project. An amount of 30.48 billion yuan had been earmarked for the construction of eastern and central routes.

7.3 Risks and Mitigation Strategies for SNWT Project

The project had raised many environmental concerns with respect to loss of antiquities, the displacement of people and the destruction of pasture land. The plans for further industrialization raised serious concerns of pollution in the diverted water. To mitigate pollution risk, the Chinese government had allocated $80 million to build treatment facilities in the Jiangud, Huai'an, Suqian and Xuzhou region of the Jiangsu province. Approximately 260 projects were initiated for pollution reduction and providing drinking water in the areas of the diversion project. The industries sectors of cage aquaculture and turmeric processing have been banned in the catchment area of Danjiankou. As a result, thousands of farmers involved in turmeric cultivation and factory workers involved in processing industry lost their daily livelihood. Another key local industry of cage aquaculture has been devastated since over 200,000 cages were removed from the reservoir. These measures had also an impact on government tax revenues. Water quality had deteriorated before the industry ban near the Danjiangkou reservoir. According to government data, the total nitrogen had increased from 0.62 mg/L to 1.55 mg/L and total phosphorus from 0.005 mg/L to 0.02 mg/L during the period 2006—2014. The protection policies implemented in the Danjiangkou area is basically aimed to address environmental and ecological concerns and achieve socio economic objectives. Danjiangkou catchment area is one the most backward regions of China. Approximately 79 percent of the counties which constitute the catchment area are classified as 'national poverty stricken counties' as compared to the 21 percent of the counties in mainland China. The majority of the indirect costs attributed with catchment protection are borne by these poorer counties. The 'turmeric town' of China, Yunxi in the region had contributed one third of average GDP for its parent prefecture, Shivan by 2014. The SNWT project highlights the importance of adoption of best practice protection in the Danjiankou basin to simultaneously protect the local environment and reduce the regional wealth and income inequalities. China has in principle a policy tool to reduce the costs to local communities of keeping catchments clean. The "ecological compensation' policy advocates payments for ecosystem services with the 'polluter pays' principle.

Thousands of people lost their habitat due to the construction of dams and reservoirs related to the project. There was ecological damage to the natural environment. The region was prone to earthquakes thereby increasing the probability of extensive damage to the project. There was also chances of water wastage due to significant evaporation from canals and reservoir. To facilitate the flow of water from Hanjiang River to northern region, the dams of the reservoir were raised to the highest level of 125,000 mu. Approximately 8333 hectares of land in Hubei were submerged.

There are viewpoints which suggest that diversion of water from the Yangtze would affect hydropower projects such as the Three Gorges Dam. Some analysts suggest that western route of any form is unnecessary. It is important to understand the changes in climate, population, society, environment while analyzing engineering solutions.

7.4 Project Structuring

A special limited company was established to cover the construction, operation and maintenance of the main project and a water supply company was founded in each province to manage the local administration and components of infrastructure. The project owner was the South to North Water Transfer company. The construction contractors were the Hanjiang Water Resources and Hydropower. The project management was done by government organization such the State Development and Planning Commission, the Ministry of Water Resources, the Ministry of Construction, the State Environment Protection Administration and the China International Engineering Consultant Corporation. Infrastructure development plans are being provided by GCW Consulting. The design and planning for the eastern route is provided by the Tianjin Hydroelectric Investigation and Design Institute. Changjiang Water Resources Commission is responsible for the middle route and

Yellow River Conservancy Commission for the western route. The construction work on the eastern route is done by Hanjiang Water Resources and Hydropower and by Danjiangkou Water Resources on the middle route.

7.5 Project Status

The extensive planning and research of the project involved different ministries, organizations and institutes of Chinese government. Approximately 62 years after the South North Water Transfer project was initiated, the middle route began the supply of water from the Danjiankou reservoir in December 2014. In the first phase, the middle route was expected to transfer an average of 9.5 billion cubic meters of water per annum to the regions of Henan, Hebei, Tianjin and Beijing which would be utilized by about 50 million people. Danjiangkou's catchment area, comprised of 95,000 square kilometers of land was administered by three different provinces of Hubei, Henan and Shaanxi. The central route which was completed in the year 2014, takes water over 1400 kilometers from Hubei province to Beijing and Tianjin. The eastern route started delivery of water from Jiangsu to Shandong and Tianjin in the year 2013. The studies for the western route commenced during 2018. The Yellow River Commission initiated an evaluation of the trends in water supply in Yellow river basin and water saving schemes. The official western route would cover a mountainous region of 3000 to 4000 metres above the sea level.

The central and eastern routes have transferred a total of 29.7 billion cubic meters of water to the north and consisted of 3.9 billion cubic meters of water through the eastern route and 25.8 billion via the central route. The first phase of the central route is projected to deliver 9.5 billion cubic meters to the northern region annually of which 3.77 billion cubic meters will be sent to Henan, 3.47 billion cubic meters to Hebei, 1.24 billion cubic meters to Hebei and 1.24 billion cubic meters to Beijing. About 120 million people have benefitted from the project. More than 40 major cities take water delivery which is transferred from south. Approximately 73 percent of water for Beijing is derived from South and 100 per cent of water for Tianjin region is sourced from south. The quality of surface water delivered through eastern route is above the level III national standard. Therefore, the water is suitable for human usage and agricultural purposes.

Further Reading

1. https://www.water-technology.net/projects/south_north/
2. https://www.thethirdpole.net/en/regional-cooperation/can-chinas-south-north-water-transfer-project-and-industry-co-exist/?gclid=EAIaIQobChMI7tvbsMPE8AIVgu_tCh0pvQ0 WEAAYASAAEgJHZvD_BwE
3. https://chinadialogue.net/en/nature/11762-vast-river-diversion-plan-afoot-in-western-china-2/
4. http://www.xinhuanet.com/english/2019-12/11/c_138623551.htm
5. https://news.cgtn.com/news/2020-12-13/China-s-South-to-North-Water-Diversion-Project-benefits-120m-people-WbgKTKWKZi/index.html

Case 4: Dubailand Project

Dubailand is one of the most ambitious leisure development project in the world which is estimated to cost $64.3 billion. It is a tourism, entertainment and leisure complex being built in Dubai and owned by Tatweer of Dubai Holding. The Dubai Holding company is a global investing corporation with a number of real estate projects. The company focuses on different sector such as financial services, consultancies, hospitality, theme parks etc.

The project was announced in year 2003. The development of the work was on hold during the 2008 economic crisis and resumed by mid-2013. Approximately $55 billion has been raised for the work. The project was designed to gain synergy from the strategic location of Dubai as the gateway for Europe and Asia. The project was based on the strategy of the government to diversify into non-oil sector and promote tourism. Dubailand will be the world's most ambitious tourism, leisure and entertainment destination.

The Dubailand project envisioned is a development project which spans over 2 billion square feet in size with 45 mega projects and 200 sub projects. The project received approximately AED 20–25 billion from the private sector for the first phase investment. Dubailand is a developing city and there is no definite completion date for the entire project. Dubailand is strategically located and is situated on the Emirates Ring Road and is in close proximity to other land marks like Burj Al Arab. Dubailand is subdivided into six zones for effective management. These zones represent different cultural and socio economic mix along with product diversity. The total investment in Dubailand was estimated at US $88.4 billion or AED 325 billion. The project is often described as "bursting with architectural steroids". Dubailand project was estimated to host a population of 2.5 million people once completed. The Residential projects in Dubailand is spanned over three million square feet in different projects such as Rukan, The Falcon City, The Tiger Wood, the Sky Courts Tower and Dubailand Oasis among others.

The zones are discussed as given below:

Attractions and Experience World:

The projects under this zone include anchor theme parks, the Global Village, themed water parks, Kids City and Giants World. The zone covers 145 million square feet. The project will be twice the size of Walt Disney World Resort and will be the largest collection of theme parks in the world. The Sahara Kingdom theme park will cover 460,000 m^2 and combines high end virtual and physical theme park rides. The attractions will include state of art gaming zone, IMAX theater, and integrated live and virtual entertainment shows along with a retail zone, four hotels and residential accommodations.

8.1 Retail and Entertainment World

This zone consists of the development energy center, destination of family entertainment and innovative retail concepts in a themed environment. Projects include Flea Market, World Trade Park, Auction World and Factory outlets. The zone consists of 45 million square feet.

8.2 Themed Leisure and Vacation World

The zone is designed for quality vacation village residences and resort hotels. This zone focuses on creative themed development concepts in exotic location of desert but adjacent to major leisure and entertainment facilities. The themed leisure and vacation world covers 311 million square feet. The projects include Women's world, Destination Dubai, Desert Kingdom and Andalusian Resort & Spa.

8.3 Eco Tourism World

Eco Tourism World is focused on preserving the desert heritage of Dubai, creating a habitat for animals and covers 806 million square feet. Projects include Desert Safari, Sand Dune Hotels, Desert Camps and Dubai Heritage Vision.

8.4 Sports and Outdoor World

The zone covers 206 million square feet and provides an arena for outdoor sports activities. The zone focuses on building facilities to host world events such as soccer, cricket, rugby etc. The projects include indoor and outdoor venues such as Dubai Sports City, Emarat Sports World, Plantation Equestrian and Polo Club Autodrome and Dubai Golf City.

8.5 Downtown

This zone is the gateway for the overall development in Dubailand and consists of the business and administrative district. The zone will boast of huge impressive gateways and water cascades. The projects include Mall of Arabia-the largest mall in the world, City Walk, Virtual Game World which is cyber centric with 3D interactive games. City Walk consists of art displays, wide boulevards, street cafes and theaters, lush parklands, lawn museum and common garden.

Dubailand uniqueness lies in its combination of different entertainment, leisure, sports, retail and other tourism attractions.

8.6 Strategic Alliances

In 2008, DreamWorks announced plans to build a theme park in Dubailand. In the same year Tatweer entered into a strategic alliance with SixFlags to build the 5000,000 square feet Six Flags Dubailand theme park. Tatweer also announced the launch of Freej Dubailand which consists of hotels totaling 2600 keys and feature retail, food and beverage outlets along with numerous entertainment attractions. The proposed Marvel Superheroes theme park will comprise nine retail outlets with over 40 food and beverage outlets. Tatweer had a strategic alliance with Merlin Entertainments Group to build a Legoland park in Dubailand. The project was expected to cost 912 million AED and would feature 40 interactive rides, shows and attractions.

Dubai Properties Group took over Dubailand from Tatweer. Six Flags and DreamWorks later on dropped out of their projects. Dubai Miracle Gardens with 72,000 square meter was opened in year 2013. In 2016, Legoland Dubai and Motiongate Dubai was opened at Dubai Parks and Resorts. Table 8.1 highlights different projects undertaken in Dubai land.

8.7 Cancelled Projects

Many projects such as Six Flags Dubailand were the part of projects which were cancelled. Projects such as Pharaohs Theme Park, Universal Studios Dubailand, F1-X Theme Park Dubai, Tourism World, Aviation World, Giants World, Six Water Parks, Astrolab Resort and Great Dubai Wheel were also cancelled.

In 2018, China Machinery and Engineering (CMEC) secured a $150 million turnkey engineering, procurement and contracting (EPC) contract from Bahrain based GFH Financial group for the construction and financing of up to 85% of California Village which is its Dubailand based project. Under the terms of contract, Chinese banks provide financing under an insurance policy issued by Chinese state government agencies. California Village is a high-end mixed-use development and gated communities located in Dubailand with more than 200 private villas and 400 branded residences.

Table 8.1 Proposed projects under different zones in Dubailand

Attractions & Experience World	Retail and Entertainment World	Themed Leisure and Vacation World	Eco-Tourism World	Sports and Outdoor	Downtown
Akoya Oxygen	Dubai Outlet City	Women's World (LEMNOS)	Al Sahra Desert Resort	Dubai Sports City	City of Arabia
Bawadi	Black Market	Destination Dubai	Sand Dune Hotel	Emerat Sports World	Mall of Arabia
Fantasia	Flea Market	Desert Kingdom	Al Kaheel	Extreme Sports World	Restless Planet
Falconcity of wonders	World Trade Park	Andalusian Resort and Spa	Bio World	Plantation Equestrian and Polo Club	Wadi Walk
IMG Worlds of Adventure	Auction World		Animal World	World Dubai Motor City which includes Dubai Autodrome	Elite Towers
Legends of Dubailand	Factory Outlets			Dubai Golf City	City Walk
Global Village	Dubai Lifestyle City			Dubai Snowdome	
The Trump World Golf Club					
Kids City					

Further Reading

1. https://en.wikipedia.org/wiki/Dubailand
2. https://propsearch.ae/dubai/dubailand
3. https://www.worldconstructionnetwork.com/news/cmec-secures-150m-epc-contract-for-dubailand-project/
4. https://www.arabianbusiness.com/dubailand-takes-shape-186124.html

Case 5: International Space Station

The International Space Station (ISS) is the largest technology project of all time and demonstrates the peaceful international use of space for scientific and industrial research. This huge orbiting laboratory had received contributions from the USA, Russia, Canada, Japan and the member states of the European Space Agency (ESA). The ISS is a modular space station in low Earth orbit. It is a multinational collaborative project which involves five participating space agencies: NASA (United States), Roscosmos (Russia), JAXA (Japan), ESA (Europe) and CSA (Canada). The contractual agreement for the project in terms of ownership and use of the space station is governed by intergovernmental treaties and agreements. ISS serves as a microgravity and space environment research laboratory and scientific experiments are conducted in different sectors such as astrobiology, astronomy, meteorology, physics and other fields. The ISS also serves as testing center for spacecraft systems and equipment required for long duration missions to Moon and Mars. The station is categorized into two sections-the Russian Orbital Segment (ROS) which is operated by Russia. The other section is the United States Orbital Segment (USOS) which is operated by US and other nations.

The project which involved a common digital workplace was perhaps one of the first examples where teams from all over the world who speak different languages could work on exactly the same thing. The parts required for the project was built in different countries with sections of the station launched into space and then assembled in orbit. It took more than 40 spaceflights to build the station which started operation since the year 2000. The station revolves in low orbit at an average altitude of 400 kilometers with a speed of 28,000 kilometers per hour which is equivalent to circling the globe in every 90 minutes.

Over 200 astronauts from 18 countries have visited the station and conducted more than 2500 scientific experiments which covered subjects from microbiology and physics to astronomy and meteorology. The space station travels approximately 8 kilometers every second. The space station's mass is 419,725 kilograms.

By 2015, NASA and space agencies of Russia, Japan, Europe and Canada have hosted investigators from 83 nations to conduct over 1700 investigation in the long term microgravity environment on board the ISS. Extreme conditions in the ISS space environment include exposure to extreme heat and cold cycling, ultra-vacuum, atomic oxygen, and high energy radiation. Astronauts on ISS frequently venture out to conduct research and in these spacewalks, they spend often five to eight hours. Approximately more than 200 spacewalks have been conducted. Russian astronaut Anatoly Solovyev had spent 82 hours and 22 minutes on his 16 spacewalks.

The IIS project delivers lessons in global cooperation and stakeholder management. The development of the project was initiated in the year 1993 by NASA, ESA, Russian and Japanese space programs by pooling their resources with support from 16 countries. The space was assembled in the year 1998. Over the next ten years $100 billion was invested with US's contribution amounting to half of the total investment. During this period over one million pounds of hardware were invested in the space project. The station is equipped to support a crew of 7 at an estimated cost of $7.5 million a day per person.

The ISS serves as an educational platform to promote sciences and bridge the gap between different cultures. The highly complex collaborative nature of the project signifies the importance which the stakeholder management plays in large scale global projects. The ISS when completed weighed over 450 tons and took 136 fights on seven different types of flight vehicles to be assembled. It took 10 years and more than 30 missions to assemble. It is the realization of scientific and engineering collaboration of five major space agencies representing 15 countries. The space station is approximately the size of a football field with permanently crewed platform orbiting 250 miles above earth. It is four times as large as the Russian space station Mir and five times as large as the US Skylab.

Germany is the major ISS partner of ESA from Europe. Germany is the biggest financial contributor of the project from Europe. Germany contributes approximately 41 percent of the European infrastructure dedicated to the scientific use of the space station. The German Aerospace Center (DLR) is responsible for the coordination of German ESA activities related to ISS programmes in relation to the structure, enterprise and use of station. Germany has also contributed towards the ISS project through the establishment of the Columbus Laboratory and the development of the Automated Transfer Vehicle. Germany also provides support for the data management for the Russian module Zarya and robotic arm for the Russian part of the ISS. German scientists are also involved in the research with respect to breeding of protein crystals, plasma and radiation in biological aspects.

In 1993, USA invited Russia to join the international space station program. By that time Russia had the greatest experience in space station design, construction and management. Russia also had highly experienced engineers with sensitive knowledge in rocket technology.

In 2018, the station's operation authorization was extended to 2030 with the funding secured until the year 2025. Statistics suggest that by November 2020, 242 astronauts, cosmonauts and space tourists from 19 different nations had visited the space station. This included 152 Americans, 49 Russians, 9 Japanese, 8 Canadians and 5 Italians.

9 Case 5: International Space Station

Table 9.1 Milestones of the project

Year	Milestones
1983	The USA and its partners in Europe, Japan and Canada had initial discussion about the possibility of a joint space station
1984	The ISS project envisaged under the leadership of President Reagan
1985	The ESA Council of Ministers approved European participation in the American space station
1988	International agreement was signed among partners.
1997	ESA and NASA signed a principle agreement wherein Europe agreed to supply additional equipment, including two connecting nodes for station modules and laboratory equipment, to the USA.
Nov 1998	A Russian proton rocket named Zarya was launched as a part of ISS project
1998	The first ISS component was launched in 1998,
Dec 1998	US built component of ISS launched. It was the first Space Shuttle launched as a part of the assembly of the station.
1993	USA invited Russia to join the international space station programme.
Nov 2000	The first long term residents resided onboard the station for several months after being launched from the Baikonur Cosmodrome.
Feb 2001	The primary research laboratory for US payloads established in ISS
2005	US Lab module in ISS recognized as Newest US National laboratory
2008	Columbus Laboratory, the European Space Agency becomes part of the ISS. European Columbus module was docked to the ISS.
March 2008	First Japanese Kibo laboratory becomes part of the ISS
Nov 2010	ISS celebrates 10 year anniversary
Feb 2011	NASA introduces cooperative agreement
July 2011	Center for the Advancement of Science in Space was selected by NASA to manage the ISS National Lab
2013	The first ISS National Lab Research Flight was established. The ISS National Lab's protein crystal growth (PCG) series of flights were initiated. Lab announced finding such as protein can be grown as crystals in space with nearly perfect three dimensional structures which are useful for the development of new drugs.

Source: https://www.issnationallab.org/about/iss-timeline/

Space expeditions run up to six months from launch until undocking. Expeditions 1–6 involved three person crews each. Expeditions 7–12 were restricted to two each following the failure of NASA Shuttle Columbia. Again from Expedition 13 onwards the crew size was increased to six by 2010. Table 9.1 showcases the major milestones for the project.

The building of international space stations faced huge risks and challenges. It was in fact a new form of international cooperation. The partners of the project had to solve challenging issues such as the technological concepts, the usage of stations, legal and intellectual rights related to the project. Thus the project had to face technology risks, legal and structural risks. One of the biggest challenges was the conduct of experiments without infringing intellectual property rights. In 1988 an international agreement was signed to resolve these issues and the agreement was one of the largest documents related to any international cooperation. The cooperation was intended for peaceful purposes.

The presence of humans onboard ISS have provided a foundation for numerous educational activities in sciences, technology, engineering and mathematics (STEM subjects). Over 43 million students from 64 countries around the world have participated in ISS related educational activities. Projects such as Earth Knowledge-based Acquired by Middle Schools (EarthKAM) have allowed for global student, teacher and public access to space through student image acquisition.

ISS provides an ideal opportunity to test new business relationships. It provides an opportunity to shift from a paradigm of government funded contractor provided goods and services to a commercially provided government as a customer approach. This facilitates the creation of a more commercially oriented market in low Earth orbit. It has the scope to create new stakeholders in spaceflight and provides new economic opportunity.

Space Station Facts

242 individuals from 19 countries have visited the International Space Station. The space station has been continuously occupied since November 2000. An international crew of six people live and work while traveling at a speed of five miles per second, orbiting Earth about every 90 minutes. In 24 hours, the space station makes 16 orbits of Earth, traveling through 16 sunrises and sunsets. Peggy set the U.S. record for spending the most total time living and working in space at 665 days on Sept. 2, 2017. The living and working space in the station is larger than a six-bedroom house (and has six sleeping quarters, two bathrooms, a gym, and a 360-degree view bay window). To mitigate the loss of muscle and bone mass in the human body in microgravity, the astronauts work out at least two hours a day. Astronauts and cosmonauts have conducted 232 spacewalks for space station construction, maintenance and upgrades since December 1998. The space station has an internal pressurized volume equal that of a Boeing 747.

More than 50 computers control the systems on the space station. More than three million lines of software code on the ground support more than 1.5 million lines of flight software code. In the International Space Station's U.S. segment alone, more than 1.5 million lines of flight software code run on 44 computers communicating via 100 data networks transferring 400,000 signals (e.g. pressure or temperature measurements, valve positions, etc.).

Source: https://www.nasa.gov/feature/facts-and-figures

9.1 Cost of the Project

The International Space Station was built at a cost of $160 billion dollars. The ISS project is often described as the most expensive project ever constructed. By 2010, the total cost incurred was about $150 billion. US is the major contributor for the project. NASA's budget towards the ISS was approximately $58.7 billion (inflation unadjusted) during the period 1985–2015. Russia's contribution amounted to $12 billion. Europe and Japan contributed $5 billion each while Canada contributed $2 billion. The cost of 36 shuttle flights to build the station was estimated to be $50.4 billion. It can be estimated that on the assumption of 20,000 person-days of use from 2000 to 2015 by two to six person crews, each person day would cost $7.5 million for the project mission.

In the year 2021, NASA unveiled the Commercial LEO Destination (CLD) project with plans to award up to $400 million in total to maximum four companies to develop private space stations. This program was in extension to its Commercial Cargo and Commercial Crew Program wherein three companies facilitated the transport of cargo and astronauts to the International Space Station. NASA has transferred the responsibility of cargo and crew transportation to private companies. SpaceX and Northrop Grumman had send the cargo spacecraft to the ISS. SpaceX and Boeing had launched astronauts to ISS. CLD program has resulted in cost savings for NASA. NASA spends about $4 billion a year to operate the ISS. In 2020, NASA estimated that the commercial crew program had resulted in cost savings in the range of $20–$30 billion. Another motivation for the CLD program is the ISS's aging hardware as much of the space station's core structures were manufactured in the 1990s.

9.2 Structuring of the Project

The ISS program is structured as a complex set of legal, political and financial agreement between 15 nations which are involved in the project. The agreement deals with the matters related to ownership and governance; rights to crewing and utilization; responsibilities for crew rotation and resupply of the ISS. These agreements combine the five space agencies and their respective international space station programmes. The agreement stipulates the nature of interaction between the members which range from maintaining station operations in terms of traffic control of spacecraft and utilization of space and crew time. The ISS is the most politically and legally complex space exploration programme in history. The 1998 Space Station Intergovernmental Agreement stipulated the primary framework for international cooperation among members. A series of subsequent agreements governed other aspects of the station which ranged from jurisdictional issues to code of conduct among visiting astronauts. According to Outer Space Treaty, the United States and Russia are legally responsible for all modules launched by these countries. During March 2015, Roscosmos and NASA entered into an agreement for collaborating on the development of a replacement for the current ISS. Boeing's contract with NASA as prime contractor for ISS was extended and Boeing extended its services under the contract for station's primary structural hardware to the year 2028. In 2018, the Leading Human Spaceflight Act was passed for extending the operations of the ISS to the year 2030.

The primary layer which establishes the obligations and rights between the ISS partners is the Space Station Intergovernmental Agreement (IGA) which is an international treaty signed on January 28, 1998 by 15 governments who were involved in the space station project. The member nations involved in the project consisted of Canada, Japan, the Russian Federation, the United States and eleven members of the European Space Agency (Belgium, Denmark, France, Germany, Italy, The Netherlands, Norway, Spain, Sweden, Switzerland and UK).

IGA also incorporated a second layer of agreements between the partners which were referred to as Memoranda of Understanding (MOUs) between NASA and each of the four other partners. NASA is the designated manager of the ISS. The MOUs focusses on the roles and responsibilities of the partners in detail. The third layer consists of bartered contractual agreements or the trading of the partners' rights and duties. A fourth legal layer of agreements implements and supplements the earlier MOUs.

Further Reading

1. International Space Station: For Showing That Space Exploration Transcends Global Politics (Most Influential Projects: #26) (2019). PM Network, 33, 54–55.
2. https://www.geniusproject.com/blog/famous-projects/the-international-space-station-project-where-no-project-manager-has-gone-before/
3. https://www.issnationallab.org/about/iss-timeline/
4. ISS - the largest technology project of all time: an outpost of humanity in space, https://www.dlr.de/content/en/missions/iss.html
5. https://www.dlr.de/content/en/articles/missions-projects/iss/iss-history.html
6. https://www.britannica.com/topic/International-Space-Station
7. "International Space Station Overview". ShuttlePressKit.com. 3 June 1999.
8. NASA. 26 June 2007. Archived from the original on 23 January 2008.
9. https://en.wikipedia.org/wiki/International_Space_Station_programme
10. International Space Station www.nasa.gov/station
11. Station Science www.nasa.gov/iss-science
12. Reference Guide to International Space Station, Utilization Edition 2015, NASA.
13. Michael Sheetz, NASA wants companies to develop and build new space stations with up to $400 million in grabs, https://www.cnbc.com/2021/03/27/nasa-commercial-leo-destinations-project-for-private-space-stations.html

Case 6: Al Maktoum International Airport

Al Maktoum International Airport is an international airport under construction in Jebel Ali in Dubai, United Arab Emirates. Al Maktoum International Airport is also known as Dubai World Centre. Dubai World Centre is Dubai's airport of the future. The airport is an important part of Dubai South which is a proposed residential, commercial and logistics complex. The phase 1 of the airport was opened on June 27, 2010 for cargo operations. The first flight was an Emirates Sky Cargo Boeing 777F which landed after a flight from Hong Kong. Passenger flights started operations in October 2013. In 2013, the passenger flights started operations with Wizz Air followed by Jazeera Airways, Gulf Air and later Qatar Airways. The Airport currently have 27 passenger carriers operating an average of 108 flights weekly to 44 destinations. The airport also serves 36 freight operators.

By 2013, the airport had capacity to handle 5–7 million terminal passengers. On completion of the entire project in the year 2027, the project will be composed of transport modes, logistics and value added services in a single free economic zone. The Airport covers an area of 14,000 hectares. The projected annual capacity of the airport is estimated to be 12 million tons of freight. This airport will be the world's largest global gateway with capacity to handle more than 160 million passengers per year. The airport has the capacity to handle 160–260 million passengers. The airport would support the emirate's aviation, tourism, commercial and logistics requirements for the next fifty years. The multi modal logistics hub was envisaged to provide significant benefits to the economy of Dubai. Dubai World Central is the first aerotropolis of the region which provides multi modal transportations solutions and international connectivity. The new airport was established to complement additional structures of the larger Dubai World Central project which included free zone commercial, residential and educational facilities. The airport is the epicenter for the greater project which consists of multiphase development of six clustered zones of the Dubai Logistics City (DLC), Commercial City, Residential City, Aviation City and the Golf City. Currently the international airport has the capacity to handle 600,000 tons per annum and operates on an A380 compatible runway of 4.5 km. The airport operates 24 hours a day. The infrastructure include 64 aircraft stands of which 10 are Code F, a state of the art ATC Tower, fire stations, line maintenance services, a fuel farm and a 66,000 square meter, single level passenger terminal. The infrastructure also includes four additional CAT III certified runways which are capable of handling four superjumbo aircraft landings.

The Phase 2 of the airport includes the construction of two automated and one non-automated cargo terminals. As a result, the total cargo capacity at Al Maktoum International Airport is expected to be 1.4 million tons per annum. An exhibition area designated as the new permanent home of the Dubai Airshow is being built in this phase. Airport is expected to have five runways and four terminal buildings. The airport is expected to be the largest airport in the world in terms of both physical size and passenger volume.

Cargo carriers such as Aban Air, ACI, Aerospace Consortium, Aviation Service Management, Coyne Airways, Euro Asian Services, Gatewick, Ramjet, Reem Style, Rial Aviation, Rus Aviation, Sonic Jet, Sun Global, Skyline and United Aviation Services had entered into agreements to use the new airport.

Under the proposed plan, the airport will have three passenger terminals which will include two luxury facilities—one dedicated to Emirates and the second one to other carriers and the third one will be dedicated to low cost carriers. The features will include multiple concourses, executive and royal jet centers, hotels and shopping malls. Al Maktoum International Airport will be linked to the existing Dubai International Airport by a proposed high speed express rail system and will be served by Dubai Metro along with Dubai World Central light railway. It was expected that UAE will become the primary air hub for transiting travelers from the Asia Pacific Region, South Asia, Greater Middle East, Africa, Europe and Australia. The airport will be surrounded by a logistics hub, golf resort, trade and exhibition facility with three million square meters of exhibition space, commercial district and residential area. The airport will have parking slots capacity for 100,000 automobile vehicles.

The new airport is equipped with different concourses and possess a 91-metre-high air traffic control (ATC) tower which is the tallest freestanding ATC tower in the GCC region. The ATC tower is equipped with the latest avionics and navigational aids. The airport will showcase a new era of smart airport systems and passenger centric facilities. The West Terminal building will host origin and destination passengers with dedicated halls for first, business and economy class passengers. The 14 station Automated People Mover (APM) will seamlessly carry travelers from terminals to concourses as well as between concourses and allows transfer passengers to reach connecting flights through the shortest path. In its final configuration structure, the platform is designed to handle 260 million passengers per year and 15 million tons of cargo. Phase 2 of the project will involve concourse 2, the south support facilities, the second control tower and the expansion of the north support facilities and the west terminal. Phase 2 will have a combined built up area of 5.4 million square meter. In terms of the master plan, the final configuration will have two large terminals at west and east side of the platform in addition to the existing passenger terminal building. The option of curbside check in with baggage drop in automated carts facilitate passengers to be hands free even before entering the terminal. A seamless movement up to APM will be feasible for passengers on account of quick border crossing facilities and non-intrusive security checks with advanced biometric systems. All the four concourses at DWC will be a mega structure with a built up area of 2.3 million square meter and 2.7 kilometer long. Each concourse will equal the length of three concourses at Dubai International Airport (DXB). In the central piazza of the concourse, large areas are reserved for shops, restaurants and other entertainment facilities. The airlines first and business class lounges will be set at the upper level. The 100 boarding gates of each concourse are to be lined along the piers with the spine linking the three nodes thereby facilitating access to the aircraft through multiple boarding bridges. Baggage will be processed through an underground network of galleries and batch centers. The facility will enable to handle 30,000 bags per hour. There will be five parallel runways for code F aircraft of which four runways will be spaced by more than 1500 metres to facilitate four simultaneous parallel aircraft operations. The 4.5 kilometer runways will be equipped with the most advanced aircraft guiding system. The second control tower will be set at the center of the airfield. The infrastructure at the airport is based on the standards of LEED Gold for sustainability. The new airport's terminals and concourses will depend completely on clean energy sources like photovoltaic solar panels. High performance insulated buildings will be enveloped by solar glazing to control energy inputs. Traffic management system will be based on intelligent systems. The Airport's footprint is 65 sq km. The built up square meter area of all facilities combined is 19.4 million. There are 400 contact gates across four concourses.

According to Airports Council International (ACI) data, the number of passengers who arrived at Dubai International Airport approximately doubled from 37.4 million in 2008 to 68.9 million in 2014. By 2020, the aviation sector was expected to account for 37.5% of Dubai's GDP which amounted to US$53.1 billion. It was further estimated that aviation sector will contribute US$ 88.1 billion towards Dubai economy by the year 2030 which will account for 44.7% of the GDP.

10.1 Financing of the Project

The total cost of Al Maktoum International Airport is estimated to be $82 billion by the government. Dubai World Central which is often described as the world's most expensive urban development project was valued at $33 billion. Another estimate suggest that the project would need $36 billion. In August 2010, the Department of Civil Aviation (DCAA) announced plans to raise USD 1.6 billion through a sukuk (Islamic bond) to fund the first phase of construction. A consortium of local and international banks was involved for raising the capital required for the project.

The project has utilized export credit funding facilities from countries which are major exporters of equipment and technology for construction of airports. Under the arrangement, the financing was provided by export credit agencies which had given finance under significant long term payment plans. The build operate transfer (BOT) model is also being considered for the development of different systems in AlMakotum International Airport. Project finance model is also used wherein

Table 10.1 Contract packages value in year 2010

Project name	Contract value
DCAA—Al Maktoum International Airport—Cargo Terminal	USD 75,700,000
DCAA—Al Maktoum International Airport—Central Utility Complexes	USD 108,000,000
DCAA—Al Maktoum International Airport—First Fuel Farm	USD 30,000,000
DCAA—Al Maktoum International Airport—First Runway Package	USD 274,000,000
DCAA—Al Maktoum International Airport—Passenger Terminal and Control Tower	USD 201,900,000

Source: http://www.zawya.com/projects/project.cfm/pid060707061036?cc

contractors are funded through banks during construction. Securitization of airport assets to generate revenues directly is another option for the project. Long term bond issuance and sukuks are also being considered. In September 2014, the Dubai government had approved a $32 billion investment to expand the Al Maktoum International Airport. The facility carried a margin of 200 basis points across both the international and local tranches. In 2014, UK Export credit agency (UKEF) had issued export guarantees which was valued at $2 billion for expansion of the project.

In the year 2016, Dubai government secured $3 billion in long term financing for expansion of the airports in the country. HSBC was the financial adviser for the deal. The deal consisted of a $1.63 billion, seven-year conventional loan and a $1.48 billion equivalent, seven-year common lease based structure ijara facility denominated in dirhams. Joint mandated lead arrangers and joint book runners consisted of twelve international and local banks. These banks included Abu Dhabi Commercial Bank, Abu Dhabi Islamic Bank, Bank of China, Citibank, Dubai Islamic Bank, First Abu Dhabi Bank, HSBC, Industrial and Commercial Bank of China, Intesa Sanpaolo, JPMorgan, Noor Bank and Standard Chartered. The funding will be raised by a combination of Dubai state departments such as the Department of Finance, state-owned fund Investment Corporation of Dubai, and the Dubai Aviation City Corporation. Funds are expected to be raised from conventional and Islamic sources.

The joint venture of Dar Al Handasah Shair and Partners and Aéroports de Paris Ingenierie (AdPi) is the PMC of the project. Table 10.1 gives the details of the values of contract package. Table 10.2 list the milestones of the project.

10.2 Risks Perspectives

In an overall perspective, the project faces challenges in terms of macroeconomic risks. Cost escalation would result due to construction delay. Economic slowdown and covid pandemic had serious impact on the aviation sector and the future demand

Table 10.2 Milestones of the project

Year	Events
2004	Project was launched
2006	The master plan was prepared by Dar Al Handasah Shair and Partners.
Feb 2006	The construction contract was awarded to Al Naboodah Contracting for the first runway package.
Sept 2006	The construction contract was awarded to the JV of Arabtec Construction and Max Bogl for the cargo terminal package.
Feb 2007	The construction contract was awarded to the JV of Arabtec Construction and Max Bogl for the passenger terminal and control tower.
Nov 2007	The construction of the first runway was completed.
Jan 2008	DCA extended the contract of Hill International to provide consultancy services to Al Maktoum International Airport (JXB) and Dubai International Airport (DXB) for three years.
Q4 2008	The construction of the cargo terminal was completed.
April 2009	The number of runways was scaled down from 6 to 5.
September 2009	The construction of the central utility complexes package was completed
H1 2010	The construction of the control tower was completed.
Dec 2010	The construction of the passenger terminal was completed

Source: http://www.zawya.com/projects/project.cfm/pid060707061036?cc

for air traffic depends on the recovery from the pandemic and revival of tourism sector.

Further Reading

1. https://web.archive.org/web/20100831130710/http://www.dwc.ae/site/Dubai_World_Central_celebrates_inauguration_of_Al_Maktoum_International_Airport.html
2. https://www.dubaiairports.ae/corporate/about-us/dwc-dubai-world-central/
3. https://www.webcitation.org/6LLUPyRmT?url=http://www.dwc.ae/project-details/al-maktoum-international-airport/
4. https://blog.seattlepi.com/aerospace/2010/06/28/dubai-opens-second-airport/?source=rss
5. Zeidan, Ghaleb (2009, November 9) pr2live.com Dubai Aviation City Corporation Executive Chairman outlines Dubai's strategic focus on transport and logistics at SITL Dubai 2009
6. Al Maktoum International Airport, Dubai (DWC/OMDW)". Airport Technology. 2011-06-15.
7. https://www.airport-technology.com/projects/al-maktoum/
8. https://daep.gov.ae/our-airports/al-maktoum-international-dwc/dwc-the-ultimate-airport/
9. https://www.constructionweekonline.com/article-40708-how-is-al-maktoum-international-airport-financed
10. https://www.constructionweekonline.com/article-40708-how-is-al-maktoum-international-airport-financed
11. https://www.reuters.com/article/us-dubai-airports-loans-idUSKCN18A0IV
12. https://propsearch.ae/dubai/al-maktoum-international-airport
13. http://www.zawya.com/projects/project.cfm/pid060707061036?cc
14. https://www.nortonrosefulbright.com/en-gr/knowledge/publications/cb41e7ae/dubais-al-maktoum-international-airport-en-route-to-becoming-the-worlds-largest

Case 7: California High Speed Rail Project

California High Speed Rail (CAHSR or CHSR) is a publicly funded high speed rail system which is under construction in the US State of California. The system is planned to run from San Francisco to the Los Angeles basin under three hours with speeds of over 200 miles per hour. CHSR in its pathway will connect Anaheim Regional Transportation Intermodal center in Anaheim and Union Station in Downtown Los Angeles with the Salesforce Transit Center in San Francisco via the Central Valley. The system will eventually extend to Sacramento and San Diego covering 800 miles with 24 stations. In order to meet the transportation needs of the modern century, the High Speed Rail Authority have plans to invest billions of dollars in local and regional rail lines. California high speed rail system is aimed to connect the mega regions of the California state and make immense contribution to the economic development of the region in a sustainable environmental context. The aim is also to create jobs and preserve agricultural and protected land. The project is owned and managed by the State of California though the California High Speed Rail Authority (CHSRA). The CAHSRA was established by an act of the California State Legislature and was delegated to present a high speed rail plan. The plan termed Proposition 1 A was approved in the year 2008. Approximately $9 billion bond was issued for the construction of the first leg of the project. The California high speed rail system will connect 8 of the 10 largest cities in the State of California. California' corridors are among the busiest in the nation with 5.7 million people using train services in 2020. The system is designed in such a way that in blended or shared corridors, trains will be slowed to 110 miles per hour as per regulations and in other areas the train speed will reach 220 miles per hour. High speed rail will be run on 100 per cent renewable electric energy. In 2008, the project was estimated to cost $40 billion. Electrified high-speed trains traveling at speeds of more than 200 miles per hour will connect California's cities, making a trip between Los Angeles and San Francisco in under three hours.

The project assumes immense significant in the context that the California's population is expected to grow to more than 50 million by the year 2060. It is estimated that every year $28 billion is lost in time and fuel due to travel congestion.

Table 11.1 Comparative cost analysis: phase 1

	Base cost	Low cost	High cost
High Speed Rail	$80 billion	$63 billion	$98 billion
Equivalent cost in Highway/Airport	$153 billion	$122 billion	$199 billion

Source: 2019 Equivalent Capacity Analysis Report/CHSRA 2020 Business plan

California cities such as Los Angeles, San Francisco and San Jose rank among the top most gridlocked cities in the nation.

California's Department of Finance estimation suggest that the population will grow to almost 45 million people by 2050. The highways and roads in the California's metropolitan areas rank among the busiest in the nation and are nearing, or already exceeding, their capacity. California State Rail plan 2018 suggest that interregional travel is forecast to increase to almost 550.5 million trips annually by 2040 on all modes of travel.

The partnership between the California High Speed Rail Authority (CHSRA) in cooperation with the Federal Railroad Administration (FRA) for the development of the 800-mile-high speed rail system to serve California's major metropolitan areas was announced by US Department of Housing and Urban Development (USHUD), US Department of Transportation (USDOT) and US Environmental Protection Agency (USEPA). The Authority had signed a comprehensive Sustainability policy in September 2013 to honor industry sustainability and stakeholder commitments. The authority board adopted an updated sustainability policy in March 2016.

The investment in transportation infrastructure is a key to stimulate economic recovery after every crisis since the Great Depression. Investment in transportation infrastructure jobs is again the need of the hour to combat the growing unemployment on account of the pandemic covid.

The alternate infrastructure to the California High Speed Rail System is estimated to be very costly in nature. To provide the same capacity, the alternate system would require 4300 new highway lane miles, 115 additional airport gates, and 4 new airport runways. This alternate system is expected to cost more than $158 billion with a 50-year maintenance cost of more than $132.8 billion. Table 11.1 gives the details of the capacity analysis report of the project.

11.1 Economic and Social Impact of the Project

During the period 2006–2020, the California High Speed Authority had made investments of $7.24 billion for planning and constructing the first high speed rail system in the US. This investment facilitated the creation of jobs and boosted economic activity in different ways. The direct and indirect impacts induced statewide economic activity by ploughing back money into local and regional economies. The investment supported 54,300 to 60,400 job years of employment and generated $10.5 to $11.4 billion in total economic activity. The investment also led to $3.9–$4.4 billion in labor income. The economic output is in the range of $10.5 billion–$11.4 billion. Construction employment and training opportunities bolstered

11.2 Program Expenditure

Table 11.2 California high speed rail project: economic impact

	Employment (job-years)	Labor income	Economic output
Direct effects	4800–4900	$410 M– $420 M	$1140 M– $1160 M
Indirect effects	2100	$170 M	$510 M–$520 M
Induced effects	2800–2900	$170 M– $180 M	$520 M–$530 M
FY 2019–2020 total	9600–9900	$750 M– $770 M	$2160 M– $2210 M
Program total (July 2006–June 2020)	54,300–60,400	$3900 M– $4400 M	$10,500 M– $11,400 M

Source: California High Speed Rail System, Technical Supporting Document

economic development. Approximately 700 private sector firms had been contracted to work on the maintenance yard and others to operate and maintain the system. During the fiscal year 2019–2020, the project created 9900 full time jobs. As of July 2020, 560 small businesses started operations on account of the project. Approximately 55 per cent of the total project expenditure was accounted in areas of disadvantaged communities throughout California. The project related construction activities have supported over 5600 job years in the Central Valley region during the fiscal year 2019–2020.

With a few employees' decades ago, the Authority now provides thousands of jobs across all functions from planning and environmental clearance to engineering and construction. This sustained employment had generated substantial economic benefits in different parts of the country. Though maximum proportion of expenditure is accounted by California State, the project has also impacted the economies of other US states though material purchases. Companies located in other states have also benefited from the program. From the initiation of the project, at least companies based in 41 different states have worked directly on the program and contributed in all spheres including planning to engineering and construction.

As of June 2020, the California High-Speed Rail Program has invested $195.6 million outside California. Since 2018, the CHSRA have doubled the total number of construction jobs created by the project from 2600 to more than 5200.The Silicon Valley to Central Valley line of the High Speed Rail project is expected to create 220,000 job years of employment, $17 billion in labor income and $50 billion in economic output. The Phase 1 System is expected to create 624,000 job years of employment, $46 billion in labor income and nearly $131 billion in economic output. Table 11.2 discusses the economic impact of the rail project.

11.2 Program Expenditure

The program investments are categorized into five general expenditure categories. The construction category includes final design, construction administration, utility relocation, site clearing and civil works construction. Construction expenditure

Table 11.3 Program Expenditure in millions of dollars

Period	Expenditure in million dollars
Fiscal year 06/07–15/16	2380
2016–2017	1140
2017–2018	1200
2018–2019	980
2019–2020	1540
Program Total	7240

Source: California High Speed Rail System, Technical Supporting Document

includes Design Build (DB) contractors, California State Route 99 relocation project and parts of project and construction management contract costs. The planning/environmental expenditure includes regional consultant (RC) and environmental and engineering costs. The tasks under the planning/environmental category cover the preparation of project site, specific environmental impact report etc. Program administration expenditure include authority expenses and rail delivery partner/program management team contract costs. The real property acquisition expenditure includes right of way (ROW) support services (mapping, surveying, appraisal, negotiation and acquisition) contract costs, relocation expenses and land acquisition purchase payments. Other expenditures include Resource Agencies (RA), Third Party Agreements (TPA), legal, financial services and other miscellaneous contracts costs. Table 11.3 highlights the expenditure for the project.

11.3 Sources of Financing

The project has two major funding sources for the high speed rail program. The primary source which is the largest is termed Proposition 1A was authorized by the State in the year 2012. The second source of funding is a one time and ongoing 25 per cent appropriation of Cap and Trade proceeds through 2030. In 2008, the Proposition 1A provided $9.95 billion for high speed rail planning and construction. The High Speed Rail Authority received $ 9 billion and $0.95 billion was allocated to local high speed connectivity projects which was implemented by California Transportation Commission. In 2017 the Department of Finance, California approved four funding plans and allocated $3.7 billion under Proposition 1A funds. Under the funding plans, $2.6 billion was allocated for the central valley, $600 million for the Caltrain Peninsula Corridor Electrification project in Northern California and $77 million for the Rosecrans/Marquardt Grade Separation project in Southern California. In April 2020, a funding plan for $423 million was approved for the Link Union Station (Link US) project. With this allocation, all bookend funding to regional construction projects in Southern California and San Francisco Bay area was completed. By December 2020, the Authority had used approximately 99 percent of the authorized $2.6 billion Proposition 1A Central Valley construction funds. The Authority has received a total of $3.7 billion in Cap and Trade funds. For the completion of environmental review for the Phase 1 system, an allocation of $3.5 billion in federal funding commitments was made. The funding was also meant to construct the 119-mile central valley segment between Madera and Poplar Avenue.

11.4 Sustainability Initiatives

The high speed rail system is central to the state's climate policies. The electrified high speed rail will transform California's transportation system. High speed rail's zero emission trains will be powered by 100 percent renewable energy. The stations and high speed rail related facilities are designed to be net zero energy and energy net positive thereby increasing the environmental benefits. In December 2020, the Authority received national recognition for its sustainability initiatives when the Envision platinum rating was awarded by the Institute for Sustainable Infrastructure. The California High Speed Rail program is the largest transportation infrastructure project in terms of capital investment and geographic area to receive an Envision award for sustainable infrastructure.

Over time, the average annual greenhouse gas emissions savings from an operational high speed rail system in California will take roughly 400,000 passenger vehicles off the road. The High-Speed Rail Program's key sustainability achievements include recycling 97 percent (183,290 tons) of all construction waste to date and net-zero tailpipe greenhouse gas emissions during construction through carbon sequestration projects.

11.5 Major Milestones

The 51 mile Caltrain Peninsula Corridor Electrification project which represent the first phase of the high speed rail development in Northern California was allotted $714 million for electrification purposes. The work on the Los Angeles Union Station is in progress with respect to track upgrades and the authority had contributed $18 million towards the environmental review. The project also has witnessed the substantial completion of the first construction package involving a 22-mile stretch through Kern County to Poplar Avenue in the Central Valley. The construction is completed or under progress on 83 of 93 structures and on 106 of 119 miles of guideway by the end of year 2021.The upcoming milestones include completion of environment documents on 291 miles of the nearly 500 miles from San Francisco to Los Angeles. The testing of electrified high speed system is expected to commence by 2025 and certification process is to be completed by the year 2027. The electrified high speed train is expected to be in service by the end of the decade.

11.6 Risk Inherent in the High Speed Rail Project

The project cost estimation had been controversial. Initially the cost estimated was $40 billion in the year 2008. In 2012, the Authority revised the expected expenditure of the project to $68.4 billion. In 2018, the authority again revised its estimate to $98.1 billion with expected service from Los Angeles to San Francisco to initiate by the year 2033. Hence inflation is a major risk for the project.

The Covid-19 pandemic is a force majeure event. Construction package has been significantly impacted and the delays in construction activities are requiring schedule adjustments such as pushing schedules to later dates. The Authority recognizes the risks and past challenges associated with right-of-way delivery and has made significant process improvements. Passage of Senate Bill 1172, allowed the Authority to directly acquire right of way through purchase and eminent domain, initially reduced processing times by an average of 75 days.

The primary challenge to the completion of the project is funding. Sufficient funding to construct the entire system has not been provided to the Authority. The Legislature has not yet appropriated the remaining $4.2 billion in Proposition 1A funds. The Cap and Trading program provides the additional source of funding for the high speed rail program through 2030. The receipts for Cap and Trade funding are volatile in nature and hence can be lower than forecasted. This auction based revenue source of Cap and Trade is contingent upon market factors and hence difficult to predict with certainty the results of future actions. The project also faces different legal risks. There are chances of potential litigation and risks on account of adjudicatory administrative processes related to project funding, environmental clearances, property acquisition and contract disputes. Litigation had already affected the construction costs and schedules in the Central Valley Segment. The project faces future risks due to technological changes. Effective design of track and systems for final operation is a function of effective adoption of new technological advancement. Latest technology adoptions for solving problems related to connections to the power grid for high speed rail electrification is important for the success of the project.

11.7 Risk Mitigation Strategy

The program has increased its focus on risk contingency of its baseline budget. An enterprise risk management program is being implemented by the authority which includes the creation of a risk committee and strengthening of expertise in risk analysis. A stage gate project is implemented to bring more structure to the project as the project evolves through the planning, design and construction phase. Each contract is structured around a series of Notices to Proceed (NTP). This approach ensures that each step in the contract can only proceed when the Authority has the funding necessary to deliver and necessary prior work has been completed. Further, the Board of Directors and the State Public Works Board must approve each NTP. Essentially, the NTP structure and process provides a "risk check" to ensure that the

Table 11.4 Phase 1 high, medium and low ridership by year (riders in millions)

Ridership level	2033	2034	2035	2040	2045	2050	2055	2060
High ridership	17.9	36.4	41.9	50	52.6	55.2	58.1	61
Medium ridership	12.8	27.8	32.0	38.6	40.5	42.6	44.8	47.
Low ridership	10.3	21.3	24.5	29.3	30.8	32.3	34	35.7

Source: California High Speed Rail Authority Business Plan 2020, Chap. 7 Forecasts and Estimates, Page 139

Table 11.5 Phase 1 high, medium and low farebox revenue by year (YOE $ in millions)

Revenue level	2033	2034	2035	2040	2045	2050	2055	2060
High revenue	1688	3614	4369	6290	7476	8885	10,560	12,552
Medium revenue	1163	2562	3100	4484	5329	6334	7528	8947
Low revenue	980	2163	2618	3787	4501	5350	6359	7558

Source: California High Speed Rail Authority Business Plan 2020, Chap. 7 Forecasts and Estimates, Page 139

contract is carefully managed and that there is consistency between the multiple NTPs. This type of contract facilitate a single contractor to design, integrate, construct and maintain the project for a period of 30 years and provide the interfaces between the train, the signal system and power system. The primary risk involved is with respect to contract costs, including maintenance costs which are ought to be paid through necessary operating agreements with a service provider. To mitigate this risk, the Authority have executed a Memorandum of Understanding with the proposed interim service provider prior to executing any Track and Systems contract. To mitigate risks affecting the track and systems procurement, the Authority would introduce a phase approach to install the track and systems in the central valley so as to mitigate cost risks and improve construction efficiency.

The tables below provide the ridership and revenue results for Phase 1. Both ridership and revenue results assume one month of full phase 1 operation in the year 2033. The future year of expenditure (YOE) estimates assume an escalation of 3 percent per year from June 2019. Tables 11.4 and 11.5 discuss different estimates of the project statistics in different years.

Further Reading

1. https://www.buildhsr.com/get_the_facts/
2. https://hsr.ca.gov/programs/economic-investment/
3. Cost of California's High Speed Train Just Skyrocketed Again, Daily Wire Jan 17 2018.
4. Ralph Vartabedian, Cost for California bullet train system rises to $77.3 billion, Los Angeles Times, March 9, 2018.
5. California High Speed Rail Authority Economic Impact 2021.
6. California High-Speed Rail Authority Fiscal Year 2019-2020 Impact Analysis Technical Supporting Document Economic Impact Methodology Documentation January 2021
7. California High Speed Rail Authority 2020 Business Plan.

Case 8: London Cross Rail Project

In the nineteenth century, the Regents Canal company highlighted the important role railways will play in London in future. The origination of the idea of Crossrail can be attributed to the 1974 London Rail study. The report was published by the then Greater London Council and Department for Environment. The 1974 Rail study proposed the construction of the northern tunnel to link the British Rail's western region lines west of Paddington to the Eastern region lines east of Bethnal Green. It was also proposed to construct a southern tunnel to connect the southern region's central division services via stations at Victoria, Piccadilly, Leicester Square, Black friars, Monument and London bridge. The proposal aimed to offer an exciting solution to the future problems of overcrowded public transport system in central London. The study however estimated the cost of such a project to be £300 million. More than an idea, the cross rail project was a scheme just waiting for its time. In 1980, a British Rail discussion paper proposed an Inter-City link across London featuring three route options and estimated cost was £330 million. The proposal also suggested linking the existing infrastructure north and south of London through a deep bore tunnel beneath in the center of the capital instead of focusing on the east and west. By late 1980s, it became clear that the looming threat of underground congestion in the existing tube and rail was becoming a reality. In 1989, the government commissioned and published the Central London Rail study report which suggested the development of the East West Crossrail connecting Wimbledon to Hackney via Chelsea and Thameslink. In October 1990, the government entrusted the British Rail and London Transport to develop the east west Crossrail scheme. The cost of the Crossrail scheme was over £ 2 billion at 1993 prices. In November 1991, a private bill was introduced in the parliament. It was expected that the cost of the project would be borne by the passengers who would benefit through the fares they paid and through the contributions from property developers who would benefit from the improved infrastructure. However due to the onset of recession, Parliament rejected the Bill in May 1994. In July 1994, it was announced that the Crossrail project would be considered under the Transport and Works Act (TWA) system. The general viewpoint that emerged was that there were no cheap alternatives to Crossrail.

The government commissioned the Strategic Rail Authority to conduct London East West study for analyzing the requirements for the London route. The London East West study recommended to implement the Crossrail project. The shadow strategic rail authority London East West study commissioned in December 1999 had estimated that the peak hour passenger growth is estimated to be 15 percent in the next 20 years and off peak travel to double in the same period. The freight demand was expected to rise by 80 percent during the above period. The Government's proposed 10 Year Plan target was to increase rail travel by 50 percent. Many lines in both the National Rail system and the London Underground are overcrowded. The level of operational risk is expected to increase due to the forecasted growth in the number of passengers. On account of economic growth, the peak period congestion on the rail network has increased over a period of time. The shadow report estimated that the growth in the peak period between 2000 and 2020 for National Rail Network travel in the South East will be approximately 15 percent. The growth in traffic in the off peak period is estimated to be in excess of 100 percent. Central London was forecasted to be the destination for two thirds of trips. In the off peak period, the West end districts of Marylebone and Westminster were the most popular destinations.

Crossrail Ltd. was established in the year 2001 to build the new railway line known as the Elizabeth line through central London. The company was entrusted with the task of the project definition work on the Crossrail link and feasibility study of the possible Hackney Southwest London scheme. The initial budget for the project was set at £154 million. Crossrail Limited is the wholly owned subsidiary of Transport for London (TfL). The company was established as a 50/50 joint venture company between Transport for London and the Department for London. On completion of the project, the rail system will be run by TfL as part of London's integrated transport network. The Crossrail Hybrid Bill was submitted to Parliament in the year 2005 and Royal Assent was received in year 2008. Crossrail Ltd. has a Health and Safety Management System and an Environmental Management System certified to OHSAS 18001 and ISO 14001 respectively.

12.1 Features of the Project

Crossrail Limited is constructing the Elizabeth line, the new railway of London and the South East which connects Reading and Heathrow in the west to Shenfield and Abbey Wood in the east through 42 km of new tunnels. The Crossrail project is currently Europe's largest infrastructure project in Europe. The new Elizabeth line will be fully integrated with London's existing transport and will be operated by Transport for London. The Elizabeth line will cover more than 100 km from Reading and Heathrow in the west through central tunnels across to Shenfield and Abbey Wood in the east. It is estimated that 200 million annual passengers will use the Crossrail system. The new rail line will cover 41 stations including additional

10 new stations at Paddington, Bond Street, Tottenham Court Road, Farringdon, Liverpool Street, Whitechapel, Canary Wharf, Custom House, Woolwich and Abbey Wood. The construction project was expected to add an estimated £ 42 billion to the economy of the United Kingdom. Crossrail project have consumed over 130 million working hours so far.

The project will bring increased capacity and improved connectivity. The Elizabeth line will increase central London capacity by 10 percent and reduce congestion at many London underground stations. It will facilitate the ease of doing businesses by improving connectivity. The Elizabeth line will make the accessibility of international gateways easier. For example, the travel time from London Heathrow to the City of London (Liverpool Street) will be reduced from 55 minutes to 34 minutes. The Elizabeth line will facilitate 1.5 million more people within a range of 45 minutes' travel of the existing major employment centers of the West End, the City and Canary Wharf. Approximately 95 percent of journey will have step free access from platform to street level and for the majority of interchanges with other London underground and national rail services.

In a span of three years, eight giant tunnel boring machines had burrowed below the streets of London to construct the 42 kilometer new rail tunnels. Over 200,000 tunnel segments were used to line the 42 kilometers of tunnels.

Crossrail is one of the landmark infrastructure projects ever undertaken in the UK. The project—Elizabeth line aims to improve the journey across London by easing congestion and offering better connections from east to west region. Elizabeth will bring transformation change in the way people travel around the capital. During the construction which began in the year 2009, more than 200 archaeologists have unearthed over 10,000 objects from 40 locations spanning 55 million years.

This capacity enhancement project will have service length of 118.5 kilometers. The tunnel length in Central London will be approximately 16 kilometers. The gauge size is 1435 mm. The expected service frequency is estimated to be 24 trains per hour each way. Though the Crossrail project is known as a major tunneling project, over 75 percent of the 100 kilometer route is above the ground. At 656 feet (200 meters) long, Crossrail trains will be almost double the size of current London underground trains. Trains are designed for 1500 passengers. Over 35 million work hours have been completed on the Crossrail project. Approximately over 10,000 people are engaged in more than 40 construction sites.

12.2 Sources of Financing

A funding requirement of £15.9 billion was initially estimated in 2007. The cost of the project would be borne by the Government, the Mayor of London and London businesses. The funding requirement was revised to £17.6 billion in the year 2018. In the year 2019 the funding requirement was further increased to £17.8 billion (Table 12.1).

Table 12.1 Components of funding

Sources	Funding Amount in £ million
Department of Transport (direct funding) (DfT)	4960
Business rate supplement borrowing and direct contribution	4100
Network Rail financing for work on existing network	2300
Transport for London (TfL) direct funding	1900
Loan from DfT to GLA	1300
Loan from Dft to TfL	750
Sale of surplus land and property	550
Community Infrastructure levy	300
Developer contribution	300
Dft additional funding to Network Rail	290
City of London Corporation committed funding	250
Network Rail funding	220
Dft additional funding	150
TfL additional funding	150
Contribution from GLA	100
Voluntary funding from London businesses	100
Heathrow Airport Limited (HAL)	70
Total	**17,790**

Source: National Audit Office analysis of departmental information and Department of transport, London

12.3 Social and Economic Impact of the Project

The project is expected to create at least 75,000 opportunities for businesses and would results in employment generation of approximately 55,000 full time jobs. Companies all over UK would benefit from the project. Approximately 96 per cent of the contracts have been awarded to firms based within UK. Of these 62 percent are outside London. About 62 per cent of the businesses which received the contracts are small and medium enterprises. Crossrail project established an accredited Tunnel Safety Card (TSC) for standardized tunneling health and safety training. The Tunneling and Underground Construction Academy (TUCA) established by Crossrail is a purpose built training facility which supports the development of skills related to tunnel excavation and underground construction. Approximately 20,000 people received training from TUCA. Crossrail Ltd. along with Network Rail, Bombardier Transportation and MTR Crossrail had created more than 1000 apprenticeships during the Crossrail project. The partnership between Crossrail and Job Centre Plus provided employment to 5000 people. The Young Crossrail programme in partnership with local schools along the route provided the engineering insights about the project to over 40,000 students. About 96 percent of the contracts awarded by Crossrail were to UK companies with 62% of suppliers based outside London.

The Elizabeth line is expected to facilitate creation of over 300,000 new jobs in key employment hubs of London. The town centers of Ealing, Woolrich, Ilford and Romford are being rejuvenated with the construction of new residential houses and offices. It is estimated that 90,599 and 180,000 new homes will be constructed along the route by 2021 and 2026 respectively. Crossrail was involved in the integration function of design for 12 major property developments along the rail project route to create over three million square feet of high quality office, retail and residential space. These initiatives are expected to generate over £ 500 million towards funding for the Crossrail project.

12.4 Sustainability Initiatives of the Project

Over three million tons of excavated material from the tunnels was used to create a new 1500 acre RSPB nature reserve in the Wallasea Island in Essex. Approximately 84 per cent of construction machinery in the central section was fitted with pollutant reducing emission controls. Over 98 per cent of material excavated from sites was reused.

12.5 Project Progress

The project is in the final stages. It is expected to start the passenger operation services by the first half of the year 2022. Crossrail achieved a milestone when it commenced timetabled trial running in the central operating section. The trail running programme involves integrated trials to test the safety and reliability of the rail line. The final phase known as Trial Operations involves testing in real time scenarios with passengers onto trains. After the opening of the central section, full services across the Elizabeth line will be initiated. The assurance regime for Elizabeth line is complex and requires huge volume of handover assurance and documentation. The assurance regime requires the integration of 500,000 individual railway assets such as public address systems, smoke alarms and CCTV cameras. Approximately 200,000 documents for assurances and handover process are required to be completed for the successful safety certification of the rail project.

12.6 Risks in the Project

The principal risks to which the project is exposed include safety programme delivery, commercial, organizational, stakeholder and financial risks. Transport for London (TfL) had modelled the impact of Covid pandemic on revenue scenarios based on Imperial College's study. It is estimated that the passenger revenues are forecasted to reduce in the range of £1.4 billion to £ 3.5 billion by the end of 2020/21. In 2016, United Kingdom voted to leave the European Union. The TfL Group sources relatively few goods from the European Union. However, supply chain risks

Table 12.2 Chronology of construction works

Period	Event
April 2009	17 firms had secured 'Enabling Works' Framework Agreement
May 2009	Piling work started in proposed Canary Wharf Station
September 2009	Preparatory work for the £1 billion developments at Tottenham Court Road station initiated
2010	Crossrail announces contracts worth £1.25 billion for the construction of 18 kilometer of twin bore tunnels underneath central London. The Tunnels West contract was awarded to BAM Nuttall, Ferrovial Agroman and Kier Construction (BFK). The Tunnels East contract was awarded to Dragados and John Sisk & Son. Contracts were awarded to civil engineering companies for the second round of enabling works such as "Royal Oak Portal Taxi Facility" Demolition and Demolition works for Crossrail Bond street station.
2011	The remaining tunneling contract (C310) was awarded to Hichtief and J Murphy & Sons. Tunnelling and Underground Construction Academy was established in Ilford. A contract was awarded to a joint venture of BAM Nuttall Ltd. and Van Oord UK Ltd. to ship excavated material from the tunnel to Wallasea Island for construction of new wetland nature reserve.
2013	Restoration of Connaught Tunnel done
June 2015	Boring of the railway tunnels was officially completed
September 2017	Installation of track was completed
February 2018	First test train run between Plumstead and Abbey Wood conducted
May 2018	TfL took over Heathrow Connect services from Paddington to Heathrow
August 2020	Crossrail announced that the central section would be ready to open by the first half of year 2022
May 2021	Trial running on Elizabeth Line commenced

Source: Collated from different sources

which includes management of subcontractors may be affected due to the Brexit decision. Project can be exposed to short term risks which include potential disruptions to operations and commercial contracts and exposure to foreign exchange rate risks and interest rate risks. According to one estimate, the cost of the project would escalate to £18.25 billion, more than £2 billion as estimated in the original budget. Table 12.2 shows the chronology of the progress of construction work.

Further Reading

1. https://www.crossrail.co.uk/news/articles/crossrail-project-update
2. https://www.crossrail.co.uk/news/publications
3. https://www.crossrail.co.uk/news/crossrail-in-numbers
4. https://www.crossrail.co.uk/project/our-plan-to-complete-the-elizabeth-line/
5. Shadow Strategic Rail Authority East West Report 2000
6. Crossrail Annual Report 2020
7. https://www.railway-technology.com/projects/crossrail/

Further Reading

8. https://www.bbc.com/news/uk-england-london-53054052
9. Ed Owen, Crossrail enabling works frameworks announced, https://www.newcivilengineer.com/latest/crossrail-enabling-works-frameworks-announced-09-04-2009/
10. Gerald Neil, Work officially starts on Crossrail, Contract Journal, 15 May 2009.
11. Peter MacLennan, Crossrail award major tunneling contracts worth £ 1.25 billion, https://www.crossrail.co.uk/news/articles/crossrail-awards-major-tunnelling-contracts-worth-125bn
12. https://www.bbc.com/news/uk-england-kent-22168938
13. http://www.tunnelsonline.info/news/tfl-takes-on-tuca-230317-5769436/

Case 9: Beijing Daxing International Airport

The iconic starfish structure of Beijing Daxing International Airport is the largest single structure airport terminal in the world. It is China's new largest airport with an area of 700,000 square meters and cost involved for its construction was £8.8 billion. The airport is estimated to carry 170 million passengers by the year 2025. The Airport is built on the border of Beijing and Langfang. The airport is located 40 miles south of Beijing Capital International Airport. Beijing Capital International Airport is positioned as the second busiest airport in the world. This airport is running at full capacity. The new Beijing International airport is expected to ease the congestion of flights between Beijing and the rest of the world. The airport has the capacity to handle 300 takeoffs and landing per hour. All major China air carriers such as China Eastern, China Southern, China United and Air China airlines have presence in Daxing airport. The new Beijing Xiongan Intercity railway connects Daxing airport to Beijing city center in 20 minutes and the Daxing airport subway connects Beijing in 19 minutes. The Beijing-Xiong'an high-speed railway will connect Beijing's West Railway Station with Daxing Airport, completing the trip in 20 minutes The airport serves as the hub for China United Airlines. It is forecasted that by 2025, the airport will have four runways and 268 parking bays which will accommodate 620,000 flights and handle 72 million passengers per year. The airport has the world's largest terminal spanning 7.5 million square feet which is equivalent to 98 soccer fields. With runways and annexes, the whole surface area covers 18 square miles. The Beijing Daxing International Airport is also known as "the starfish. The glimmering structure resembles a giant starfish from top with six curved spokes spreading out from a central hub. Inside the core, an expansive rolling atrium is supported by eight giant C shaped pillars each with a 350-foot-wide skylight at the top. The innovative feature of starfish design is that the passenger doesn't need to walk more than 10 minutes from the core to the furthest gate in each wing.

The airport's first commercial flight was a China Southern Airlines A380 service to Guangzhou.

The official approval for the construction of the Airport by given by the National Development and Reform Commission on December 22, 2014. The airport was to be designed with 7 runways of which six were for civilian use and one for military purposes. The cost of construction was initially estimated to be at least 70 billion RMB (US$11.2 Billion).

The master plan of the airport was prepared by Netherlands Airport Consultants (NACO). The airport has a ground transportation center which provides inter airport transportation system and connects the airport to high speed rail, metro and bus services. The terminal building was executed by the Beijing Institute of Architectural Design. China IPPR International Engineering is responsible for security and baggage system. Hong Kong design studio Lead 8 was the lead designer of the integrated service building.

The major contractors involved in the project include China Electronics Engineering Design Institute, Civil Aviation Electronic Technology, The Third Rail Survey, Design Institute Group Corporation etc. The suppliers for the project included Xsight Systems, T-Systems, Schindler, Thales, Beijing EasySky Technology and Oasys.

The interior of the airport is designed to replicate a small city with amenities such as luxury duty free retail and restaurants, pet hotels, childcare facilities and work spaces. Facilities are in place such that over 80 per cent of all check ins with biometric scanners are handled by about 400 self-service check in kiosks. Passengers need not have to walk more than eight minutes to arrive at the designated gate. Zoeftig's quality Zenky Plus seating solutions are designed for passenger's comforts. The Zenky Plus seating solution has been placed in different zones such as the North West, South West and South Central Zones which houses the international departures. Beijing Daxing Airport is also characterized by high tech features. Huawei Technologies, China Eastern Airlines and China Unicom have introduced a 5G based smart travel system which will support facial recognition at security gates and check along with paperless luggage tracking service. Artificial intelligence is being deployed with smart robots along with regular airport staff.

The construction project was completed in a time period of four and a half years. The construction work started on December 26, 2014. The Airport became operational on September 26, 2019. The domestic and international terminals are stacked on top of each other. By mid of this decade, China Southern have plans to run 200 planes a day. By 2020, Daxing had handled 84,000 fights and now serves 129 destinations in China alone.

The airport is 46 kilometers south of Tiananmen Square, 26 kilometers west of downtown Langfang and 65 kilometer south of Beijing Capital International Airport. The airport has become a hub for Sky Team alliance airlines. It has the largest single building airport terminal. The airport was named as best airport for hygiene measures in Asia Pacific in the year 2020 by Airports Council International.

There are currently four runways and 79 airport stands. There are plans of total seven runways in future. The airport facilitates the operations of both one twin aisle and two single isle planes. The total passenger traffic in year 2019 was 3,135,074 and 16,091,449 in year 2020. The airport's unique design incorporates two tier departure and arrival platforms. It is the world's largest integrated transport hub. It is estimated that by 2040, approximately 100 million passengers and 20 million tonnes of cargo will be received by the airport on a yearly basis.

13.1 Structuring of the Daxing Airport

Capital Airports Holding Company (CAH) is the wholly owned entity of the Civil Aviation Administration of China (CAAC) which operates airports of Beijing Capital International Airport, Beijing Daxing International Airport, 40 airport companies and other companies.

13.2 Construction Cost

The airport construction cost was approximately US$17.47 billion and other projects in the periphery costed US$46.2 billion. The total cost was approximately US$63 billion. The project of Daxing airport was funded by the Chinese government.

13.3 Financing

The total investment for the project was estimated to be 79.98 billion yuan with 50 per cent from capital investment which included 18 billion funding from the Civil Aviation Administration of China (CAAC) and 6 billion yuan from Capital Airports Holding Company (CAHC). The project intended to seek funds from the private sector. National Reform and Development Commission (NRDC) and Ministry of Finance will contribute towards remainder of the funds which are allocated through central government budget. CAHC also raised funding for non-capital investment through financing by banks.

Bond were issued to finance the airport project. Approximately 4 billion yuan of the bond issue was used to acquire land and provide for housing demolition for the project. Additional bonds of value 6.7 billion yuan were used to finance the construction of the building for the project.

13.4 Development Fund

A development fund for Beijing Daxing International Airport economic zone was established in 2019 to raise 50 billion yuan (US$ 7.1 billion) for developing the airport economic zone. The fund would be used for major investment projects such as infrastructure, public services, regional services, urban management and other airport related industries. Beijing New Aerotropolis is the key platform for developing the airport economic zone. Beijing Daxing Airport Economic zone covers 50 square kilometers within Beijing and 100 square kilometers in Hebei province with three major divisions of service area, logistic area and technological innovation area. This area aims to become a leading service provider for Beijing Daxing Airport by the year 2035.

13.5 Economic Impact

China is the most populous country in the world and the public demand for aviation is a function of the size of its middle class population. According to China's Civil Aviation Administration, the annual passenger traffic had reached 1.26 billion in the year 2018. According to International Air Transport Association (IATA), China will overtake US as the world's largest aviation market by the year 2022. The urban population in China has increased from 19 per cent in 1980 to 58 percent in 2017. The middle class population is estimated at 400 million people constituting less than one third of China's total population.

According to the Civil Aviation Administration of China (CAAC), the airport will contribute 900 billion yuan to the regional economy. By 2025, the airport will receive 72 million passengers with an economic profit of 130 billion yuan (19 billion US dollars).

The construction of Daxing airport was aimed to reduce the economic imbalances across the Beijing Tianjin Hebei region. In the northern region of Hebei province where Daxing airport was situated, the infrastructure was far behind Beijing and Tianjin. The new airport was supplemented with good transport links to strategic destinations such as Langfang in Hebei and the "city of the future" Xiong'an New District. In its report, the commercial aviation organization Air Transport Action Group estimates that the global aviation sector creates five jobs in goods and services supply chains and tourism for every one job directly generated in aviation sector. Daxing Airport is expected to create 144,000 new jobs in Southern Beijing and Langfang thereby providing a boost to the local economy.

The government had plans to convert the Southern suburbs to new super city for economic growth and prosperity. The focus was on major regeneration of the southern provinces of Beijing which included Tianjin and Hebei provinces. These regions traditionally relied on farming and with the new connectivity in terms of airport and high speed rail system from Xiong'an area, several government establishments were relocated to this region. The new airport adds immensely to the air capacity in China.

13.6 Potential Risks

Environmental concerns in terms of carbon emission have been a source of concern for the project. Aviation accounts for three percent of global emissions. According to the UN organization, International Civil Aviation Organization (ICAO), for every 5 per cent growth in air travel, the carbon emission by the sector will account for one quarter of the carbon budget. On account of environmental and economic concerns, experts are suggesting that the focus should be on integrating the existing transportation networks. Earlier the routes between Beijing, Tianjin, Nanjing, Shanghai and Jinan were lucrative for airlines with numerous daily flights between cities. But with the advent of high speed rail, the demand for flights have come down in the region. The number of flights between Tianjin and Shanghai has dropped from 40 to 10 per day. Such reductions were observed in other regions too. According to international aviation industry, high speed rail has an absolute advantage over flying at distances between 150 and 800 kilometers. During the five-year plan 2016–2020, 74 airports were expanded or newly built in China.

The lack of airspace is largely blamed for the frequent delays suffered by the flyers. The Civil Aviation Administration of China (CAAC) had in the year 2019 estimated that flight delays in Chinese airspace had increased by 50 percent with 71 percent of flights only taking off on time. Passenger volume, air traffic control are some factors which had contributed for delays. According to FlightStats report, in 2019, the five global airport hubs with longest average delay time in the range of 84–97 minutes were all in mainland China.

The airport was spread over 18 square miles of land and it estimated that approximately 20,000 people were displaced for the construction of the project. The process was simpler in China compared to other countries since all land is owned by the state.

Further Reading

1. https://www.zoeftig.com/our-work/seating-system-case-studies/daxing-international-airport-beijing
2. Daxing International Airport Website
3. Jiang, Steven (September 18, 2019). "Beijing's new mega-airport ready to open". CNN Travel.
4. http://www.chinadaily.com.cn/a/201809/14/WS5b9ba783a31033b4f465628d.html
5. https://www.straitstimes.com/asia/east-asia/new-beijing-airport-to-open-on-oct-1-2019-able-to-accommodate-620000-flights-per-year
6. https://www.theguardian.com/environment/2011/sep/08/beijing-aviation-hub-mega-airport
7. https://www.airport-technology.com/projects/beijing-daxing-international-airport-china/
8. Civil Airports Statistics Reports 2019/2020.
9. https://www.cntraveler.com/story/inside-beijing-daxing-international-airport
10. https://chinadialogue.net/cities/11563-what-does-beijing-s-new-mega-airport-mean-for-emissions/?gclid=EAIaIQobChMIkIGh89Dz8AIVRertCh00aApZEAMYAiAAEgJnqPD_BwE
11. https://globetrender.com/2019/11/11/beijing-daxing-could-be-the-most-innovative-airport-in-the-world/
12. https://www.tripzilla.com/beijing-daxing-airport-open/96175
13. http://www.china.org.cn/china/2019-11/22/content_75434911.htm
14. https://airport.nridigital.com/air_jul19/beijing_daxing_airport_a_giant_prepares_for_take-off
15. https://www.cnbc.com/2019/09/26/beijing-daxing-airport-takes-china-closer-to-being-worlds-largest-aviation-market.html
16. https://economictimes.indiatimes.com/news/international/business/lawmakers-issue-bond-to-finance-third-airport-in-beijing/articleshow/49116398.cms?from=mdr

17. http://www.xinhuanet.com/english/2019-06/21/c_138162774.htm
18. http://www.icscc.org.cn/upload/file/20190628/20190628081713_43291.pdf
19. https://www.chinatravelnews.com/article/87291
20. https://simpleflying.com/beijing-new-airport-passenger-numbers/

Case: 10 Jubail II Industrial City

Jubail Industrial City is the largest civil engineering project in the world today. It is the largest industrial city in the world. Jubail was a fishing village until 1975. The government then decided to build the Jubail Industrial city. The first part of the megaproject termed Jubail I was initiated in the mid-1970s in the Eastern province of Saudi Arabia on the Persian Gulf. It included construction of facilities such as steel mill, petrochemical plants and refinery. Jubail I is a classic example for urban planning with dozen shopping centers and schools. Jubail has the largest combined desalination and power plant in the world. The desalination plant called Saline Water Conversion Corp (SWCC) is the largest producer of desalinated water in the world. In the year 2019, SWCC entered Guinness World Record with production of 5.6 million cubic meters of desalinated water every day. In terms of economic output, Jubail I produces 7 percent of the world's petrochemical products and contributes more than 11 percent towards Saudi Arabia's non-oil GDP. Jubail II is located about 8 kilometers west of Jubail I. During the peak period of early 1980s, the Jubail Industrial city project had a workforce of 50,000.

The city covers 1016 square kilometers and consists of industrial complexes, harbor and port facilities. Energy intensive industries are located in the city. The city of Jubail is close to economically important areas such as Ras Tanura, Ras al-Khair and Dammam. Major energy companies such as Sabic Al Jubail Petrochemical Company, Arabian Petrochemical company, Jubail United Petrochemical company, Saudi Aramco Total Refining and Petrochemical Company and the $20 billion Sadara Chemical Company petrochemicals complex are located in the city. In the mid-1970s the Bechtel Company was commissioned to engineer the construction of the new city. The government agencies of General Petroleum and Mineral Organization (PETROMIN) and the Saudi Basic Industries Corporation (SABIC) were the government agencies overseeing the project. The industrial city is composed of 16 primary industries. The industrial sectors included steel, gasoline, diesel fuel, petrochemicals, lubricating oil, and chemical fertilizers. The entire industrial zone covered 132 square km. Module paths and cooling water canals were built throughout the city. In June 2016, Bechtel signed a five-year extension with the Royal

Commission to extend its services related to the Jubail project. The expansion project involves the construction of residential accommodation, educational facilities, infrastructural facilities such as roads, bridges, hospitals and utilities. The total population of the city was 684,531 in the year 2021. The fourth largest petrochemical company SABIC is located in Jubail city.

The industrial city of Jubail is connected to other cities through the two major highway of Dhahran Jubail Highway and Abu Hadriyah Highway. One of the current highway project in progress is the Jubail-Qassim express high and the project would reduce the travel distance between Jubail and Qassim by about 500 km. There are plans in place to connect the city of Jubail to Dammam through a division of the Saudi Landbridge project. The two seaports constructed in Jubail are the Jubail Commercial Seaport and the King Fahd Industrial Seaport. The city is served by King Fahd International Airport. Jubail Airport is an airfield located 25 km west of Jubail city and serves as a naval base for the eastern fleet of the Royal Saudi Navy. The two other airfields located in Jubail city are the Abu Ali Airport and King Abdulaziz Naval base.

Jubail II consists of an 83 km square industrial development in the city of Jubail,490 km northeast of Riyadh. The project was initiated in the year 2005. The new development when completed is expected to double the population of the city. The construction is spread over 22 years in four phases. Phase 1 is completed and consists of eight blocks of industrial land development. The phase 2 and 3 include 7 blocks with support industries and power facilities. Phase 4 is dedicated to development of four blocks for aluminum and smelting industries. The project required 35 million cubic meters of earth removal. Both the Jubail I and Jubail II are designed and managed by Bechtel. Jubail is a major player in the global energy market. The project is aimed to double the size of the Jubail Industrial city by approximately 6200 hectares. The cost of construction of Jubail industrial city is estimated to be $18 billion dollars. It is planned to add over 50,000 residential units by the year 2026. The total infrastructure cost is estimated to be $80 billion. The estimated cost to construct the new Jubail II refinery was approximately US$10 billion. The number of barrels of Arabian heavy crude oil to be processed by the refinery was $10 billion.

Jubail II industrial city is being developed in four phases. The construction of first phase of the industrial city was initiated in the year 1977. The first phase is spread over 40.86 km square and consists of 19 primary industries which produces products such as refined oil, petrochemicals, steel, glass and aluminium. Phase 1 saw the construction of major industrial projects like the $750 million (SR 2.6 billion) plant which produces ethylene vinyl acetate and low density polyethylene. It is a joint venture between Saudi International Petrochemicals and Korean Hanwha Chemicals Corp. One of the landmark project of the Phase II was the establishment of the $14 billion Satorp refinery wherein the workforce consisted of 43,000 people per day during the peak of the project. The mega refinery Satorp covers 4 km square and the estimated cost of construction was $14 billion. The refinery is structured as a joint venture between Saudi Aramco and France's Total Fina. Saudi Aramco have ownership stake of 62.5 percent and Total's equity stake in the project is 37.5

percent. The refinery has a capacity to process 400,000 barrels of oil per day into petrol, diesel, jet fuel and other products. In later stages, plans are in place to construct a downstream chemical complex with 26 different manufacturing units costing $19.3 billion in infrastructural development. Royal Commission set up in the year 1975 is entrusted with the task of developing and maintaining the Jubail Industrial City. An area of 17 Km square has been allotted for the fourth and final phase of Jubail II. Other projects include $800 million (SR 3 billion) Jubail Chemical Industries and $533 million (SR 2 billion) Saudi Arabian Fertilizer Co.

Phase III of the project include the construction of the Sadara chemicals complex which is a joint venture between Saudi Aramco and Dow Chemical Co. This joint venture has 65 per cent equity ownership by Saudi Aramco and the rest 35 percent equity stake is owned by Dow Chemical Co. The chemical complex is a $19.3 billion eight km square complex with 26 different manufacturing plants. In the core structure of complex, there is an ethylene cracker and polyethylene plant which produces products such as glycol ethers, propylene glycol, low and high density polyethylene and elastomers. Sadara chemicals joint venture raised $12 billion in debt funding and the contribution from equity partners was $6.8 billion. Both the complexes were developed by Bechtel. Jubail's seawater cooling network is a complex network of pipe system which consists of 28 pumps and have the capacity to handle 25 m3 of water per day. This cooling system is one of the biggest in the world. Jubail city uses a network of three 11 km long canals for cooling purposes.

One of the most ambitious project is the development of new city center near Mardumah. The project is spread over 2.75 km square. The Royal Commission is making investments worth $18 billion in the new city center and expects the population to be around 1.3 million by the year 2040. Other major developments include the construction of the army and naval bases.

The transportation system of the Jubail city consists of six lane highway between Jubail and Dammam. Many roads and towns were created within the project. More than 530 miles and 60 bridges were built during the construction phase. The construction involved combination of tunnels, highways and superstructures. The earthwork process of construction involved 30 million cubic meters of aggregates. The project saw the installation of 16 feet diameter pipelines to carry water from the sea into the industrial site at a rate of 200,000 cu m per hour. It is also home to the world's largest Independent Water and Power Project (IWPP). This desalination plant will process 800,000 cubic meters of water for cities in the Eastern province and generate 2750 megawatts of electricity. The project also includes two large ports built on an artificial harbor enclaved by 11 miles of breakwater. The construction also consists of a 5.6 mile by 984-foot causeway with a four berth open sea tank terminal, a dry bulk terminal with nine berths, a service quay and a module import facility.

Jubail II project consists of residential accommodation for 120,000 residents; education centers which include an 18,000-student 'greenfield' university and other social infrastructural facilities. The Ras Al Khair Industrial City which was planned in year 2009 have an area of 124 plus square miles. Jubail Industrial City Airport covers an area of 29 plus square miles. The project also involved expansion of the

King Fahd Industrial port for both commercial and industrial business. The main highway between Dammam and Jubail which is six lanes wide is the epicenter of development.

The construction of King Fahd Industrial port in Jubail Industrial city in the year 1974 led to Saudi Arabia's transformation from a raw material exporter state to an oil/gas industrial producer. The port was designed to import raw materials for local industries and export industrial products such as petrochemicals, refined petroleum products, chemical fertilizers etc. The port can accommodate ships which can transport solid and liquid materials in the range of 6000-110,000 tons; petrochemicals in the range of 2000-80,000 tons; chemical tankers for refined petroleum products in the range of 12,000-360,000 tons and LPG carriers in the range of 1000-80,000 tons. The bulk cargo terminals are operated by Saudi Aramco company, Sabtank and Satorp.

14.1 Industrial Incentives

The Saudi government provides investment benefits and incentives for companies which establish their divisions in Jubail Industrial City. The Saudi Industrial Development Fund gives medium to long term interest free loans to new industrial establishments. The fund also provides funding for established companies for expansion purposes. Industries have access to fuel sources and feedstock at competitive prices. The investment benefits also consist of availability of necessary infrastructure, long term lease agreement and social infrastructure.

14.2 Green Initiatives

There were efforts for a mega recycling initiative across all 50 contract sites for this project. There were initiatives to reduce waste by 8000 tons. Saudi government has implemented a comprehensive initiative for Jubail to monitor its air and water quality, manage solid and industrial waste. In every five minutes, nine stations measure the air up to 30 components which include carbon monoxide and ammonia. About 13 stations with electronic probes measures factors such as salinity, dissolved oxygen, temperature and acidity. Jubail's wastewater is recycled and reused for landscaping purposes which has led to Sabkhat al-Fasl emerging as a popular bird watching destination that draws over 20,000 birds during peak migration period.

14.3 Challenges and Risks

The challenges for the project are huge. Jubail Industrial city covers 1016 square kilometers. The construction of the city involved levelling of entire dunes and relocation of more than 35 million cubic meters (1.2 billion cubic feet) of sand which was environmentally a challenging task. The economic downturn may affect the development work associated with the project.

14.4 Status Quo

The Southern part of Jubail II is 75 percent complete while the work on the north sector have started. The government has announced plans for Ras al Zawr Minerals Industrial city in the northern region to make contribution toward the mineral and metals sector.

14.5 Economic Impact

The establishment of the industrial city laid the foundation for economic diversification and facilitated the country to enter the international markets with industrial products. Jubail City have attracted investments in primary and secondary industries and saw joint venture companies from different regions of the world establishing their firms. Jubail had been named as the Middle East city with best economic potential by leading business publications such as Financial Times, Foreign Direct Investment Magazine etc. Jubail II project is expected to attract investments worth SR224 billion. The infrastructure investment will be nearly SR14.25 billion ($3.8 billion). The project will double the size of the existing industrial zone. Employment generation in terms of 55,000 new jobs is expected from the project. The workforce involved during the peak period of the project was 50,000. Jubail City had attracted foreign investment worth $46 billion which accounted for 50 percent of the total investment received by the country. Jubail City is the largest convertor of natural gas to value added petrochemicals in the world with a share of seven percent of the global market. Jubail City houses 17 major primary industries and facilitates the operation of 150 secondary, support and light manufacturing industries.

Further Reading

1. Juan Rodrigues , Jubail II Industrial Area is World's Largest Civil Engineering Project, https://www.thebalancesmb.com/worlds-largest-civil-engineering-projects-844606
2. https://www.bechtel.com/projects/jubail-industrial-city/
3. Swanson, S. A. (2010). The Royal Commission & Bechtel Corp., Jubail Industrial City, Saudi Arabia. *PM Network, 24*(2), 38–41.
4. Bernie Roseke, Jubail 2 is the World's largest Industrial Project,https://www.projectengineer.net/jubail-2-is-the-worlds-largest-industrial-project/
5. https://www.meed.com/jubail-industrial-city-3/
6. https://www.aapa-ports.org/unifying/landing.aspx?ItemNumber=21049&navItemNumber=20767#
7. https://www.arabnews.com/node/1455641/saudi-arabia
8. https://www.thebalancesmb.com/worlds-largest-civil-engineering-projects-844606

9. https://mawani.gov.sa/en-us/SAPorts/Jbeil/Pages/default.aspx
10. https://www.arabnews.com/saudi-arabia/news/664951
11. https://www.arabnews.com/node/291908
12. https://www.constructionweekonline.com/article-25566-site-visit-jubail-industrial-city

Case 11: Hong Kong Zhuhai Macao Bridge (HZMB)

The Hong Kong Zhuhai Macao Bridge (HZMB) consists of the 12 km Hong Kong Link road, 29.6 km main bridge and 13.4 km Zhuhai Link road. The total length of the bridge is 55 km. HZMB is the longest bridge cum tunnel sea crossing in the world. Operating 24 hours a day, this bridge connects major cities in the Pearl River Delta within a three-hour commute from Hong Kong. It will take only 40 minutes to commute the distance of approximately 42 km from Hong Kong port to Zhuhai Port and Macao Port.

This bridge tunnel system consists of a series of three cable stayed bridges, an undersea tunnel and four artificial islands. It is the longest open sea fixed link in the world. The bridge passes through the Lingding and Jiuzhou channels and connects the cities of Hong Kong, Macua and Zhuhai located on the Pearl River Delta. The design of the bridge was such that life span was estimated to be 120 years though biggest sea bridges are designed to last 100 years. The construction work on the project started on December 2009. The bridge was opened to public on 24th October 2018.

The main bridge is basically a dual three lane carriageway which is approximately of 30 kilometers length comprising a sea viaduct section of approximately 23 km and a tunnel section of approximately 7 kilometers. The viaduct section is comprised of three cable stayed bridges named Qingzhou Channel Bridge, Jianghai Channel Bridge and Jiuzhou Channel Bridge. Qingzhou channel bridge is the longest among them with a length of 458-meter long. The highest part of the Qingzhou channel bridge was designed in the shape of an auspicious Chinese knot. The weight of steel tower of the Jianghai Channel bridge was approximately 3100 tonnes.

HKZMB project is undeniably an extraordinary feat of engineering. It is built to withstand a magnitude eight earthquake, a super typhoon and strikes by super-sized cargo vessels. The bridge underwent a natural test when it withstood the super typhoon Mangkhut in the year 2018. The steel used in the project was 4.5 times the amount used in San Francisco's Golden. The most technical challenge for the project was the construction of a four-mile-long submerged tunnel.

To minimize the impact of disturbance to marine life and environmental sustainability, initiatives such as precast and prefabrication techniques were adopted during the construction process of the work. For example, pile caps, steel bridge decks and steel towers were manufactured off site and transported to the construction site for erection. The construction of the steel tower involved the integral erection method which was used to overcome challenges during construction in terms of water current, wind speed and operation of navigation channel. The amount of steel used for the steel bridge was equivalent to the total weight of sixty Eiffel Towers. Approximately 420,000 tonnes of steel was used in the project. The total bridge deck area covered 700,000 square meters which was equivalent to 98 football pitches. The total weight of the bituminous materials used in road surfacing work was approximately 100,000 tonnes.

The tunnel is made of 33 elements which are huge hollow blocks measuring 590 feet long, 125 feet wide and 37 feet high. Each element weighs 80,000 tons which is equal to the weight of an aircraft carrier. The tunnel runs between two artificial islands each measuring one million square feet.

According to the Hong Kong Zhuhai Macao Bridge Authority statistics over 4000 vessels consisting of passenger ferries to container ships cruise its waters every day. In the first three years of operation, 250 taxi licenses would be issued for travel over the bridge. Of these, 150 will be in service between Zhuhai and Hong Kong. Special bridge traffic licenses are also being issued to private cars in quota systems in the three regions. The speed limit has been set at 62 miles (100 kilometers) an hour.

The construction process faced huge challenges and risks. Technical risks were involved in the project as the immersed tube tunnel is placed in open sea at a depth of 45 meter and had to overcome unstable wind speed and water current conditions during the placement of tunnel segments. The tunnel segments were precast at the precasting yard on Gushan Island and transported by tug boats to the construction site. The largest lifting barge in the world was used to install the final connection which weighed around 6000 tonnes. Workers performed welding and grouting works inside the tunnel segments.

15.1 Hong Kong Link Road (HKLR)

HKLR is the link road which connects the Main bridge and the Hong Kong Port. The link road is a dual 3 lane carriageway which consists of land and marine viaducts of 9.4 km; a tunnel of 1 km and road section of 1.6 km. The construction work involved adoption of various construction plant and methods to erect the precast deck segments. For the Scenic Hill Tunnel, the construction methods of Drill & Blast, Mining, Box Jacking and Cut & Cover method were involved for the project. The most difficult and complex among the tunnel works was the box jacking operation undertaken beneath the Airport Express Line (AEL). The ground strengthening work took one year for completion to minimize the impact on the AEL.

The main challenge of the HKLR was the construction of the viaduct along the ecologically sensitive Sha Lo Wan headland. A mega straddle carrier was used to construct long span viaduct 180-meter long.

15.2 Hong Kong Port

Hong Kong Port was built on reclaimed land of 130 hectares at the waters off the north east of the Hong Kong International Airport. The airport infrastructure consists of a passenger clearance building, vehicle clearance plazas and public transport interchanges. The passenger clearance building is close to the busiest airport of Hong Kong. Due to the closeness to the airport, challenges were encountered for the design and construction of the passenger clearance building. The airport height restrictions imposed severe constraints on the design of the passenger clearance building. The roof is formed by 45 large scale prefabricated modules. The District Cooling System at Hong Kong port have an estimated annual savings in electricity consumption of 3.5 million kilowatt hour with a corresponding reduction of 2500 tonnes of carbon dioxide per annum. The HZMBus shuttle service runs 24 hours a day with bus departure frequency of every five minutes.

The Hong Kong Zhuhai bridge took nine years of construction for completion.

15.3 Financing of the Project

The total cost of the main bridge was $7.56 billion. Funding in terms of bank loans amounted to $4.32 billion. The remaining funding of $3.24 billion were sourced from the government of mainland China, Hong Kong and Macau. Hong Kong's funding amount exceeded $9 billion as Hong Kong spend an additional $4.57 billion on its Boundary Crossing Facilities and $3.19 billion on a link road from the main bridge to the boundary crossing (Table 15.1).

The Bank of China was the lead bank of the consortium which provided the loan for the main body of the Hong Kong Zhuhai Macao Bridge. Bank of China provided $3.23 billion for the main bridge construction. Hong Kong and Macao banks were part of the financial consortium.

Table 15.1 Sources of Financing

S No	Sources	Amount
1	Bank Loans	$4.32 billion
2	Zhuhai (China)	$1.43 billion
3	Hong Kong	$1.38 billion
4	Macau	$0.43 billion
	Total	$7.56 billion

Source: HKZM Bridge Authority/HKTDC

15.4 Economic Impact of the Project

The bridge initiative was a part of the Chinese government's plan to drive the economic and social integration of the Greater Bay area. The Greater Bay Area is home to 68 million people and covers 21,800 square miles in central southern China and includes 11 cities that consist of Hong Kong, Macau and nine cities across Guangdong province. The area covers less than one percent of the land area of China and accounts for less than 5 per cent of the population and contributes 12 per cent towards China's GDP.

The bridge linked the three economic heavy weights which had different social systems and economic structures. The bridge connected the economic belt of the Guangdong Hong Kong, Macao Greater Bay area. The bridge became an economic circle which united Hong Kong's financial services, Guangdong's industrial manufacturing and Macao's entertainment industry. The HZMB project was envisaged as a part of China's strategy for the creation of an economic hub for the development of the Pearl River Delta area known as Greater Bay area. In the year 2015, Zhuhai's Henggin was designated as a free trade zone area.

Before the construction of the bridge, transportation from Hong Kong to Zhuhai was possible only after detouring via several cities including Shenzhen and Dongguan. The bridge construction was a part of Chinese policy of One Country, Two systems. The commissioning of the HKZM bridge was expected to bring development to Hong Kong's largest outlying island Lantau which was often known as the double gateway of the landing point of both the bridge and Hong Kong's international airport. The bridge slashed journey times between the three cities from three hours to 30 minutes thereby connecting them within an hour's commute of each other. There is lot of disparity in economic distribution between Pearl River Delta's east and west coast. The eastern side cities such as Hong Kong, Shenzhen and Dongguan are more economically developed compared to cities in the western side such as Zhuhai, Jiangmen and Zhingshan. The bridge would facilitate the transportation of goods produced by manufacturing units on the west side to be exported from air and sea ports located on the east side. It has to be noted that Hong Kong's international airport is the busiest cargo airport in the world. The construction of the bridge is also expected to give a boost to the tourism industry. With the opening of the bridge, tourists from China and other parts of the world could travel from Hong Kong's airport to Macau and the mainland in about 45 minutes. Macau is the largest gambling city in the world. Zhuhai is referred to as China's Florida due to its balmy climate and lush vegetation. The offshore island of Henggi is witnessing construction of holiday resorts, theme parks and golf courses for promotion of tourism. There is much potential for the region to emerge as the most attractive tourism hub of China.

15.5 Risks Inherent in the Project

There were concerns raised with respect to restrictive criteria and administrative paperwork related to the usage of bridge by the people. The drifting of parts of the reclaimed artificial island which houses the Hong Kong Boundary Crossing Facilities (HKBCF) caused a delay in the completion of the HZMB project. The challenges faced by mainland contractors was with respect to construction of immersed tubes for the project. On account of increased labor costs, material costs and changed designs, the HZMB project had a cost overrun of ¥10 billion by the year 2017. Enviornmental concerns were also raised as the seawall constructed to protect the artificial island appeared to be dislodged based on the footage taken by drones. Environmental conservationists at WWF Hong Kong have attributed the construction of bridge for the dwindling number of white dolphins in the area near the bridge. It is estimated that dolphins found near waters of Lantau were the worst hit with numbers dropping by 60 percent during the period 2015–2016. There were also criticism from different quarters that the construction of the bridge was a political act in the wake of the 2014 pro-democracy protests which rocked Hong Kong and the bridge was a means by Beijing to tighten its grip on the city. The project's work safety record had been criticized. Seven workers had died and 275 had been injured while working on Hong Kong's link road and boundary crossing facility.

Further Reading

1. https://www.hzmb.gov.hk/en/
2. https://www.hzmb.gov.hk/en/project/main-bridge.html
3. https://www.arup.com/projects/hong-kong-zhuhai-macau-bridge
4. Xinhua Headlines: World's longest cross-sea bridge opens, integrating China's Greater Bay Area http://www.xinhuanet.com/english/2018-10/23/c_137553194_2.htm
5. Sarah Lazarus, CNN, The $20 billion 'umbilical cord': China unveils the world's longest crossing -crossing bridgehttps://edition.cnn.com/2018/05/04/asia/hong-kong-zhuhai-macau-bridge/index.html
6. http://news.xinhuanet.com/english/2009-04/14/content_11186292.htm
7. Jonathan Cheng, China Builds Bridge to Link Southern Cities, https://www.wsj.com/articles/SB126088119555891949?mod=googlenews_wsj

Case 12: Gotthard Base Tunnel (GBT) 16

Gotthard Base Tunnel (GBT) is the world's longest and deepest rail tunnel in Switzerland. It was officially opened in the year 2016 after almost two decades of construction work. This gigantic project work was aimed to revolutionize the European freight transport system. The 57 km (35 mile) twin bore Gotthard base tunnel provides a high speed rail link under the Swiss Alps between northern and southern Europe. The tunnel is designed as the first flat low level route through the Alps. The new rail link is a major milestone in the history of Switzerland and Europe. The vision for a new rail line through the Alps originated during the 1950s. The construction work began in the year 1999. The Gotthard tunnel emerged as the longest tunnel in the world surpassing Japan's 53.9 km Seikan rail tunnel and the 50.5 km Channel tunnel which links the UK and France. The two single track Gottthard Base Tunnel links the Erstfeld in the Uri canton and Bodio in the southern canton of Tessin. The design of Gotthard Base Tunnel took 25 years and the project took 17 years for construction.

The mega project was endorsed by 64 percent of Swiss voters in a referendum in 1992. In the same year, the New Rail Link through the Alps (NRLA) programme was approved for building two base tunnels. In 1994 the public also supported a proposal from environmental groups to move the transportation of all freight travelling through Switzerland from road to rail. To mitigate adverse environmental effects, the Swiss constitution incorporated Protection of the Alps in 1994. The test operations for Gotthard Base Tunnel began in October 2015. The tunnel was officially opened in June 2016. Commercial train services began in December 2016.

This longest tunnel in the world is also the deepest traffic tunnel with up to 2300 meters of rock above it. It is also the first flat low level route through the Alps with a maximum height of 550 meters (1804 feet) above sea level. The tunnel covers up to 2.3 km below the surface of the mountains above and through rock. The construction was an engineering marvel as 73 different types of rocks were subjected to blasts. These rocks included hard rocks like granite as well soft as sugars. Over 28 metric tonnes of rock was excavated from the site and then broken down to make the concrete for building the tunnel. Approximately 30 million tonnes of granite were used before laying almost 250 miles of steel rails and thousands of miles of cables for power, signaling and communication systems. Temperatures can reach 104F (40 degrees Celsius) inside the tunnel and huge fans blow cooling air through the tunnels to maintain the atmosphere.

The course of the tunnel is flat and straight unlike winding up through the mountains like the old rail and road tunnel which was in operation since the year 1980. By avoiding the curves and spiral of the classic route, the Gotthard Base tunnel shortened travel by 40 Km.

The base tunnel consists of two bores with two track crossovers and multiple interconnections for foot access between the bores. The base tunnel is approximately 600 meter lower than the old line summit. Intermediate shafts were sunk to allow for simultaneous tunneling on several fronts. Tunnel boring machines were used for the creation of the tunnel along with some drilling and blasting works. The final part involving 7.7 km from Erstfeld was started in year 2007 and the work at Amsteg was completed in year 2009. The two ends of the tunnel was connected after 14 years and involved approximately 2500 workers for construction. The planning of the project allowed for advances in freight vehicles to allow for speeds up to 160 km/hr. through the tunnel.

The Ceneri Base Tunnel (CBT) is the final section of the high speed rail link. CBT creates an uninterrupted rail route from the Dutch North Sea port of Rotterdam to the Italian city of Genoa on the Mediterranean. Two multi-function stations at Sedrun and Faido facilitated trains to cross between two tunnels in the event of maintenance or emergencies. The planning of the project involved division of the two main tunnels and 180 cross passages into five construction phases. Gotthard base tunnel project comprises of 152 kilometers of tunnels and shafts.

The tunnel created a mainline rail connection between Rotterdam in the Netherlands and Genoa in Italy. The journey time for travelers between Zurich and Milan were reduced by an hour.

The developers of the project were Alp Transit Gotthard AG which was a 100 per cent Swiss Federal Railways (SBB) subsidiary. Alp Transit Gotthard AG was established during May 1998. Construction was split into five sections each with a designated consortium. Other companies involved in the project included Transurb, Erico and Klimat Fer. Transurb provides rail and urban mobility solutions and rail simulation dedicated to training. ERICO is a leading designer manufacturer and marketer of precision engineered specialty metal products in rail applications. Klimat Fer provides HVAC air conditioning systems. A consortium of ABB and TLT Turbo received $45 million contract to provide a ventilation system for the Gotthard base tunnel. Siemens obtained the contract for providing the tunnel control and fire protection systems for the railway tunnel. Norma supplied pipe couplings to connect the rainwater pipes in the tunnel. Nokia was the partner responsible for furnishing telecommunications and tunnel control technology. High speed trains can travel at a speed of 200 to 250 kilometers per hour through the Gotthard base tunnel.

16.1 Cost and Financing of the Project

The estimated final cost of the project was SFr 9.4 billion ($9 billion) for the Gotthard and SFr2.24 billion for the related 15.4 km (9.6 miles) Ceneri tunnel project. The final cost exceeded the original estimates. The Swiss parliament had made provisions for uncertainties related to the project. The project costs amounted to over $12 billion (£8.3billion). The financing of the project is done by means of value added taxes, fuel taxes, road charges on heavy vehicles. Other sources include state loans which are to be repaid in a decade time. Funding sources included a new road tax. In 2009, the Swiss parliament increased the credit facility for the new rail link to CHF 19.1 billion. The funding for the financing of public transport infrastructure was approximately 30 billion CHF. Out of this amount, 13.8 billion CHF was allocated to finance lost funding with respect to the construction of the NRLA. About 75% of the funding was from the public transport fund, the remaining 25 per cent of the investment are financed through private capital market. This investment will be paid back by the operator of the project. The project financing structure ensured a secure financing for the project. The project didn't face any delays on account of lack of financial resources. Cost escalation were the result of upgradation of the project to incorporate new safety measures and state of the art technologies, extra costs related to geotechnical impact and cost increases due to contract awards and construction. The evolution of the final costs and its financial impact were monitored by ATG on a quarterly basis and reported to control authority every six months. The increase in credit amounted to 9.9 billion CHF from 6.3 billion CHF of which half of the extra costs came from variations resulting from orders issued by the Swiss Office of Transport.

16.2 Economic Impact

The New Rail Link through the Alps (NRLA) contributed a new dimension in mobility for Switzerland. It strengthened Switzerland's connectivity in Europe by linking the northern and southern parts of the continent with tunnels through the Lotschberg, Gotthard and Ceneri mountains. Goods carried on the route by a million lorries a year was replaced by the train system. Approximately 260 freight trains and 65 passenger trains pass through the tunnel every day. The economic benefits include hurdle free movement of goods and enhanced contribution towards tourism sector. The project was a part of Switzerland's strategic plan to transfer maximum freight from road to rail to address environmental concerns. Approximately 80 percent of freight transport between Italy and other nations in EU is through the Alps. Before the operation of the Gotthard base tunnel, approximately two third of the freight traffic was through road all along the Brenner (Austria), Fréjus and Mont Cenis (France) and Gotthard (Switzerland) transport corridors. Neighboring countries were committed to provide high speed rail corridors to serve as connections to the Gotthard tunnel.

It is observed that the road traffic through the Alps currently doubles every eight years. Heavy traffic congestion is observed throughout the year. The newly constructed two NEAT axes at the Gotthard and Lotschberg mountains will facilitate the doubling of freight capacity from its current 20 million to around 50 million tonnes per year. On account of the flat rail concept, bigger trains of larger capacity and weight of 4000 tonnes instead of the current 2000 tonnes can be operated on the new line. The freight trains can travel at speeds of up to 160 km/h on the new line which is twice the speed of trains operated earlier. The new rail link has the capacity to operate 260 freight trains through the Gotthard mountain range every day. Freight companies will be benefitted as the firms will gain more capacity, lower costs and shorter journey on this key trans-European axis. GBT is a part of wider project known as New Trans Alpine Railways to provide flatter higher capacity rail links between Northern Europe and Italy. Through the tunnel project, Swiss government made a huge investment for smoothing the flow of freight between Europe's major economies while ensuring that rail system remains as a competitive option for moving goods. The rail route provides an alternate to air travel.

16.3   Structuring of the Project

The Swiss parliament had passed a project related legal framework which formed the basis for the construction of the corridor of the NRLA. The Swiss Federation was the sponsor of the project and entrusted with the task of financing and supervision of the NRLA. The developers of the project were Alp Transit Gotthard AG (ATG) which was a 100 per cent Swiss Federal Railways (SBB) subsidiary. The SBB-CFF-FFS was the sole shareholder of the ATG and the future operator of the new railway link. The consultants, contractors and suppliers were contracted with ATG.

16.4   Risk Management of the Project

The designer acted as a direct agent of the client. The design and the general and local construction supervision were run by the client, ATG, and its consultants. Contractors were generally only commissioned to carry out the construction works defined by the client's designers. The civil engineering activities and services related to the provision and commissioning of mechanical, electrical and plumbing works were contracted according to classic model applied in Switzerland for underground works. Adjustment of deadlines are made on account of geological risks and production risks attributed to contractor actions. The conflict management process is designed to act through progressive levels starting from the lowest level of construction site and reaching up to the level of the advisory arbitration. The management of geology related risks by the client and its consultants along with the unit prices remuneration mechanisms contributed to the success of the construction of the Gotthard Base Tunnel. Table 16.1 lists the biggest tunnels in the world. Table 16.2 highlights the salient features of the tunnel project. Table 16.3 gives the major timelines of the project.

16.4 Risk Management of the Project

Table 16.1 Biggest tunnels in world

Serial No	Tunnel	Country	Year completed	Length
1	Gotthard Base Tunnel,	Switzerland	2016	57.5 km
2	Seikan Tunnel	Japan	1988	53.9 km
3	Euro Tunnel	France-UK	1994	50.5 km
4	Yulhyeon Tunnel	South Korea	2015	50.3 km
5	Lotschberg Base Tunnel	Switzerland	2007	34.6 km
6	New Guanjiao Tunnel	China	2014	32.6 km
7	Guadarrama Tunnel	Spain	2007	28.4 km

Source: Collated from different sources

Table 16.2 Salient features of the Gotthard base tunnel project

Dimensions	Features
Construction Period	17 years
Length	57.1 km
Cost	$12.5 billion
Employment	2600
Length of drilling machine used	410 meter
Amount of concrete used	4,000,000 cubic meters. Equivalent to 84 Empire State Building
Maximum Freight amount	377,000 tonnes per day. Equivalent to 15,080 shipping containers.
Copper cable	3200 km

Source: Swiss government, Alp transit & BBC

Table 16.3 Milestones

Year	Event
1872	Construction of the first rail tunnel through the Gotthard is initiated. Swiss engineer Louis Favre is in charge.
1882	The longest railway tunnel in the world with length of 15 Kilometers starts operation.
1969	Construction of the first road tunnel through the Gotthard begins.
1980	The first road tunnel is opened to traffic. The tunnel connects Göschenen with Airolo.
1996	The first preparatory and exploratory work for the Gotthard Base Tunnel begins in Sedrun.
1998	The Swiss government approves financing for the New Alpine Transversal (NEAT).
1999	Excavating activities begin in Sedrun with the first blasting works.
2003	Tunnelling work with the four Herrenknecht Gripper TBMs begins.
2006	Ceneri Base Tunnel work is initiated.
2009	Mechanized tunneling is successfully completed in the north.
2010	Main breakthrough Tunnel in the Eastern tunnel between Sedrun and Faido completed.
2011	Main breakthrough in the Western tunnel between Sedrun and Faido completed
2016	The Gotthard Base Tunnel work completed
2020	Opening of Ceneri Base Tunnel

Further Reading

1. htttps://www.alptransit-portal.ch/en/overview
2. Gotthard tunnel: World's longest and deepest rail tunnel opens in Switzerland, June 2016 https://www.bbc.com/news/world-europe-36423250
3. https://www.railway-technology.com/projects/gotthard-base-tunnel/
4. https://www.herrenknecht.com/en/references/referencesdetail/gotthard-base-tunnel/
5. https://www.dw.com/en/the-worlds-longest-rail-tunnel-the-gotthard-base-tunnel/a-19293039
6. https://www.commscope.com/resources/case-studies/the-gotthard-base-tunnel/
7. https://edition.cnn.com/travel/article/trans-alpine-rail-tunnels/index.html
8. Davide Fabbri. Engineering Achievements Risk, Contract Management, and Financing of the Gotthard Base Tunnel in Switzerland, Engineering 5(2019),379–383.

Case 13: Channel Tunnel UK

Channel tunnel is also known as the Eurotunnel. The 50 km long channel tunnel link Folkestone Kent in England with Coquelles Pas de Calais in northern France. The tunnel extends beneath the English Channel at the Strait of Dover. The tunnel is the only fixed link which connect the island of Britain with the European mainland. The tunnel connects the city of London by train to Paris, Lille, Brussels, Amsterdam and Cologne through Eurostar and Thalys train lines.

The initial plans to establish a fixed link between Great Britain and the rest of the continent was formulated during the mid-seventeenth century. After the initial plan, over twenty-five reports were prepared for the tunnel project but were abandoned due to financial or military reasons. In mid 1970s, a project which was about 90 percent state funded was also abandoned due to economic recession. During September 1981, an Anglo French project group was set up to assess the various suggested links for the tunnels and bridges. The franchise was signed in Paris in 1987 between the French and British government for constructing the tunnel which was known as Anglo French Treaty. In 1990, the service tunnel was completed, followed by the main tunnel in 1992.

The Channel tunnel is composed of three tunnels: two for rail traffic and a central tunnel for services and security. Passengers can travel either by ordinary rail coach or by their own motor vehicles which are loaded on special railcars. The train speed at tunnel can be at a maximum of 160 km per hour. The journey takes around 35 minutes. It took more than five years to complete the project with over 13,000 workers involved in the project. The tunnel has been named as one of the seven wonders of the world.

The idea of a Eurotunnel under the English Channel originated long back. In the year 1986, the idea was revived. The project was financed by a consortium of British and French corporations along with banks. The operating company of the tunnel is called Eurotunnel. The work on the project started on both sides of the Strait of Dover during the period 1987–88. The work was completed in year 1991. The tunnel was officially dedicated for traffic on May 6 1994. The tunnel crosses under the channel between Coquelles near the French port of Calais and Folkestone in the English county of Kent.

It is the only fixed link between the island of Great Britain and the European mainland. The channel tunnel is a symbol of major civil engineering feat involving complex transportation system. It is the longest undersea tunnel in the world with length of 37.9 kilometers. The tunnel is 75-meter-deep below the sea bed and 115 meter below the sea level at its lowest point. The speed limit for trains operating through the tunnel is 160 km/hr.

The Eurotunnel consortium, consisting of the Channel Tunnel Group (CTG) and France-Manche (FM), was awarded the project in January 1986. Eurotunnel was selected partly on account of the fact that it offered the highest level of safety through a three-tunnel design which included two tunnels for train transit, and a tunnel in the middle for maintenance and safety evacuation.

The tunnel is managed and operated by Getlink which was formerly known as Groupe Eurotunnel. The European public company based in Paris operates the Eurotunnel shuttle vehicle services. High speed Eurostar passenger trains, the Eurotunnel Shuttle for road vehicles and international freight trains operate through the tunnel. High speed railway lines of the LGV Nord in France and High Speed 1 of England are connected end to end through the tunnel. 4G mobile services are available in the tunnel.

Four types of trains basically use the tunnel. Le Shuttle services of Eurotunnel is used for cars, coaches and caravans. LeShuttle for trucks. Eurostar, the passenger service is operated by the British, French and Belgian railways. Rail freight services are operated by the British, French and Belgian railways. Each shuttle travels at 140 km/hr. The normal crossing time is 35 minutes and the service operates 24 hours a day throughout the year.

Approximately 2.5 million Eurostar passengers travelled through the channel tunnel in year 2020 which represented a decline of 77 percent in traffic over the whole year. About 1736 rail freight trains operated through the tunnel in 2020. Around 208 million Eurostar passengers have travelled through the tunnel since the year 1994.

About 4.9 million cubic meters of chalk marl and shale were excavated during construction and used for creation of a 30-hectare nature reserve in the foot hills of white cliff of Dover in Kent. The travel figures suggest that the equivalent of six times the population of UK have crossed through the tunnel since its completion in the year 1994.

17.1 Cost and Financing

The project was considered the most expensive construction project ever proposed in UK. The procuring authority was Government of United Kingdom and Government of Republic of France. The project was basically funded with hundred percent project finance with no governmental subsidies. The original cost estimated was about GBP 4.8 billion in the year 1985. By the completion time, the cost for the project reached GBP 9.5 billion. The project was financed entirely by private sector capital. Five banks formed the TransManche Link consortium to provide the financing. Shareholders also made investment in the project. The bank consortium consisted of two UK banks (Midland and Natwest) and three French banks (Credit Lyonnais, Banque Nationale de Paris and Banque Indosuez). In 1986, a private placement of shares for institutions (Equity 2) was launched in year 1986. As a result, the shareholdings of 15 original promoters were reduced to minority shareholdings. The European Investment bank participated as a co financier in the project. The project witnessed a large syndication of banks in which the group of 50 banks who underwrote the deal syndicated it successfully to over 200 banks. Syndication of additional £1.8 billion credit facility was facilitated by four agent banks namely Midland, Natwest, Credit Lyonnais and Banque Nationale de Paris. European Investment Bank (EIB) also offered £300 million parallel line of funding. The debt was structured in 12 tranches to facilitate different currencies and different types of loans. Advances and letters of credit amounted to £6.8 billion under junior credit facilities. Parallel loans by EIB and ECSC amounted to £300 million and £200 million respectively. Advances in terms of senior credit facilities amounted to £647 million. The co-financing facilities of £1 billion offered by EIB and FFr 2 billion offered by Credit National were secured by letters of credit under the junior credit facilities.

17.2 Structuring

The channel tunnel project was designed as a concessional public private partnership. The project was structured as Design, build, finance, maintain, operate and transfer (DBFMOT) model. Eurotunnel is acting as the Anglo French holding company of the Channel Tunnel Group Ltd. and France Manche SA is the client and operating authority of the Channel Tunnel. Its monopoly on the franchise for the fixed link expires in year 2042. The Anglo French Treaty and Concession agreement set the framework within which Eurotunnel operates. The treaty established the setting up of a binational Intergovernmental Commission (IGC) and safety authority to monitor Eurotunnel's compliance with the concession agreement. The concession agreement for Channel Tunnel establishes the role and rights of the two governments and operator IGC. The concessionaires of the Channel Tunnel have the right and obligation to develop, finance construct and operate the channel tunnel for a period of 66 years. In the year 1997, it was extended to 99 years until 2086. The nature of structuring is without recourse to government funds or government guarantees of financial or commercial nature. The concessionaires are free to determine their tariffs and commercial policy and type of services to be offered. Another feature of the agreement is that laws relating to control of prices and tariffs will not apply to the prices and tariffs of the fixed link. According to the Railways Usage contract, Eurotunnel is expected to make half tunnel capacity available to the British, French and Belgian railways for operating Eurostar and freight trains. In return the railways require to pay a fixed charge along with tolls which is based on the volume of traffic passing through the tunnel. Railways are also required to make a contribution towards Eurotunnel's operating costs. A minimum charge level system was introduced to ensure a guaranteed level of cash flow to Eurotunnel over the first 12 years of operation. The Railway usage contract, the Treaty of Canterbury and the concession agreement were the major security arrangement designed for the project. The design and build contract was awarded by Eurotunnel to binational organization—TransManche Link (TML). The organization was composed of a consortium of five banks and 10 construction companies. The construction group was composed of five French companies (TRANSMANCHE) and five UK companies (TRANSLINK). Thus the project had 15 founding shareholders which were evenly divided between English and French. Maitre d'Oeuvre (Mdo) is an independent consulting firm which advises IGC, the banks and Eurotunnel on construction safety.

The passenger trains are run by Eurostar, which is owned by public companies namely SNCF with 55 percent share ownership; London and Continental Railways (LCR) with 40 percent and SNCB with 5 per cent ownership. LCR shares were transferred to UK government in year 2014. Again the government shares were sold to a consortium in the year 2015.

17.3 Risks Mitigation

The attempts by migrants to illegally enter United Kingdom reached crisis proportion during the period 2015. Nine people lost lives on account of the attempt. Controversies erupted on account of issues of human right violations, illegal immigration and diplomatic disagreements. The UK and France stepped up security measures to prevent illegal immigrants from attempting to crossover. During construction phase the tunnel had mechanical issues. The weather conditions had also temporarily disrupted its operations. Cost escalation of over 80 per cent was incurred for the project by the time of its completion. Cost escalation was attributed to construction cost problems, delays in equipment delivery and testing problems. Problems had also risen due to changes in design of the project during construction undertaken to enhance the safety of the project.

The Euro tunnel project had structured its debt obligations, revenue receipts and payments in currencies of both Euro and pound sterling to mitigate currency fluctuations. Revenue contributions from passenger traffic are skewed more towards pound sterling while freight traffic revenues are accounted more in euros. Customer credit risk is managed on the basis of UK and Eurozone credit policy.

The IGC composed of even French and UK government representatives oversee the channel tunnel's operations and implement regulatory aspects on the basis of relevant EU legislation even after the Brexit.

17.4 Impact of the Project

The project was aimed at providing an alternate travel option which was faster than ferry and affordable than air travel. The project had immense economic and political implications particularly with reference to trade and tourism. The project was expected to strengthen ties between UK, France and rest of the European union.

Improved communication and regional employment generation were the significant contributory factors on account of the project. About 26 per cent of goods traded between UK and continental Europe go through the channel tunnel which represent a value of € 138 billion per year. The trade value of goods transported through the tunnel was estimated to be 26 per cent of the total EU and UK trade by year 2016. The trade connectivity have provided the opportunity to offer products at a cheaper cost. One million e commerce delivery parcels travel through the tunnel each day. Over 380 million tonnes of freight have been transported on board truck shuttles and on rail freight trains via the tunnel since its opening in year 1994. Approximately 80 million vehicles have boarded the shuttle ever since it was opened. Eurotunnel project have facilitated transport infrastructure improvement of road and rail network system in UK and France. It was one of the best infrastructural projects with less impact on environmental ecosystem as the tunnel was constructed about 40 meter under the seabed thereby reducing the risk of air pollution.

17.5 Problems Faced by the Project

On account of imprecise specification of tunnel boring machines, the tunneling work was initially delayed. The contractor also faced challenges with respect to logistical support for boring machines and cost controls. Problems also cropped up with respect to changes in terminal and fixed equipment work. Additional expenses due to underestimation of rolling stock also led to cost escalation.

The estimate revenue calculations from the project were far away from the reality. Stiff competition from existing ferry operations affected the revenue and market share of Eurotunnel. In its first year of operation in 1994–1995, the company reported a loss of USD 1.4 billion on account of lower revenues from passenger and freight and huge interest burden on its debt amount of $12.2 billion.

The company had to renegotiate the terms of the debt with its creditors. The problems for the project was manifold. The project couldn't attract business on account of high access charges. The interest payment burden on the debt of £6 billion was very high. Low volume of passenger and rail traffic than estimated added to the problem. Eurotunnel proposed a refinancing scheme based on debt for equity restructuring with a French legal protection in terms of safeguard procedures. The process involved stoppage of the repayment of debt process for six months and allowed the use of the operating revenue to finance the restructuring effort. The reorganization plan enabled the company to reduce its debt from £ 6 billion to £ 2.8 billion. Eurotunnel project obtained a net profit of US $ 1.4 million for the first time in the year 2007 when the refinancing plan was completed. Under the terms of the

Table 17.1 Milestones of the project

Year	Events
1802	First design of cross channel revealed
1834	First rail tunnel proposed for steam trains
1880	Attempts were made for tunnel excavation
1960	The Channel Tunnel Study Group makes a proposal of railway tunnel, bored or submerged, comprising a twin rail tunnel with a service tunnel
1973	Franco-British Channel Tunnel Treaty giving mandate to the Channel Tunnel Group to lead the study and preparatory construction work
1975	Cancellation of the works by UK Government for financial reasons and oil crisis.
1981	Resumption of the work, and the governments setting up a joint working group to study technical and economic aspects of a fixed link
1985	Start of a call for proposals, and selection of Eurotunnel as the winning proposal for the project
1986	Treaty of Canterbury between the UK and French Governments, and the Concession Agreement authorizing Eurotunnel as the contractor for the project.
1987	Boring of service tunnel initiated
1994	Official opening of the project
1997	A nature reserve created from the debris involved in construction. Eurostar lines extended to Brussels.
2006	100 millionth customer on Eurotunnel passenger shuttle
2009	50 million crossed the channel through the Eurotunnel shuttles
2014	Eurotunnel celebrate 20th anniversary of operation
2015	New orders to facilitate travel by two million trucks by the year 2020. Eurostar lines extended to Avignon, Lyon and Marseille
2018	Approximately 80 million vehicles have passed through the tunnel since the operations began. 8 Eurostar lines extended to Amsterdam

Source: https://www.eurotunnel.com/uk/build/; Getlink reports

restructuring plan, interest which cannot be paid when due in cash is settled in notes which doesn't bear interest for next nine years. Table 17.1 lists the major timelines for the project. Table 17.2 highlights the fixed link statistics related to the project.

17.5 Problems Faced by the Project

Table 17.2 Fixed link traffic statistics

Year		2007	2008	2009	2010	2011	2012	2013	2014
Truck Shuttles		1,414,709	1,254,282	769,261	1,089,051	1,263,327	1,464,880	1,362,849	1,440,214
Passenger Shuttles	Cars	2,141,573	1,907,484	1,916,647	2,125,259	2,262,811	2,424,342	2,481,167	2,572,263
	Coaches	65,331	55,751	54,547	56,507	56,095	58,966	64,507	63,059
High Speed Trains	Eurostar Passengers	8,260,980	9,113,371	9,220,233	9,528,558	9,679,764	9,911,649	10,132,691	10,397,894
Rail Freight trains	Trains	2840	2718	2403	2097	2388	2325	2547	2900

2015	2016	2017	2018	2019	2020
1,483,741	1,641,638	1,637,280	1,693,462	1,595,241	1,451,556
2,556,585	2,610,242	2,595,247	2,660,414	2,601,791	1,399,051
58,387	53,623	51,229	51,300	50,268	14,382
10,399,267	10,011,337	10,300,622	10,971,650	11,046,608	2,503,419
2421	1797	2012	2077	2144	1736

Source: Getlink press release Eurotunnel traffic and revenue

Further Reading

1. https://www.britannica.com/topic/Channel-Tunnel
2. http://www.ferryto.co.uk/ports/Folkestone.html
3. https://www.eurotunnel.com/uk/build/
4. https://www.getlinkgroup.com/content/uploads/2019/09/110118Eurotunnel-traffic-and-revenue.pdf
5. https://cdn.gihub.org/umbraco/media/3754/the-channel-tunnel.pdf
6. Flyvbjerg, B. (2014). What You Should Know About Megaprojects, and Why: An Overview.
7. Finnerty, J.D. (2012). Chapter 18 Case Study: The Eurotunnel Project (in: Project Financing – Asset-Based Financial Engineering). John Wiley & Sons, Inc., Hoboken, New Jersey.
8. Grant, M. (1997). Features: Big Project Financing – Financing Eurotunnel. Japan Railway & Transport Review No. 11, pp. 46–52. East Japan Railway Culture Foundation (EJRCF). Tokyo. Retrieved from https://www.ejrcf.or.jp/jrtr/jrtr11/pdf/f46_gra.pdf
9. TRANSMANCHE: Bouygues, Dumez, Spie-Batignolles, La Société Auxiliaire d'Entreprises (SAE), La Société Générale d'Entreprises (SGE)
10. TRANSLINK: Balfour Beatty Construction, Costain UK, Tarmac Construction, Taylor Woodrow Construction, George Wimpey International.
11. Eurostar.com, Behind the scenes. Available at: https://www.eurostar.com/uk-en/about-eurostar/our-company/behind-the-scenes
12. Anguera, R. (2006). The Channel Tunnel – An ex post economic evaluation. Retrieved from: https://ideas.repec.org/a/eee/transa/v40y2006i4p291-315.html
13. Connectivity across borders: Global practices for cross border infrastructure projects, Case study: The Channel Tunnel, Global Infrastructure Hub, https://cdn.gihub.org/umbraco/media/3750/full_report.pdf

Case 14: Doha Metro

The Doha Metro is a new state of the art, automated rail network located in the city of Doha. The metro development is a part of Qatar's National Vision 2030. Doha metro is the backbone of Qatar's integrated public transport system to promote the use of public transport system in the country. Doha metro is basically an underground metro. The metro system has two phases. The first phase involved the construction of 3 lines—Red, Gold and Green with 37 stations. The first phase was completed in year 2020 and opened to public. The future phases involve the construction of an additional line and expansion of existing ones. In an architectural sense, the stations signify the heritage of the country with vaulted spaces design which were inspired by traditional Bedouin tents. The largest station, Msheireb falls at the heart of the Doha Metro.

Doha Metro is designed as one of the most advanced rail transit systems in the world developed by Qatar Railways Development Company. By December 2019, the metro rail project has a completion status of 76 km network with 3 lines and 37 stations. All the sporting venues associated with the 2022 Soccer World Cup in Qatar are connected with rapid transit system (Light Railway System) under construction.

In the year 2009, Qatari Diar and Deutsche Bahn had signed a joint venture to develop a railway network in Qatar. Qatar Rail have the exclusive ownership for the project. Deutsche Bahn and its global arm DB Engineering & Consulting is the main consultant for the project. The work on the project started in the year 2013. Salini Impregilo was given the contract to construct the Red Line north segment from Msheireb to Al Khor North. QDVC and Porr were given the contract to construct the Red line south segment and green line. In the year 2014, a consortium of firms such as Larsen & Toubro, Aktor, Yapi Merkezi, STFA Group and Al Jaber Engineering were awarded the contract to design and construct Doha Metro Gold line.

The Red Line covers 40 km from Al Wakra in the south to Lusail in the north. This line connects Hamad International Airport at Terminal 1 to the center of the city. The line has 18 active stations with major ones of West Bay, Katara and Qatar University. The Red Line has two interchange stations for the metro lines-Al Bidda for interchanges between Red and Green and Msheireb for interchanges between all three lines. It also provides interchange stations between the Metro and Tram with Legtaifiya and Lusail QNB. The Green Line runs east from Al Mansoura to Al Riffa in the west. There are 11 stations along the line with the major ones being Education City, Hamad Hospital, Al Shaqab and Qatar National Library. Gold line runs from the east to west from Ras Bu Aboud to Al Aziziyah. There are 11 stations on the gold Line route with major stops at the Qatar National Museum, Souq Waqif, Sport city and Al Aziziyah.

The 18 km Lusail Tram has 4 lines, 25 stations and 1 Lusail Tram depot for operation, maintenance and storage facility.

The three lines are of approximate 76 km in length. Doha metro is one of the fastest driverless trains in the world. The metro is one of the main pillars of the larger Qatar Rail network which would connect Qatar to the rest of the GCC region. Major portion of the project is underground. The red and green lines included elevated and at grade sections.

When fully complete, the project is expected to cover a network of 300 km with the establishment of four metro Lines-Red, Green, Gold and Blue. Phase I of the project consisted of the construction of the Red, Green and Gold lines and 37 stations. Phase II added the Blue line to the network. By the year 2026, another 60 additional stations are expected to be added to the metro network. Phase 2 also involves the construction of a 150 km high speed connection to Bahrain. Each line of the Doha metro has been tendered as a separate package with its own project management consultant (PMC).

Phase 2 involves the construction of a 150 km high-speed connection to Bahrain. Phase 3 involves the development of a 165 km passenger and freight national network linking Dukhan to Al-Shamal and Doha. There are also plans for a light rail network in the Lusail City development in North Doha.

The metro network will cover the greater Doha area and will connect town centers, main commercials and residential areas throughout the city. The ground work is done using 21 tunnel boring machines (TBM). Each of the TBMs for the Doha Metro measures 7.05 m in diameter and 120 m in length. Qatar Rail holds the Guinness World Records for the title of having the largest number of tunnel boring machines which operates simultaneously in a single project. The Metro system is operated as a system with automatic train operation known as Grade of Operation (GoA 4). GoA is unattended train operation (UTO) where starting and stopping, operation of doors and handing of emergencies are fully automated without any on train staff.

Doha metro as a part of Qatar Integrated Railway project has one of the fastest driverless train systems in the world with speed of 100 km/h. The metro network basically aims to create an efficient and reliable service which encourages the use of public transport as a valid alternative to private transportation.

The three connections of Gold Line, Red Line and Green Line converge through the Msheireb subway station. Approximately 82 km of tunnel routes and 25 stations were connected to suburbs and the stadiums for the 2022 World Cup by the year 2020. In the final phase, the Doha metro system will have 4 metro lines and approximately 100 stations. The construction of the Msheireb subway station involved four main levels at a depth of up to 40 m. Msheireb station is the biggest station within the Qatar Rail's Doha Metro development project. The construction work was carried by SOQ Joint venture (Samsung C&T, OHL, QBC).

The metro network is being operated and maintained by RKH Qitarat, a JV of Hamad Group, Keolis and RATP Dev. The rail cars were supplied by Mitsubishi Corporation in collaboration with Kinki Sharyo. Thales supplied advanced communications based train control (CBTC), signaling, telecommunications and automatic fare collection systems. Hitachi was responsible for the delivery of special maintenance vehicles for the inspection of railway tracks and electric train lines.

The Central Planning Office in Doha is the nodal agency responsible for coordination and supervision of all infrastructural projects in Qatar. The total ridership estimate for the year 2026 when the operationalization of the entire metro project is complete is expected to be 60,000 passengers.

18.1 Structuring

The operations and maintenance of Dubai Metro is entrusted with RKH Qitarat for a period of 20 years which is a joint venture formed by Hamad Group with 51% ownership and French transit operators Keolis and RATP Dev with 49% partnership. Qatar Rail is the owner of the Dubai Metro.

DB International and Qatari Diar Real Estate Investment company had developed the conceptual design for the project. UK based Turner & Townsend are the project management consultants and US based Parsons Brinckerhoff is the strategic project manager.

18.2 Financing

The $35 billion rail projects are funded through government sources. The consortium for building the $4.2 billion gold line of Doha Metro secured syndicated funding worth over $1 billion from a group of banks in the year 2014. The funding was provided by Qatar's Barwa Bank with the First Gulf Bank and Qatar International Islamic bank serving as lead arrangers for the financing. A syndicate led by Mashreq bank and mandated lead arrangers of Barwa bank, Qatar Islamic bank and Union National bank had lent US$576 million for the construction of a section of the Doha metro.

18.3 Significance of the Project

The project is a part of the Qatar government's strategic plan for modernization of Qatar's economy. The EUR 130 billion investment plan of the rail transit system is aimed at attracting public and private investments for economic diversification and reduce Qatar's dependency on natural gas exports. The project is part of the larger railway network envisaged for the development of GCC through passenger and freight rail transport systems. The Qatar Rail metro network is aimed at creating a world class public transportation network and improving the existing urban connectivity and accessibility. The first ever underground rail system is designed to alleviate traffic and congestion problems. According to some estimates, delays due to congestion costs Qatar economy between 1 and 2% of GDP each year. The metro system will contribute towards the Qatar 2030 National Vision for economic and social progress. The other two major rail projects are the Lusail Tram and the long distance rail.

18.4 Risks Involved in the Project

When the project was conceptualized, there was no local rail infrastructure firms in Qatar to bid for contracts. The state owned company had to seek international partners. These international contractors had wide expertise in building rail network, but lacked knowledge of local laws and regulations. To mitigate the risk, the government allowed international contractors to bid through joint ventures in partnership with local companies in order to navigate local market issues, laws and regulations. During the period of construction, Qatar faced a major regional diplomatic crisis with neighbors. In 2017, four Arab countries imposed a land, air and sea blockade on Qatar. The blockade has not impacted the work of Qatar Rail. Table 18.1 list the timeline of the metro project.

18.5 Main Contractors of the Project

Jacobs Engineering was the project management and consulting engineering contractor for the red line. The contract for Gold line and main stations were awarded to Louis Berger and Egis Rail. Hill International was responsible for management of the Green Line. The value of these contracts amounted to $313.16 million. The contract for the design and construction of the 13 km of twin bore underground tunnels and seven underground stations in the northern region of Red Line was awarded to the consortium led by Italian construction giant Impregilo and included other firms such as SK Engineering & Construction of South Korea, Galfar Engineering and Contracting company of Qatar. The build design contract of southern region of red line was awarded to the consortium led by QDVC which was a joint venture between Qatari Diar and Vinci Construction Grands project of France. The consortium included GS Engineering and Construction of South Korea and Al Darwish Engineering of Qatar. The consortium was also entrusted with the contract to design and build a 12.8 km dual tube underground between Msheireb station and New Doha International Airport. The design and construction of the green line between Msheireb and Al Rayyan stadium was carried by the consortium of Austrian contracting firm Porr, Saudi firm of Binladin and HBK contracting company. The

Table 18.1 Time line of Doha Metro Project

Year	Event
2008	Qatari Diar Real Estate Investment commissioned the German national rail company Deutsche Bahn (DB) to design a rail network for Qatar. The international arm of Deutsche Bahn, DBI prepared the design of the rail network in association with Qatari Diar.
2009	In November 2009, Qatari Diar and DB formed a joint venture (JV) Qatar Railways Development Company for the implementation, development and management of the design of the railway plan. Qatari Diar held 51% and DBI held 49% shares in the joint venture of the company.
2011	Qatar Rail bought all the shares held by DBI in the Joint Venture
2014	In 2014, Qatar Rail took the first delivery of the TBM machine which is manufactured by Germany's Herrenknecht.
2015	A consortium of Mitsubishi Heavy Industries (MHI), Mitsubishi Corporation, Hitachi, Kinki Sharyo and Thales were awarded the turnkey contract of construction of the fully automated driver less metro system. The project involved delivery of 75 sets of three car trains, tracks, platform screen doors, railway yard, signaling system, power distribution, tunnel ventilation and telecommunication
2017	Qatar Rail received the prestigious ITA award from the International Tunneling and Underground Space Association. The first four train sets of the Doha metro were delivered.
2018	With an additional 35 train orders, the total fleet to be supplied by Rail carrier Kinki Sharyo reached 110.
2019	Approximately 76 km of metro network were completed with the 3 of gold, red and green lines and 37 stations.

construction contract for building two major stations in Msheireb and Education city was awarded to the consortium of Samsung C&T, Obrascon Huarte Lain (OHL) and Qatar Building Company (QBC). The $3.3 billion contract for the design and construction of the Gold line was awarded to the consortium led by Greek firm Ellaktor. The other firms in the consortium included Yapi Merkezi and STFA from Turkey, Larsen & Toubro from India and Al Jaber Engineering company from Qatar. Atkins was the lead designer for the Gold line and Red South underground lines. UNStudio was the principal architect for the Qatar Integrated Railway project which had designed more than 30 stations in phase one of the project.

Further Reading

https://corp.qr.com.qa/English/Projects/Pages/RedLine.aspx
https://en.wikipedia.org/wiki/Doha_Metro
https://www.constructionweekonline.com/article-35521-qatar-rail-tbms-entered-into-guinness-records/
https://structurae.net/en/products-services/major-construction-site-at-a-depth-of-40-m-msheireb-metro-station-qatar
https://www.railway-technology.com/projects/doha-metro/
https://www.railway-technology.com/features/doha-metro-project/

https://www.arabianbusiness.com/doha-metro-gold-line-consortium-secures-1bn-funding-576738.html
https://www.gtreview.com/news/mena/me-banks-to-finance-doha-metro/
https://www.meed.com/qatar-integrated-rail-project/
https://www.globalmasstransit.net/archive.php?id=10867

Case 15: Panama Canal Expansion

The Panama Canal was opened in the year 1914. The project was instrumental in linking ship traffic between the Pacific and Atlantic Oceans. This man made canal consists of a system of artificial lakes, channels and locks and measures 50 miles long. More than 14,000 ships pass through the canal with 275 million tons of cargo in a given year. US is the final destination of approximately more than 70% of the canal's containerized cargo. On account of increased globalization and congestion in the US West coast, Panama Canal had gained a significant share of container traffic directed towards the US East coast. The American Society of Civil Engineers had ranked the Panama Canal as one of the seven wonders of the modern world. It often takes ships an average of 11.38 h to pass between the canal's two locks.

During the peak period, the vessels often have to wait 10 days before transiting through the canal. The shippers often have to shelf out an average of $50,000 per day due to sitting idle. In the global scenario, Panama Canal have two major competitors. The Suez Canal offers an alternative route between the Pacific and the Atlantic. The other competitor is the US intermodal system of overland transcontinental shipping. By the turn of the century, the intermodal system had captured over 80% of all containerized traffic between northeast Asia and the US East Coast. The Panama Canal handles as much as 5% of global trade. The U.S.-built canal was turned over to Panama in 1999 and the Panama Canal Authority (ACP) manages the operations of the canal. The canal has served more than 144 maritime routes which connects 160 countries and 1700 ports.

19.1 Expansion of the Project

The Panama Canal Expansion project officially began on September 3, 2007. The plan was approved by a referendum of the Panamanian people. It had also received support from international shipping and financial communities. The Panama Canal Authority (ACP) is an autonomous legal entity of the Republic of Panama which has the exclusive charge of operation, administration, maintenance and modernization of the Panama Canal.

The project was expected to be completed by 2014 coinciding with the 100th anniversary of the canal. The project was inaugurated on June 26, 2016. The expansion involved the construction of two lock complexes—one on the Atlantic side and the other on the Pacific side. The expansion project involved the construction of a new shipping lane with three chambers which included three water saving basins. In the expansion, excavation of new access channels to new locks and widening of existing navigational channels were undertaken. The project also involved the deepening of the navigation channels and the elevation of Gatun's lake's operating capacity. The expansion was expected to cost approximately $5.5 billion and the financing means was through a toll system along with foreign credit. The Panama Canal expansion aims to effectively double the canal's capacity by adding a new set of locks to accommodate larger container ships. The project involved the construction of a set of new locks which are 70 ft wider and 18 ft deeper than the locks in the original waterway. The length of the canal was approximately 80.5 km.

The new expanded canal enables tugboats to guide ocean-going vessels into the locks and through the canal. Vessels which enter from the Atlantic side sail at sea level to Gatun locks where they are lifted 85 ft in three steps to Gatun lake which is a large freshwater reservoir built in the middle of the isthmus.

Ships then sail for approximately 30 miles 85 ft above sea level to Pedro Miguel Locks, and then are lowered 31 ft to Miraflores Lake. After sailing another mile to Miraflores Locks, they are lowered 54 ft in two steps to the Pacific Ocean level, and sail 4 miles to reach the sea.

The expansion program involved dredging deeper shipping channels and installation of larger gantry cranes and construction of new container yards to accommodate the ultra large container ships. The work involved dredge and excavation of approximately 150 million which was more than half the quantity during the original canal construction. The largest contract for the project was won in a competitive bid by Grupo Unidos Por el Canal (GUPC) with a value of $3.12 billion which was approximately more than half of the total cost of the project.

Of late the global shipping was being dominated by post Panamax ships which were too large to transit through the original canal. By the year 2009, about 40% of oceanic container shipping was accounted by post Panamax. This led to the development of alternate routes and undermined the Panama's central role in transoceanic shipping. The ever rising volume of traffic had turned Panama Canal into a clogged bottleneck. The new lock system facilitated the new Panamax container ships to carry more than twice as much cargo on account of longer, wider and deeper draft with specifications of 160 ft wide, 1200 ft long and 49 ft deep. The Cocoli and Agua Clara Locks added a third lane to the Panama Canal for the transit of Neopanamax vessels. Half of the traffic through the expanded canal represented containerships followed by liquefied petroleum gas (LPG) carriers and liquefied natural gas (LNG) carriers. The locks also facilitate the passage of other segments such as bulk carriers, tankers, car carriers and passenger vessels.

The original canal continues to operate handling the Panamax size ships of specifications meant to accommodate by the original infrastructure. The Neopanamax size for the new lane is approximately 1200 ft long, 168 ft wide and 47 ft deep. The new locks can accommodate New Panamax vessels, which can transport up to 12,000 containers stacked as tall as a 15-story building.

19.2 Sources of Financing

The cost for the expansion project of Panama Canal was estimated to be US$5250 million. The financing needs was expected to be met from internal funds and external financing. The internal financing sources through the operation of the canal was expected to raise an amount of US$2950 million. The external financing was meant for raising US$2300 million. During December 2009, ACP entered into a common terms agreement with five development agencies for a loan agreement valued at US$2300 million. The loan agreement was for a period of 20 years with 10-year grace period which permitted disbursements on the basis of lenders costs aligned with the execution of the expansion program. Financing was secured from the IFC, European Investment Bank, the Japanese Bank for International Cooperation, the Inter-American Development and the CAF (Corporación Andina de Fomento). The significance of the project for global trade is reflected through the subscription participation in terms of multilateral and bilateral agencies. IFC's financing contribution involved a $300 million 20-year loan to the Panama Canal Authority.

19.3 Impact of the Project

The Panama Canal expansion project have significant impact on shipping routes, port development and cargo distribution. The impact is significant on the fast growing container trade whereby the expanded canal facilitates larger vessels to transit the canal. This would provide an alternate route for vessels to carry cargo away from the congested West Coast. The cargo volume was expected to increase by an average of 3% per year and thereby doubling the 2005 tonnage by 2025. The main catalyst for the expansion of the canal had been the increased world trade particularly with Asia. The expansion project impacts the trans American shipping in three ways. The higher volume of goods movement through the canal would decrease transportation costs and reduces the distance of global shipping routes. Panama canal's importance in terms of regional shipping networks will be enhanced. As the canal traffic increases, there would be corresponding rise in transshipment wherein the goods are transferred to smaller ships which provide service to shallower harbors in cities. The three ports of the canal namely Balboa, Colon and Manzanillo will link distribution centers such as Shanghai with smaller shipping hubs such as Barranquilla in Colombia. The project expansion would provide an alternative route for shipping agricultural products from the interior United States to East Asian markets thereby increasing the importance of the Mississippi River corridor compared to the overland routes to Pacific ports. It is estimated that 90% of the LNG world's fleet now transit through the Panama Canal thereby providing the opportunity for LNG producers in the United States to send natural gas to Asia at competitive prices. LPG vessel traffic has become the second largest segment of traffic through the Neopanamax locks. The expanded canal had offered greater connectivity to world maritime trade. Panama's economy benefits immensely from the expansion project. Panama could emerge as the primary transshipment hub for the western hemisphere. US businesses were expected to benefit from the expansion project as approximately 60% of all cargo passing through the canal has an origin or destination in the US. Giant bulk vessels using the new route had lower transit times and operating costs. In the year 2018, this new segment contributed 9.5% year on year increase in tonnage. By 2018, the average size of containerships transiting the waterway had increased by 28%. One of the cited cost advantage for carriers using the Panama Canal have been the faster all water transit times from Asia compared with the Suez route. Big ships which transit through the Pacific end of the canal gets the opportunity to load containers which originate in Panama's free trade zone as well as the agricultural products from Central and South America.

According to Panama Canal Authority, the canal expansion resulted in job creation of 30,000 new jobs of which 7000 was construction related jobs.

19.4 Risks Involved in the Project

Environmental impact studies were commissioned with respect to the risks involved in the project. Environmental concerns were raised with respect to flora, water quality and sediment formation. The expansion project has provided environmental leadership in the maritime industry through prioritization of water savings and reduction of carbon emissions on account of shorter routes. The amount of water in the canal is a function of the annual rainfall received in the region. On account of El Nino effect, water shortage has prompted the canal authority to impose weight limits on ships passing through the existing locks three times in year 2016. Water conservation and management had been a major area of concern for Panama Canal Authority. Each transit requires the use of an average of 52 million gallons of fresh water of which 22 million gallons is released into the sea. The water source from the two reservoirs also are the sources of drinking water for Panama. Due to climatic changes rainfall scarcity is a potential challenge. In terms of navigation challenges, the neo Panamax ships might face problems while transiting through the Corte Culebra which is a narrow passage with many tight turns and sheer rock walls. It is also suggested that the maneuverability of the vessels would be comprised making accidents very likely due to the lock's narrow dimensions. The canal could face competition in future from a new 278 km canal in Nicaragua being built by a Chinese firm which will be longer, deeper and wider than the Panama Canal.

Further Reading

Kevin Knight, The Implications of Panama Canal Expansion to U.S. Ports and Coastal Navigation Economic Analysis, IWR White paper, December 2008, pages 36.
ACP Expansion Report, Global Insight.
Brian Davis, Rob Holmes, Brett Milligan, December 2015, https://placesjournal.org/article/isthmus-panama-canal-expansion/?gclid=EAIaIQobChMIkYTYmf218QIVyu3tCh0HNgSTEAAYASAAEgJ1ffD_BwE&cn-reloaded=1
"Cracks in Lock May Delay Panama Canal Expansion," Container Management, August 25, 2015
"The Panama Canal: A Plan to Unlock Prosperity," The Economist, December 3, 2009
Expansion of Panama Canal to Create 7,000 Jobs," Latin American Herald Tribunal
ACP, Environmental Impact Statement, Panama Canal Expansion Project, Third Set of Locks [pdf], 2007, Chapter 3, 108
https://micanaldepanama.com/expansion/
https://www.dcvelocity.com/articles/30335-has-the-panama-canal-expansion-changed-anything
https://www.npr.org/2016/06/25/483523910/the-5-billion-panama-canal-expansion-opens-sunday-amidst-shipping-concerns
https://www.wsp.com/en-RO/projects/panama-canal-expansion
https://www.asme.org/topics-resources/content/panama-canal-expands-to-meet-demand
https://www.cepal.org/sites/default/files/publication/files/37039/S1420341_en.pdf
https://www.bbc.com/news/world-latin-america-36635198
https://conference-service.com/pianc-panama/documents/agenda/data/abstracts/en/abstract_0056.html
https://www.ifc.org/wps/wcm/connect/news_ext_content/ifc_external_corporate_site/news+and+events/news/multilateral+institutions+to+lend+%242.3+billion+for+panama+canal

Case 16: Three Gorges Dam—The World's Largest Hydroelectric Plant

The construction began in the year 1994. Three Gorges Dam which was commissioned in the year 2013 is the largest hydroelectric dam in the world in terms of electricity production. The dam has a generating capacity of 22,500 megawatts (MW). The dam is located in the Xilingxia Gorge which is one of three gorge of the Yangtze River in Hubei province in China. The Three Gorges dam have an inspiring structure. It is one of the few man-made structures on Earth which is visible to the naked eye from space according to NASA. The 26 power generating units with a generating capacity of 700 MW are designed to produce a total of 84.7 BkWh/year. Three Gorges dam with 2.3 km long is one of the world's largest dams. Over 40,000 workers were involved in the project which took 17 years for completion. The construction was phenomenal in sense that approximately 28 million cubic meters of concrete were used for its construction. Spillway gates have been installed along the concrete shoots which hurl water over 100 m downstream.

A dam on the Yangtze River in central China's Hubei Province was first proposed in the year 1919 by then President of the Republic of China Sun Yat Sen. The three gorges dam refers to 120-mile stretch of limestone cliff along the upper reaches of Yangtzi River.

The dam has a height of 185 m and is 2309 m wide. The dam has created the Three Gorges Reservoir which has a surface area of 400 square miles and extends upstream from the dam in 600 km. The gorge covers 1 million square kilometers of drainage areas and averages a runoff of 451 billion cubic meters annually. The operations of the dam are done by 32 main power generators. The construction work was completed in the year 2008.

China Three Gorges Corporation (CTGPC) is the legal entity responsible for the construction, operation and financing of the project. The first underground unit became operational in the year 2011. In the year 2012, all 32 hydro units were commissioned to generate a total of 22,500 MW output. The output from the dam project of 85 TW/h. is close to one tenth of the current Chinese requirements for power generation. Chinese Electric Power Company was responsible for the management of the generation aspect of the project. Eight turbines were developed by a consortium of ABB, Alstom and Kvaerner and the remaining six by GE, Siemens and Voith. Each turbine has the capacity to produce electricity worth 4.2 million yuan ($525,000) a day. When the reservoir achieves its optimum water depth of 148 m, the turbines will be able to produce 700,000 kWh a day.

The final estimation cost of the project was expected to be US$22.5 billion (180 billion yuan) On the basis of estimation of electricity produced at a price of 0.25 yuan per kWh, the project was estimated to recover the investment cost when the project generates 1 trillion kWh of electricity.

20.1 Funding and Costs of the Project

The construction of the Three Gorges Dam cost amounted to ¥249 billion (US$37 billion) (Table 20.1).

The static investment is based on the price level at the end of May in 1993. Static investment includes engineering fees of construction and installation, equipment and tools, basic reserve fees etc. Dynamic investment includes the sum of estimated investment required by the whole Three Gorges Dam project. It includes loan interests in construction period, adjustment tax for investment direction, price and interest rate and reserve fees for price rise etc.

The funding came in the form of loans from China State Development bank, national debts, corporate bonds, revenues sourced from electricity power of Gazhouba Dam. Funding was also sourced from Three Gorges Project Construction Fund which collected an additional electric charge of ¥0.003 per kWh since 1992. In 1994, the charge was changed into ¥0.004 per kWh; and ¥0.007 per kWh in benefited areas of Three Gorges hydropower station since 1996. In later stages, the revenues from the partially operated Three Gorges hydropower station also became the sources of funds.

The Three Gorges Dam became breakeven by the year 2003 when power generating units were started. Until 2018, the annual power produced by the Three Gorges hydropower station had exceeded 100 billion kWh and generated income of ¥300 billion ($44 billion).

Table 20.1 Cost estimates

Three Gorges Dam cost	Static investment	Dynamic investment
Pivotal project	¥50 billion (US$7.3 billion)	¥126.4 billion (US$18.4 billion)
Power transmission and transformation	¥32 billion (US$4.7 billion)	¥36.5 billion (US$5.3 billion)
Immigration and resettlement	¥53 billion (US$7.7 billion)	¥85.7 billion (US$12.5 billion)
Total	¥135 billion (US$20 billion)	¥249 billion (US$37 billion)

Source: https://www.travelchinaguide.com/river/three-gorges-dam-cost.htm

20.2 Significance of the Project

Three Gorges Dam is the largest hydropower project in the world. The project was aimed at the economic growth of China along with objectives of flood management along the Yangtze River. One of the primary objectives of the project was the control of flood. According to statistics from the National Development and Reform Commission (NDRC) of China, the total hydroelectric generating capacity stood at 115 GW before the first phase of the Three Gorges hydro power plant was completed. The advocates of the dam suggest that the dam will be a boost for Yangtze River trade which basically accounts for about 80% of China's inland shipping. It is stated that the dam plays an important role in environmental protection as million tons of plastic bag wastes are prevented from flowing out to sea. The engineers have created a mechanism called garbage lapping tongue to prevent the trash from damaging power generators. The dam area has two ship locks to support freight traffic and support the movement of over 18 million tonnes of freight per year. The construction of the dam has minimized the risk of flooding by a mechanism of releasing the water through a contained and controlled process. For economic growth, the project witnessed the construction of the biggest ship locks in the world which receives over 150 freight ships per day over the Yangtze river. The Three Gorges Dam is expected to provide enough power for the growing Chinese economy and contribute towards reduction of toxic emissions. Coal consumption has been reduced by approximately 30% per year on account of the project.

Chines authorities have estimated that over 300,000 people were killed in the twentieth century's largest Yangtze River floods. According to estimates, the dam will protect some 15 million people from flood waters as well as 1.5 million acres of farmland.

20.3 Challenges and Risk

The project posed several ecological dangers, technical challenges and human rights issues. The project costed around $28.6 billion and took two decades for completion. The project displaced more than 1 million people along the Yangtze River. The efficacy of the dam in preventing destruction from huge floods is often questioned. During the recent floods, over 3.67 million residents have been displaced and 54.8 million people were affected causing economic losses of over $20.5 billion. The Chinese authorities have stated that the dam has been successful in intercepting the flood waters. According to the dam's operator China Three Gorges Corporation, the dam has intercepted 18.2 billion cubic meters of potential flood water. According to sources, the dam was able to reduce the speed and extent of water level rises on the middle and lower basins of the Yangtze river. The dam which is located on an upstream section of the Yangtze river helps in prevention of the flooding downstream by diversion of water in a huge reservoir and then controlled release of water takes place through its sluice gates. The 660 km reservoir connects the upstream through the narrow valleys of the Three Gorges dam. It is estimated that "once a century flood" of more than 244 billion cubic meters of water or twice the volume of Dead sea water can pass through the Three Gorges dam in 2 months.

The work on the project was stopped by the State Environmental Protection Administration when it failed to meet national environmental guidelines. The project was launched after 3 years of preparation in terms of technical planning, environmental and water protection. Over 7000 people were relocated from the construction site. The dam's 410-mile-long reservoir flooded about 244 square miles of land which covered thousand towns and villages. About 1.3 million people were relocated. The displaced people were offered new homes and jobs but the efforts were plagued by widespread local corruptions and complaints. Environmentalists have raised concerns about the harmful environmental effects as the dam has reduced downstream nutrient and sediment flow and had negative impact on neighboring river and sea ecosystems. The sediment loading reached half of pre dam levels. This trend would create problems for coastal fishing grounds and increase erosion in wetlands.

Further Reading

https://www.usgs.gov/special-topic/water-science-school/science/three-gorges-dam-worlds-largest-hydroelectric-plant?qt-science_center_objects=0#qt-science_center_objects

https://www.power-technology.com/projects/gorges/

Nectar Gan, China's Three Gorges Dam is one of the largest ever created. Was it worth it? CNN. August 2020. https://edition.cnn.com/style/article/china-three-gorges-dam-intl-hnk-dst/index.html

https://www.waterpowermagazine.com/news/newsbeyond-three-gorges-in-china

https://www.nationalgeographic.com/science/article/china-three-gorges-dam-how-big

https://constructionglobal.com/construction-projects/building-the-three-gorges-dam. Three Gorges Dam: the world's largest hydroelectric power plant

Case 17: One World Trade Center

One World Trade Center (One WTC) is the main building of the rebuilt World Trade Center complex in Lower Manhattan, New York City. This new structure has the same title as the North Tower of the original World Trade Center which was destroyed in the terrorist attacks of September 11, 2001. One WTC is the tallest building in the United States and the sixth tallest in the world. The steel frame of One World Trade Center is higher than the 1250-ft-high Empire State Building which is the second tallest building in USA. It is 408 ft taller than its predecessors.

The structure is situated on 16-acre original World Trade Center. The building is surrounded by West Street to the west, Vesey Street to the north, Fulton Street to the south, and Washington Street to the east. Skidmore, Owings & Merrill owned by David Childs is the architect of the building. The building has a total height of 1776 ft. The building has 94 stories with the top floor numbered 104. It occupies approximately 3 million square feet which includes 2.6 million square feet of new Grade A office space spread across 71 floors. It is most expensive new office tower with cost exceeding $3.8 billion. The tower's construction consists of steel and concrete.

The towers are designed as framed tube structures thereby facilitating tenants open floor plans unhindered by walls. In 2009, the Port Authority changed the official name of the building from "Freedom Tower" to "One World Trade Center". One World Trade Center is designed with sustainable architecture features. The building structure and interior is built from recycled materials which include gypsum boards, ceiling tiles. Approximately 80% of the tower's waste products are recycled. The Purcell phosphoric acid fuel cells generate 4.8 MW of power and its waste steam generates electricity. The project has implemented a number of safety measures to protect against any accident or terrorist attack. Long term protection has been provided by the reinforced concrete base along with 3 ft (91 cm) thick reinforced concrete walls in all stairwells, elevator shafts, risers and sprinkler systems. There are also stairwells exclusively dedicated to firefighters, biological and chemical filters through the ventilation system along with pressurized stairwells. The work for the project started in year 2006 when the lease agreement between the Port

Table 21.1 One World Trade Center in numbers

Concrete used	200,000 cubic feet
Exterior glazing	1 million square feet
Structural steel used	40,800 metric tones
Office space	2.6 million square feet

Authority of New York and New Jersey (the owner of the World Trade Center) and Larry Silverstein (the leaseholder of the complex) became effective. The project was completed in the year 2014. Design architecture was provided by Minoru Yamasaki & Associates. The Port Authority provided design services for site utilities, foundations, basement retaining walls and paving. The service core in World Trade Centre 2 is oriented from north to south. The One World Trade Center recaptures the New York skyline and the design solution is an innovative mix of architecture, structure, urban design, safety and sustainability. The tower rises from a cubic base with its edges chamfered back and have a faceted form composed of eight elongated isosceles triangles. In the middle, the tower forms a perfect octagon in plan. The building design was provided by Skidmore, Owings & Merrill (SOM). The prism like shape is intended to interact with natural light. Seven World Trade Center the first rebuilt structure near Ground zero was completed in year 2005. This tower is 52 storied and 741 ft tall. Table 21.1 gives construction statistics for the project.

The world trade center transportation hub occupies 800,000 square feet to serve 250,000 pedestrians every day. The tower mainly functions as an office building. The first 19 floors are designed as protective base. The office spaces occupy floors from 20 to 90. The floors above the 90th floor are mechanical floors. The floors from 100th floor to 103rd floor are occupied with observation decks and restaurants. The antenna atop the roof floor is used for telecom communication. The Conde Nast media group is the building's biggest tenant.

21.1 Cost of Funding

The tower's construction cost amounted to $3.9 billion. The redevelopment costs for the entire 16-acre site had risen by 35% from $11 billion in the year 2008 to $14.8 billion in 2012. The site also received more than $6 billion in tax breaks and other deal sweeteners. The tower's construction was partly funded by approximately $1 billion of insurance money received by Silverstein Properties for the losses in the September 11 attacks. The State of New York provided the additional source of funding which amounted to $250 million. The Port Authority raised $1 billion through the issue of bonds. Funds were raised by Port Authority through bridge and tunnel tolls during the period 2011–2015.

21.2 Risks and Challenges

The project was marred by different political challenges and ever lengthening construction delays. The continuous delays have led to the site in the middle of Lower Manhattan to be boarded up for more than 10 years. Construction cost overruns also occurred for the project work.

21.3 Ownership

The project was developed by the Port Authority of New York and New Jersey which are bi state public agency. The Port Authority of New York and New Jersey owns the majority stake in the building as well as the ownership of the 16 acres of land which the Ground Zero encompasses. In 2010, the Real Estate corporation Durst Organization acquired 10% stake in the One World Trade Center. The developer Larry Silverstein is the long term leaseholder of the World Trade Center site.

Further Reading

https://en.wikipedia.org/wiki/One_World_Trade_Center
Morgan, B, 2021, World Trade Center Officially New York's New Tallest Building, https://www.forbes.com/sites/morganbrennan/2012/04/30/1-world-trade-center-officially-new-yorks-new-tallest-building/?sh=71f8c2542bbb
https://www.wsj.com/articles/SB10001424052970203920204577191371172049652
https://www.som.com/projects/one_world_trade_center
Kenneth Lewis, Nicholas Holt, Case Study One World Trade Center, New York
https://thetowerinfo.com/buildings-list/one-world-trade-center/

Case 18: Making of the Tallest Building—Burj Khalifa

Burj Khalifa, the iconic structure in UAE is the tallest manmade structure in the world. The 162 story tower with a height of 828 m above the metropolis of Dubai is the world's tallest building. The project was completed in the year 2010. It took 6 years for the completion of the project which involved over 12,000 workers during the peak period of the project. Emaar properties, one of the largest real estate companies in the world is the master developer of the project. The Burj is more than twice the height of the Empire State Building and almost three times the size of the Eiffel Tower.

The design combines the local cultural influences with cutting edge technology. Burj Khalifa accommodates offices, retail spaces, residential units and a Giorgio Armani hotel. The Y shaped floor plan maximizes views of the Arabian Gulf. In the ground level, the tall tower is covered by green space, water features and pedestrian friendly boulevards. Burj is the Arabic word for tower. The overall design was based on the theme of patterning systems embodied in Islamic architecture and geometries of regional desert flower called Spider Lily (Hymenocallis).

The three pronged design consists of three elements around a central core with the elements spiraling upwards. The tower was designed by the architectural firm Skidmore, Owings & Merrill which designed the Willis Tower (Sears Tower) and the new One World Trade Center in New York.

Burj is composed of sculpted volumes arranged around a central buttressed core and is built of reinforced concrete and covered in glass. The tower rises from a flat based and setbacks occur in an upward spiraling pattern thereby reducing the building's mass and forms a spire.

The structure has a total built-up area of 5.67 million square feet. The residential space accounts for 1.85 million square feet. The prime office space measures over 300,000 square feet. This is in addition to the area occupied by the Armani Hotel Dubai and the Armani Residences.

The Armani Hotel Dubai based in Burj is the world's first hotel to be designed by Italian fashion legend Giorgio Armani which reflects minimalist style with muted gray interiors, sumptuous fabrics and Japanese wooden floors. All the 160 rooms and

Table 22.1 World records held by Burj Khalifa

Tallest Freestanding structure in world
Largest number of storeys in the world—200 plus with 160 habitable storeys
Highest occupied floor in the world
Highest outdoor observation deck in the world
Tallest service elevator in the world
World's highest swimming pool in a building
Highest positioned revolving doors ever installed in a façade worldwide.
World's highest restaurant
World's highest New Year display of fireworks
World's largest light and sound show staged on a single building

Source: https://www.burjkhalifa.ae/img/FACT-SHEET.pdf

Table 22.2 Project facts

Location	Dubai, UAE
Project completion year	2010
Site area	104,210 m^2
Project area	454,249 m^2
Number of stories	162
Building height	828 m
Market	Commercial, Office, Hospitality, Mixed use, Residential

Source: https://www.burjkhalifa.ae/img/FACT-SHEET.pdf

suites of the hotel are spread over the entire 39th floor with each decorated with bespoke furnishings and state of the art structure. At the top which spreads across Levels 148, 124 and 125 provides exclusive access to the highest outdoor observatory in the world.

The construction of Burj Khalifa was based on sustainable practices to reduce material usage and waste through the adoption of structural and construction efficiencies. The tower has a 'sky sourced' ventilation system in which the cool less humid air is drawn in through the top of the building. The tower has one of the largest condensate recovery systems in the world. Table 22.1 highlights the world record statistics held by Burj Khalifa. Table 22.2 gives the project details.

The design of Burj Khalifa was based on technologically advanced, highly efficient and environmentally sustainable MEP system which provides a healthy indoor environment. The tower has one of the world's highest pressure chilled water system with a 460 psi (3.2 Mpa). This innovative cooling condensate can provide 14 Olympic sized swimming pools of fresh water annually. The system also provides a centralized high quality filtration for quality air circulation and reduces the maintenance needs. The high performance curtain wall protects the building structure from summer heat and provides radiant thermal comfort. A "life boat" vertical transportation system with advanced monitoring and controls is in place to withstand emergency events.

Burj Khalifa was an international collaborative project as more than 60 contracting and consulting companies around the world were involved in the project. Over 12,000 workers and contractors representing over 100 nationalities were involved in the project. According to Emaar estimates, the construction has absorbed 22 million man hours. The construction team consisted of companies such as Samsung Engineering from South Korea, Besix from Belgium and Arabtec from the United Arab Emirates.

The three-part design was effective in facing the windy challenge as the spiral floors could break the wind currents around the building which results in a stable structure. As the building spirals in height, the wings set back to provide different floor plates. This setback arrangement provides a different width to the tower for each differing floor plate. This stepping and shaping of the tower has the effect of disrupting the flow of wind over the height of the building. In terms of foundation, the tower's superstructure is supported by large reinforced concrete mat which is in turn supported by 192 bored reinforced concrete piles. The mat is 3.7-m-thick and was constructed in four separate pours totaling 12,500 cubic meters of concrete. Approximately 45,000 m^3 of concrete, weighing more than 110,000 tons, were used for the foundation of the structure. The overall construction process involved the usage of 330,000 m^3 of concrete and 39,000 tons of steel rebar.

The total weight of aluminum used on Burj Khalifa is equivalent to that of five A380 aircraft and the total length of stainless steel bull nose fins is 293 times the height of Eiffel Tower in Paris.

The mechanical floors house the electrical sub stations, water tanks, pumps and air handling units which are essential for the operations of the building. These mechanical floors typically serve the 15 floors above and below them.

The Burj Khalifa's water system supplies an average of 946,000 L (250,000 gallons) of water daily. At peak cooling, Burj Khalifa will require about 10,000 tons of cooling, equal to the cooling capacity provided by about 10,000 tons of melting ice.

The tower has 57 elevators and 8 escalators. The building service/fireman's elevator with a capacity of 5500 kg is the world's tallest service elevator. The sky lobby is an intermediate floor where residents and guests can change from an express elevator to a local elevator which stops at every floor within a segment of the building.

The impressive attraction of Burj Khalifa lies in its telescopic spire which is made of 4000 tons of structural steel. The spire was constructed from inside the building and jacked to its full height of over 200 m (700 ft) using a hydraulic pump. The top four floors of the Burj have been reserved for communications and broadcasting which occupy the levels just below the spire.

The exterior of the tower and its two annexes are made of 28,261 glass cladding panels. The work on Burj Khalifa project was completed after 1325 days after excavation work started in January 2004. The publicly accessible observation deck with an outdoor terrace is based after 124 storeys up. The project holds a world record for concrete pumping in which concrete was pumped to 606 meter's height. Approximately 31,400 tons of rebar were used for the construction of Burj Khalifa.

Outside the building, a fountain system was designed at a cost of US$217 million which is illuminated by 6600 lights and 50 colored projectors. It is the world's largest choreographed fountain.

22.1 Project Finance

Mashreq bank, Emirates Bank International and Abu Dhabi Commercial bank formed a syndicate to finance the project in the year 2005. The syndicated banks signed a financing agreement with the Construction contractor Samsung Corporation and its project partners Belhasa Six Construct and Arabtec. Approximately 90% of saleable space was sold off plan. The construction cost was estimated to be US$1.5 billion.

22.2 Significance of the Project

The construction of Burj Khalifa tower is one of the most successful projects in the Middle East. It was planned by the Dubai government to place Dubai as the hub for finance, trade and tourism. The building was part of new development called Downtown Dubai which was designed to be the centerpiece of large scale, mixed use development. The project was themed on the basis of the government strategy to diversify from oil based economy to have focus on service and tourism sectors.

Further Reading

https://edition.cnn.com/travel/article/burj-khalifa-dubai-guide/index.html
https://www.som.com/projects/burj_khalifa
https://www.som.com/projects/burj_khalifa__mep
https://www.boonedam.com/inspiration/burj-khalifa
https://www.constructionweekonline.com/projects-tenders/article-7400-how-the-burj-was-built
https://www.burjkhalifa.ae/img/FACT-SHEET.pdf

Case 19: Shanghai World Financial Center

The Shanghai World Financial Center (SWFC) is one of the tallest mixed use skyscraper in the World. The tower is built in the Pudong district of Shanghai. The construction took 11 years for completion. It was designed by the American architectural firm Kohn Pedersen Fox Associates of New York. The building was inaugurated in the year 2008. During its completion period, it was the second highest building after the Taipei 101 financial center building in Taiwan. Shanghai World Financial Center has 101 stories and reaches a height of 1614 ft (492 m). SWFC ranks second in Shanghai in terms of height and fifth in Mainland China after Shanghai Tower, Shenzhen Ping—an International Finance Center, Tianjin Golden 117 Tower, Guangzhou Chow Tai Fook Center. SWFC is the tenth tallest building in the world in terms of standard height. The developer Mori Group is the owner of the SWFC. SWFC is located very close to Jin Mao Tower. The most significant feature of the design is that the huge trapeziform aperture on the top portion is used to lessen the impact of wind pressure. The building has a total of 380,000 square meters of floor areas and can accommodate 20,000 people. The design life of the tower is expected to be 50 years.

The SWFC based within the Shanghai's Pudong New area is positioned at the very heart of the Lujiazui Finance and Trade zone which has the potential to develop into a major Asian center for international finance and trade. SWFC overlooks the 100,000 square meter Shanghai Central Park. The center is located in an area which houses government agencies, securities and commodities exchanges, leading banks and trading companies. The location is linked to excellent transportation and urban infrastructure which include the Shanghai Pundong International Airport.

The Shanghai World Financial Center is designed as a giant square column in which two of its sides have been beveled from opposite corners and gradually taper closer and form a narrow rectangle at the top. The structure is supported by large diagonally braced corner columns made up of mixed structural steel and reinforced concrete in the outer wall and a reinforced concrete inner core wall. A series of radiating beams at intervals connect the two structures. The exterior sheathing is a curtain of double paned mirror glass. The building is designed to withstand earthquakes and high winds from typhoons.

Construction of the building which began in the year 1997 was held up due to the Asian financial crisis and was resumed in the year 2003. The structural framework was completed in the year 2007. Approximately 70 floors of the tower are devoted to office space.

SWFC is a mixed use building which consists of offices, stores, hotel, meeting rooms and observatory. There are three observation decks on the 94th, 97th and 100th floors. The three underground floors are used for parking with a capacity of 1100 parking spaces. Stores and restaurants are based in the first and second floors. Floors 3–5 are occupied by meeting rooms. The floors starting from 7th to 77th are meant for office spaces. The hotel Park Hyatt occupies the floors from 79th floor to the 93rd floor. The hotel features 174 rooms and suites. The floors above the 93rd floor are for mechanical use. The observation deck based on 100th floor is ranked as the third highest observation deck in the world.

23.1 Construction

The construction contractors for the project was Shanghai Construction Group and China State Construction Engineering Corp Third Engineering division. The construction cost amounted to $1.2 billion. Table 23.1 gives the SWFC project details.

23.2 Sustainability Initiatives

SWFC have deployed advanced technologies to create a sustainable office building. The zoned air conditioning system minimizes energy consumption and the use of multilayered glass in the curtain wall enhances HVAC effectiveness. SWFC combines three structural systems and perimeter megastructure consisting of perimeter columns, beams and braces. These structures provide high safety against the threat of earthquakes and strong winds. Two mass dampers consisting of 150-ton counterweight are installed on the 90th floor to reduce building sway. To conserve

Table 23.1 Project highlights

Project site area	30,000 m^2
Building site area	14,400 m^2
Total gross area	381,600 m^2
Number of floors	101 floors above ground and 3 underground floors
Height of the building	492 m
Project owner	Shanghai World Financial Center Co Ltd
Project architect	Mori Building Co
Completion date	2008

energy, the SWFC have curtain walls made of double paned glass. These walls provide effective insulation against hot and cold weather. Human surveillance and electronic security systems provide a fully integrated and comprehensive security package. SWFC is equipped with 44 double deck elevators for vertical transport across floors in the building.

SWFC houses the office building for many international companies in banking, insurance, securities and fund management such as Ernst & Young, Morgan Stanley, BNP Paribas, Commercial bank, Bank of Yokohama, Sumitomo Mitsui Banking and Korea Development Bank. SWFC received the Best Tall Building Overall and Asia & Australasia awards from the Council on Tall Buildings and Urban Habitat.

23.3 Significance of the Project

The SWFC was planned with the aim of building an international financial center which would serve as a critical driver for the Chinese economy. The financial center was positioned at the heart of the Lujiazui Finance and Trade Zone in the Pudong New Area of Shanghai, a district being strategically developed by the Shanghai city government and the government of China. The mixed super tall building was envisioned to provide leading edge offices to meet global company requirements based on the policy of international openness in the financial field. The building was designed under the concept of the "global magnet" to emerge as the Asia's premier financial and information centers.

Further Reading

https://www.britannica.com/topic/Shanghai-World-Financial-Center
https://thetowerinfo.com/buildings-list/swfc/
http://www.swfc-shanghai.com/?l=en
https://www.mori.co.jp/en/company/press/release/2008/11/20081128140101000736.html

Case 20: Dolphin Gas Project

The Dolphin Gas project is one of the largest trans border energy projects in the GCC region. Dolphin Gas project is the only international gas network in the GCC region which connects three countries Qatar, UAE and Oman. The project involved the transportation of natural gas via pipeline from Qatar to the neighboring countries of United Arab Emirates and Oman. This was the first major regional energy network created in the GCC region. The value of the project was estimated to be $7 billion. The project was completed in two phases. The construction of the project was started in the year 2002. The first phase witnessed the development of two platforms in Qatar's North field, two multi-phase offshore sealines to the processing facilities and the gas treatment and compression plants at Ras Laffan in Qatar. The second phase involved the construction of 364 km subsea pipeline to transport gas to UAE coast. The cost of the second phase was $3.5 billion. The second phase of the project was completed in the year 2006. The pipeline became operational in the year 2007. The pipeline has the capacity to carry up to 3.2 billion cubic feet of Qatar natural gas a day to UAE for a period of 25 years.

The project proposal was initiated by the UAE Offsets Group (UOG) of Ministry of Defense, UAE. In 1998, UOG proposed that Qatar would serve as the exclusive supplier and marketer of Qatari gas in UAE and Oman. In 1999, Mobil Oil and Qatar signed a Memorandum of Understanding with UOG which resulted in the long term supply and purchase agreement which facilitated UOG to obtain gas and condensate by products.

Dolphin Energy is the constructor and operator of the project. Mubadala Development Company of Abu Dhabi federal government have an ownership stake of 51% in Dolphin Energy and the rest 24.5% stake is owned by Total Fina of France and Occidental Petroleum of USA. Dolphin Energy was established in the year 1999 and provides 2 billion standard cubic feet of natural gas every day to the Sothern Gulf region. The construction cost for the Dolphin Gas project amounted to US$6.2 billion. In the Dolphin gas project, Dolphin Energy is involved in the three key stages of production process—upstream, midstream and downstream. Dolphin Energy's upstream activities takes place in Ras Laffan Industrial City where the firm's gas processing and compression facilities receive and process gas from Qatar's North Field. Dolphin Energy produces raw natural gas from 30 deep wells in Qatar's offshore North Field. The two offshore unmanned platforms Dol-1 and Dol-2, situated in the North Field, extract the gas through 30 deep wells. The two 36-in. sealines connect Dolphin Energy's two production platforms to the gas processing plant at Ras Laffan Industrial City. This system has the capacity to transport up to 2.6 billion standard cubic feet per day of raw gas to the Ras Laffan plant. It is stated that the gas processing and compression plant at Qatar's Ras Laffan Industrial city is the largest single build plant in the world. The downstream operations of the company involve reception, metering and distribution of gas to the customers in the UAE and Oman. The major Gas network under Dolphin Energy consists of the Taweelah Receiving Facilities(TRF), the Eastern Gas Distribution System(EGDS), the Al Ain Fujairah Pipeline and the Taweelah Fujairah Pipeline. Dolphin Energy have implemented Advanced Subsea Intervention & Support Technology(ASSIST) pipeline repair system to minimize disruption and restoration of gas after the occurrence of any accidental events. Dolphin Energy meets approximately 30% of the UAE's energy requirements. The total investment in the Dolphin gas project is estimated to be US$6.2 billion.

JCG Middle East FZE, the wholly owned subsidiary of JGC Corporation of Japan was the EPC contractor for the gas processing and compression plant at Ras Laffan. The plant became operational in the year 2006. The plant extracts hydrocarbon liquids like condensate and NGL products from the wet gas received from North field and processes it for sale. The compressed dry gas is then transported through the pipeline for export to the UAE. JCG also offers it services as maintenance contractor and its specific responsibilities involve training of operations staff and maintenance.

The compression trains for the plant project were supplied and commissioned by Rolls Royce Energy systems of the UK. The plant has the capacity to compress over 2 billion cubic feet of methane. The propane, butane and the condensate are sold in open market. Ethane is supplied to Qatar Petroleum. The Automation Applications and Systems at Dolphin plant was done by Honeywell Middle East and its main subcontractor Trust Technical Services in the year 2006. Scand Power was awarded the contract for the sea line pipeline management system and the export and distribution pipeline contract was awarded to Energy Solutions along with the gas distribution management system contract.

The upstream FEED contract for the North field wells were carried out by Foster Wheeler Sofresid. The FEED work involved construction of the offshore production complexes, two multiphase sea lines for the transportation of wet gas to shore, the onshore receiving facilities, gas processing and export gas compression facilities. During the period 2005–2006, a total of 24 wells were constructed to provide raw gas to Dolphin plant.

In 2004, EPC contract for the construction of two offshore platforms was awarded to J Ray McDermott Middle East. The work for the contract involved the fabrication, installation and connection of the offshore production platforms to the sealines. In the same year, the EPC Contract for the sealines were awarded to Saipem of Italy which is a subsidiary of the Eni Group. The contract work involved installation of two 36-in. diameter concrete coated sealines for the transportation of natural gas, hydrocarbon liquids to Ras Laffan processing plant. The twin sealines which became operational in the year 2006 transported the unprocessed natural gas and hydrocarbon liquids from the offshore plants to the processing plant.

The EPC (design and installation) contract for the 364 km subsea export pipeline from Qatar to UAE was given to Saipem during March 2004. The pipeline transport the natural gas from the Ras Laffan based Dolphin Plant to the facilities terminal at Taweelah in the UAE. The contract for the procurement of the line pipes was awarded to Mitsui company of Japan. This contract involved the supply of high carbon steel line pipe of approximately 400,000 tons. The EPC contract for gas reception at Taweelah was awarded to Abu Dhabi based Technip and Al Jaber Energy services consortium of UAE. The facilities at Taweelah include three parallel gas receiving trains and equipment, metering facilities, control buildings and warehouses. The value of this EPC contract was approximately $62 million.

A 118 miles long pipeline was constructed from Al Ain to Fujairah with a capacity to carry 20 billion cubic meters of natural gas a year. A 240 km pipeline was constructed between Taweelah gas receiving station and Fujairah for supply of gas to Fujairah F2 power and water desalination plant. In 2006, two EPC contracts were awarded for the Eastern Gas Distribution System in the UAE.

In 2004, the UAE and Omani government signed a pipeline agreement to facilitate the transmission of natural gas between the two countries. The agreement also confirmed the role of Dolphin Energy Ltd as the owner and operator of the gas pipeline which connects Oman with Fujairah of UAE.

24.1 Significance of the Project

The project laid the foundation for economic cooperation between GCC nations of UAE, Qatar and Oman. The project envisaged regional economic and political integration. The North Field has facilitated Qatar to become a major regional exporter and international gas player through liquefied natural gas (LNG) exports. The Gulf region accounts for 40% of the world's natural gas reserves. The natural gas demand has witnessed increasing trend on account of anticipated changes in domestic usage. By 2006, it was estimated that approximately 19% of the world's total gas reserves were found in the North Field region.

Gulf countries earlier were reluctant to invest in new gas production for their domestic markets due to the government control over the pricing policy. Rapid economic growth in the region which led to huge oil exports created new focus for substitution of oil with gas in the domestic economy. In Oman the domestic prices of natural gas were kept artificially below the international market rates. Diversification strategy have facilitated the expansion of natural gas based industries such as petrochemicals, power generation and use of natural gas as a feedstock for oil recovery projects in Oman. The economic and political future of Qatar basically depends on the way in which the gas resources are exploited. Qatar didn't have the technical capacity to develop the natural gas reserves. Qatar offered equity stakes to International Oil companies for the development of North Field reserves in the form of energy companies, project financiers, engineering, procurement and construction contractors. Qatar entered into contracts to ship LNG worldwide on a spot and long term basis to avoid both political and commercial risks on account of pipelines. The GCC countries have substantial energy demands due to oilfield reinjection, industrial and consumer power usage.

24.2 Financing

Initially Dolphin faced difficulties for securing outside financing. Hence the equity partners provided sources of funding for the project's early expenditures. Dolphin Energy Ltd entered into a $2.45 billion bridge loan agreement with a consortium of 20 local regional and international banks. Bridge loans are short term loans obtained to finance construction expenditures. These bridge loans were structured as multi tranche deal with non recourse project financing, bonds and Islamic financing. In the year 2005, Dolphin entered into an Islamic financing agreement with 14 financial institutions to provide $1 billion to partially fund the construction expenditures. At that time, this Islamic financing was the largest ever Sharia compliant oil and gas transaction. Islamic financing was used for the first time for the funding of the upstream operations. The Islamic tranche was secured for a period of 4 years.

24.3 Major Risks for the Project

The project faced setbacks due to political disagreements and territorial disputes. Iran often accused Qatar of overproducing the Qatari side of the North Field. Increased tensions can contribute toward oil and gas infrastructure risks. In the year 2005, Saudi Arabia denied permission to extend the Dolphin Project to Kuwait as the undersea pipeline required transit across Saudi border. As a result, Qatar and Kuwait were forced to abandon the project after they had finalized negotiations including gas price. International Oil Companies were initially reluctant to take part in the project due to lack of sovereign guarantee or state backed loan guarantee. Qatar Petroleum had reservations as the FOB price of $0.87mn/BTU ex-Ras Laffan, and the delivered CIF (cost, insurance, freight) price of $1.30mn/BTU was considered low.

Further Reading

https://www.hydrocarbons-technology.com/projects/dolphin-gas/
http://www.dolphinenergy.com/press_news_releases_29_march2004.htm
https://www.dolphinenergy.com/
https://www.dolphinenergy.com/operations

https://www.mubadala.com/en/what-we-do/petroleum-and-petrochemicals/dolphin-energy
https://gulfnews.com/business/energy/dolphin-project-to-benefit-uae-and-qatar-economies-1.283947
Justin Dargin (2008), The Dolphin Project: The Development of a Gulf Gas Initiative, NG22, Oxford Institute for Energy Studies. ISBN 978-1-901795-69-1.
See Persian Gulf Region: Natural Gas, Energy Information Administration. Available at http://www.eia.doe.gov/emeu/cabs/Persian_Gulf/NaturalGas.html
See Qatar: Background, Energy Information Administration (May 2007). Available at http://www.eia.doe.gov/emeu/cabs/Qatar/Background.html

Case 21: Bhadla Solar Park

According to Institute for Energy Economics and Financial Analysis (IEEFA) report, half of the world's largest 10 solar parks which are currently under construction are based in India. Bhadla project was commissioned in the year 2017. India had pioneered the concept of ultra-mega power plant (UMPP) in a single solar industrial park. The Ministry of New and Renewable Energy (MNRE) had initially set a target for 40 industrial solar parks with a combined capacity of 20 GW and the target was doubled to 40 GW by the year 2022.

Bhadla Solar Park is the largest solar park in the world as of the year 2020. The park has a total capacity of 2245 MW. The park is spread over a total area of 5700 ha. It is located in Jodhpur district in Rajasthan, India. The park has a total capacity of 2245 MW. A 300 MW project at Bhadla III Solar park became fully operational in year 2020. A large number of institutions such as Rajasthan Solar Park Development Company Ltd (RSPDCL) owned by Rajasthan Renewable Energy Corporation Ltd (RRECL); Saurya Urja Company of Rajasthan which is a joint venture between the government of Rajasthan and IL&FS Energy Development company; Adani Renewable Energy Park Rajasthan which is a joint venture between the government of Rajasthan and Adani Renewable Energy Park (a subsidiary of Adani Enterprises) are the main stakeholders of the project. Table 25.1 provide details of the phase wise projects commissioned in Bhadla Solar Park.

Phase I of the project witnessed the commissioning of 65 MW of projects. In Phase II, the projects with capacity of 680 MW were commissioned. In the year 2016, the Solar Energy Corporation of India issued tender for the 750 MW of projects which were developed in two phases: 500 MW under Phase III and 250 MW under Phase IV under the National Solar Mission. Rajasthan Solar Park Development Company Ltd is responsible for the development of first two phases. Saurya Urja Company of the State of Rajasthan is responsible for the development of Phase 3 and Adani Renewable Energy Park for the Phase 4 development.

The total investment on the project was approximately $1.4 billion. The work on the solar park project was started in July 2015 and the first phase was commissioned in October 2018. The project was developed under the Ministry of New &

Table 25.1 Phase Wise Projects commissioned in Bhadla Solar Park

Development agency	Phases	Capacity (MW)
Rajasthan Solar Park Development Company	Bhadla-I Solar Park	65
Rajasthan Solar Park Development Company	Bhadla-II Solar Park	680
Surya Urja Company of Rajasthan	Bhadla-III Solar Park	1000
Adani Renewable Energy Park Rajasthan Ltd	Bhadla-IV Solar Park	500

Source: Mercom India Research

Renewable Energy (MNRE) scheme for the development of solar parks and ultra-mega solar power projects. National Thermal Power Corporation (NTPC) and Solar Energy Corporation of India (SECI) have signed 25-year power purchase agreement with developers. In third phase, the solar power plants are developed by Hero Future Energies, Softbank Group, ACME Solar and SB Energy. Azure Power, ReNew Solar Power, Phelan Energy Group, Avaada Power and SB Energy are developing solar power plants under the fourth phase. The power evacuation system of the solar park is developed by Powergrid Corporation of India and the state owned transmission company TRANSCO. Powergrid Corporation established grid substations and pooling stations at Bhadla.

The Bhadla solar park is India's largest solar park with total installed capacity expected to surpass 2000 MW. In 2020 with the commissioning of 330 MW solar power project, the Bhadla solar park became fully operational with installed capacity of 2245 MW. The Bhadla solar park hosts 260 MW state which is commissioned by state owned National Thermal Power Corporation. The project was initiated by the state owned energy company NTPC and the Solar Energy Corporation which comes under the Ministry of New and Renewable Energy.

25.1 Financing

The construction of transmission lines from solar park to the national grid is financed under the Rajasthan Renewable Energy Transmission Investment Programme (RRETIP) which is coordinated by the Government of India, the Asian Development Bank(ADB) and the Clean Technology Fund. The Clean Technology Fund of the Climate Investment Funds(CIF) along with Asian Development Bank have plans to invest $200 million in large scale solar infrastructure projects in India of which Bhadla Solar Pak is the largest.

25.2 Contracts for the Project

Rays Power Experts is the engineering, procurement and construction (EPC) contractor for the development of 140 MW capacity in Phase II of the solar park project. Vikram Solar was the EPC contractor for the 130 MW solar power plant in Phase II. Larsen & Toubro received the contract to establish a 100 MW solar power plant in

Phase III from SB Energy in the year 2018. Ecoppia had a contract with SB Energy to install 2000 robotic solar panel cleaning equipment across five sites in Phase III & Phase IV.

25.3 Impact of the Project

Solar infrastructure projects are basically facilitating India to reduce its dependence on imported fossil fuels. In energy deficient rural areas, the solar projects are emerging as clean power source than petroleum based kerosene for indoor lighting. Bhadla Solar Park is aiding economic growth and job creation in the areas close to the project. The project has provided an impetus to the local service industry. The Government of India aims to produce 100 GW of solar power to electrify 75 million households by the year 2022. As a part of its sustainable future initiatives, the government has increased its renewable energy targets. To meet India's commitment towards Paris Climatic Agreement 2015, the government have committed to shift its power mix to 40% non fossil fuel based energy sources by the year 2030. The country plans to increase its renewable energy capacity to 275 GW by the year 2027. Rajasthan, the north western state of India has one of the most ideal conditions for solar power in the world on account of higher solar incidence as well as vast tracts of barren land. Asian Development Bank have invested $800 million in Rajasthan Renewable Energy Transmission Investment Program (RRETIP) to develop solar power. The program has a multi tranche financing facility funded by up to $300 million from ADB, $200 million loan and grant from Clean Technology Fund(CTF) and counterparty funding from the state government. The investment program has the ability to add 4300 GW of new renewable energy capacity to the grid and would result in an estimated greenhouse gas emission reduction of 5.4 million tons of carbon dioxide equivalent per year. The Bhadla Solar Park employs around 1000 people.

25.4 Feasibility of Solar Power

With new solar power tariffs of $0.03 per kWh introduced in the year 2017, solar power has become one of the cheapest source of electricity for India which was well below the coal's average tariff of $0.04 per kWh. According to estimates, if 3% of wasteland is made available, India's exploitable solar energy potential would be in the range of 750,000 MW. Solar parks are not labor intensive and less complicated to operate. Solar power plants take less time to become functional. In case of thermal power plant, it takes 5–6 years to be operational, while in the case of nuclear power plant the period can extend to 10 years. For solar plants like Bhadla, the electricity producing units took only 9 months for becoming operational. By 2014, the prices of photo voltaic systems declined by almost 20% compared to the 2008 levels. As a result, generation of electricity from solar systems have become a financially viable alternative. During the period 2008–2014, the global installed capacity of solar electricity has increased by six times.

25.5 Challenges for the Project

The project faced local constraints in terms of availability of suitable land in desert, road design, topographic challenges, geotechnical limitation, water availability, power transmission and social issues.

Further Reading

https://mercomindia.com/world-largest-solar-park-bhadla/
https://www.nsenergybusiness.com/projects/bhadla-solar-park-rajasthan/
https://www.adb.org/sites/default/files/project-documents/45224/45224-002-dpta-en_0.pdf
https://indianexpress.com/article/india/bhadla-solar-park-rajasthan-catching-the-sun-india-biggest-solar-energy-park-jodhpur-power-plant-hot-winds-sand-storms-4709314/
https://www.business-standard.com/article/economy-policy/india-s-ultra-mega-solar-parks-offer-500-700-billion-investment-potential-120051401022_1.html
https://ieefa.org/record-setting-2-2gw-solar-park-in-india-now-fully-operational/

Case 22: Tengger Desert Solar Park China

Tengger Desert solar park is one of the world's largest solar park in the world with solar generation capacity of 1.5 GW. The park covers over 43 square kilometers. It is situated in Zhongwei which is located in China's northwestern Ningxia province. With the establishment of Tengger Desert solar park, China's installed capacity rose over 176 GW. China is the global leader in terms of installed capacity with 32% of the global capacity. Chinese power sector faces challenges like transmission bottlenecks, oversupply and problems associated with electric grids. China is the world's largest manufacturer of solar panel technology. The International Energy Agency statistics suggest that more than 60% of the world's solar panels are made in China. The Chinese government focusses on solar energy as the clean source of energy. Approximately two thirds of electricity produced in China is from coal. In 2018, the capacity factor of Chinese solar equipment was approximately 15%. The low capacity factors were attributed to weather factors and huge transmission losses. China aims to have 35% clean energy supply in terms of its total energy needs by the year 2030. It is estimated that China will account for nearly half of all global renewable energy by the year 2022.

Tengger Desert Solar Park was established by the China National grid and Zhongwei Power Supply Co. The owners and developers also include Tianyun New Energy Technology Co. Ltd., Beijing Jingyuntong Technology Co. Ltd., Ningxia Qingyang New Energy Co. Ltd., Qinghai New Energy Co. Ltd. and Zhongwei Yinyang New Energy Co. Ltd.

The park supplies power to over 600,000 homes. The development work started in the year 2012 and comprised 45 interconnected grid project. The project was commissioned progressively over the 2011–2017 period. The park is also known as the "Great Wall of Solar ". The Tengger Desert is an arid natural region which covers about 36,700 km and is located in the inner Mongolia Autonomous region of China. The solar field itself covers 1200 km of land area. Tengger solar park consists of over 50 individual solar power plants.

When the Tengger Desert solar plant became functional, much of the solar capacity went unused due to low demand in the sparsely populated region around the plant. There were also transmission issues.

The project combined the development of photovoltaic and desert control and contributed towards water saving agriculture along with grid connected PV power station in the desert.

The photovoltaic industrial park is divided into the desert in Zhongwei city, photovoltaic, PV manufacturing industry, agricultural greenhouse area and sightseeing for planning area. The entire project had a total investment of 20 billion yuan. The industrial park was able to increase the grid capacity by 2.8 billion per year. The project achieved an output value of over 7 billion yuan which resulted in annual savings of more than 1.1 million tons of standard coal. In 2018, Tengger's contribution to China had a combined 174 GW of installed solar capacity.

Further Reading

https://earthobservatory.nasa.gov/images/145159/solar-powered-china

https://www.bbc.com/future/article/20180822-why-china-is-transforming-the-worlds-solar-energy

Tengger Desert Solar Park: For Building the Great Wall of Solar (Most Influential Projects: #48) (2019). *PM Network, 33*, 92.

https://www.semprius.com/largest-solar-farm/

https://www.focalsolar.com/2014/10/deserts-of-tengger-desert-is-emerging-largest-photovoltaic-power-plant-photo/

Case 23: Millau Viaduct—The Tallest Bridge, France

Millau viaduct is one of the largest cable stayed bridges in Europe. It is the tallest bridge in the world with a structural height of 336.4 m. In 2012, Mexico's Baluarte Bridge surpassed Millau as the world's highest cable-stayed bridge. The bridge spans 2 km valley in the Massif central mountain range. The bridge is 2.4-km-long and 270 m above the river at its highest point. Millau duct forms the final link in the A75 highway from Paris to Barcelona. The bridge forms the part of the A75-A71 autoroute axis from Paris to Beziers and Montpellier. The subsidiary Compagnie Eiffage du Viaduc de Millau (CEVM) of Eiffage was awarded the primary contract for the construction of the bridge during August 2001. Eiffage Group is a specialist in civil engineering and metal construction.

The project involving the construction of a road bridge to span river and gorge valley was designed to reduce congestion near the Tarn valley due to traffic on the route from Paris to Spain. Millau Viaduct forms the main entrance to the Gorges Valley and connects the Causse du Larzac and the Causse Rouge which are the limestone plateaus. This bridge holds several records such as the highest pylons in the world (245 m and 221 m), the highest bridge tower in the world (343 m) and the highest road bridge deck in Europe (270 m).

The bridge was inaugurated on 17 December 2004. By December 2017, 5 million vehicles passed through the viaduct. The road has two lanes in each direction. The structure crosses River Tarn and spans the huge gap from one plateau to the other. The bridge is taller than the Eiffel Tower. The structure was designed by Sir Norman Foster and the Europe Etudes Gecti—SERF—Sogelerg group.

Each of the sections spans 342 m and its columns range from 75 m to 235 m in height over the river Tarn. The deck, masts and multi span cables were all build in steel. The structure is such that the seven piers of the Millau Viaduct were sunk in shafts of reinforced concrete in pyramidal shape and divided in an overturned V shape. Moreover, the shrouds were anchored and distributed in semi harps. High pressure hydraulic cylinders and pumps were used to push the deck spans. PC synchronized lifting system was used to lift the auxiliary piers. Enerpac was contracted to provide the supply for the hydraulic system for lifting and pushing the bridge spans and piers for the bridge. Millau Viaduct is not straight to rectify the sensation of floating for drivers. The curve for the road is 20 km in range designed to provide slight incline of 3% to improve visibility for drivers of vehicles.

The bridge is considered as one of the greatest engineering achievements in the modern world. In the year 2006, the bridge received the outstanding structure award from the International Association for Bridge and Structural Engineering. The construction of the Millau Viaduct involved the use of the most advanced techniques in the public works space. Laser, GPS, translators, self-climbing formwork, high performance concrete and innovative materials were used for the project work. Eighteen launching operations brought the two parts of the deck above the Tarn.

Construction for the bridge began in October 2001. The work for the deck started by February 2003 and was completed by May 2004. The deck was constructed from high grade steel instead of concrete. The bridge is supported by multi span cables which are placed in the middle. For the purpose of expansion and contraction of the concrete deck, 1-m empty space is designed at the extreme points. Each column is split into two thinner and more flexible columns below the roadway thereby forming an A frame above the deck level. The Millau Viaduct weighed approximately 290,000 tons. The construction work consumed approximately 127,000 m^3 of concrete, 19,000 tons of steel-reinforced concrete and 5000 tons of pre constraint steel basically cables and shrouds. For security purposes, a 3-m-wide emergency lane was designed so that the drivers were hindered from observing the valley from the viaduct. Side screens were constructed to reduce the effects of the wind by approximately 50%. The bridge otherwise would have been exposed to winds of up to 151 km/h. The project witnessed an extension work in the year 2005 involving the installation of 30 km/h electronic toll collection lanes and payment lanes with recycling. An 18 km lane consisting of toll plaza which includes a CCTV connection provides the technical and administrative services to the project. Piers were built with Lafarge high performance concrete. The tallest pylon was 803.7 ft and was mounted by PAECH Construction Enterprise from Poland.

The construction consortium composed of the Eiffage TP company which provided the concrete resources, the Eiffel company which provided the steel roadway and the Enerpac company which facilitated the roadway's hydraulic support. Appia company was entrusted with work related to the bituminous road surface on the bridge deck and Forclum was responsible for electrical installations. Freyssinet the subsidiary of the Vinci Group installed the cable stays. Eiffage Concessions was responsible for the management of the project. The steel road deck and the hydraulic action of the road deck were designed by the Walloon engineering firm Greisch from Belgium.

Piles, apron, pylons and guy wires are fitted with a multitude of sensors to detect the slightest movement of the viaduct and measure its resistance. The project has used measuring instruments such as anemometers, accelerometers, inclinometers and temperature sensors.

The bridge is made up of two slim pylons and a light deck and touches the valley below at only seven points though the construction required 85,000 m^3 of concrete and 36,000 tons of structural steel. Toll plaza has 16 lanes of traffic, 8 in each direction.

27.1 Financing and Construction Cost

Approximately 400 million euros was spend on the construction of the bridge. The 6 km toll plaza had incurred an additional cost of 20 million euros. The builder Eiffage financed the construction under a concession agreement to collect the tolls for 75 years until 2080. The concession agreement stipulated that in case of high revenues, the French government can assume control of the bridge as early as the year 2044.

27.2 Risks for the Project

Many organizations such as the World Wildlife Fund (WWF), France Nature Environment and the National Federation of Motorway users opposed the project for different reasons. Some viewed the project as technically unsustainable as questions were raised about the capability of pylons to support the structure. Some suggested that the viaduct would not solve Millau's congestion problems. Some thought that the project will not be financially viable as the project will not break even. At the peak of the work, around 600 people were engaged for the work. The project took 3 years for completion.

27.3 Economic Benefits of the Project

The Millau Viaduct is a classic example of an exemplar in infrastructure design. The successful integration of the project into the landscape has resulted in Viaduct becoming a major tourist attraction and the town of Millau experienced significant economic boost. The local economy received a boost from the Millau Viaduct. Annual tourist visit is in the range of 1 million visitors. The concession returns were above the predicted levels. By 2019, the profits from the project to Eiffage amounted to 24 million euros per annum. The current toll is 8.60 euros which rises to 10.80 in summer for light vehicles. Table 27.1 highlights the main features of the project.

Table 27.1 Features of the project

Length	2460 m
Width	32 m
Maximum height	343 m; 19 m more than the Eiffel Tower
Radius of curvature	20 km
Height of the highest pier (P2)	245 m
Height of pylons	87 m
Number of piers	7
Length of spans	2 side spans with 204 m span
Number of guy ropes	154 (11 pairs per pylon arranged in a single monoaxial layer)
Tension of the stay cables	900–1200 tons
Weight of the steel deck	36,000 tons or 5 times the Eiffel Tower
Volume of concrete	85,000 m^3, or 206,000 tons
Construction cost	400 million euros
Duration of the concession	78 years (3 years of construction and 75 years of operation)
Guarantee of work	120 years

Source: http://www.leviaducdemillau.com/version_html/construction.html

Further Reading

https://www.roadtraffic-technology.com/projects/millau_viaduct/

France 'completes' tallest bridge. news.BBC.co.uk. BBC News. 29 May 2004. Retrieved 2 May 2017.

https://web.archive.org/web/20130706200013/http://www.leviaducdemillau.com/version_html/construction.html

http://www.leviaducdemillau.com/version_html/construction.html

http://www.bridgesdb.com/bridge-list/millau-viaduct-bridge/

http://tag-on-line.blogspot.com/2019/02/millau-viaduct-raises-millions.html

https://nic.org.uk/app/uploads/NIC_Value-of-Design_double.pdf

Case 24: Jiaozhou Bay Bridge

Jiaozhou Bay Bridge in the eastern China's Shandong province is one of the longest bridges in the world. The record has now been overtaken by the $15 billion ocean crossing bridge—Macau Zhuhai bridge which is the longest ocean crossing bridge currently in the world.

The length of the bridge is 26.7 km. It is the part of the 41.58 km Jiaozhou Bay Connection Project. The bridge transects the Jiaozhou Bay and reduces the journey distance between Qingdao and Huangdao by 30 km thereby decreasing the travel time from 40 min to 20 min. Thus the project connected the eastern and western areas of the Qingdao region in China. The bridge which was opened in June 2011 is the longest sea bridge in the world. The construction of the bridge was completed in a 4-year period. The design of the bridge is T shaped with the main entry and exit points in Huangdao and the Licang District of Qingdao. The construction of the bridge used 450,000 tons of steel and 2.3 million cubic meters of concrete. The bridge is supported by 5238 concrete piles. The project has 5127 punching bored concrete piles. The three navigable sections of the bridge consist of the Cangkou Channel Bridge to the west, the Dagu Channel Bridge to the east and the Red Island (Hongdao) Channel Bridge to the north. The length of the Cangkou bridge was 260 m. The Cangkou channel bridge is the first ocean interchange in China. Cangkou and Red Island bridge are cable stayed bridges while the Dagu channel bridge is a single tower self-anchored suspension bridge which spans 260 km. The Jiaozhou bay tunnel runs beneath the Qingdao Bay bridge. The tunnel with length of 5550 m was constructed along with the bridge. The construction of the six lane two-hole tunnel took approximately 3.5 years for completion. The bridge was designed to withstand earthquakes of 8 magnitudes on Richer scale. It could also withstand the impact of a 300,000-ton vessel and strong typhoons. The lifespan of the bridge is expected to be 100 years. It is the largest to be constructed on frozen waters in China.

The 110-ft-wide bridge cost more than 10 billion yuan ($1.5 billion). According to the Guinness record, the Jiaozhou bridge is 2.5 miles longer than the Lake Pontchartrain Causeway in Louisiana. The bridge had the capacity to carry more than 30,000 vehicles each day. Over 20,000 people were engaged in the construction of the project in two teams.

The construction was completed in two phases. Phase I which involved the construction of the Cangkou bridge, Red Island bridge and Dagu Channel bridge covered 28.8 km. The work on the two interchanges at Licun River and Red Island, the three spans and toll stations in Qingdao were also completed in the first phase. The first phase was completed in the year 2010. The Phase II of the project involved the construction of the road on the bridge, power supply and distribution, fencing, lighting, housing and landscape.

28.1 Financing Cost

According to the official state run television company CCTV, the project cost amounted to CN¥10 billion (US$1.5 billion). Other sources reported costs which were as high as CN¥55 billion (US$8.8 billion).

28.2 Structuring of the Project

The design work of the bridge was done by Shangdong Guausu Group. Shandong Hi Speed Qingdao Highway a subsidiary of Shandong High Speed Group was entrusted with the task to construct, operate and manage the bridge. The agreement was for a period of 25 years. The toll collection rights for the Jiaozhou Bay Expressway and the advertising operation rights were entrusted to the company. The company also had the toll collections rights for the tourism development and operation rights of the Qingdao Bay Bridge and Jiaozhou Bay Expressway.

28.3 Economic Benefits

The construction of the bridge provided better connectivity between the two fast growing industrial regions on the either side of the bay thereby boosting the local economy. This construction aided in the economic development of Qingdao as one of the coastal cities. Earlier the Huangdo region was connected to the city of Qingdao through a ferry service across Jiazhou Bay. Ferry services were not able to meet the requirements on account of increasing passenger and cargo levels. The bridge formed the starting point of the Qingdao Lanzhou Expressway. The bridge could have crossed the English Channel which is 32 km wide at its narrowest point.

Further Reading

Qingdao Bay Bridge Design-Innovation-Technologie. wutancn.com. 2013.
David Eimer (8 January 2011). "China builds world's longest bridge". The Daily Telegraph.

https://www.nbcnews.com/id/wbna43588234
https://www.roadtraffic-technology.com/projects/qingdao-bridge/
A marathon span: China opens world's longest bridge over water. NBC News. 2011.
https://www.bbc.com/news/world-asia-pacific-13976281

Case 25: Trans-Siberian Railway

Trans-Siberian Railway is the longest single rail system in the world. It connects Moscow in the west with Far East city of Vladivostok and passes through the cities of Perm, Yekaterinburg, Omsk, Novosibirsk, Krasnoyarsk, Irkutsk, Chita and Khabarovsk. The project covered a distance of 9289 km. The project was originally conceived by Tsar Alexander III. The construction work of the railroad began in the year 1891. The project had great significance in the economic, military and imperial history of the erstwhile Soviet Union. The project connected Moscow to Vladivostok in the year 1904. In 1916 an alternate route was built within the Russian Territory. The completion of the railroad project led to the industrialization of the Siberian region. The trans Manchurian line came under the control of the Chinese region after World War II. During the period 1974–1989 construction was completed on the Baikal Amur Mainline. There are three rail routes that traverse Siberia from Moscow. The Trans-Siberian route from Moscow to the Pacific terminus of Vladivostok. The Trans-Mongolian route connects Moscow to Beijing via Ulaanbaatar, Mongolia. The Trans Manchurian route connects Siberia and Manchuria to Beijing. Thus the Trans-Siberian railway spans across three countries and crosses the two continents of Europe and Asia. The Trans-Siberian Railway is one of the most impressive engineering feats in modern history. The Trans-Siberian Railway or the Great Siberian Route is the main railroad artery which connects the European part of Russia with Siberia and the far east regions. The Trans-Siberian Railroad connects two parts of world and connects five federal districts of the Russian Federation. The European part of the project covers approximately 19% of the total length of the railway while 81% is covered by the Asian region. Covering over 5 million square miles, the region constitutes 77% of Russian land but yet has only a population of 36 million. This world's longest train route traverses eight time zones from Moscow to Vladivostok. Trans-Siberian Rail system introduced computer tracking system to monitor the movement of containers along the railway.

It was the cause of a major war which led to the Russia Japanese rivalry. The Trans-Siberian Railway was the pet project of the Russian government to develop the underexploited region of Siberia. The project facilitated Russia to harvest the natural resources of Siberia and expand trade with East Asia. The Russian intentions became a matter of concern for the Japanese policymakers. Before the development of the project, the Siberian infrastructure for the military and economic expansion to the Pacific area was limited. The Russian geopolitical influence altered with the construction of the Trans-Siberian Railway in the year 1891. Finally the scenario precipitated into the Russia-Japanese war. The war killed between 130,000 and 170,000 soldiers and transformed East Asian geopolitics. Russia ceded large amounts of territory to Japan and its Pacific fleet was devastated. Japan emerged as the dominant military power in Asia after the war. During the first world war, Siberia became a very important strategic area and US intervened into the Russian war with attempts to remove the Czech legion from Siberia.

The project faced huge challenges like the hilly landscapes, frozen ground, swamps, cold weather conditions. The skilled workers for the project were recruited from the central regions of the country. Approximately 89,000 people were employed for the construction of the rail project.

The first trains started operational from Moscow to Vladivostok even before the completion of the entire Trans-Siberian Railway project. The committee for the construction of the Trans-Siberian Railway had estimated the value of the project at 350 million rubles in gold.

During the second world war, the railroad facilitated the delivery of cargo and military forces to the war zone and served as the main transportation source for the evacuation of the civilian population from the occupied territories. After the post war period, the Siberian Railway was modernized.

29.1 Economic Benefits

The Trans-Siberian Railway had the longest history of commercial freight operation between Europe and Far East. The Americans believed that the railway system had created conditions favorable for American exports. The introduction of containerization in world market proved advantageous to both shipping and railway sector in the Soviet bloc as it provided the fastest and cheapest route from Far East to Western Europe and vice versa. On account of containerization and intermodal transport, Trans-Siberian Railway provided the cheapest alternative route compared to the deep sea route from Europe to the Far East. Meanwhile, the Trans-Siberian Railway system also gained the confidence of Japanese and Western European transport communities. The trans rail route provided transit for cargo transferred from Soviet border stations to ports in Japan and other regions in South Asia. The Trans-Siberian Railway gave an impetus to Siberian agriculture and facilitated substantial exports to the central Russia and Europe. The rail line remains the most important transportation link within Russia with approximately 30% of exports maintained through this rail line. The system also attracts foreign tourists through the route. By the beginning of the year 1985, Trans-Siberian Railway introduced regular express block train services with 52–55 wagons which could carry up to 110 TEU. This system proved to be an advantage over sea transport.

The Trans-Siberian railroad have become the backbone of the Russian rail network facilitating the passenger traffic and turnover of goods. The Trans-Siberian railroad covers more than 80% of Russia's industrial and natural resources region. Now the Trans-Siberian network provides a modern double track electrified railway line with access to China and Mongolia. The project had a significant impact on economic development and led to the growth of circulation of goods. The Russo–Japanese war during the period 1905–1906 created hurdles for economic development. The railroad capacity during the war was mere 13 trains per day. After the war, the wooden rails were replaced with metal rails and number of trains as well as the size of carriages were increased. The rail line was also extended to cover all regions of Russia.

The Trans-Siberian rail celebrated 100th anniversary in the year 2001. The centenary in the year 2001 also marked the one thousandth train journey to Finland via the Trans-Siberian region. In the year 2018, North Korean government announced its intend to connect the railways between the Koreas. If the project is successful, the shipments by land along the popular trade route from Seoul to Rotterdam would take just 10 days as opposed to the 30 days needed by sea.

29.2 Sources of Financing

The financing of the project was done with increase in taxes and money supply for wages and equipment expenditures. The economy was also opened up for foreign investment from France, Britain and the United States.

29.3 Challenges of the Project

The project was hampered by harsh climatic conditions. The project work had to be carried out through large rivers and lakes which run through the Siberia region and other waterlogged regions or regions filled with permafrost. Huge challenges were faced in the Baikal region as mountains were blown up for the construction of railway tunnels and railway bridges. The construction cost was huge and man power supply was a big challenge. Construction workers were drawn from the ranks of exiled prisoners, soldiers and peasants. In spite of the challenges, approximately 600 km of railroad were laid every year. The project was completed in a period of 12 years.

During the period 1980–1989, the overall movement of containers via the Trans-Siberian Railway remained stable. After the year 1989, major political problems between Soviet Union and East European countries created problems for the Trans-Siberian Rail system. The development of the Trans-Siberian Rail system was affected by the disintegration of the erstwhile Soviet Union as all of the Baltic ports left the Soviet Union.

The current challenge lies in the problem of optimizing the Trans-Siberian capacity. The major portion of freight traffic between east and west takes place through sea lanes. Through modernization of its services, the Trans-Siberian rail system could emerge as a highly competitive alternative to sea transport.

29.4 New Developments

The Russian authorities are focusing on the development of Baikal Amur Mainline which is termed as the cousin to the Trans-Siberian railway which spans about 4300 km from the town of Tayshet to the Pacific Ocean. The Russian Railways is investing over $17 billion over a decade to boost the transport of goods and raw materials from Asia to Europe.

Further Reading

https://www.britannica.com/topic/Trans-Siberian-Railroad
https://wikitravel.org/en/Trans-Siberian_Railway
https://www.vox.com/world/2016/10/5/13167966/100th-anniversary-trans-siberian-railway-google-doodle
https://www.thetranssiberianexpress.com/blog/trans-siberian-railway-history-facts
https://reconasia.csis.org/struggle-behind-trans-siberian/
https://www.transsiberianexpress.net/train-info/history-of-the-trans-siberian-railway
https://www.gsd.harvard.edu/2019/04/moving-monument-landscape-architects-reimagine-the-trans-siberian-railway/
Slepven, I. (1996) "The Trans-Siberian Railway", History Today, 46, pp.134–145.
Soviet Shipping Journal (1982) "Trans-Siberian Container Service", February, 25–27.
Helmer, J. (1999) "Moller weights future of Russian intermodal route", Journal of Commerce, 2 August
Lloyd's Maritime Asia (1990) "Trans-Siberian Railway: Contest on the Orient Express", December.
Cargo Systems (2002) "Baltic Ports" March, p.13.
Anastasia Liliopoulou, Michael Roe, Irma Pasukeviciute, Trans-Siberian Railway: from inception to transition European Transport \ Trasporti Europei n. 29 (2005): 46–56
https://www.cs.mcgill.ca/~rwest/wikispeedia/wpcd/wp/t/Trans-Siberian_Railway.htm

Case 26: Pan-American Highway

The Pan American Highway, the longest road on earth is a network of roads which stretches across the Americas and measures approximately 48,000 km in total length. It is one of the biggest adventures in the world. This network of highways connects North America and South America. According to the Guinness World Records, the Pan American Highway is the world's longest motor able road. Except for the Darien Gap, the road links almost all of the Pacific coastal countries of the Americas in a connected highway system. Darien Gap is the rainforest break of 106 km in length between southeast Panama and northwest Colombia. It is necessary to take a ferry to cross the Darien Gap. The gap is 96 km long and 50 km wide which stretches from the Atlantic to the Pacific on the border between Panama and Colombia. The region consists of undeveloped swampland and impenetrable rainforest inhabited by indigenous tribes, Colombian guerrillas and exotic wildlife. The road trip offers the most diverse scenery on the planet. It is the most popular overland route in the world. The Pan American Highway is unique in the context that it passes through diverse climates and ecological characteristics. Pan American Highway passes through dense jungles to arid deserts and barren tundra. The Pan American Highway spans from Prudhoe Bay Alaska in North America to South America and passes through cities of Puerto Montt and Quellon in Chile and Ushuaia in Argentina. Beyond the West and North of the Darien Gap, the roadway known as the Inter American Highway passes through Central America and Mexico. The inter-American Highway from Nuevo Laredo Mexico to Panama City covers 5390 km. Thereafter it splits into several branches and ultimately leading into the Mexico United States border. The official section of the highway runs from Laredo in Northern Mexico to the Argentine capital Buenos Aires. The Pan American Highway runs through 14 countries. The road trips start in Prudhoe Bay Alaska and stretches to the tip of Argentina in Ushuaia. The highest point in the road is Cerro de la Muerte which is at 11,322 ft above the sea level. The northern part of the road goes through Canada, United States, Mexico, Guatemala, El Salvador, Honduras, Nicaragua, Costa Rica and Panama. The Southern part crosses Suriname, Guyana, Brazil, Venezuela, Colombia, Ecuador, Peru, Chile, Argentina, Bolivia, Paraguay and Uruguay. The highway aimed to foster closer and harmonious relationship among different nations in the Americas. The highway connects almost all of the Pacific coastal countries. The Pan-American Highway which connects the North and South America, crosses six time zones and four climatic zones. Large scale projects such as highways can have significant linkages to other national projects operating at other scales.

The concept of building a highway emerged at the Fifth International Conference of American States in the year 1923. In the year 1928, the sixth international conference of American states held in Havana issued its approval of building a road across the continent. On July 29, 1937, the American countries such as Argentina, Bolivia, Chile, Colombia, Costa Rica, Salvador, Guatemala, Honduras, Mexico, Nicaragua, Panama, Peru, Canada and United States signed the Convention on the Pan American Highway for the construction of the highway. There are two US entry points on the original route of the highway. Early travelers had accessed the Pan American Highway in the north through Washington and in the South through Texas. Assuming the gasoline cost of $3 per gallon cost, the total travel on the road would cost $2415.

The First part of the highway was completed in Mexico in the year 1950. Prudhoe Bay in Alaska is the starting point of the Pan American Highway if the direction is north south. The first 662 km follows the Dalton highway to Fairbanks. The first official section of the Pan-America Highway starts at the Mexican city of Nuevo Laredo. By 2007, only 54 miles remain to build.

World War II acted as a catalyst for the development of the highway. Land connections between the US and the Panama Canal zone became crucial for military security. In the 1950s, US Congress stressed the importance of highway for the social development of the region which could act as an important deterrent to the communist expansion in Latin America. By 1940, the United States had a strong presence in Central America especially in Panama. The US owned and operated both the Panama Canal and the Panama Railroad.

30.1 Financing

The financing for the highway from the Costa Rican border to Panama City was provided by the government of Panama. Financing to the extent of $15 million was provided by government of Panama and $5 million was provided by the US government. US financing of the project in the region was due to the fact that the highway would connect various military installations and bases which are located in the interior places surrounding the area. In 1940, the US Congress provisioned appropriate funds for completing a 1550-mile stretch of the Inter American Highway which involved governmental expenditure of $20 million over a period of 5 years. In 1941 a new Export Import Bank loan which totaled $4.6 million was contracted for the early completion of the Costa Rican link in the Pan American highway. Costa Rica was obliged to pay only $2.5 million of the construction costs. In the same year, Salvador received $1,250,000 Export-Import Bank loan to complete the Salvadorian section of the Pan American highway. In 1955, the world bank provided loan to Peru which amounted to $5,000,000 with an interest of 4.5% per annum. US EXIM bank was a major financier of the project in Mexico, El Salvador, Honduras, Nicaragua, Costa Rica and Ecuador.

30.2 Benefits of the Project

The project had huge strategic economic importance. The project resulted in political, cultural and economic exchanges between different countries in the Americas. The project also contributed in enhancing the tourist potential of the Americas region.

30.3 Risks Attributed to the Project

The project faced lots of challenges like lack of funding, war and governmental support. Environmental concerns were huge on account of the highway project. The increased colonization of forested areas was one of the serious negative impact on account of the project. The region along the project line witnessed entry of loggers and small farmers. In summary, the construction of the road segment promoted uncontrolled colonization and deforestation. The uncontrolled colonization of the region will lead to deforestation, disruption of fragile tropical forest equilibria, soil erosion and degradation. Protected forest areas will experience direct impact of colonization. Trafficking in wildlife is another threat on account of the project. The region also witnessed illegal arms shipment from Panama to Colombia. The highway project required a sophisticated system of controls—immigration, public and animal health, border security, customs, wildlife protection, control and enforcement of protected areas to address the challenges on account of the project.

Further Reading

https://www.ucf.edu/pegasus/pan-american-highway/
https://www.lonelyplanet.com/articles/the-pan-american-highway-the-ultimate-road-trip
https://www.britannica.com/topic/Pan-American-Highway
https://www.dangerousroads.org/north-america/usa/4638-pan-american-highway.html
https://www.worldconstructionnetwork.com/features/the-pan-american-highway-from-alaska-to-argentina/
https://www.encyclopedia.com/humanities/encyclopedias-almanacs-transcripts-and-maps/pan-american-highway
Koch, Wolfgang. "Beyond the End of the Road." Americas 40 (July-August 1988), 44-49
http://www.smithsonianeducation.org/scitech/impacto/graphic/panama/article_2.html
wiki-commons:Special:FilePath/PanAmericanHwy.png?width=300

http://www.fjcollazo.com/documents/PanAmerHiwyRpt.htm

Gruel, V. M. The opening of The Pan-American Highway. Tourism and stereotypes between Mexico and United States, http://www.scielo.org.mx/pdf/estfro/v18n36/2395-9134-estfro-18-36-00126-en.pdf

https://repository.law.miami.edu/cgi/viewcontent.cgi?referer=&httpsredir=1&article=1067&context=umialr

https://www.exim.gov/about/history-exim/historical-timeline/full-historical-timeline

Case 27: Port of Shanghai

The Port of Shanghai is situated in the middle of the eastern coastline of the Chinese mainland. It lies in the intersection of the T shaped water transport network which comprises the Yangtze River known as the golden waterway and coastal transport channels. The port of Shanghai is well connected with accessibility to the southern and northern part of China's coastal areas, oceans across the world, the Yangtze River basin, inland rivers of Jiangsu, Zhejiang and Anhui provinces and Taihu Lake basin. The Port of Shanghai has immense geographical significance with well-connected road and railway networks.

The Port of Shanghai was originally known as Shen or Hudu during the fifth and seventh centuries AD. It was given the official city status by the Yuan Dynasty in the year 1927. From the year 1684 onwards customs duty was collected for foreign trade. By the year 1735, the port became the most significant port in the Yangtze region. The rules and regulations for maritime policy was implemented in the Port of Shanghai through different treaties such as Treaty of Nanjng in 1842, Treaty of the Bogue in 1843 and the Sino American Treaty of Wangsai in 1844. In the year 1949, the port came under the control of China. During this period, the port witnessed large scale restructuring activities.

The container terminals of the Port of Shanghai are distributed in three port areas of Yangshan, Waigaogiao and Wusong. There are altogether 49 container berths, 176 container gantry cranes and 7.58 million square meters of container yard. The Port of Shanghai is the busiest port in the world in terms of cargo tonnage and consists of a deep sea port and river port. The port area is 3619.6 km^2. In 2019, the cargo throughput was 542.46 million tons. The port is located in the middle of the 18,000 km long Chinese coastline.

Shanghai International Port (Group), Ltd (SIPG), the operator of public terminals in the Port of Shanghai was established in the year 2003 through the restructuring of the Shanghai Port Authority. It was listed on the Shanghai Stock Exchange during the year 2006. SIPG is the biggest listed company in port operations in China. The major functions of SIPG include port handling operation, integrated logistics service, port related service and investment business. The industrial chain of port logistics comprises warehousing, storage, shipping and agent services. SIPG have 12 Shanghai branches, 3 internal organizations and 31 second tier subsidiaries. SIPG hold the responsibility for operation and management of the public terminals in the port. SIPG handles domestic, national and international cargo transportation. The operator is also responsible for maintaining, manufacturing and leasing containers as well as building, managing and operating port facilities. One of the main businesses of SIPG include terminal operation for bulk and general cargo. This business includes stevedoring of bulk cargo, general cargo and special cargo, roll on/roll off for wheeled cargo and cruise terminals. These operations are basically handled in the port areas of Luojing, Wusong, Longwu, Waigaoqiao and North Bund area.

In 2019, the container throughput of the Port of Shanghai amounted to 43.03 million in the year 2019. By 2019, the company held 142.177 billion yuan in total assets, 9.062 billion yuan in net profit. The market capitalization in A shares market amounted to 133.712 billion yuan. In 2019 the port handled 542.46 million tons of cargo.

The strategy of the port is focused on the development of the Yangshan Deepwater port to strengthen the 13th Five-year plan period. The strategic aim of the port includes the development in Yangtze river and develop the port logistics which feature vertical integration of port, shipping and cargo businesses. SIPG is also involved in the development of highly efficient cargo collection and distribution network with extensive access to both river waterways and maritime routes for building a port logistics hub.

There are two bulk cargo terminals and three break bulk terminals located in the Luojing, Wusong and Longwu areas. The cruise terminal covers an area of 160 km^2 and has an 850 m long quay wall and four large berths. This cruise terminal's annual handling capacity is 1 million passengers. The services offered include pilotage, tugboat, agency and port information technology service. The three main container port areas of the Port of Shanghai are Wusongkou, Waigaoqiao and Yangshan. The terminals are over 13 km long quay length. It consists of 43 berths and 156 quay cranes. The container port area of Wusongkou is managed by Shanghai Container Terminals Company (SCT) which is a joint venture of Hutchison Port Holdings Limited (HPH) and SIPG. The three container terminals operated by SCT include Zhanghuabang Terminal, Jungong Road Terminal and Baoshan Terminal. The services provided by the terminal company include container cleaning and management, storage and transport along with inland goods storage and electronic data interchange. Shanghai Pudong International Container Terminals, SIPG Zhendong Container Terminal Branch, Shanghai East Container Terminal Company and Shanghai Mingdong Container Terminals Ltd have the responsibility to operate the Waigaoqiao area. Shanghai Pudong operates in 500,000 m^2 area. This container port area has 147 container handling equipment and machinery, 36 RTG, 10 quay cranes, 73 container trucks and 11 forklifts. The major activities of Shanghai Mingdong include container handling, storage and transfer. The Yangshan Deepwater port is operated by the Shanghai Shengdong International Container Terminal company. This terminal has the capacity to handle containerized cargo of 2.2 million TEU. The terminals contribute towards the economic development of regions in the

Yangtze river valley and also act as distribution centers for the remote regions of the port.

The Port of Shanghai is the second busiest seaport in the world. The Port of Shanghai is a municipality within province status in the People's Republic of China. It is also one of the most popular tourist destination in the world.

31.1 Yangshan Deepwater Port

The port of Shanghai has witnessed over 40 years of development. Though Shanghai had made big progress in the field of port infrastructure, the container handling capacity was limited. On account of demand of more ports and terminals, the construction work on the new port project Yangshan island was initiated in the year 2002. The Yangshan Island is approximately 30 km from Shanghai. Shanghai and Yangshan Island was connected to Shanghai through 32.5 km bridge built on the sea. The bridge can handle six lines at a design driving speed of 80 km/h. It took 35 months to complete the construction of the bridge. To avoid block in the shipping line, a navigation hole of approximately 40 m from the water surface was constructed in the middle of bridge. Ships with over 10,000 tons can pass through the hole safely. There are two other holes to facilitate the passage of ship with size of 1000 tons and 500 tons. Bigger ships need to make a detour trip to travel through this area. A wind energy plant was also setup on the bridge to provide 100,000 kW/h. electricity power.

The Shanghai Deepwater project consisted of three parts-the Yangshan Deepwater port, the Donghai Bridge and the Luchao New Harbor city. The project had strong backing of the central government of the People's Republic of China.

In order to increase the capability of the marine shipping traffic, the port was designed to accommodate 200,000 tones tankers and 10,000 TEU container ships.

Yangshan Deepwater port was developed in four phases due to insufficient water depth at the port. The Deepwater port is located 30 km from the mainland. The first phase of the terminal was completed in the year 2005 with an investment of $7.5 billion. The terminal has a water depth of 16 m and five berths. The second terminal was completed in the year 2006 with investments of $7 billion. The second terminal has the capacity to handle 2.1 million TEU and uses four berths. The phase III of the terminal began operations in the year 2008. The phase IV is the world's largest and advanced automated container terminal and began operations in the year 2017. This terminal handled 2 million TEU in its first year of operation.

The total investment for the project amounted to ¥70 billion Chinese Yuan. The ports also had 50 deep water berths for containerships with annual loading capacity of 15 million TEU. There were provisions for oil and gas tanker ship loading zone.

The master plan envisaged the completion of the project by the year 2020. The man made area increased by 18 square kilometers and deep water coastal line increased by 22 km. The project made the port the biggest and busiest terminal in the world.

31.1.1 Financing of the Project

The budget for the first phase was estimated to be 14.31 billion RMB (1.73 billion USD). The port was developed by the Shanghai Tongsheng Investment (Group) which is jointly owned by the Shanghai International Group Co Ltd, the Shanghai Port Administration and the Shanghai State Owned Assets Operation co. A consortium of five domestic banks namely China Construction Bank, the State Development Bank, Bank of China, the Industrial and Commercial Bank of China and the Shanghai Pudong Development Bank provided 7.5 billion RMB in loans for the first phase construction to the Shanghai Tongsheng Investment Group. Another consortium consisting of the above five banks and five other lending institutions provided 17 billion RMB (2.06 billion USD) credit line for the port construction till the year 2020.

31.1.2 Project Challenges

Combining and extending the islands for the deep water project through land reclamation was a huge challenge for the project. According to world bank report, the contribution by the port to the environmental problems of Shanghai are very small in relation to those of industry, power and households. The port contributes marginally to this pollution, mainly through accidental oil spills and spillage of coal and other bulk cargo (fertilizer); these are most likely to occur during mid-stream cargo operations.

31.1.3 Future Milestones

Luchao Harbour city was planned as 1 of the 11 satellite towns in the new phase of Shanghai urban planning. The Harbour city is situated in the south east corner of Nanhui district which is about 30 km away from the island Yangshan port and 55 km from downtown Shanghai. The city is designed as an ecological and coastal city with a maritime culture. In future the handling capacity of the Port of Shanghai is expected to reach 40 million standard containers which would make up to one tenth of world capacity and higher than the capacity of nine major ports in US combined.

Further Reading

https://en.portshanghai.com.cn/Strategy.jhtml
https://en.portshanghai.com.cn/TeminalHanding/index.jhtml
https://en.portshanghai.com.cn/AboutUs/480.jhtml
https://www.ship-technology.com/projects/portofshnaghai/

Further Reading

https://journals.library.mun.ca/ojs/index.php/prototype/article/view/429
Jing Xu, Yangshan Island Deep-Water Port Project, Shanghai, China, Journal of Undergraduate Engineering Research and Scholarship, Vol 1 2013, https://journals.library.mun.ca/ojs/index.php/prototype/article/view/429
https://documents1.worldbank.org/curated/en/345671468018595391/pdf/multi-page.pdf
https://www.sinoptic.ch/shanghaiflash/texts/pdf/200303_Shanghai.Flash.pdf

Case 28: Sakhalin Project–II

Sakhalin I project consisted of the development of the Odoptu oil and gas field and the Chayvo gas field which was developed during the period 1977–1979. Sakhalin II involved the development of the Piltun Astokhskoye and Lunskoye oil and gas fields.

Sakhalin II is termed as one of the largest integrated export oriented oil and gas projects in the world. It is also the first offshore gas project of Russia. The project is operated by the Sakhalin Energy Investment Company Ltd. The project is owned by Gazprom, Shell, Mitsui and Mitsubishi. The infrastructure of the project includes three offshore platforms, an onshore processing facility, 300 km of offshore pipelines, 1600 km of onshore pipelines, oil export terminal and liquefied natural gas (LNG) plant. It is oil and integrated LNG. By 2017, the LNG capacity was 11.49 million tons. Foreign companies hold shares in Sakhalin Energy through their subsidiaries. The ownership structure consisted of 27.5% (minus one share) by Shell, 50% (plus one share) owned by Gazprom, 12.5% owned by Mitsui and 10% owned by Mitsubishi.

Sakhalin II has been one of the most technically complex projects undertaken in the global oil and gas industry. For the development of the two oil fields, large scale infrastructure for the extraction, transportation, processing and marketing of hydrocarbons were put in place. These infrastructures consisted of three fixed offshore platforms, offshore and onshore pipeline systems, an onshore processing facility, two booster stations, an oil export terminal with a tanker loading unit, a liquefied natural gas (LNG) plant with an LNG jetty, and gas transfer terminals.

Sakhalin II is Russia's first liquefied natural gas plant. Sakhalin II was the result of the visualization of the state policy on the gas industry development for an integrated gas production, transportation and supply system in Eastern Siberia and the Far East. The project included the development of the Piltun—Astokhskoye and Lunskoye oil and gas fields in the sea of Okhotsk under the production sharing agreement. The Trans-Sakhalin pipeline system carries extracted oil and gas via an onshore processing facility to the Prigorodnoye production complex which consists of an LNG plant and an oil export terminal. The Molikpaq (Piltun-Astokhakaya-A) platform is the first offshore oil production platform in Russia. During the period 1999–2008, the platform was the core facility of the Vityaz production complex. The function of the production complex included oil drilling, production and offloading along with support and exploration activities. The production of oil was carried out during ice free periods which was for approximately 6 months per year. Oil is transferred from the Trans-Sakhalin pipeline system to the oil export terminal of the Prigorodnoye production complex through the Molikpaq platform. The largest platform within the Sakhalin II project is the Piltun Astokhskaya B platform. The platform is operational under severe climatic conditions. The Trans Sakhalin pipeline system's function involve delivery of hydrocarbons to the LNG plant and oil export terminal of the Prigorodnoye complex.

The Lunskaya A (LUN-A) platform is the first offshore gas production platform in Russia which contributes towards major gas production in Russia. The platform facilitates operations such as oil, condensate and gas separation which includes gas treatment for transportation to the LNG plant. The LNG plant comprises two production trains and general service facilities. The production trains are utilized for gas treatment and liquefaction. The design capacity of the plant is 9.6 million tons of LNG per year.

32.1 Environmental Safety

The project has implemented engineering solutions to ensure structural safety. The offshore platforms were designed to resist loads caused by earthquakes. Structural strength reserve is also provided at the LNG plant. Cradle mechanism involving sliding pendulum are structured to ensure safe operation of offshore platforms. Pioneering technologies have been used in the Sakhalin project for addressing the environmental concerns. Table 32.1 highlights the major milestones of the project.

Sakhalin II hold many records. The offshore oil platform Molikpaq was the first to be installed in the Russian region. The two platforms Piltun Astokhkoye-B (PA-B) and Lunskoye A (LUN-A) are the first of their type to be installed. The LNG plant is the first plant of its type in Russia. Approximately 4% of the world's LNG supply is accounted by Sakhalin II. The main customers for oil and LNG exports are Japan, South Korea and China. The gas from Sakhalin II are sold under long term contracts to customers in Asia Pacific and North America. The stakeholders including Gazprom and Shell have entered into mutual interest contract whose scope lies for growth opportunities, purchase of third party gas by Sakhalin Energy and acquisition of exploration blocks in the area for enhancing the prospects for Sakhalin II project.

The construction work of the project was completed during the year 2009 and the LNG plant was officially inaugurated in 2009. Over 25,000 people were engaged for the construction work of the project. Sakhalin II was Russia's first ice class offshore oil and gas platform. This project involved the use of first foreign investment for the implementation of large scale project in Russia.

Table 32.1 Project pipeline

Time period	Milestone
April 1994	Establishment of Sakhalin Energy
June 1994	Production Sharing Agreement between Sakhalin Energy, the Government of Russian Federation and Administration of Sakhalin Region signed to develop the Piltun-Astokhskoye and Lunskoye oil and gas fields.
1996	First Phase of Project launched
1999	Production of oil from the Piltun Astokhskoye field initiated
2003	Phase II initiated for the development of Piltun-Astokhskoye and Lunskoye fields
2007	Gazprom becomes partner for the Sakhalin II project
2009	The first Russian LNG plant was commissioned in Sakhalin. The production capacity was 9.6 million tons of LNG per year.
2015	Gazprom and Shell sign the memorandum to construct the third production train of the LNG plant for the Sakhalin II project.

Source: https://www.gazprom.com

By the end of the year 2020, the PA-B platform had 20 production wells, 8 water injection wells, and 2 cutting re-injection wells. The PA-B platform has produced more than 141 million bbl. of oil since the commencement of oil field development.

32.2 Risks and Challenges of the Project

The project exists in a subarctic environment which is ecologically and socially sensitive. The 800 km pipelines which carries oil and gas from the fields in the north of the island to ice free export terminal passes through earthquake zones and crosses over 1000 watercourses which are ecologically sensitive.

As a result of environmental and social initiatives, Sakhalin II project implemented the recommendations of the scientific review panel set by the International Union for Conservation of Nature and rerouted the offshore pipelines to minimize the risks of oil and gas developments in Whale habitats. Sakhalin Energy has been proactively educating the community about the rules of behavior in the vicinity of the pipeline system.

32.3 Economic and Social Significance of the Project

Sakhalin II laid the foundation for Russia to emerge as a leading energy exporter to the energy markets of the Asia Pacific region. The project also contributed towards substantial social investment for local community development. The development agenda covered safety, education, healthcare, protection of environment in terms of biodiversity. The share of Sakhalin LNG in the year 2020 was approximately 3.3% of global demand and 4.6% of the demand in the Asia Pacific region. By April 2020, the Molikpaq platform have produced 300 million bbl. of oil since the oil production started in the Astokh area of the Piltun Astokhskoye field in the year 1999. The PA-A platform has produced over 308 million bbl. of oil.

The production sharing agreement stipulates that the state retain the ownership rights to the field and grants the investor the exclusive right to develop the mineral resource. In 2020, Sakhalin Energy allocated US$2.5 billion to the Russian Federation as royalties.

32.4 Structuring of the Project

In 1994, Sakhalin Energy signed the production sharing agreement for the development of Piltun Askokhskoye and Lunskoye Oil and gas fields with the Russian Federation government and Sakhalin Oblast Administration. This agreement termed Sakhalin-II PSA defined the terms and conditions for the exploration, development, production, processing and transportation of hydrocarbons. This agreement was the first production sharing agreement undertaken in Russia. The agreement Sakhalin II PSA stipulated the retention of the sovereign right of ownership of the oil and gas fields to Russia and Sakhalin Energy was required to invest the funds for exploration and development activities. The Russian government have the right to audit the investor's expenses. The Sakhalin II PSA stipulated a specific tax regime for project development. The production sharing under the Sakhalin II project was initiated in the year 2012. Approximately 60% of LNG produced by Sakhalin II project is supplied to Japan. In the year 2020, the Sakhalin II project achieved performance of 178.6 standard LNG shipments.

Further Reading

https://www.gazprom.com/projects/sakhalin2/
https://www.shell.com/about-us/major-projects/sakhalin/sakhalin-an-overview.html
http://www.sakhalinenergy.ru/en/company/psa/
Sakhalin Sustainable Development Report GRI Report 2020.

Case 29: Ichthys LNG Project

This project is one of the most significant oil and gas project in the world. It is unique in the sense that it covers the whole chain of development and production involving subsea, offshore, pipeline and onshore. The project is structured as a joint venture between INPEX group companies (the Operator), the major partner Total Energies and the Australian subsidiaries of CPC Corporation Taiwan, Tokyo Gas, Osaka Gas, Kansai Electric Power, JERA and Toho Gas. The Ichthys Field is estimated to have reserves of 12 trillion cubic feet of gas and 500 million barrels of condensate. The project is located about 220 km offshore Western Australia and 820 km south west of Darwin. The Ichthys field is spread over 800 square kilometers in water with average depth of 250 m. The gas and condensate from the Ichthys field are exported to onshore facilities in Darwin through an 890 km pipeline. The condensate is shipped to the global markets through a floating production, storage and offloading system which is permanently located near the Ichthys field in the browse basin. Ichthys project is one of the most complex liquefied natural gas projects in the world with the longest subsea pipeline in the Southern Hemisphere. It is the second largest global LNG player in the private sector. The project covers the entire LNG production chain with deep offshore production facilities, two floating production units, gas pipeline and liquefaction plant.

In the offshore, the gas and condensate are extracted from the Ichthys field from the Browse Basin which is located 200 km off the northern coast of Western Australia. The semi-submersible platform (central processing facility) where gas and liquids are separated is the largest in the world which weighs 120,000 metric tons. The condensate is transferred to the production storage and offloading unit (FPSO) where it is processed, stored and exported to different markets. The gas pipeline which covers 882 km of sea and 8 km of land transports the gas to the liquefaction plant. In onshore the Bladin Point plant is equipped with liquefaction trains with annual capacity of 8.9 million metric tons. It is estimated that there are 3 billion barrels of oil equivalent in the Ichthys field reserves.

The production for the project was commenced in July 2018. The project was designed with the capacity to produce 8.9 million tons of LNG and 1.65 million tons

Table 33.1 Ownership stakes

Company	Stakes in percentage
INPEX	66.245
TOTAL	26
CPC	2.625
Tokyo Gas	1.575
Osaka Gas	1.2
Kansai Electric	1.2
JERA	0.735
Toho Gas	0.42

Source: https://www.jera.co.jp/english/business/projects/ichthys

of LPG per annum. It was expected to produce more than 100,000 barrels of condensate per day during peak production time.

It is the first time that a major Japanese company (INPEX) had undertaken an ambitious project. The project became a national priority for Japan which is the world's largest importer of LNG. In the year 2012, Chubu Electric Power Company (Chubu) through its Australian subsidiaries acquired 0.735% participating interest in the exploration and development of the Ichthys gas condensate. Shares were also acquired in the liquefaction company Ichthys LNG Pty in 2012. A purchasing contract for 1.54 million tons of LNG per year over 15 years also became operational. The liquefaction plant is located in Darwin. The gas and condensate field is located offshore the northern coast of Western Australia. The production capacity of the condensate is approximately 100,000 barrels per day during peak period. Table 33.1 highlights the ownership stakes for the project company.

Inpex owns approximately 66% of Ichthys and Total owns 26% of the project. The rest of the ownership is shared by five Japanese and one Taiwanese energy utility company. The initial cost of the project was assumed to be US$34 billion and the production was expected to start in the year 2017. The cost of the Ichthys LNG project escalated to US$45 billion. The junior partner sold 4% interest in Darwin based project to Inpex for US$1.6 billion in the year 2018.

The life of Ichthys project is expected to be 40 years and expected to produce 8.9 million tons of LNG and 1.6 million tons of LPG. The liquefaction plant located onshore is the first plant in the world which uses combined cycle technology.

33.1 Risks Involved for the Project

The project faced major cost overruns and delays during the construction phase. The production process was delayed as two huge offshore vessels which Inpex had constructed in Korea didn't arrive on the location of Kimberley coast on time. Delays were experienced in commissioning of the vessels. The oil and gas safety regulator NOPSEMA had to intervene due to electrical work issues. Cost escalation also resulted due to capital expenditures. The project was hit with multiple delays and a major industrial accident. The maintenance of equipment for an operational life of more than 40 years is an infrastructural challenge. The project faces the challenge of survival of offshore climate in Browse basin which is known for its cyclones.

33.2 Economic Impact

The demand for gas in Asian markets was expected to be 6% on average. Asian region became the fastest expanding market by the year 2020. It is the biggest import region accounting for over 70% of consumption. The project has made immense contribution towards the development of Australian economy. A comprehensive industry participation plan is in place to boost the use of local labor and skill training across the northern territory and Australian region. About 250 sub contracts were awarded by the lead onshore contractor and its Tier 1 contractors to firms based in Northern territory. The industry plan also encourages Aboriginal and Torres Strait Islander (ATS) business participation in the project. Icththys LNG is also involved in developing training and education institutes.

33.3 Contractual Agreements

With respect to the project, sales and purchase agreements were in place with shipments becoming operational in the year 2017. The project's production over the 15-year period were already been sold to buyers in Japan and Taiwan. Approximately 70% of contracted Ichthys gas will be supplied to Japanese utilities. INPEX and Total affiliate would consume 1.8 metric MMTpy of LNG.

33.4 Health Safety and Environment Measures

The joint venture participants have set a goal of zero harm to the workforce and environment. The Ichthys project have a charter among the contractors to promote safety measures. On the onshore fabrication yards, the project has recorded 18 MM worker hours without lost time injury. The scientific environmental program of the project monitors and records the changes in dredging and marine construction activities. The Ichthys project has allocated AU$92 million towards environmental benefits package for the protection and management of the marine and terrestrial environment. The joint venture participants had donated AU$3 million to Charles Darwin University to accelerate the development of North Australian Center for Oil and Gas.

Further Reading

https://www.inpex.com.au/projects/ichthys-lng/
https://www.jera.co.jp/english/business/projects/ichthys
https://thewest.com.au/business/energy/inpexs-ichthys-lng-cost-blows-out-another-us5-billion-ng-b881050751z
https://totalenergies.com/energy-expertise/projects/oil-gas/lng/ichthys-a-bold-lng-project-off-the-coast-of-australia
http://www.gasprocessingnews.com/features/201406/ichthys-lng-combines-three-mega-projects-in-one.aspx

Case 30: Kashagan Oil Field Development Project

In 1997, a consortium of major international oil firms and Kazakh State signed a 40-year agreement North Caspian Production Sharing Agreement which was designed to govern the project and develop the oil field. The Kashagan oil field is the first major offshore oil and gas development project in Kazakhstan which covers three fields of Kashagan, Kairan and Akoty. Kashagan Phase I commenced production in the year 2016. The Kashagan Field has one of the largest oil discoveries with approximately 9–13 billion barrels of recoverable oil. This shallow water oil field lies approximately 80 km offshore from the city of Atyrau in 3–4 m of water. The Republic of Kazakhstan was formerly part of the Soviet Union and became an independent country in the year 1991. The Kazak oil field covered an area of 75 km by 45 km and contained both oil and gas.

The operator of the project is North Caspian Operating Company NV (NCOC). It was subsequently named as Agip Kazakhstan North Caspian Operating Company. The project reached production levels of over 200,000 barrels per day by mid-2017. The estimated cost of Kashagan Phase 1 was approximately US$ 55 billion. On account of technical complexity, the North Caspian project would be developed in phases.

The operator North Caspian Operating company (NCOC) is a joint venture between state owned KazMunai Gas, Shell, Total, Eni, Exxon Mobil, CNPC and Inpex. NCOC is responsible for the North Caspian Sea Production Sharing Agreement. Table 34.1 shows the ownership stakes for the project company.

KMG was 100% owned by the Kazakh state. The Kashagan oil field was discovered during the year 2000 and is located in water depths between 3 and 4 m. In 2001, the drilling of Kashagan West 1 and Kashagan East 2 took place. During the period 2002–2003, smaller oil fields Kalamkas Sea, Kairan, Aktoty and Kashagan were also discovered in the NCSPA license block. With 75 km long and 45 km wide, the Kashagan water field which covers 2678 km square in the Caspian Sea is stated to be one of the world's biggest oil discoveries during the past 50 years. The highly pressurized Kashagan reservoir located 4.2 km beneath the seabed is

Table 34.1 Ownership stake in the joint venture

Companies	Equity ownership (%)
KazMunai Gas (KMG)	16.9
Shell	16.8
Total	16.8
Eni	16.8
Exxon Mobil	16.8
CNPC	8.3
Inpex	7.6

estimated to contain more than 35 billion barrels of oil of which 13 billion barrels are recoverable.

The work on the construction of D Island which is the largest among all artificial islands built on the Kashagan field was started in the year 2002 and the drilling activities were initiated during the year 2006. The Kazakhstan government had approved the Kashagan development plan in the year 2004. The onshore and offshore installation works were completed during the period 2006–2008. The offshore hook up works were completed in 2010 and the gas injection modules were installed on the D Island during the year 2012. The Kashagan oil and gas field became operational in the year 2016.

The D Island serves as the offshore processing and production hub for the field. Approximately half of the gas produced is reinjected into the reservoir while the remaining gas and crude oil are piped onshore to the Bolashak plant for final processing. Kashagan phase I involved a total pipeline network of 510 km. The offshore field is to be developed in subsequent phases as part of the full field development program which would raise the output to 1.5 million barrels of oil a day. Kashagan Phase I includes 40 wells which consists of 20 wells which are operated from A to D Islands and the rest from the EPC islands. The bulk of crude oil which are processed at the Bolashak plant are transferred into the Caspian Pipeline Consortium (CPC) pipeline system which functions as the main export network for the Kazakhi crude. The crude is carried from the Tengiz onshore oil field to the Novorossiisk port on Russian Black sea. The sour gas is purified from hydrogen sulphide and the resultant sweet gas is used for onshore and offshore power generation. The rest of gas produced is marketed as sales gas via the Kaz Trans Gas pipeline. The Sulphur produced at the oil field is exported by rail through a dedicated rail loading facility at Eskene West.

The Kashagan phase I development achieved 180,000 bopd production capacity in early-2017. By 2019 the phase I design capacity was further increased to 380,000 bopd. By August 2019, the Phase I of the field have produced a cumulative total of 30 million tons of crude oil, more than 8.44 billion cubic meters (bcm) of gas, and 1.75 million tons (Mt) of Sulphur.

NCOC have plans to increase the output to 500,000 bopd by 2027. The full development plant involves drilling of 35 drilling centers, 2 offshore processing hubs, 3 offshore gas plants, large scale onshore processing facility with multiple oil trains and gas sweetening plants of approximately 1000 km of infield pipelines, power cables and 500 km of trunk lines.

34.1 Main Contractors

The contract for management of onshore construction works was awarded to North Caspian Constructors (NCC)—a joint venture of Fluor, Tekfen Construction and Gama Group in year 2005.

During the year 2015, ERSAI Caspian contractor, the subsidiary of Saipem was awarded $1.8 billion contract for the construction of two 95 km pipeline which connected the D island of the Kashagan field with Karabatan onshore plant. Saipem and Aker Solutions were awarded $2.6 billion contract for the installation and commissioning offshore production facilities during the year 2009. KBR provided project management services for the Phase I of the project and also facilitated the conceptual design for Phase II and Phase III. McDermont provided FEED services for the Kashagan full field development plan. Worley Parsons along with CB&I and Aker Solutions was awarded an updated FEED services contract for phase II development during the year 2010. Bateman Litwin was awarded the EPC contract for the construction of the 270 MW power station and utilities plant at Eskene West. The contract for the construction of rock islands was awarded to Boskalis-Archirodon joint venture in year 2003. ENKA along with its Kazakh partner MSS was involved for the offshore civil construction works. Middle East based Consolidated Contractors Company (CCC) was also involved in construction activities. Rosetti Marino was entrusted with the work to carry out fabrication, testing and hook up works for the processing hub at Island D. Renco was responsible for design, delivery and commissioning of local equipment on EPC2 and EPC3 islands. Kitek construction was engaged for the installation, maintenance and pre commissioning of power distribution systems. The contract for the construction of construction of oil and gas export pipelines for the project was awarded to Kaz Stroy Service and Punj Lloyd. KTR WG Turbine services which was a joint venture between Wood Group and KazTurbo Remont (KTR) was awarded long term contract to provide maintenance services for the turbines and compressors of the project. GE, Siemens and Rolls Royce provided the turbines and compressors for the project.

34.2 Production Sharing Agreement (PSA)

Typically, there were four major provisions envisaged in the production sharing agreement between the consortium of oil firms and the state. The agreement stipulated that IOC would pay a royalty to the state based on gross production. After net royalty deductions, the oil firms were entitled to receive a pre-determined share of production to recover the capital expenditure and operating costs which is known as cost of oil. The remaining portion of profit oil was shared between the host government and the IOCs at predetermined rate. The IOCs had to pay the income tax on its share of profit oil. The Caspian agreement envisaged equity share in the project for the government subsidiary KasMunai Gas instead of royalty. According to the agreement, the IOCs would initially receive 80% of the crude output to cover the costs for exploration, development and operations and then the percentage to fall to 55% after payback was achieved. The remaining output termed profit oil would be divided using weighting factors such as project's R factor, cumulative output and internal rate of return. In the initial phase, the share of profit oil for the consortium of oil firms were 90% and would decline to 10% on the basis of actual performance. The PSA also contained provisions for investor protection and dispute redressals. The host government was entitled to profit income tax in the range of 30–60% based on project's realized IRR.

34.3 Risks and Challenges

The safety engineering and logistics challenges in a harsh offshore environment makes Kashagan project one of the largest and most complex industrial projects in the world. The initial production had to be suspended due to gas leakage and defects in onshore section of the gas pipeline. It is estimated that upstream investment in the Caspian region is expected to fall by 2030. The commercialization of the project faces challenges due to deep water gas discovery in Azerbaijan area. Another challenge is in terms of generation of economic returns as FDI-based brownfield and green field projects generally generate before tax IRR of less than 20%. The project faces challenges in selling Caspian oil to core export destination such as European Union.

The project faced a number of environmental and social risks. Project construction and subsequent potential accidents could endanger the pristine coastline and the biodiversity of the Caspian region which consist of diverse flora and fauna with 60% of species unique to the Caspian Sea. The Caspian Sea is also major migratory route for birds flying from Asia to Siberia. Preservation of environment is a key challenge while developing the oil and gas field in this region. The field was rich in toxic hydrogen sulphide and oil trapped in small compartments made the project extremely challenging.

The development of the Kashagan field represented a unique combination of technical complexity and supply chain coordination in extreme climatic environment where temperatures can drop below $-30\ °C$ in winter and rise to $+40\ °C$ in summer. This part of Caspian freezes for nearly 5 months a year. Drifting ice and ice souring on the seabed requires adoption of innovative technical solutions for construction, production and logistics of oil field. The Kashagan reservoir is located at a depth of 4200 m below the sea bed and is highly pressurized. The light crude oil extracted from the Kashagan oil field has a high sour gas consisting of hydrogen sulphide and carbon dioxide. This poses challenging operating environment for the project in terms of safety.

Table 34.2 Project milestones

Time period	Milestones
December 1993	North Caspian Sea Production Sharing Agreement (NCSPSA) conducts one of the largest 2D seismic surveys in oil industry.
November 1997	Republic of Kazakhstan and consortium of major global oil and gas firms enters into a legal framework for the largest FDI in the history of Kazakhstan.
2017	20th anniversary of the signing of the NCSPSA.

There were political and geographic challenges of exporting crude from Kazakh to western markets. Being a green field project, the project faced two types of completion risks—the scope for schedule delays and significant cost overruns. The project also faced operating risks such as reserve risk. There were uncertainty regarding the kind of oil and the amount of oil contained in the reserves. There were also chances of force majeure risks. The project also faced throughput risk and market risks due to fluctuating oil prices. The project may also face sovereign risks in the form of creeping or expropriation risks. Table 34.2 lists the major milestones for the project.

Further Reading

https://www.nsenergybusiness.com/projects/kashagan-oil-field-development/
https://jpt.spe.org/caspian-oil-and-gas-leverages-strengths-to-survive-in-a-low-carbon-world
https://www.offshore-mag.com/regional-reports/middle-east/article/14205990/caspian-sea-megaprojects-facing-uncertain-future
https://www.ncoc.kz/en/ncoc/about
www.barrows.com
Benjamin Esty, Florain Bitsch, The Kashagan Production Sharing Agreement (PSA) 9-213-082, Harvard Business School Case Study, September 2013.

Case 31: Barzan Gas Project

Barzan gas project is a joint venture between Qatar gas and Exxon Mobil. The project is valued at $10.4 billion. RasGas is the project manager and responsible for operating the plant. The project work was initiated in the year 2011. The joint venture agreement and development and fiscal agreement by the two joint venture partners were signed during January 2011. The project consists of total of six trains. In the first phase, the project produced 1.7 billion cubic feet a day (bcfpd) of pure natural gas.

During the construction period, the project employed over 20,000 people. The project site covered over 3 square kilometers. The Barzan LNG plant is located in the North field in Ras Laffan Industrial city which is about 80 km north east of Doha city. The plant plays a vital role by providing natural gas for infrastructural development such as power plants, desalination plants, New Doha Airport and Sea port. The project is envisaged in the Qatar National Vision 2030.

The Barzan gas project was designed to be developed in three phases. The total capacity was 6.2 bcf per day of natural gas. The first phase had a capacity of 1.7 bcf per day of natural gas. The phases two and three had a capacity of 2 bcf per day and 2.5 bcf per day of natural gas respectively.

The project would extract gas from the Qatar's North Field which is estimated to hold recoverable reserves of 900 trillion cubic feet and represent approximately 10% of the world's known gas reserves.

The onshore facilities at the project site consists of a gas processing unit, sulphur recovery unit to remove impurities from the natural gas and natural gas liquids recovery unit. This NGL recovery unit produces methane, ethane, propane, butane and condensate. The ethane produced is used as a feedstock for petrochemical industries. The offshore site is equipped with three offshore wellhead platforms, subsea pipelines which extends 300 km and subsea cables which stretches 100 km. The platform was fabricated at Hyundai Heavy Industries site at Ulsan, Korea.

Exxon Mobil provided the project management and technical expertise for the project by providing key personnel for the project. Exxon Mobil had also licensed its proprietary Flexsorb SE technology to achieve 99.4% sulfur recovery in Qatar.

35.1 Financing the Project

The project was financed through 30% equity and 70% syndicated loan from banks and credit export agencies. The financing deal consisted of a $3.34 billion commercial bank loan with the involvement of Skadden, Arps, Slate, Meagher & Florm LLP as counsel, $850 million Islamic finance, $2.55 billion financing facility from export credit agency (ECA). The ECA financing was arranged by banks and guarantees were provided by Japan, Korea and Italy. Allen & Overy were the advisors for the ECA deal. Royal Bank of Scotland was the financial advisor for the deal. The legal advisor for the sponsors was White & Case.

35.2 Contractors for the Project

Chiyoda Corporation was responsible for the Front End Engineering Design (FEED) and execution planning for the project. The contract for thermal insulation services valued at $25 million was awarded to Cape. Air energi provided the consultancy services for the project. The engineering, procurement and construction (EPC) contract for development onshore was awarded to Japan Gas Company. The offshore development and pipeline installation works were done by Hyundai Heavy Industries. The offshore development cost amounted to $900 million.

35.3 Project Structuring

Qatar gas and Exxon Mobil signed the memorandum of understanding for the project in the year 2007. Following this, the environmental, social economic and health impact assessment (ESHIA) for the project was also completed. Further the joint venture agreement (JVA) and the fiscal agreement (DFA) were signed between the two companies in the year 2011. The Barzan project is owned by the local Barzan Gas Company. The ownership structure consists of 93 per by Qatar Petroleum and 7% by Exxon Mobil. The project is managed and operated by local Ras Gas company (RasGas) which is one of the world's leading producers of liquefied natural gas (LNG). RasGas is 70% owned by Qatar Petroleum and 30% owned by ExxonMobil RasGas.

The onshore facilities are constructed in two phases. The two processing trains are estimated to produce 1.4 billion standard cubic feet of sales gas per day (Bscfd). The RasGas's overall production capacity would be increased to 11 Bscfd thereby making the project one of the world's biggest single gas processors. The project aims to contribute towards Qatar National Vision 2030 which aims for overall industrial development of Qatar.

Barzan onshore project will produce about 22,000 barrels per day (bpd) of field condensate, 6000 bpd of plant condensate, 34,000 bpd of ethane, and 10,500 bpd of propane and 7500 bpd of butane.

The offshore segment of the project consists of installation of three wellhead platforms, one living quarters platform, 300 km of subsea pipelines and 100 km of subsea cables to transfer gas to new gas processing plant at Ras Laffan Industrial city and 30 drilling wells.

35.4 Risks and Challenges

Gas pipeline leakage can cause environmental damage. The launch of Barzan project was repeatedly delayed. There was a gas leakage in one of the project's upstream pipelines. In 2015, the project was delayed due to technical challenges.

35.5 Economic Contribution of the Project

The project aims to contribute towards the economic development of Qatar. The project is a part of the $200 billion infrastructure upgrade. The population growth has driven up demand for electricity. To meet the electricity demand, Qatar have focused on natural gas production through the offshore Barzan gas project. The production output from Barzan is basically used for target achievements in power and water sector. The natural gas supplied from Barzan project will be a reliable source of energy for the economic development of Qatar. During the peak period more than 30,000 people worked on the project. Qatar is the world's leading exporter of liquefied natural gas and holds the third largest gas reserves in the world which is estimated at 16% of the global reserves. Gas sector accounts for two thirds of Qatar GDP and provide 80% of export earnings. Table 35.1 highlights the major milestones for the project.

Table 35.1 Project timelines

Period	Milestones
2010	Project development announcement
Jan 2011	The offshore facilities development deal is awarded to Hyundai Heavy Industry valued at $90 million.
Jan 2011	Onshore gas processing facilities awarded to JGC
Dec 2011	Financial settlement made with $3.2 billion equity and $7.2 billion debt which included $850 financing from Islamic banks
2015	Main contract completion

Source: MEED

Further Reading

https://www.hydrocarbons-technology.com/projects/barzan-gas-project-ras-laffan-qatar/
https://www.offshore-technology.com/projects/barzan-gas-project-north-field/
http://www.gasprocessingnews.com/news/gas-leak-delays-start-up-of-qatars-barzan-gas-project.aspx
https://www.meed.com/barzan-gas-project/
William Bill, Essa Matar, Al Kuwari, Barzan Gas Project: Clean Source of Energy Supporting Qatar, International Petroleum Technology Conference, Jan 19-22 2014, Doha Qatar.
https://www.oceanteam.eu/wp-content/uploads/2021/03/25_OTG_BarzanOnShoreProject.pdf
https://www.exxonmobil.com.qa/en-QA/Energy-and-environment/Energy-resources/Natural-gas/Development-of-domestic-gas

Case 32: Australian Japan Cable

During September 1999, Telstra, Teleglobe and Japan Telecom entered into a Memorandum of Understanding to develop the Australian Japan Network project. This submarine cable system was valued at $520 million.

During 1999 three cables dominated the Australian traffic market. SEA-ME-WE-3 offered access to United States from the west coast of Australia via Japan or China. PacRim East and PacRim West offered access to United States from Australian East coast.

The Australian Japan Cable Network (AJCN) is a subsea cable system which offers connectivity and bandwidth options with diverse landings in Australia, Guam and Japan. The AJCN was established in the year 2000 with an expected design life of 25 years. The network was established as a private cable company to design, construct, market and operate the 12,700 km submarine fibre optic cable network from Sydney, Australia to Japan via Guam. The optical fibre submarine cable offers connectivity from Australia to Japan via Guam. This project was completed under budget and on time. The AJC network was designed as an optical fibre ring to provide cable resilience and cost effectiveness. The safe sections of the route between Sydney and Guam and between Guam and Japan was designed using a single sheath.

In deep water of more than 4000 m, the fibers are laid in a single sheath. In shallow water landing points, a branching unit is used to separate the fibers and are then diverted to separate cable stations. In the event of an outrage involving shallow water branches, the traffic can be routed via the in country connection and other shallow water branch. The network uses SDH MSP ring technology to minimize cable failure due to fishing activities. The AJCN had an initial design capacity of 320 Gbit/s. The route for AJCN via Guam was chosen to provide safe deep water path. The selection of the landing station sites was chosen to provide optimum connectivity between AJCN and existing and future submarine cable systems. The AJCN was upgraded with 40G technology in the mid-2012 and 100G technology during the period 2013–2014. AJCN was upgraded with 5000 Gbit/s capacity during the year 2018. The design capacity of AJCN is 10,000 Gbit/s approximately with coherent transmission technology.

AJC provides services for Carrier and ISP segments in terms of providing quality high speed bandwidth to Tier 1 domestic and international carriers and to Tier 2 and ISP providers. AJC also provides services to mobile service providers and content/search engine providers. It provides direct route between Japan and Australia via Guam and alternate routes to USA, Asia and Europe via onward connectivity options.

In terms of network connectivity, this 12,700 km optical fibre ring cable network provides 10 Gbit/s wavelengths with a design capacity of up to 64 waves per fibre pair and uses dense wavelength division multiplexing technology. AJC also enable onward connectivity on submarine cables which are colocated in the same cable station as AJC.

The Australian Landing points consist of AJC Oxford Falls Cable Station, AJC Paddington Cable Station. The Guam Landing Station consists of AJC Tanguisson Cable Station and AJC Tumon Bay Cable Station. Japan Landing Station consists of AJC Maruyama and Shima Cable Station.

The AJC network is monitored by the AJC NOC and landing stations. Approximately 93% of the cable network is under deep water. About 9000 m of cable lie in the deepest water.

AJC network provided less costs to retailers and wholesalers. High quality sponsors had executed the project. The option of pre-sales was the most attractive feature for the stakeholders of the project.

Submarine cable system consists of physical cable, repeaters and transmission equipment. Cable system owned by different companies can be housed in a single landing station. Submarine cable system became the primary medium for transoceanic transmission since satellite transmission had limited capacity, poorer quality and higher prices. The faster growth in capacity led to fall in prices at a rate of 20–40% per year.

36.1 Financing of the Project

The source of financing was combination of equity along with project finance debt facility provided by a consortium of banks. A major part of the debt was secured by pre sales and the rest was repaid through subsequent capacity sales.

Financing of cable systems are done through three structures-clubs, private deals with carrier sponsors and private deals with non-carrier sponsors. In the 1990s, the financing of new cable systems was done through large clubs comprising of up to 90 sponsors. As a result, carriers contributed only small amount in terms of equity participation. By mid 1990s, the business model of private carrier deal structure gained prominence. In this structure, two to three carriers formed limited partnership to finance cables through a mix of debt and equity. This private carrier structure created a new wholesale market for capacity.

In the 1990s, the submarine cable manufacturing equipment market consisted of only couple of manufacturers with almost 80% dominated by top three suppliers.

Telstra's initial estimation to build the system was $520 million. The company expected the system to have a life of 15 years. The upgrades to the system was estimated to cost $25 million per 40 Gbit/s. Telstra decided on a private carrier deal using project finance structure to fund the construction. ABN AMRO was the financial adviser for the deal.

36.2 Opportunities, Risks and Challenges

The submarine cable systems industry witnessed slow, cyclical growth over the years its period of history. During the 1990s, the telecommunication industry witnessed exponential growth and significant changes in cable technology. Worldwide deregulation, technological changes with respect to voice and data application and internet have transformed the telecommunication industry. As a result, the need for more transmission capacity increased and submarine cables emerged as a viable low cost solution. At the same time, rapid improvements in cable technology and price declines made investments in submarine cable industry risky in terms of profit generation.

The AJC project faced challenges of marine installation, directional drilling for Sydney landing and making of terrestrial routes for closing the fibre ring in Sydney and Guam. The AJC network had incurred three submarine faults since operational in year 2001. This fault was in line with industry expectations for such a cable network.

36.3 Project Ownership

The AJC group holding company, Australia Japan Cable Holdings Ltd is owned by Communications Global Network Services Ltd, Softbank Corp (Formerly Japan Telecom), Telstra and MFS Globenet Inc.

The sponsor Teleglobe was the main carrier of the project while Japan Telecom was the borrower for the project company. Telstra held 40% of the shares of the project company. During the project time, Telstra was Australia's leading telecommunications and information services company. The transmission infrastructure of Telstra included both satellite and submarine cable transmission.

Further Reading

https://ajcable.com/ajc-network/history-timeline/
https://caseism.com/australia-japan-cable-structuring-the-project-company-85402
Benjamin C Esty, Carrie Ferman, Australia Japan Cable: Structuring the Project Company, Harvard Business School, 9-203-029. 2003.

Case 33: Addis Ababa–Djibouti Railway

In the year 2007, the Technical Advisory Group (TAG) under Ethiopia's Ministry of Transport was formed to create a framework for the modernization of the railway network in Ethiopia. In the year 2010, an agreement for the modernization of the Addis Ababa-Djibouti Railway was signed between Ethiopia and China under Belt and Road Initiative. In the same year, the MoU for the development and operation of Standard Gauge Railway Line between Ethiopia and Djibouti was also finalized.

This project is located in Djibouti and Ethiopia. It is the first electrified standard gauge railway project in Africa. This project is part of the Belt and Road Initiative. In the year 2012, the government of Ethiopia and Djibouti signed a bilateral agreement for the development and operation of the standard gauge network.

The state owned companies Ethiopian Railway Corporation (ERC) of Ethiopia and Société Djiboutienne de Chemin de Fer (SDCF) of Djibouti have ownership rights for the project. The project was structured under design, build, maintain and operate (DBMO) model and was constructed by China Railway Group (CREC) and China Civil Engineering Construction Corporation (CCECC). These companies were entrusted with the responsibility for operating the railway for a period of 6 years after the construction completion. The project started commercial operations in the year 2018. During October 2015, the project was opened for freight services and the passenger services became operational in October 2016. The value of the project was estimated to be $5.1 billion.

37.1 Highlights of the Project

This new modernized project has emerged as the main transport corridor for Ethiopia which connect to the Port of Djibouti. The railway project consists of 753 km electrified single gauge line which connects Ethiopia's capital Addis Ababa with the Port of Djibouti. Approximately 90% of the international trade of Ethiopia is handled by the Port of Djibouti. The new gauge line has replaced the 1-m gauge railway line which was over 100 years old. The rail project connects the Ethiopian cities of Adama and Dire Dawa. The project was the first overseas railway project constructed by Chinese companies under international standards of 1435 mm gauge line and electrification at 25 Kv1. The maximum running speed of passenger train was 120 km/h. The maximum running speed of freight train was 80 km/h.

37.2 Economic Significance of the Project

The port of Djibouti is the main central port for Ethiopia. This gateway accounts for over 90% of the international trade. Infrastructural development like investments in road and rail along the gateway of Djibouti corridor contributes towards reduction in transportation costs and time savings. With infrastructural development, the manufacturing export capabilities of Ethiopia can be improved through foreign direct investment. From the 1990s onwards, Chinese companies have been making investments in African countries. Under the Belt and Road initiatives, China aims to strengthen its trade routes and enhance investments in African region. The Chinese investment in Addis Ababa–Djibouti Railway project is focused on this investment strategy. This project has immense socio economic and macro-economic benefits. This railway system has emerged as the primary national mass transportation system. After the implementation of the project, the Ethiopian government have adopted 5-year plan for economic structural transformation in terms of development of dry ports, rail, road networks and air transport system. The plan also envisaged the development of 34 km light rail system for Addis Ababa. The new rail project has immensely led to the long haul transport of freight with reduced travel times. It is estimated that travel times have been reduced from up to 50 h to 10 h. The passenger and freight tariffs rates under rail system have become very competitive compared to road transport system. The current import rate is USD 0.046 per ton km and the export rate is USD 0.023 per ton km. The trade volumes between the two nations are forecasted to grow on account of reduction in transportation costs and delivery time. Rail transport will account for approximately 75% of the market share of trade. The currency capacity of the Addis Ababa rail system is 11.2 million tons of freight which is estimated to increase to 24.9 million tons by the year 2025. The cargo capacity is estimated to reach four million tons by the year 2035. The rail system requires expansion of the handling capacity for oil, bulk cargo and containers at the Port of Doraleh which is the extension of the Port of Djibouti. The project would contribute towards the consolidation of economic ties between the two nations of Ethiopia and Djibouti. The project is vital for rail and port infrastructure development of Djibouti. In the year 2019, the service sector in Djibouti which included the transport sector accounted for 76% of GDP. The project will aid the development of rural regions in terms of rural employment generation. Approximately 2000 local workers were employed for infrastructure and rolling stock maintenance following the project completion. The project has boosted the performance of the international trade corridor in terms of exports and imports. The new project line contributed towards reduction in regional disparities which existed in both nations. The project facilitated technology transfers. The local employees were trained in technical universities in China.

37.3 Financing of the Project

The equity contribution for the project which amounted to 30% of the project financing was sourced by the governments of Ethiopia and Djibouti. The debt financing which comprised 70% was sourced through concessional loans from China's Exim bank, the China Development bank and the Industrial and Commercial Bank of China. The security arrangements included credit guarantee insurance obtained by the governments of Ethiopia and Djibouti for their loan financing. The project cost was approximately USD 5.09 billion.

37.4 Significance of the Project

The landlocked Ethiopia was characterized by high transport and trade costs which became a barrier for the export focused industrial development of Ethiopia. The economic development of Ethiopia was retarded due to lack of industrial and manufacturing sectors. The economy depended on international trade. The rail line was pivotal for sustainable development of the region. The economy of Djibouti heavily depended on international trade and was driven by port services. The rail line will improve the transport connectivity for the port of Djibouti by facilitating fast distribution corridor.

37.5 Risk Mitigation Strategy

The project faced revenue risks due to lower usage in terms of lower traffic volumes and had also faced exchange rate risk. Exchange risk was due to structuring of revenues and costs in different currencies. The project's debt was structured in US dollars while the revenues, construction and operation cost were denominated in Ethiopian Birr. In order to mitigate repayment risks, the Chinese banks took initiatives such as restructuring of the Ethiopian debt and extended the repayment period from 15 to 30 years.

The project supervision and control functions were entrusted to the Joint Railway Commission constituted by the state owned companies ERC and SDCF.

Further Reading

Reference Guide, Global Infrastructure hub, Connectivity across borders, Global practices for cross-border infrastructure projects February 2021

Tesfaye, A. (2020): China in Ethiopia: The Long-Term Perspective, Chapter 5

The Guardian (2018), Available at: https://www.theguardian.com/global-development/2018/may/12/ethiopia-railway-boom-promises-turn-to-dust

World Bank Group (2019): Djibouti Overview, https://www.worldbank.org/en/country/djibouti/overview

Global Construction Review (2015): https://www.globalconstructionreview.com/markets/ethiopia-steams-ahead-vision-modern-n8a8t8i8o8n8al/, accessed on 01-06-2020

Case 34: Port Mann Bridge Vancouver

In the year 2006, the Ministry of Transportation and Infrastructure, British Columbia launched the Gateway Program which was an integral part of the British Columbia's Pacific Gateway Strategy. The existing Highway 1 corridor from Vancouver to Langley was one of the three priority corridors identified in the Gateway program. This corridor was the busiest and most economically critical route in Greater Vancouver. The original bridge built in the 1960s was designed for 850,000 people. It is now the only major east west corridor to serve approximately 2.5 million population of Greater Vancouver. Port Mann bridge alone carry approximately 127,000 vehicles per day. This represented an increase of 65% since 1985 when the daily traffic was about 77,000 vehicles. The new bridge was necessitated due to traffic congestion in both directions which was 13 h on an average weekday. It was stated that the daily traffic on the Port Mann Bridge was 20% higher than on San Francisco's Golden Gate Bridge. The population of Vancouver is expected to grow to 900,000 over the next 25 years.

The Port Mann Bridge was constructed to tackle the traffic congestion and enhance the traffic mobility in Vancouver. The project involved the replacement of the existing Port Mann Bridge and widening of the Trans-Canada Highway and its interchanges. The project covered a total distance of 37 km. The construction work for the project started in the year 2009 and was completed by 2013. The construction contract for the project was given to Peter Kiewit Sons and Flatiron Constructors under a design build form of agreement. The investment for the project was approximately $3.3 billion. The new bridge is the widest long span bridge in the world measuring 65 m.

The original Port Mann bridge was constructed in the year 1964 and had four lanes. The new bridge had 10 lanes in total. There was a future plan to introduce a light rapid transit line beneath the main deck. The new project reduced the travel time by approximately 30% thereby saving 1 h of travel on daily basis. The project facilitated the introduction of highway rapid bus service facility. The new bridge was opened during July 2015. The project had improved the cycling and pedestrian facilities on the bridge.

The newly constructed Port Mann Bridge was composed of three major sections. The first section consisted of the cable stayed 850-m-long main bridge across the Fraser River. The second section featured the 350-m south approach at Surrey. The third section consisted of the 820-m northern approach at Coquitlam. The north and south span superstructure consists of steel field sections, per cast panels and stay cables. The two towers of the bridge stood at 160-m-high which facilitated navigation clearance of 42 m. About 144 cable stays extend from each 535-foot-tall tower. The north and south approaches were composed of 1158 segments which weighed 80 ton each and were erected by a 720-ton self-launching gantry.

The construction of the new Port Mann Bridge involved 13,000 ton of structural steel, 157,000 m^2 of concrete, 25,000 ton of asphalt, 28,000 ton of rebar and 108 caissons. The project used 288 cables which covered approximately 48 km. Around 16 km of pile and 5 km of drilled shafts were used as support structures. A structural monitoring system was implemented to calibrate structural responses on account of any seismic activity. The other features of the project included widening of seven Highway overpasses, replacement of nine highway interchanges etc. The project also covered the construction and rebuilding of 15 new overpasses and underpasses along with five ramps. This new 10 lane cable stayed bridge was constructed using the balanced cantilever method. The project also included the upgradation of 23 miles of Highway 1 on each side of the Fraser River.

British Columbia government provided $1.5 billion for the project. Tolls collected at the new bridge will be the source of cash flows expected to cover the financing costs. The project was implemented to alleviate traffic congestion and reduce travel times. The total design and construction cost was estimated to be $2.46 billion. The DB Partner Kiewit/Flatiron General Partnership was a joint venture between Peter Kiewit Sons Co and Flatiron Constructors Canada Ltd. The consultants for the project included T Y Lin International and International Bridge Technologies. The modular expansion joints and disc bearings for the bridge were provided by Mageba and R J Watson. H5M—the design joint venture between Hatch Mott Macdonald Ltd and MMM Group provided the on shore design services for the project. Mainroad Infrastructure Management Ltd was the O&M contractor for the project.

38.1 Project Agreement

The project contractor was selected on the basis of two stage selection process which consisted of a Request for Qualifications (RFQ) stage and a Request for Proposals (RFP) stage. The province entered into a fixed price, design build agreement (DB) with Connect BC Development Group's design builder—the Kiewit/Flatiron General Partnership for the design and construction of the new 10 lane Port Mann Bridge and Highway 1 improvements. Connect BC Development Group represent the Macquarie Group consisting of Macquarie Bank Ltd, Macquarie Infrastructure Group and Macquarie Infrastructure Partners. In the year 2008, the Transportation Investment Corporation (TI) was established by the Province to act as the authority and concessionaire for overseeing the implementation of the project. Under the DB model, the province entered into a DB agreement and the lead contractor took the responsibility of preparing the detailed design of the project and undertook the construction Under the model, the private partner had to apply tolls within the tolling framework set and regulated by the province. In the scenario of actual revenues from the tolls exceeding expectations, a revenue sharing mechanism between the government and private partner was included in the project. For effective management of the corridor, performance incentives were also included in the agreement. The risk of cost overruns and schedule delays were the responsibility of the contractor.

The project DB agreement promoted public interest by specifying performance standards, incentives and penalties for not conforming to standards. The agreement stipulated significant liquidated damages for late completion. Penalties were applied for non adherence to the traffic management plan and noncompliance measured against delivery of all contractual agreements.

38.2 Project Benefits

The project was aimed at reduction of congestion and travel time; improvement of safety and accessibility. The project also facilitated transit service along with expansion of networks and transportation choices for high occupancy vehicles, cyclists and pedestrians. According to project estimation, the benefits from the project on account of reduced travel times, vehicle operating costs and improved safety was estimated at $5 billion on present value terms. This analysis was based on discounted cash flow analysis over a project life of 35 years using a 6% discount rate. The project resulted in employment generation for 8000 people and contributed over $800 million to provincial gross domestic product. The project provided the first bus service across the Port Mann Bridge in more than 20 years. The RapidBus service which was a joint initiative of the province and TransLink allowed passengers to commute from Langley to SkyTrain in Burnaby in less than 25 min. The project also provided significant safety improvements along the transportation corridor. By 2010, Kiewit had awarded more than $500 million in subcontracts to 100 firms based in the province of British Columbia. This represented about 20% of the total design build agreement value. In terms of long term benefits, the competitiveness of the goods movement in the region will be improved. The transportation costs of goods and services for consumers were reduced. The productivity of workers was enhanced through reduction of travel time of service providers. The air quality improvement was another benefit on account of reduction of congestion related vehicle emissions. The project had introduced tolling as part of a suite of congestion reduction measures to manage traffic growth over time and improve the effectiveness of highway movement.

38.3 Environmental Assessment

The project was subject to environmental assessment in terms of environmental and socio community impacts. The mitigation and compensation measures were also proposed in the environmental assessment. The project received an environmental assessment certificate under the B C Environmental Assessment Act and Canadian Environmental Assessment Act.

38.4 Risk Mitigation

The DB partner was responsible for risks associated with design and construction, utilities, traffic management, environmental management and quality assurance. Force Majeure risks was shared between the DB partner and the government. The government was responsible for risks related to property acquisition and corridor environmental aspects. The risk related to tolling revenue, toll collection and tolling system were taken by the government of province. The risks related to operations and maintenance were retained by the government. The construction cost risk and schedule completion risk remained with the DB partner. The DB agreement envisaged payment to DB partner through construction milestones based on the work progress. The Province had capped its annual expenditure exposure in terms of maximum annual payment amount.

Further Reading

https://www.roadtraffic-technology.com/projects/port-mann-bridgehighway-1-project/
https://www.flatironcorp.com/project/port-mann-bridge-highway-1/
Project Report: Achieving Value for Money Port Mann/Highway 1 Improvement Project https://www.infrastructurebc.com/files-4/documents/PMH1-2011/PMH1_Project-Report_14March2011.pdf

Case 35: Chernobyl New Safe Confinement Project

The Chernobyl nuclear power explosion on 26th April 1986 was the worst ever nuclear accident in the world. The reactor hall of unit 4 was destroyed by a massive explosion and radioactive material was released which affected large part of Eastern and Western Europe. The disaster affected large parts of Ukraine, Belarus and Russia. The disaster caused huge damage to the environment. The explosion caused deaths of 30 workers and firemen at the Chernobyl nuclear power plant. The long term health consequences of the accident are still a debatable topic. Over 200,000 people were evacuated from the vicinity of the destroyed reactor. An exclusion zone of 30 km length is in place ever since the accident took place.

A worldwide review of nuclear safety standards and regulatory processes was held following the accident and the critical role of international community in nuclear safety programmes was stressed upon. As a result, agencies such as European Bank for Reconstruction and Development were roped in for creation of nuclear safety programs. Ukraine faced a formidable challenge in terms of decommissioning of the three remaining reactor units, the loss of arable land and health issues for victims.

In the year 2016, the establishment of New Safe Confinement radically transformed the accident site. Chernobyl's New Safe Confinement (NSC) is a unique design and construction project in the context that such a huge structure was constructed for the first time at a heavily contaminated site. The project was aimed at the safety of the explosion site with the provision for the dismantling of the ageing shelter and management of the radioactive waste within the shelter. NSC have been handed to the Ukrainian government after systems installation, testing and commissioning of the project. In late 2020, the Chernobyl Shelter Fund related to the project was closed.

NSC is a remarkable example of an extraordinary feat of engineering. The structure weighs 36,000 tons and is 108 m high, 162 m long. The structure has a span of 257 m. The frame of the structure is a huge lattice construction of tubular steel sections which are supported by two longitudinal concrete beams. The structure is equipped with a heavy duty crane for the future dismantling of the shelter and waste management. The construction of the structure was carried out by a joint venture of French engineering firms Bouygues and Vinci. The first waste canister containing highly radioactive spent nuclear fuel from the Chernobyl nuclear power plant was successfully processed and could be safely stored for at least next 100 years. The New Safe Confinement is the largest moveable land based structure ever built.

The Shelter Implementation Plan (SIP) on the New Safe Confinement was initiated in the late 2010 and the structure was completed and placed during November 2016.NSC is designed to prevent the release of contaminated material from the present shelter and also protects the structure from adverse natural calamities and extreme weather. The structure is strong enough to withstand a tornado. The risk of corrosion is eliminated by the technically superior ventilation system. The work involved collaboration with local subcontractors across the world. The arch was made of structural elements which were designed in Italy. The crane system was manufactured in the US. The arch cladding contractor came from Turkey. The lifting and sliding operations were done by Dutch firm. All the contracts were awarded in accordance with the EBRD's procurement policies and rules related to Bank's Environmental and Social policy.

The first phase of the Shelter Implementation Plan focused on the engineering work for development of conceptual solutions for confinement strategy for fuel containing materials in the shelter. During the first stage of the plan, infrastructural facilities such as projects, roads and other utilities which were prerequisites for safety at the decommissioned nuclear sites were developed.

The New Safe Confinement is an integral part of the Shelter Implementation. The construction was financed by the Chernobyl Shelter Fund which was managed by the EBRD on the behalf of the contributors to the Fund. EBRD was entrusted by the international community to manage funds to transform Chernobyl into a safe and secure state after decommissioning the nuclear plant.

The liquid waste treatment plant retrieves highly active liquids from current storage tanks, processes them into a solid state and transferred into containers for long term storage. There were several limitations in the technical and financial provisions for the decommissioning process.

The initiative for the establishment of the Chernobyl Shelter Fund was taken by the G7 governments, the European Commission and Ukraine during the 1997 G7 summit in Denver.

39.1 Financing

The cost of Shelter Implementation Plan amounted to 2.1 billion euros and was funded by contributions from 45 countries, the European Commission and the EBRD. The EBRD is also involved in the management of Nuclear Safety Account which is used for decommissioning of two infrastructure facilities at the nuclear site. The work on the processing of the spent fuel assemblies from reactors and enclosing then in concrete modules for a minimum period of 100 years had incurred cost in excess of 400 million euros. The liquid radioactive waste treatment plant was the first EBRD managed project in Chernobyl. EBRD has contributed its own resources which amounted to 715 million euros to make Chernobyl environmentally safe. The Nuclear Safety Account had committed 280 million euros, provided by 18 donors, to decommissioning and safety projects in Chernobyl. The EBRD had provided 235 million euros to support the construction of the ISF-2 project. The first phase of the Shelter Implementation Plan was funded by the United States and European Union. The member countries which made contributions to the Nuclear Safety Account include Belgium, Canada, Denmark, European Union, Finland, France, Germany, Italy, Japan, the Netherlands, Norway, Russia, Sweden, Switzerland, the United Kingdom, Ukraine and the United States. By the mid of 2018, the Nuclear Safety Account received approximately 440 euros million in total.

Further Reading

https://www.ebrd.com/what-we-do/sectors/nuclear-safety/chernobyl-new-safe-confinement.html
https://www.ebrd.com/what-we-do/sectors/nuclear-safety/chernobyl-overview.html
https://www.ebrd.com/what-we-do/sectors/nuclear-safety/chernobyl-decommissioning-power-plant.html

Case 36: Kashiwazaki Kariwa Nuclear Project, Japan

Kashiwazaki Kariwa nuclear station is the largest nuclear power station in the world. The project was started in the year 1980. The nuclear power plant is operated by the Tokyo Electric Power Company (TEPCO). The nuclear power project with seven reactors have generating capacity of 8212 MW and can produce electricity to 16 million households. The plant has the capacity to satisfy about 5% of Japan's total power demand. The project site of 4.2 km^2 is located in the Niigata Prefecture city of Kashiwazaki and the town of Kariwa which was approximately 135 miles north west of Tokyo situated on the coast of the Sea of Japan. Kashiwazaki is the world's first advanced boiling water reactor. It receives cooling water from the coast of the Sea of Japan. The plant is owned and operated by Tokyo Electric Power Company (TEPCO). The last two units were the first Advanced Boiling Water Reactors ever built. In 1996, the nuclear plant became the first plant to employ an advanced boiling water reactor for commercial use. The advanced boiling water reactor was designed by General Electric and is a Generation III reactor. It has an average output of 1315 MW and power rating of 1356 MW. Low enriched uranium is used as the nuclear fuel in all the reactors. Kashiwazaki Kariwa possess seven conventional nuclear reactors each with an average output of 1067 MW and power rating of 1100 MW. By 2010, the nuclear power sector had provided more than 11% of Japan's total energy requirements.

Kashiwazaki Kariwa is the world's fourth largest electric generating station behind the three hydroelectric plants of Itaipu, the Three Gorges Dam and Guri Dam. In terms of net electrical power rating, it is the largest nuclear generating station. Kashiwazaki municipality's revenues which were directly related to the nuclear power plant was approximately ¥8.0 billion in the year 2018.

As of January 2021, the Kariwa plant employs over 6300 people which include utility personnel and staff of independent contractors. Japan is an earthquake prone area. During October 2004, an earthquake measuring 6.9 on the Richter scale struck the Niigata Prefecture which killed 40 people and damaged 6000 homes. However, the Kashiwazaki Kariwa nuclear plant withstood the tremor.

Kashiwazaki was built according to earthquake resistance standards. The nuclear plant was safe from another major earthquake which hit on July 16th 2007. The 2007 earthquake led to leakage of radioactive substances into the air and water. This was the second strongest earthquake which happened near a nuclear plant. The epicenter of the earthquake was approximately 19 km from the nuclear site. During August 2007, investigators from the International Atomic Energy Agency (IAEA) carried out inspection of site and recommended that the plant's safety measures performed well. During the period of shutdown, TEPCO was forced to run a natural gas plant. The demand for more fuel for Japan led to increase in carbon dioxide output which inversely affected the ability of Japan to meet the Kyoto Protocol on Climate Change with respect to global warming. Kashiwazaki-Kariwa was unaffected by the March 2011 earthquake and tsunami, which damaged TEPCO's Fukushima Daiichi plant.

The nuclear plant which has been in operation since the year 1985 was closed until the safety checks following the earthquake were completed. The plant was reopened in May 2009 after complete shutdown for 21 months following the earthquake. All the seven units are built along the coastline. TEPCO had invested ¥1.2 trillion in upgrading the Kashiwazaki-Kariwa plant for addressing safety concerns.

The project had economic advantages in terms of limited impact of refueling outages of individual units on the plant's total net power production.

In June 2020, TEPCO and Toshiba signed a memorandum of understanding (MoU) to form a new company KK6 for the construction of the safety precautions at Unit 6 of the power plant. Unit 6 and 7 are the first boiling water reactors to comply with the revised regulatory standards which are recommended by the Japanese Government. In the same period, TEPCO applied to the Nuclear Regulation Authority to amend the safety regulations for the large building for Unit 7 reactor building. The last unit became operational in the year 1994.

In April 2021, Japan's Nuclear Regulation Authority (NRA) had issued an administrative order to TEPCO which prevented it from transporting nuclear fuel stored at the Kashiwazaki Kariwa or loading into reactors due to a series of security breaches at the nuclear site. Kashiwazaki Kariwa was among the many nuclear plants in Japan which were shut down in the aftermath of the accident at Fukushima in the year 2011. According to new business plan released by TEPCO in July 2021, Japan's Kashiwazaki Kariwa project will not be restarted until fiscal 2022. TEPCO also had plans to invest up to $27 billion by fiscal year 2030 for decarburization efforts. The plan was designed to raise funds for compensation, decontamination and decommissioning following the 2011 Fukushima nuclear disaster. Tokyo Electric Power Co have spent nearly 1.17 trillion yen on safety measures which included reinforcement of piping at buildings housing the seven reactors at Kashwazaki Kariwa nuclear power plant following the 2007 Chuetsu Offshore earthquake. The amount is estimated at around 17 times the company's 2013 cost estimate of 70 billion yen.

40.1 Structuring and Financing of the Project

The major creditors for TEPCO include financial institutions such as Sumitomo Mitsui Financial Group, Mitsubishi UFJ Financial Group and Mizuho Financial Group and the Development Bank of Japan. For the units 6 and 7 construction, TEPCO had assumed the overall management of the project in a split package contract approach. A joint venture of manufacturers such as Toshiba, Hitachi and General Electric carried out the main design and construction work. The civil work and the main building work was done by a building joint venture. The mechanical work was done by Hitachi and General Electric. For Kashiwazaki Kariwa 6 and 7 units, TEPCO had established basic requirements for Quality Analysis based on extensive K-67 Steering Committee Schedule co-ordination meeting. The construction duration of the Kashiwazaki 6 and 7 units was 51.5 months.

Further Reading

https://en.wikipedia.org/wiki/Kashiwazaki-Kariwa_Nuclear_Power_Plant
https://www.power-technology.com/projects/kashiwazaki/
https://world-nuclear-news.org/Articles/Tepco-anticipates-delay-in-Kashiwazaki-Kariwa-rest
https://www.reuters.com/article/japan-nuclear-tepco-idCNT9N0GD01Q20130930
https://www.eia.gov/todayinenergy/detail.php?id=28392
https://mainichi.jp/english/articles/20191116/p2a/00m/0na/004000c
https://www.neimagazine.com/news/newstepco-business-plan-defers-restart-of-kashiwazaki-kariwa-npp-8936701
Nuclear Energy Agency, Nuclear New Build: Insights into Financing and Project Management, https://www.oecd-nea.org/upload/docs/application/pdf/2019-12/7195-nn-build-2015.pdf. OECD.
https://www.ft.com/content/57bdef2e-2d1b-4d06-8163-830f17764219
https://www.nippon.com/en/in-depth/d00687/

Case 37: Kudankulam Nuclear Power Plant, India

The Kudankulam Nuclear Power Plant (KNPP) is established in the Tirunelveli district of Tamil Nadu, one of the southern state of India. Nuclear Power Corporation of India (NPCIL) is the operator of the project. It is the largest nuclear power plant in India. The reactors at Kundankulam were placed under the safeguards of the International Atomic Energy Agency (IAEA).

In the year 1998 NPCIL and Rosatom finalized the reactor design and engineering supervision arrangements for the construction of KNPP phase 1 project. Rosatom is the state atomic energy corporation of Russia and have competencies across the entire nuclear fuel cycle. The company has the largest foreign project portfolio in the world with 35 power units at different stages of implementation in 12 countries. Rosatom is the largest producer of electricity in Russia which covers over 20% of the country's energy needs.

The Phase 1 of the project saw the commissioning of two 1000 megawatt (MW) pressurized water reactor (PWR) based on Russian technology. The construction of Phase 1 started in the year 2001. The concrete work for Unit 1 and Unit 2 was started in the year 2002. The first two units were commissioned in the year 2013 and 2016 respectively. The current nuclear power generation capacity of all 22 nuclear power reactors in India is 6780 MW.

The project agreement for additional four units for the nuclear plant was signed between India and Russia during December 2008. The construction work for the third and fourth unit was started during the year 2016 with operationalization plans by 2022–2023. NPCIL and Atomstroyexport (ASE) entered into a general framework agreement for the construction of the fifth and sixth units during June 2017. The units are expected to be commissioned during 2025–2026 period. In 2021, the government announced that unit 5 and unit 6 of KNPP are scheduled to be completed in 66 and 75 months respectively. The scope for employment generation in the two reactors is approximately 250 people through contractors and 6000 people during the construction processes.

On the event of commissioning of all the six units, the power plant will have a combined capacity of 6000 MW. The project has an estimated production life of 60 years which could be extended for another 20 years.

41.1 Financing Cost

The original cost of the first two units was US$1.75 billion. Later it was revised to US$2.29 billion. Phase 1 financing cost amounted to US$ 2.47 billion. Russia had advanced a credit of US$ 0.85 billion for the construction of the two units. The sanctioned cost for the Unit 3 and Unit 4 of the project was INR 39,849 crore (US $5.29 billion). The third and fourth reactors at Kudankulam financing consisted of export finance of US $3.5 billion. The amount would be enough to finance 85% of the value of works, supplies and services. A further credit line of $800 million was made available to cover fuel supplies. These credit lines carried an interest of 4% per annum and the terms for repayment was spread over 14 years and 4 years respectively from 1 year after the start of power generation. Indian government took up credit offers which amounted to US$3.06 billion which represented 53% of the estimated total project cost. The total cost of the project for the six units is estimated to be around US $16.3 billion.

The sanctioned cost for Unit 5 and Unit 6 was INR 49,621 crore (US$6.60 billion). On account of liability issues, the cost of units 3 and 4 was more than twice the costs of the units 1 and 2. The fifth and sixth units' construction is estimated to cost US $6.65 billion. Indian Prime minister Narendra Modi and Russian President Vladimir Putin had signed the agreement for the two new reactors on the sidelines of the annual summit meet in 2017. The project would be funded with 70% debt and 30% equity. The Russian government will lend India USD 4.2 billion to cover the construction cost. The equity portion will be funded by NPCIL or government of India. Atomstroyexport will build the reactors.

41.2 Pricing of Nuclear Power

The first unit of the plant supplies power at a rate of INR 3.89 per unit. In 2015, NPCIL announced the price of 4.29 per unit.

41.3 Power Distribution

Tamil Nadu, the southern home state where the power plant is situated is allocated 50% (925 MW) of the power generated. The neighboring states of Karnataka, Kerala and Puducherry share 35% of the power generated. Karnataka receives 442 MW; while Kerala and Puducherry receives 266 MW and 67 MW of power from nuclear plant. The rest 15% of the unallocated generated power is added to the central pool.

41.4 Risks and Its Mitigation

The project had experienced significant delays. The first unit of the Phase 1 of the project was commissioned in 2013 only though the work was started in the year 2001.The total cost of setting up two units of the nuclear power plant had escalated from INR 13,000 crore to INR 16,000 crore.

A Comptroller and Audit General of India (CAG) report stated that more than eight years of delay in starting the commercial operation of KKNPP had caused a loss of over US$1.33 billion to the Nuclear Power Corporation of India. The report also alleged that NPCIL's inappropriate careless financial spending provided undue financial advantage to Russian company Atomstroyexport (ASE), the contractor for setting up the project. The report also cited multiple instances of avoidable payment of interest on borrowings and non-transparency in availing loans and lapses in tariff fixation process.

During the time surrounding the commissioning of unit 1, the project experienced delay on account of persistent protests by locals and nuclear activists over safety concerns with respect to potential radiation threats and issues related to nuclear waste disposal. There were concerns as KNPP was located in a tsunami prone area. The population within the 30 km radius of the nuclear power plant was approximately one million. The safe evacuation of the population in the event of any nuclear disaster would be a challenging task. The People's Movement Against Nuclear Energy (PMANE) was the main campaigner for the anti Kundankulam project. The arrest of Russian officials for sourcing substandard materials for nuclear equipment and identification of four faulty crucial valves in reactors at Kudankulam strengthened the opposition to the plant.

The construction work was stopped during October 2011 due to the protests. The work resumed in March 2012 with the permission of the Tamil Nadu government. In May 2013, the Indian Supreme Court dismissed the petitions filed by nuclear activists over the safety of the nuclear power plant and gave the green signal for the commissioning of the first two units.

KNPP is the first nuclear power plant in India to use the imported PWR technology. The other nuclear power plants in India use the pressurized heavy water reactor or boiling water reactor technology. The advanced version of the Russian developed PWR nuclear technology based VVER -1000 type reactors (water-water power reactors) are used by KNPP. This VVER technology has the credentials of completion of more than 1500 reactor years of operating time.

KNPP uses AES-92 (V-466) model which is the latest version of the third generation VVER-1000. The adoption of this technology have facilitated active and passive multi layered safety measures such as passive heat removal system, hydrogen recombiners, core catchers and quick boron injection system. The system also uses active safety provisions such as the use of neutron absorbing control rods for reactivity control. The passive safety system uses factors such as pressure differentials, gravity or natural convection for protection against malfunctions in emergency situations. A series of passive hydrogen re-combiners convert abnormal production of hydrogen into water. AES-92 has a double protective containment with the inner envelope made of steel and the outer one made of heavy reinforced concrete steel. The adoption of such a system prevents the release of radioactive materials into the environment during natural catastrophe incidents. A water sprayer system is equipped in the inner containment to ease the steam pressure in the reactor.

41.5 Contractors for the Project

Atomstroyexport, the subsidiary of the Russian State Nuclear Energy Corporation Rosatom is responsible for the technical design, construction, supervision and technical support for commissioning of the reactors. Atomstroyexport is also responsible for training for operation and maintenance and supply of equipment and materials. Bharat Heavy Electricals deals with the configuration of machines at the plant. NPCIL is responsible for construction, erection and commissioning of the projects. HCC India took part in the construction works related to Unit 1 and Unit 2.

Further Reading

https://www.power-technology.com/projects/kudankulam-nuclear-power-plant/
https://timesofindia.indiatimes.com/city/chennai/Kudankulam-power-to-cost-4-29/unit/articleshow/45712143.cms
https://pib.gov.in/PressReleasePage.aspx?PRID=1605939
https://www.thehindu.com/news/national/Kudankulam-units-3-4-cost-more-than-doubles-over-liability-issues/article10928559.ece
https://www.business-standard.com/article/economy-policy/kudankulam-s-2-new-units-to-cost-rs-50k-cr-russia-to-fund-half-of-it-117060200422_1.html
https://www.world-nuclear-news.org/Articles/Finance-for-next-Kudankulam-units
https://www.hindustantimes.com/business-news/npcil-spent-rs-706-crore-more-on-kudankulam-nuclear-plant-component-finds-cag/story-Va4dfaauRV3MMi5MnF6MvK.html
https://www.thehindubusinessline.com/news/national/construction-of-kudankulams-fifth-and-sixth-reactors-to-be-completed-in-5-6-years/article35483253.ece

Case 38: Boundary Dam Power Station

The Boundary Dam is an 824 MW coal fired power plant located in Estevan in Saskatchewan, Canada. The power plant consists of six production units and is owned by SaskPower. Saskatchewan Power Corporation (SaskPower) is the main electric utility company in Canada established by the provincial government in the year 1929. The firm manages over $11.8 billion in assets. It operates three coal-fired power stations, seven hydroelectric stations, six natural gas stations, and two wind facilities, and has partnerships with 21 independent power producers for a total capacity of 4211 MW. Boundary Dam is the largest project undertaken by SaskPower.

In the year 1959 Unit 1 and Unit 2 were commissioned with total capacity of 123 MW. Unit 1 had 62 MW and Unit 2 had 61 MW capacity. The next two units were added in the year 1970 with a combined capacity of 278 MW. In the year 1973, the fifth unit was commissioned with a capacity of 139 MW. The sixth unit was commissioned in the year 1978 with power generation capacity of 284 MW. Unit 1 and Unit 2 was decommissioned in the year 2013 and 2014 as per the guidelines of federal rules on carbon dioxide emissions. The unit 3 was scheduled for decommissioning in the year 2013 after operational service of 45 years. A retrofit for the installation of the Carbon Capture and Storage (CSS) equipment was proposed and adopted instead of decommissioning the unit. This strategy was aimed to extend the life of Unit 3 by 30 years.

In the year 2014, the adoption of CCS technology in Unit 3 led to the transformation of the energy landscape in the Boundary project. Unit 3 was converted into a 120 MW producer of base load power electricity. CCS technology was able to reduce 90% of greenhouse gas emissions produced from Unit 3 of the plant. CCS technology is vital for maintaining the long term sustainability of coal production globally. Boundary Dam power station became the first power station in the world to successfully use the CCS technology. The adoption of the technology facilitated the reduction of atmospheric pollution by preventing the entry of approximately four million tons of carbon dioxide into the atmosphere which was equivalent to taking one million vehicles off the road for a year. The unit 3 have the capacity of 115 MW which is enough to light approximately 100,000 homes in Saskatchewan. The adoption of CCS technology was able to reduce Sulphur di oxide emissions from the coal processes by up to 100% and the carbon dioxide emission by 90%. The estimated investment for CCS technology was $1.2 billion.

The CCS technology adoption in Unit 3 was motivated by the endorsement by the Carbon Sequestration Leadership Forum in 2009. The CCS technology adoption was executed as a Public Private Partnership between the Canadian government, the government of Saskatchewan, SaskPower and other private companies. The project was named as one of the National Geographic magazine's 10 Energy Breakthroughs in the year 2014. The carbon capture facility can reduce greenhouse gas emissions by up to one million tons of carbon dioxide each year. It can capture 90% carbon dioxide, 100% Sulphur and 50% of the NOx and other harmful particulate matters.

The Unit 3 retrofit had incurred a cost of approximately Can $354 million and was self-financed by SaskPower. The installation cost for the CCS equipment amounted to Can $ 1.4 billion. The boundary project had received $240 million from the federal government. The total funding for the project from the federal government amounted to $1.467 billion. The retrofit adoption in Unit 3 led to the replacement of the existing steam turbine generator with new generator which is integrated with CO_2 and SO_2 capture mechanism. The compressed carbon dioxide is transported through a 66 km long pipeline to oil recovery project in Weyburn. An agreement was signed with Cenovus Energy to purchase full volume of one million tons of carbon dioxide a year. The unused carbon di oxide was transported to an injection well and storage site which belonged to Aquistore research project managed by the Petroleum Technology Research Centre. The Sulphur di oxide collected were used as sources of feedstock for a 50 ton per day sulphuric acid plant located near the power plant. A pre-commercial-scale chemical absorption technology demonstration pilot plant has already been operating at Boundary Dam as part of the International Test Centre for CO_2 Capture. The investment made for this plant was $5.2 million. A part of the funding of $1.2 million came from the Canada/Saskatchewan Western Economic Partnership Agreement.

The total cost of the project was currently $1.5 billion up from the original cost estimate of $1.3 billion. Approximately $800 million was for the CCS process with remaining $500 million for retrofit costs. The additional revenues for the project came from generation of the sale of carbon di oxide, sulphuric acid and fly ash. In 2014, due to decreased capture rate and failure to deliver the promised carbon di oxide to Cenovus Energy, Saskpower had to pay approximately Can $ 12 million as penalties.

In 2010, the engineering, procurement and construction (EPC) contract for the CCS project was awarded to SNC Lavalin and Cansolv Technologies. Cansolv is the wholly owned subsidiary of Shell Global Solutions. The firm supplied the carbon capture process design for the project. Cansolv had also developed an innovative system for capturing sulphur dioxide at coal fired power plant which had been adopted by three facilities in China. Cenovus had also set up injection wells and build a 40-mile-long pipeline which connected the Weyburn EOR project with Boundary Dam. In 2010, SaskPower had entered into a collaborative agreement

Table 42.1 Primary project vendors and partners

Unit 3 Upgrade	
Project partner	Contribution
AB Western	Turbine island mechanical construction
ABB	New distributed control system
Babcock & Wilcox	Boiler rebuild: All new convective sections; low NOx burners .
Hitachi (MHPS)	New 160 MW turbine
Stantec	Engineering consultancy
Westwood	Electric Install
Carbon capture and compression facilities	
ABB	Distributed control system
ABB-Trax International	Control system and training simulator
Babcock Borsig Service GmbH	Flue gas cooling system
Cansolv Technologies Ltd	Amine capture technology
Cenovus Energy	Compressed carbon dioxide, pipeline and EOR storage
GEA	Water treatment system heat exchangers
MAN Turbo Diesel	Carbon di oxide compressor
Siemens	Electric motor to drive the carbon di oxide compressor
SNC Lavalin	Carbon capture facility
SPX Cooling Technologies	Cooling Towers

Source: SaskPower/Powermag.com

with Hitachi for the advancement and implementation of CCS technology for air quality control system and steam turbine generators. The custom designed gas turbine was supplied by Hitachi Canada. In 2011, Babcock & Wilcox was awarded $107 million contract for boiler retrofit. The turbine was installed by the joint venture firm established by Alberici Western Constructors and Balzer Canada. The original 139 MW project was upgraded to 160 MW. Now the net capacity after carbon dioxide capture retrofit is 110 MW. The details of major project vendors and partners is given in Table 42.1.

Further Reading

https://www.saskpower.com/Our-Power-Future/Our-Electricity/Electrical-System/System-Map/Boundary-Dam-Power-Station
https://www.saskpower.com/Our-Power-Future/Infrastructure-Projects/Carbon-Capture-and-Storage/Boundary-Dam-Carbon-Capture-Project
https://www.power-technology.com/projects/sask-power-boundary-dam/
http://sequestration.mit.edu/tools/projects/boundary_dam.html
https://www.sasktoday.ca/yorkton-news-review-archive/boundary-dam-project-is-reaping-benefits-4072267

Case 39: Boeing 787 Dreamliner Project

During Jan 2003, Boeing decided to go ahead with a development designation to develop a new super-efficient midsized airplane—the Boeing 787 with the focus on efficiency, economics, environmental performance, comfort and convenience along with e-enabled systems. The Boeing 787 was developed as a 200–250 seat airplane to provide nonstop, point to point service. The project though was expected to deliver the new airplane to customers by 2004 got delayed and the new planes entered into service by the year 2009. The 787 became the fastest selling wide body airplane in history. On Dec 15 2009, the 787 Dreamliner made its first flight from Paine Field in Everett, Washington. The 787-9 undertook the first flight on September 17 2013 and delivered the first airplane to Air New Zealand during June 2014. The 787-8 Dreamliner can accommodate 210–250 passengers on routes of 7650–8200 nautical miles while the 787-9 Dreamliner can carry passengers in the range of 250–290 on routes of 8000–8500 nautical miles. During the Paris Air Show held on June 18, 2013, Boeing launched the third member of the 787 family—787-10 Dreamliner. This series had orders for 102 airplanes from five customers. This longest aircraft of the 787 family achieved firm configuration in April 2014 and was scheduled for delivery in the year 2018. The new 787-10 has seating capacity in the range of 300–330 passengers and was designed to fly up to 7000 nautical miles. The new 787-10 aircraft covered more than 90% of the world's twin aisle routes. The engines for the 787 aircrafts were provided by General Electric and Rolls Royce.

During May 2007, Boeing opened its final assembly plant for the 787 program in Everett. The second final assembly site for the 787 Dreamliner was located at the North Charleston site which Boeing acquired from the Vought Aircraft Industries in 2008. In 2011, the 787 aircraft achieved the record for completing the longest flight for an airplane in its weight class with a 10,336 nautical mile travel.

The 787 is a groundbreaker in design, build and technology. It is the first airplane in which the composite materials form approximately 50% of the primary structure. The 787 Dreamliner can achieve 20–25% greater fuel efficiency and lesser carbon emissions. One of the unique features is the fuselage which is one-piece composite section which eliminates 1500 aluminum sheets and 40,000–50,000 fasteners per section compared to previous airplanes. The airplane has the largest windows compared to other aircrafts and possess large overhead bins, LED lighting and counters turbulence for smoother ride. The Boeing 787-9 Dreamliner is one of the world's most technologically advanced aircraft. Along with lie flat business class seats and superb premium economy section, the seats are equipped with high definition in-flight entertainment screens and in-flight Wi Fi connectivity.

Since making an entry into the commercial airline sector, Boeing 787 Dreamliner is flying more than 1900 routes and have established more than 235 new point to point routes possible. Boeing designed the 787 Dreamliner family with largest windows and provides cleaner and comfortable travel. Over 420 million people around the world have already flown in the Dreamliner. It connects the world with 150 plus new nonstop. The Boeing 787 have celebrated one million 787 Dreamliner passenger flights. The project offers the fastest for any twin aisle. It holds the record of 2.5 billion miles flown and 18 billion pounds of oil saved. Currently over 80 customers have ordered more than 1400 787 s. The family of 787 airplanes are built at the rate of 14 airplanes a month between factories in Everett, Washington, North Charleston and South Carolina.

In the year 2012, the Dreamliner team was honored with a 2021 Aviation Week Laureate Award in Aeronautics/Propulsion and the 2012 Hermes Awards for Innovation given by the European Institute for Creative Strategies and Innovation.

The first order came from the Japanese Airline All Nippon Airways in April 2004. During 2013, the airplane received its 1000th customer order when Etihad Airways ordered for 30 787-10 Dream liners.

The 787 Boeing project had ushered in a new era of composite construction and efficient wide body aircraft. The project resulted in a widespread production effort for Boeing with suppliers in several countries and two US production lines. The company opted for the smaller 200–300 capacity as a replacement for the 767 model. The 787 model aircraft was the first major commercial aircraft to use carbon fiber composite components in the fuselage and wing construction. This made the aircraft lighter with high strength.

Boeing company embarked upon a six month 'Dream Tour" by 787 aircraft for the global marketing tour in 2011. The travel covered Europe, Africa, China, Thailand, the Middle East and the United States. Table 43.1 list the technical

Table 43.1 Technical specifications

	787-8 Dreamliner	787-9 Dreamliner	787-10 Dreamliner
Passengers (two-class)	248	296	336
Range (km)	13,530	14,010	11,730
Length	57 m (186 feet)	63 m (206 feet)	68 m (224 feet)
Wingspan	60 m (197 feet)	60 m (197 feet)	60 m (197 feet)
Height	17 m (56 feet)	17 m (56 feet)	17 m (56 feet)
Engine	GEnx-1B/Trent 1000	GEnx-1B/Trent1000	GEnx-1B/Trent 1000

Source: https://www.boeing.com/commercial/787/

Table 43.2 Consolidated orders and deliveries

	Total orders	Total deliveries	Unfilled
787-8	417	377	40
787-9	893	568	325
787-10	184	61	123
Total	1494	1006	488

Source: https://www.boeing.com/commercial/#/orders-deliveries

Table 43.3 Annual 787 orders and deliveries

Year	Net Orders	Deliveries			
		787-8	787-9	787-10	Total
2004	56				
2005	235				
2006	157				
2007	369				
2008	93				
2009	−59				
2010	−4				
2011	13	3			3
2012	−12	46			46
2013	182	65			65
2014	41	104	10		114
2015	71	71	64		135
2016	58	35	102		137
2017	94	26	110		136
2018	109	10	120	15	145
2019	82	10	114	34	158
2020	20	5	36	12	53
2021	−11	2	12		14
Total	1494	377	568	61	1006

Source: https://www.boeing.com/commercial/#/orders-deliveries

specifications for the Dreamliner project. Table 43.2 gives the statistics for the consolidated orders and deliveries. Table 43.3 gives the statistics for 787 orders and deliveries.

Altogether there are 411 backlog orders for 787 aircrafts.

43.1 Scenario During the Project Development

Project development of 787 was initiated when the crude oil price was rising in the late nineties and airlines were focusing on greater efficiency. The airline industry was transforming from hub and spoke model to point-to-point model in order to overcome congestion due to growth in air traffic. The need for a new aircraft model was necessitated as Airbus was offering stiff competition to Boeing to gain competitive leadership position in the airline industry. In the 1970s when Airbus was set up,

Boeing had the monopoly in the industry. By early 2000s, Airbus started to lead in terms of number of orders. Airbus had also introduced the plan of adoption of A380XX, the largest jumbo aircraft in the world. Hence it became increasingly relevant for Boeing to introduce new product lines.

43.2 Production and Development Support

Boeing required many support structures for the product development. The development supply chain was adopted to source parts for the development of the aircraft, building the prototypes, display models and first test aircrafts. Unique software tools were used for design and coordination during development. Boeing transported the components of the 787 using modified 747 s to the assembly plants. In order to minimize changes in airport infrastructure, Boeing had the similar interface design for 787 models like that of existing family of planes such 767 and 777.

Boeing had increased the level of outsourcing and third party construction for the 787 project. The final assembly took place in North Charleston. The main wings and central wing box were manufactured by Mitsubishi Heavy Industries Japan. The main landing gear was made by Kawasaki Heavy Industries Japan and Messier–Bugatti Dowty, UK. The passenger doors were made by Latecoere, France. Boeing handles the construction of the aft fuselage section and the tail fin. Boeing uses four large fuselage transporters called Dreamlifters to transport components from Japan and Italy to South Carolina and Washington Boeing factories. In October 2020, Boeing announced that it would be consolidating all 787 productions to its North Charleston, Southern Carolina facility in the year 2021.

Boeing 787 is the first commercial aircraft to rely on composite materials rather than on aluminum alloys. Approximately 50% of materials used are carbon fiber reinforced plastic and other composites with only 20% aluminum and 15% titanium. This resulted in 20% weight reduction for the aircraft.

43.3 Financing Cost and Revenues

The original baseline cost estimated for the development of Dreamliner was US$5.8 billion. After seven years of development and cost overruns the cost was estimated to be US$ 32 billion according to Seattle Times. For strengthening global supply chain for the 787 project, Boeing bought Vought Aircraft Industries' stake in Global Aeronautica in 2008, the joint venture with Alenia of Italy which assembles 787 fuselage. The deal was valued at US$55 million. Boeing also acquired the South Carolina plant from Vought Aircraft in 2009 for approximately US$580 million. This facility was used to make composite sections for 787. Vought Industries was owned by the private equity firm Carlyle Group. The 787 program was stated to be breakeven after the selling of 1100 aircraft. The list price on a 787-9 aircraft was $249.5 million. Boeing had estimated that the total market demand for the 787 class of airplane over a 20-year period up to 2030 was 3500 planes.

43.4 Risks Inherent in the Project

The cause of delay for the project was attributed to gaps in supplier management and technical support. Boeing didn't effectively plan to provide onsite support for its suppliers. It had delegated the responsibility to sub-contractors who didn't perform the coordination work properly. As a result, Boeing had to send large number of its engineers to the sites of various Tier 1, Tier 2 and Tier 3 suppliers worldwide to solve various technical problems. Finally, the entire aircraft sub assembly process had to be redesigned. This resulted in cost escalation. The involvement of major technological innovation in the project was a source of innovation risk. The interactions in terms of new electrical systems, power and distribution channels involved in the project was a source of innovation risk. Boeing had delegated much of the detailed engineering and procurement to subcontractors. The project faced outsourcing risk as Boeing had increased the amount of outsourcing for the 787 project compared to the other aircraft projects. The extent of outsourcing was stated to be in the range of 35–50% for earlier models such as 737 and 747 compared to approximately 70% for 787 models.

The delivery schedules were delayed and the first planes were delivered after three years of delay. The tiered outsourcing risk was attributed to the fact that unlike Boeing's earlier projects of involvement of the firm in a role of integration and assembling different parts and subsystems produced by suppliers, the 787 project involved fostering partnership with approximately 50 Tier 1 strategic partners. Some strategic partners did not have the experience to manage the Tier 2 suppliers. Boeing mitigated the risk by acquiring key Tier 1 supplier like Vought Aircraft Industries and supply expertise to other suppliers. Offshoring risk was also involved in the project of manufacture of airplanes. Approximately more than 30% of 787 component parts were sourced from abroad while the foreign component part was just 5% for models like 747.

In 2019, the North Charleston final assembly plant produced 14 aircraft per month. On account of pandemic, the production had fallen to five per month by end of 2020. There were also quality control issues identified and investigated by the FAA.

Further Reading

Justin Hayward, https://simpleflying.com/how-its-made-the-787/
https://www.boeing.com/history/products/787.page
https://www.boeing.com/features/2019/12/787-1st-flight-anniversary-12-19.page
http://www.inceptone.com/posts/projects/aerospace/boeing-787#overview
https://www.forbes.com/sites/stevedenning/2013/01/21/what-went-wrong-at-boeing/?sh=1cc61867b1b7

https://www.researchgate.net/publication/329241950_Crisis_in_Boeing_787_Dreamliner_An_Investigation_from_Project_Management_Control_Perspective

Gates, Dominic (September 24, 2011). "Boeing celebrates 787 delivery as program's costs top $32 billion". The Seattle Times.

The eye of the storm. The Economist. May 14, 2016. ISSN 0013-0613.

Jonathan R. Laing (April 27, 2013). "Will Boeing's Battery Fix Fly?". Barron's.

Case 40: Shanghai Metro System

By the implementation of the 12th Five-year National Development Plan, China have made an investment of 1.23 trillion CNY with the operationalization of 2019 km metro lines and covered a traffic volume of 52.8-billion-person time.

The biggest metro system by route length is the Shanghai Metro system with 743 km. It is the second biggest metro in the world in terms of number of stations with 381 stations on 18 lines. The ridership record was 13.29 million during the year 2019. Shanghai is an international metropolis. The integrated development of urban transport and rail systems are critical for intercity integration and urban ecosystem development. Shanghai Metro carries nearly 10 million passengers each day thereby serving 52% of residents. In the year 2009, the above figure was 1.9 million. The expansion of metro lines and stations were necessitated due to the large volume of passenger flow.

Shanghai Metro network added its 7000th train during 2020. During the early 1990s, the Shanghai's first metro trains were imported from Germany. Since the year 2008, China had designed its own trains. The plan for Shanghai Metro system was designed as a result of traffic surge in Shanghai on account of economic boom in Shanghai. Initially the plan involved a 40 year phased programme which included 11 metro lines which covered over 325 km.

Metro Shanghai I and Metro Shanghai II project comprised the construction of the first two underground lines (Line 1 and Line 2) in the city of Shanghai. The construction of Line 1 was basically for the sustainable and reduction of the time spent on travel between home and place of work. The project design was planned to connect the city center of Shanghai to the outer districts by means of installation of a north south axis (Line 1) and east west axis (Line 2). The aim was to establish a long term alternative and supplement to road traffic on account of rapid increase in motorized traffic. The limited possibilities to expand the road infrastructure was hampering the further development of Shanghai. The project executing agency suggested that the share of Metro Shanghai in the total annual passenger volume in local public transport in the city of Shanghai at that time was estimated at 12%.

The first line was opened in 1995, the second line in 1998 and the third line in the year 2001. In 2007 the route length was 145 km. With the introduction of line 5, the operation of the system was split between two companies-the Shanghai Metro Operation Company and Shanghai Modern Rail Transit Company.

The main attractions, transportation hubs and commercial areas such as the Bund, Nanjing Road, Huaihai Road, People's Square, Shanghai Railway Station and Xujiahui can be reached by several metro lines. Currently there are 19 Shanghai subway lines in operation, totaling 772 km (480 miles). All metro lines are operated by Shanghai Metro Operation Co. Ltd, These lines have features such as 1435 mm standard gauge, with 1500 V dc being supplied via an overhead catenary. The standard platforms are 150–190 m long.

During December 2018, the Chinese authorities had earmarked US$43.3 billion for Shanghai's subway system over 5 years which would see the expansion of eastern city's network to 27 lines with 1100 km of route track. By the year 2023, the subway will connect Hongqiao Airport, Pudong Airport, Shanghai South Railway Station, Shanghai East Railway Station and other transport hubs. The municipal and district governments will bear some 45% of the total cost while the rest will be sourced through bank financing.

44.1 Project Milestones

The first line was opened in the year 1995 after 6 years of construction and connected the northern and southern districts of the city. In 1996, another 5.25 km was added to the existing line. The project was completed through the consortium Adtranz (now Bombardier) and Siemens. The first phase of line 2 was opened in June 2000 and the project linked the Hong Qiao International Airport and the new Pudong International Airport. The 25 km line 3, the Pearl line was opened in the year 2001. Line 4 was inaugurated during January 2006 and became a circular line in year 2007. Further lines were constructed during the post 2007 period.

44.2 Infrastructural Details

Line 1 consist of 16 station and connects the southern district at Xin Zhuang to the central railway station covering 21.4 km. Line 1 was further extended from the current terminal at Shanghai railway station to Baoshan district in the northern part of the city.

Line 2 covers 55 km long and stretches from Hong Qiao Airport to Pudong International Airport. The 39 km long Line 3 consist of 19 stations and extend from Shanghai South station to Jiangyang station.

Initially Line 1 was operated by trains which were built by the German Shanghai Metro Group consisting of Adtranz, Siemens along with AEG Westinghouse and Duwag. Platform safety doors were built for Line 4 onwards. The largest part of the fleet consisting of 348 trains were supplied by Alstom. In 2007, Bombardier received contract for 500 freight locomotives and 192 MOVIA metro cars. The contracts valued at US$ 204 million was awarded to Bombardier Transportation together with CBRC and Bombardier CPC Propulsion System Co Ltd. The signaling installations were provided by Alstom. The Shanghai Metro Corporation 2025 plan envisages a comprehensive network of 11 lines over 325 km supported by seven light rail routes consisting of 136 km. Six lines are under construction and the network is focusing on its 40-year development plan.

Schneider Electric helps Shanghai Metro across four areas: power distribution, environmental control, connectivity and service. Schneider Electric solutions help Shanghai Metro improve operational efficiency, sustainability, asset performance, feasibility data and employee productivity. LV/MV Power System helps to guarantee the stability and safety of the electrical facilities. Electromechanical Equipment Automation System (BAS) monitors the environment of the stations (ventilation, water and electricity)

The consultants for the project included DeLeuw Cather, ETC and DE-Consult.

44.3 Financing

The metro line 1 had incurred a cost of US$ 145,941,065. The EXIM bank of United States had extended a loan for an amount of US$60 million to China to finance the export of US goods and services for the construction of Shanghai Metro Phase II, Line 1. Table 44.1 gives the project details of Phase I and Phase II.

Table 44.1 Phase I and Phase II details

Metro Shanghai (Phase I)	Project appraisal (planned)	Ex-post evaluation (actual)
Start of implementation	Q 3 1988	Q 1 1988
Period of implementation	5 years	7 years
Investment costs	0.9 billion euros	1.1 billion euros
Counterpart contribution	0.6 billion euros	0.8 billion euros
Financing, of which Financial Cooperation (FC) funds	0.2 billion euros	0.3 billion euros
Metro Shanghai (Phase II)	Project appraisal (planned)	Ex-post evaluation (actual)
Start of implementation	3. Q 1 1995	1. Q 1 1996
Period of implementation	5 years	4 years
Investment costs	1.0 billion euros	1.0 billion euros
Counterpart contribution	0.7 billion euros	0.7 billion euros
Financing, of which Financial Cooperation (FC) funds	0.3 billion euros	0.3 billion euros

Source: https://www.kfw-entwicklungsbank.de/migration/Entwicklungsbank-Startseite/Development-Finance/Evaluation/Results-and-Publications/PDF-Dokumente-A-D/China_Metro_Shanghai_2004.pdf

44.4 Structuring of the Project

Four firms were responsible for financing, construction, operation and supervision of the metro construction project. Shen Tong Company was responsible for financing, construction, operation and supervision of the project. Metro construction company was in charge of metro construction. Metro operation company was responsible for metro operation. The Rail Transit Administration was responsible for metro industrial supervision.

44.5 Challenges

One estimate suggests that the average cost of development for each kilometer of subway works out to USD 78 million and metro systems in cities such as Beijing and Shanghai are struggling to service the vast loans taken for the project. In 2015, about 28 more cities in China were permitted to undertake subway and construction expansion which span 2500 km. According to the Chinese People's Political Consultative Conference research, the subway construction would cost over US$156 billion. The annual operating and maintenance costs are also on upward swing. The income from ticket sales and advertising costs will not be sufficient to pay for maintenance or the interest on its loans. Shanghai Shentong Metro Co had gross liabilities of USD 95.55 million by the end of the year 2011.

Further Reading

https://www.railway-technology.com/projects/shanghai-metro/
https://www.shine.cn/news/metro/2012252178/
https://www.travelchinaguide.com/cityguides/shanghai/transportation/subway.htm
https://www.se.com/ww/en/work/campaign/life-is-on/case-study/shanghai-metro.jsp https://www.yicaiglobal.com/news/shanghai-to-invest-usd433-billion-in-subway-expansion-over-five-years
https://futuresoutheastasia.com/comparison-of-first-metro-lines-in-asia/
https://journal.hep.com.cn/fem/EN/10.15302/J-FEM-2017015
https://www.presidency.ucsb.edu/documents/presidential-determination-ex-im-loan-china-for-shanghai-metro
https://economictimes.indiatimes.com/news/international/metro-rails-cost-more-than-space-travel-chinese-planners/articleshow/15291458.cms?utm_source=contentofinterest&utm_medium=text&utm_campaign=cppst

Case 41: São Francisco River Basin Project

The São Francisco River Basin (SFRB) is based in Brazil. The Sao Francisco River Basin is strategically important for Brazil on account of its potential in agriculture, hydropower, tourism, urban and industrial water supply. The SFRB is known as the river of national integration since it includes different variety of biomes, climatic conditions, landscapes. The river basin links the southeast part of Brazil with the northeast part. It is the fourth longest river in Latin America. The SFB have faced serious water related problems due to water conflicts for multiple uses and predominantly for food production by irrigation.

Brazil holds 12% of the available freshwater of the world. The Northeastern water-scarce area of Brazil is known as the Drought Polygon. The São Francisco River Basin (SFRB) has 58% of its area lying within the Drought Polygon. The Sao Francisco River Basin and its Coastal zone are areas of strategic importance for Brazil on account of socio economic disparities and environmental issues. The basin stakeholders face challenges in terms of the optimization of water uses for generation of electricity, shipping, irrigation, dilution of wastes and industrial water supply.

The river basin project was developed in 4 Components and 28 Activities and provided scientific and technical background for the protection of marine environment, community involvement, institutional strengthening, and human resources education and technical training and the basis for the formulation of the Strategic Action Program for the basin and its coastal zone.

The implementation agency of the integrated management of land based activities in the Sao Francisco river basin project was United Nations Environment Programme (UNEP). The regional executing agency was the Organization of American States/Office for Sustainable Development and Environment (OAS/OSDE). The local executing agency was National Water Agency of Brazil. The duration of the project was 2000–2005 period. GEF grant amounted to US$4.771 million. The government of Brazil contributed US$17.168 million. The total project cost amounted to US$ 22.214 million for the project on integrated management of land based activities.

The river basin covers an area of 636,920 km². The project was envisaged by the São Francisco River Basin Committee (CBH-SF) for the integrated management of the basin and its natural resources. The project formulated a comprehensive strategic action program for the integrated management of the São Francisco River Basin and its Coastal Zone (SAP-SF). The basin is an area of strategic and economic importance which are marked by socio economic disparities and environmental vulnerabilities. The project was basically aimed to promote an integrated approach to the planning and management of the São Francisco River Basin. The project activities would address both current and future problems affecting the basin draining and near shore marine environment. The SFRB is comprised of river, estuary and coastal areas. The river basin system faces problems such as estuarine degradation, point and non-point sourced pollution and multiple use conflicts. The strategic action plan of the project involved fostering an integrated management approach for the basin, its natural resources and coastal zone. Another aim was to strengthen the basic agency as the operational mechanism for regulating water resources and ensuring economic sustainability of water resource development. The project also focusses on implementation of programs and projects to prevent environmental degradation through sustainable economic development through the use of instruments of national water resource policy. The project involves the large scale inter basin transfer of the river to the dry regions in the four northeastern states of Rio Grande do Norte, Paraiba and Pernambuco in Brazil. The estimated cost for the project is US$ 2 billion. The project was okayed by the government of Brazil in year 2005. The project faced legal hurdles and finally the Supreme Country of the country gave permission to start the project in year 2007. The project is estimated to take 20 years for completion. The project involved construction of 722 km of conveyance systems, 591 km of canals, 20 km of pipeline, 22 km of 12 tunnel and integration of 26 reservoirs. By 1999 US dollar terms, the investment amounted to 1.49 billion.

Approximately 1.4% of the river would be diverted for the municipal water supply, industry and irrigation purpose. There are two major transfers with respect to the project. The East axis would transfer water to the Paraíba do Norte River, while the North axis would transfer water to the Jaguaribe and Piranhas rivers. The basin covers more than 2700 km from the Southeast to the Northeast and is one of the few permanent rivers in the water scarce backland. SFRB has most of its area inside the northeastern semi-arid zone.

The region has experienced steady economic growth since the 1960s due to expansion of irrigated areas which included the introduction of large hydraulic constructions and massive investment by the government. The hydroelectric potential of SFRB is estimated to be 26,336.33 MW which represent about 10% of the national potential generation and 19% of the Brazilian production. About 60% of the energy is exported from this region. The principal agency which is responsible for hydroelectric generation in SFRB is the São Francisco Hydroelectric Company (CHESF) which is the biggest national energy generator. For over 50 years, the principal groups of irrigators in the SFRB region are farmers using large sprinkler technology; agribusiness firms engaged in fruit crops for export; small farmers making use of various irrigation systems, rice producers and cultivators of humid soil. Massive government investments of approximately US$9 billion for hydropower generation and US$2 billion for public irrigation have been used in SFRB region.

45.1 Challenges and Environmental Impact

The project faced lot of controversies. It is stated by anti-project advocates that the project would benefit only rich farmers with irrigation infrastructure and do little to support rain fed farmers who are often hardest hit by drought. The critics pointed out that project was unattractive on account of insufficiency of water in the Sao Francisco River during dry season and its consequent impact on the aquatic ecosystems. There were doubts raised with respect to the impact of the project in compacting poverty and drought. The Sao Francisco River Basin had experienced water scarcity problems on account of decreasing streamflow and increasing demand from multiple sectors. Ill-conceived agricultural practices and irrigation procedures have led to salinization of soil and water. Deforestation and agricultural expansion led to changes in vegetation composition. The flora and fauna have been impacted and the nutrient cycling and sediment budgets had been disrupted. The intensification of irrigation has led to high use of agrochemicals, excessive mechanization and deforestation of the riverbanks and resulted in water pollution in the SFRB region. The construction of large dams in SFRB have led to serious negative effects in terms of reduction of sediments and resulted in coastal erosion. The changes in climate patterns and rupture of local ecosystems have made the environment more fragile.

Further Reading

Department of Sustainable Development, http://www.oas.org/dsd/waterresources/projects/SaoFrancisco_NEW_eng.asp
The bishop and the saint: Brazil's São Francisco river project, The Economist, Oct 13th 2005
Significant Base flow Reduction in the Sao Francisco River Basin Murilo Cesar Lucas, Natalya Kublik, Dulce B. B. Rodrigues, Antonio A. Meira Neto, André Almagro, Davi de C. D. Melo, Samuel C. Zipper and Paulo Tarso Sanches Oliveira *Water* **2021**, *13*(1), 2; doi:10.3390/w13010002 MDPI
Abreu, M.P., Carneiro, D.D. and Werneck, R.L.F. 1996. Brazil: Widening the Scope for Balanced Growth, World Development, 24, 241-254.
Arnell, N.W. 1994. Socio-Economic Impacts of Changes in Water Resources due to Global Warming. In Oliver, H.R. and Oliver, S.A. (eds.) The Role of Water and the Hydrological Cycle in Global Change. NATO ASI Series. Vol I 31. NATO/Springer-Verlag: Berlin. pp. 429-457
Antônio Augusto Rossotto Ioris Mansfield College, Water Resources Development in the São Francisco River Basin (Brazil): Conflicts and Management Perspectives, University of Oxford, Environmental Change Unit, MSc Dissertation. http://www.oas.org/en/sedi/dsd/iwrm/Past_Projects/Documents/Sao_Francisco_Brochure.pdf
http://web.worldbank.org/archive/website00662/WEB/PDF/KEMPERSA.PDF

Case 42: Kazan Smart City Project

Kazan is the capital and the largest city of the Republic of Tatarstan, Russia. It is the eighth most populous city of Russia. Kazan is situated at the confluence of the Volga and Kazanka Rivers in European Russia. The Kazan Kremlin is a World Heritage Site. In the year 2009, Kazan was branded as the "Sports Capital of Russia". The city was one of the host cities for the 2017 FIFA Confederations Cup and the 2018 FIFA World Cup. Seven of Russia's 14 largest cities are located within a 1000 km radius of Kazan. Kazan was the most economically diverse region within the Republic of Tatarstan with a total land area of 7075 km^2.

Kazan Smart City project is a path breaking urban development project which is designed to promote growth of investment in sectors such as high technology, medicine, education and tourism. Kazan smart city project is a greenfield development project which is being developed using the latest advancements in urban planning and engineering. The aim of the project is to transform the city into a full-fledged international business hub by means of attracting major multinational firms. Government is providing range of incentives for new investors such as corporate income tax waivers, land grants, transportation and logistics assistance. The project location is situated at major rail, water and overland corridors which connects Russia with Europe and Asia.

Kazan International Airport have registered as one of the fastest growing airports in the Russian Federation in terms of passenger traffic. In 2013, Kazan International Airport launched Aero express high speed train service to the center of Kazan. The tourist flow has been increasing by an average of 12% making the region one of the leading tourist destinations in Russia.

The development of Kazan Smart City was in conjunction with other development projects in the Greater Kazan area like the expansion of Kazan International Airport, the development of Kazan Administration Center, Innopolis and the Sviyazhsk multimodal interregional logistic center. The development of greater Kazan is being supported by two large infrastructure development projects. The first one -the ring road is being built around the perimeter of Greater Kazan. The second project is US$30 billion federal railway development program which would

Table 46.1 Kazan smart city in number

Kazan smart city gross development value	10 billion US dollars
Total area	650 ha
Projected annual tourist arrival	337,000
Population capacity	59,000
Jobs created	39,000
Number of companies/Exponents at Kazan smart city international exhibition and convention centre annually	10,000

Source: Kazan Smart City Investment Guide

link Kazan to Moscow by high speed train which would reduce the travel time from 14 to 3.5 h. For hosting the XXVII World University Summer Games in 2013, 30 new world class sports centers, a new dam, 11 new road junctions, 39 pedestrian crossings, 11 new roads, 13 reconstructed streets and 122 repaired roads were constructed. Kazan received, about four million square meters of new asphalt pavement, three new metro stations, modern airport terminals and aero express railway line. Table 46.1 gives the details of Kazan smart city statistics.

In 2012, the Development Corporation of the Republic of Tatarstan and the Malaysian consortium signed a contract to carry out design work on the development of the master plan for the Smart City Kazan project. In 2013, a memorandum of understanding was signed between the Development Corporation of the Republic of Tatarstan and Cisco for developing an intelligent master plan for the Smart City. Agreement on investment of 400 billion rubles were signed between Sberbank of the Russian Federation and the Agency for Investment Development, Republic of Tatarstan.

The Kansan smart city focus sectors are high technology, medicine, education and tourism. The format of the project is greenfield. Kazan Smart City Supervisor is the Tatarstan Investment Development Agency. Tatarstan Development Corporation is the Kazan Smart City Operator. AJM Planning & Urban Design Group is the Kazan Smart City Master Plan Developer.

Straits Consulting Engineers is the engineering consultant for the Kazan smart city project. The market feasibility for Kazan Smart City was done by Jones Lang LaSalle. The local project consultant was Tatinvestgrazhdanproekt. The project draws on Siemen's experience in implementing similar projects for development of smart cities like the Masdar city in UAE. The US based green technology firm Kronos Energy Solutions was involved in the project for the creation of innovative transport system.

The award winning master plan of Kazan smart city was designed to attract investment into high technology, medicine, education and tourism. The project covers 220 land plots with more than five million square meters of real estate for development. The Kazan Smart City development includes four phases of construction with duration of 4–5 years each. The first phase of construction includes Radiance Kazan hotel and Business Towers, Apart-Hotel, Exhibition and Convention Centre, University of Management and Hospitality, Office Centre, R&D centers and Residential Development. The construction of three large infrastructure projects consisting of the ring road, high speed rain and new second terminal of Kazan International Airport have supported the development of Kazan Smart City. The third terminal of the airport which is expected to be completed by 2025 would improve the capacity from 3.2 million to five million passengers per year. The Republic of Tatarstan have allocated nearly one billion US dollars for the basic utilities and transport infrastructure development of Kazan Smart City.

The 220 land plots of Kazan Smart City owned by the Republic of Tatarstan are available for purchase or long term lease of 49 years. The land plots are available at discounted rates during the first phase of development of Kazan Smart City. In the later phases, the land plots would be sold at their blue book value. Kazan Smart City offers a range of tax benefits for all residents. The residents of the special economic zone are entitled to further tax benefits. The general tax rate is 20%. The corporate tax rate for Kazan Smart city is 15.5%. The rate for special economic zone is in the range 0–5%.

46.1 Zones of the City

The city is divided into four main zones. The Central Business Precinct is the business and commercial hub for Kazan Smart City. This zone consists of 96 investment plots and covers 225 ha. The Kazan International Exhibition and Convention Center is the main attraction center with a total space of 40,000 m^2. Kazan Smart City's Knowledge and Education Precinct is aimed to become the center of excellence in education and research for Tatarstan and Russia. There are 89 plots and covers 209 ha of land area. The main infrastructural highlight is a 250,000 m^2 multivarsity campus for 10,000 students. The Knowledge and Education Precinct will also feature a science park which will create about 4000 jobs. The Special Economic Zone of 102 ha is planned for high technology manufacturing. There are two platforms for special economic zones. The first platform is designed for development of IT industry whereas the second platform is designed for the development of high tech manufacturing, biotechnology and medical technology. The Metropolitan park zone accounts for 17% of the development area. The Metropolitan park is designed to include vegetated parklands, park amenities, religious buildings, art and cultural facilities and cultural complexes. The park coves a land area of 107 ha.

The special economic zones are designed into high technology clusters, medical clusters, education and tourism clusters. Kazan smart city is designed along sustainable standards in terms of carbon and waste reduction, sustainable transport, water and building. The aim is to reduce the potable water consumption by 15–30% per house. The project aims to reduce earthwork volume by 80% and provide 12 m^2 green space per person.

Tatarstan Gulf Investment Company (TGIC) which is a consortium of investment companies from the Middle East have made investments in the Kazan Expo International Center for Exhibitions and Conferences as well as interregional shopping center and business park. TGT Oil and Gas Services had announced plans to invest US$ 11 million for the establishment of an engineering center in Kazan city.

Most public areas in the city are equipped with free wifi. It also works in 50 city buses and have plans to add 300 more. Unmanned electric buses based on 5G pilot zone were introduced in the year 2018. There are more than 120 electronic public services in Tatarstan.

The Republic of Tatarstan had nurtured close relations with the Persian Gulf Arab region. Several countries in the region had bankrolled $760 million into the Kazan Smart City project. The first Islamic bank in Russia, the Ak Bars bank from Tatarstan had attracted investments worth $60 million in 2011 and $100 million in 2013. In the year 2015, the Republic of Tatarstan issued a sukuk for financing a major business center in the capital of Kazan. A special purpose vehicle was created for the project smart city with respect to placement of sukuk valued at US$100–$200 million.

Further Reading

https://www.smartcity-dialogues.com/cities-umd17/kazan-russia/

Kazan Smart City Investment Guide, Tatarstan Investment Development Agency

The official start of the project «Smart City Kazan»., URL: kazan.bezformata.com/listnews/start-proekta-smart-siti/11275359

Tatyana Zakirova, Application of innovative standards of «green» construction in Tatarstan on the example of Kazan, E3S Web of Conferences 274, 01001 (2021), doi:https://doi.org/10.1051/e3sconf/202127401001

https://financialtribune.com/articles/world-economy/37146/islamic-finance-growing-in-russia

https://www.cls.ru/press-centr/publications/islamic-financing-developments-in-russia/

Case 43: Masdar City

Masdar City is the sustainable city project in Abu Dhabi, UAE. It is built by Masdar a subsidiary of Mubadala Development Company. The city is designed by the British architectural firm Foster and Partners. The city sources energy from solar and other renewable energy sources. The city hosts the headquarters of the International Renewable Energy Agency (IRENA). The city is designed as a hub for clean tech companies. In 2007, the government of Abu Dhabi announced the intent of building "the world's first zero carbon city" the custom designed settlement called Masdar.

In 2009, Al Jaber Group, the Abu Dhabi based construction and diversified holding firm had won a contract worth US$ 1.6 billion to build infrastructure for the zero carbon city. The project was valued at $22 billion. The first phase of development was estimated to cost between $5.5 billion to $6 billion. The first phase of the project Masdar Institute of Science and Technology was completed during the fall of 2010. Masdar City was envisaged as a hub for innovation, research and development to offer real world solutions in energy and water efficiency, mobility and artificial intelligence.

The Masdar City aims to be the first zero carbon city in the world. Masdar City's innovative design strategy is based on the adoption of One Planet Principles guidelines which was adopted to ensure that cities and organizations only consume their "fair share" of the earth's resources. The project commissioned by Abu Dhabi Future Energy Company would house over 1500 businesses. Masdar City's sustainability objectives include features such as use of sustainable construction material for construction of the city, construction with substantial waste diversion from landfills, low carbon footprint during the operational life of city powered by renewable energy. The city aims to maximize the use of recycled water for all regulatory approved uses. A multi model innovative personal rapid transit (PRT) transportation system is designed for transportation of people, goods and supplies. The Abu Dhabi government focusses on developing Masdar city as a global hub for research and development of renewable energy and sustainable technology. The project was scheduled to be built over seven phases. The city forms part of an ambitious plan to develop clean energy technologies. Abu Dhabi government have committed $4 billion of equity for the project.

The whole project was expected to be completed by the year 2016 but now is expected to be completed by year 2025.

47.1 Initiatives

The long term initiatives include sustainable power solutions, expansion of green spaces, enhancement, improvements to environmental performance of buildings, mobility programmes and promotion of sustainable urban agriculture.

Masdar, the Abu Dhabi Future Energy Company established in year 2006 is a global leader in renewable energy and sustainable urban development company. It is wholly owned by the Abu Dhabi government's Mubadala Investment Company.

Over 1000 businesses including multinationals, SMEs and homegrown startups exist in Masdar city. Innovate is a global initiative by Masdar City to identify and nurture the next generation of sustainable technologies. The aim of the initiative is to being together investors, innovators and Abu Dhabi's technology ecosystem. Innovate focuses on urban mobility, clean energy, agritech and food security, water, energy storage and artificial intelligence.

Cities account for 80% of the world's energy consumption and 75% of its carbon emissions. The Masdar City is a low carbon development city made up of a rapidly growing clean tech cluster, business free zone and residential neighborhood with restaurants, shops and public green spaces.

The land developers at Masdar city can choose between buying or leasing land to develop their own projects based on sustainability principles. The investment options include apartments, villas, townhouses, office buildings etc. Large firms can partner with Masdar City to develop commercial, retail, residential, recreational, educational, healthcare facilities.

Masdar City is an economic free zone and offers a hassle free environment for companies to operate. For investors, Masdar City offers 100% foreign ownership and 100% exemption from corporate and personal income taxes. There are zero import tariffs. Facilities with one stop shop exist for registration, government relations and visa processing.

To promote research ecosystem, Mohamed bin Zayed University for Artificial Intelligence was established as first research driven university that focuses on artificial intelligence. International Renewable Energy Agency (IRENA) and Siemens Middle East have established their headquarters in Masdar city using Leadership in Energy and Environmental Design (LEED) Platinum certified buildings respectively. All buildings in Masdar city is constructed using low carbon cement which utilizes aluminum. It is 90% derived from recycled sources and the design is such to reduce energy and water consumption by at least 40% compared to that of an average building in Abu Dhabi. These specifications are set in accordance with LEED and Estidama Pearl Building Rating System baselines. There are a variety of low carbon public transportation options which include the Personal Rapid Transit

(PRT), the autonomous NAVYA shuttle, electric shuttle cars, electric and public buses. The planned future transportation options include a Metro Line, Light Rail Transit (LRT) and Group Rapid Transit (GRT). There are walking, running and cycling track facilities in Masdar City.

Masdar City is a prime destination for international business. Important establishments at Masdar City include the International Renewable Energy Agency (IRENA), UAE Space Agency, Tech Park, Solar PV Plant, Seawater Energy and Agriculture System (SEAS), Emirates Nuclear Energy Corporation (ENEC).

Further Reading

Bradley Hope and Chris Stanton, Al Jaber secures Masdar deal, http://www.thenational.ae/article/20090209/BUSINESS/779661070

Dante Clemente, An overview of the world's first carbon neutral city, Issue 5 Fall 2010, https://www.catalystreview.net/welcome-to-masdar-city/

http://news.bbc.co.uk/2/hi/science/nature/7237672.stm

http://www.thenational.ae/news/uae-news/environment/masdar-city-completion-pushed-back-but-total-cost-falls

https://masdarcity.ae/en/learn/overview

https://masdar.ae/en/Masdar-City/the-city

Masdar City, The Source of Innovation and Sustainability, Brochure file:///C:/Users/Admin/Downloads/MAS_MC_Brochure_2020.pdf

Case 44: Delhi Mumbai Industrial Corridor Project

The Delhi Mumbai Industrial Corridor (DMIC) project was conceived as a symbol of Indo-Japan strategic partnership in 2006. Delhi Mumbai Industrial Corridor (DMIC) is a mega infra structure project in India covering a distance of 1438 km between the political capital (Delhi) and the business capital (Mumbai) of India. The total project cost was valued at USD 90 billion. In 2006 a MOU was signed between Government of Japan and India for the development of the project. DMIC Development Corporation (DMICDC) incorporated in the year 2008 is the implementing agency for the project. DMICDC ownership structure consists of 49% equity stake by Government of India, 26% stake by Japan Bank for International Corporation and the rest are held by government financial institutions. DMICDC is managed by a shell structure with USD 2.5 million. The project is being funded through private public partnership and foreign investment. The initial Japanese government support for the project was US$4.5 billion which was offered as a loan for a period of 40 years at a nominal interest rate of 0.1%.

The project includes 24 industrial regions, eight smart cities, two international airports, five power projects, two mass rapid systems and two logistical hubs. The project aims to create sustainable global cities with world class infrastructure to manage urbanization and large scale employment opportunities. The main objective of DMIC is to develop the corridor project as a "Global Manufacturing and Trading Hub".

Under the Phase 1 of DMC, eight investment regions are being developed –the Dadri-Noida-Ghaziabad (UP); Manesar-Bawal (Haryana); Khushkhera-Bhiwadi-Neemrana and Jodhpur-Pali-Marwar (Rajasthan); Ahmedabad Dholera Special Investment Region (SIR) in Gujarat; the Shendra-Bidkin Industrial Park and Dighi Port Industrial Area in Maharashtra. The Ahmedabad Dholera Special Investment Region is the biggest region with size of 920 km^2 in area. This region has a target residential population of two million and focuses on employment generation for 800,000 people by the year 2040.The initial amount for this project was approximately $212 million and was contributed equally by the Japanese and Indian government.

Phase 1 of the project was scheduled for the period 2012–2022. Phase 2 of the project was planned for the period 2022–2032. DMIC project goals included doubling the employment potential; tripling the industrial output and quadruple the exports in 5-year period.

Government of India had announced the establishment of the Multi modal High Axle Load Dedicated Freight Corridor (DFC) between Delhi and Mumbai which passes through six states of Uttar Pradesh, North Central Region of Delhi, Haryana, Rajasthan, Gujarat and Maharashtra. The end terminals of the project are based at Dadri in the national capital region of Delhi and Jawaharlal Nehru Port near Mumbai. The states of Rajasthan and Gujarat together constitute 77% of the total length of the alignment of freight corridor. The project was aimed to provide a major impetus to planned urbanization in India with the focus on manufacturing sector. The project focusses on development of infrastructure linkages such as pioneer plants, assured water supply, high capacity transportation and logistics facilities. In the first phase of the project, seven new industrial cities are being developed. Initially eight cities in the six DMIC states were taken up for development. DFCCIL, a Ministry of Railways, Government of India enterprise is developing the Western Dedicated Freight Corridor. The Dedicated Freight Corridor offers high speed connectivity for High Axle Load Wagons which are supported by high power locomotives.

48.1 Project Details

Under Phase 1, four cities in the States of Gujarat, Maharashtra, Uttar Pradesh and Madhya Pradesh have already implemented the project. Investments of US$2.12 billion have been made in 68 plots covering an area of 521 acres. The total developed land available for allotment to industries is 3620 acres and 3000 acres for non-industrial uses. Table 48.1 gives the details of Phase 1 of the project.

The Dholera Special Investment Region (DSIR) have been spread over an extensive area of approximately 920 km^2. This node is strategically located near the industrial cities of Vadodara, Ahmedabad, Rajkot, Surat and Bhavnagar urban. The developable area in DSIR is divided into six town planning schemes. The developable area is 567.39 km^2. The sub projects include roads and services, water treatment plant, sewage treatment plant, common effluent treatment plant and Dholera International Airport.

Table 48.1 Phase 1: under implementation and completion under DMIC

Project	Area	Location—State
Dholera Special Investment Region	22.5 km^2	Gujarat
Shendra Bidkin Industrial Area	18.55 km^2	Maharashtra
Integrated Industrial Township Greater Noida	747.5 acres	Uttar Pradesh
Integrated Industrial Township Ujjain	1100 acres	Madhya Pradesh

Source: https://www.nicdc.in/about-DMICDC

48.1 Project Details

Table 48.2 Phase 2: Under advanced stages of planning and implementation

Project	Area	Location—State
Integrated Multi Modal Logistics Hub	886 acres	Haryana
Krishnapatnam Industrial Area	2500 acres	Andhra Pradesh
Tumakuru Industrial Area	1736 acres	Karnataka
Multi Modal Logistics Hub & Multi Modal Transport Hub	1208 acres	Noida, Uttar Pradesh
Dighi Port Industrial Area	7413 acres	Maharashtra
Warangal Industrial Corridor	8000 acres	Hyderabad

Source: https://www.nicdc.in/about-DMICDC

Aurangabad Industrial City is one of DMIC's most planned greenfield and smart cities covering 10,000 acres in the state of Maharashtra. The implementation of the project is undertaken by Aurangabad Industrial Township Ltd, a special purpose vehicle between Maharashtra Industrial Development Corporation and DMICDC. The value of exports created from the project amounted to USD 11.6 billion. About 60% of land has been used for industrial purposes.

DMIC Integrated Industrial Township, Greater Noida Ltd is a special purpose vehicle incorporated as a 50:50 joint venture between National Industrial Corridor Development and Implementation Trust (NICDIT) and Greater Noida Industrial Development Authority (GNIDA). A site area of 302.63 ha have been developed for the integrated industrial township under the Dadri Noida Ghaziabad investment region of DMIC to facilitate large scale investments for commercial and industrial development.

A special purpose vehicle named Delhi Mumbai Industrial Corridor Vikram Udyogpuri Ltd had been incorporated for enhancing employment, industrial output and exports from the region. Vikram Udyogpuri is situated in Ujjain and provide infrastructural facilities. The key highlights of the project include integrated plotting for Industrial, Commercial, Public/Semi Public, logistic and recreation centers. The project is expected to create employment generation of approximately 78,000 jobs.

Table 48.2 gives the details of Phase 2 of the project. Phase 3 is likely to be initiated by 2023 and detailed master planning and preliminary engineering for projects such as Ponneri (4000 acres) and Dharmapuri Salem (1733 acres) in Tamil Nadu, Palakkad (1878 acres) are being initiated. Phase 4 projects are under conceptualization and the implementation are likely to be initiated by the year 2024. Projects under consideration in this phase include Kopparthy in Chittor district of Andhra Pradesh, Integrated Manufacturing Cluster at Prag Khurpia and Hyderabad Nagpur Industrial Corridor.

The mandate of DMICDC Ltd has been expanded to develop and implement all Industrial Corridor Projects in India and accordingly, the name has been changed to National Industrial Corridor Development Corporation (NICDC) Limited.

Further Reading

http://delhimumbaiindustrialcorridor.com/
https://economictimes.indiatimes.com/news/economy/infrastructure/make-in-india-delhi-mumbai-industrial-corridor-to-invite-first-anchor-investors-in-august/articleshow/51015748.cms?utm_source=contentofinterest&utm_medium=text&utm_campaign=cppst
Social Impact Assessment Study Delhi-Mumbai Industrial Corridor Project, Report Gautam Buddha University, Uttar Pradesh Nov 2020.
https://www.nicdc.in/about-DMICDC
http://dicdl.in/
https://www.auric.city/
https://www.iitgnl.com/
http://vikramudyogpuriujjain.com/

Case 45: Golden Quadrilateral Highway, India

Road transport accounts for 65% of freight movement and 80% of passenger traffic in India. National highways account for 40% of the total national traffic but account for just 2% of the total road infrastructure. Approximately 20% of the national highway network is four lanes and one fourth of the rural population don't have access to an all-weather road. The road network in India has three categories: (1) national highways that serve interstate long-distance traffic; (2) state highways and major district roads that carry mainly intrastate traffic; and (3) district and rural roads that carry mainly intra-district traffic.

This largest highway project ever undertaken in India was aimed at improving the Golden Quadrilateral network, the North–South and East–West (NS–EW) corridors, port connectivity and other projects. Golden Quadrilateral Highway is the fifth longest highway project in the world with total length of 5846 km. It is the first nationwide central project to build a network of four lane highways to link the metropolitan cities of Delhi, Mumbai, Kolkata and Chennai. It connects other cities such as Pune, Ahmedabad, Jaipur, Kanpur, Surat, Bengaluru, Visakhapatnam and Bhubaneswar. The Golden Quadrilateral project was launched in the year 2001 as part of National Highways Development Project (NHDP). The project consists of four/six lane express highways. The large network of highways in India are managed by the National Highway Authority of India (NHAI). The Golden Quadrilateral highway network was established as part of Phase 1 of the NHDP. The Golden Quadrilateral project has four sections. Section I connects Delhi to Kolkata. This section covers a distance of 1454 km of National Highway 2(NH2) and passes through the states of Delhi, Haryana, Uttar Pradesh, Bihar, Jharkhand and West Bengal. It connects major cities in these states such as Delhi, Faridabad, Mathura, Agra, Firozabad, Kanpur, Allahabad and Varanasi. Section II of the highway link Kolkata to Chennai and covers 1684 km. This segment consists of NH6, NH60 and NH5. This section passes through the states of West Bengal, Orissa, Andhra Pradesh and Tamil Nadu. Section III covers 1290 km stretch from Chennai to Mumbai. It comprises of parts of NH4, NH7 and NH 46 which covers cities of Mumbai, Bangalore and Chennai. Section IV is a 1419 km stretch which covers major cities such as Delhi, Gurgaon, Jaipur, Ajmer, Udaipur, Gandhinagar, Ahmedabad, Vadodara, Surat and Mumbai.

The project though planned for completion by the year 2006 got delayed by 6 years on account of land acquisition issues and renegotiations with contractors. The project was executed through a public private partnership (PPP) between NHAI and the contractors. The major contractors associated with the projects were Larsen & Toubro, LG Engg. & Construction, Nagarjuna Construction, Consortium of GVK International and BSCPL, IRCON International, Punj Lloyd, Progressive Construction, ECSB-JSRC, Madhucon Projects, Sadbhav Engg., KMC Construction, Gujarat Public Works Department, SKEC—Dodsal, MSRDC, Mumbai, Skanska Cementation India, Hindustan Construction Company, RBM—PATI, Unitech, CIDBI Malaysia and PATI—BEL etc.

Some sections on the highway are planned to be extended to six lanes. In September 2011, the infrastructure group GMR won a $1.4 billion contract from the NHAI to widen the 555 km Kishangarh-Udaipur–Ahmedabad highway from four to six lanes. The company would operate the highway for 26 years under the Design, Finance, Build and Operate Model (DFBO). Ninety percent of the original plan was implemented within 4-year period.

Golden Quadrilateral is one of the longest highways which connects the industrial, agricultural and cultural centers of India. The construction of Golden Quadrilateral has vastly improved the connectivity and transportation between major cities and ports.

After the Golden Quadrilateral project, NHAI had taken up six more highway projects. NHAI manages 55,000 km of highways. During the fifth phase of the National Highway Development Plan, the government had approved the six laning of 6500 km of four lane highways which included Golden Quadrilateral. Currently approximately 2800 km are six lane highways. Government of India have launched a new initiative called Bharatmala Pariyojana which is aimed to upgrade 35,000 km of roads in 5-year time period (2017–2018 to 2021–2022) at a cost of USD 70 billion.

49.1 Financing of the Project

The financing of the project was obtained from taxes on petrol and diesel, external assistance through market borrowing and private sector participation. The funding of the project was done through the Central Road Fund which was made out of cess on the sale of petrol and diesel. In total, the highway passes through 13 states of India. The total estimated cost of construction was around USD 8.4 billion. The highway has been built under budget. Initially Government had estimated the cost of the project to be USD 9.4 billion at 1999 prices.

Table 49.1 Golden quadrilateral segments

SL	Segment	Total length (km)	Date of completion
1	Delhi–Kolkata	1453	31st August 2011
2	Chennai–Mumbai	1290	31st August 2011
3	Kolkata–Chennai	1684	31st May 2013
4	Mumbai–Delhi	1419	31st Aug 2011
	Total	5846	

49.2 Impact of the Project

According to a study by World Bank Policy Research in 2013, for the organized portion of the manufacturing sector, the Golden Quadrilateral project led to improvements in both urban and rural areas of non-nodal districts located 0–10 km from the Golden Quadrilateral. A study appeared in Journal of European Economic Association finds that Golden Quadrilateral have increased the manufacturing sector's real income by 2.72% which is equivalent to USD 4.2 billion.

The project established faster transport network between major cities and ports and provided an impetus to truck transport throughout India. It also facilitated the industrial growth of small towns and provided opportunities for transport of agricultural produce from hinterland to major cities and ports for export. The average transportation time had come down substantially. For example, the travel time between the cities of Kanpur and Kolkata was reduced by 12 h. The project had manifold benefits such as better transportation movement for products, more options for industrial activity and reduced wastage for agricultural sector. The overall vehicle operating costs and time was reduced. Transporters could carry more loads on account of better quality roads by using multi axle trucks. The project contributed to economic growth directly through construction as well as indirectly through contributions in driving demand for cement, steel and other construction materials. Table 49.1 gives the details of different segments of the Golden quadrilateral projects.

Further Reading

https://www.roadtraffic-technology.com/projects/golden-quadrilateral-highway-network
https://indianexpress.com/article/india/atal-bihari-vajpayee-golden-quadrilateral-5310899/
Ghani, Ejaz; Goswami, Arti Grover; Kerr, William R.. 2013. Highway to Success in India: The Impact of the Golden Quadrilateral Project for the Location and Performance of Manufacturing. Policy Research Working Paper; No. 6320. World Bank, Washington, DC. © World Bank. https://openknowledge.worldbank.org/handle/10986/12170 License: CC BY 3.0 IGO.
National Highway Authority of India website: http://www.nhai.org/
https://www.businesstoday.in/magazine/focus/story/economic-benefits-of-the-golden-quadrilateral-project-41439-2013-05-04
https://concretecivil.com/golden-quadrilateral/
Jose Asturias, Manuel Garcia, Santana Robert Ramos, Competition and the Welfare Gains from Transportation Infrastructure: Evidence from the Golden Quadrilateral of India, Journal of European Economic Association, https://pedl.cepr.org/publications/competition-and-welfare-gains-transportation-infrastructure-evidence-golden, 2019.

Case 46: Hong Kong Disney Land Project

In December 1999, the Walt Disney Company and Hong Kong Government entered into an agreement to develop Hong Kong Disneyland (HKDL), the US$3.6 billion theme park complex. Disney the multinational multimedia entertainment company have Theme Parks and Resorts as one of its business segment. The company owned and operated the Disneyland projects in California and the Walt Disney World resort complex in Florida. The company also earned fees and royalties on Tokyo Disneyland and Disneyland Paris. The Hong Kong Disney land project was developed on the northeastern end of Lantau Island. The agreement specified the development of project in three phases. The HKDL project is owned and managed by Hong Kong International Theme Parks (HKITP). The park was opened to visitors during September 2005. The ownership structure of the park is such that 53% is owned by the Hong Kong government and 47% by the Walt Disney Company. The Board of Hong Kong International Theme Parks Limited (HKITP) have a membership of 11 directors. The Hong Kong SAR Government appoints five directors while the Walt Disney Company (TWDC) appoints four directors. Two independent non-executive directors are jointly appointed by the Hong Kong SAR Government and TWDC.

The project construction started in January 2003 and took 6 years for completion in phases. In 2016, Disney had announced multi year, $1.4 development plan for new themed areas, attractions and entertained from 2018 through 2023. The project budget estimation was approximately HKD 10.9 billion which would be funded by the two shareholders, the Hong Kong government and the Walt Disney company through concurrent cash equity injections. The number of themes areas would be increased from seven to nine and the number of attractions and entertainment offerings which includes castle shows, stage shows and character greetings would increase from 110 to over 130. Table 50.1 gives important timelines with respect to the progress of the project.

The park is partially located in Islands District and Tsuen Wan District and is divided into themed areas and well concealed backstage areas. The public areas occupy approximately 27.4 ha. The seven themed areas of the park are Main Street

Table 50.1 Milestones in the development of project

Period	Events
Nov 1999	The Government of Hong Kong Government announces the project for the construction of Disney's first theme park in China through a joint venture with Walt Disney Company.
Jan 2003	Construction work is initiated
Aug 2005	The new MTR to Hong Kong Disneyland Resort is inaugurated. Inspiration Lake Recreation Centre officially opened to the public
Sept 2005	The Grand Opening of Hong Kong Disneyland Resort.
Oct 2007	Hong Kong Disneyland Resort is selected as the "Top 15 World's Most Popular Amusement Parks" by Forbes.
Dec 2009	Hong Kong Disneyland Resort project expansion plan announced..
Sep 2010	Hong Kong Disneyland Resort celebrates its fifth anniversary
Dec 2011	Hong Kong Disneyland Resort receives Green Management Award
July 2012	The world exclusive Grizzly Gulch officially open
May 2013	One of the most sophisticated ride system in Disney's history "The Mystic Magneto Electric Carriage "in Mystic Manor introduced.
Oct 2014	The brand-new "Disney Paint the Night", a first-ever fully LED parade created by Walt Disney Parks and Resorts officially begins
Sept 2015	Hong Kong Disneyland Resort celebrates its tenth magical year
Dec 2015	Fairytale Forest- a new attraction in Fantasyland opens
June 2016	Wars: Tomorrowland Takeover, a Star Wars-themed seasonal event launched.
Nov 2016	HKDL announces its new expansion and development plan, which includes among other the construction of a Frozen-themed area, introduction of Marvel-themed rides, redesigning of the Sleeping Beauty Castle etc.
Jan 2017	Disney Parks' first Marvel-themed ride, Iron Man Experience officially opens. Iron Man Experience is a 3D motion simulator attraction in Tomorrowland at Hong Kong Disneyland.
April 2017	Hong Kong Disneyland Resort opens its third hotel, Disney Explorers Lodge.
Oct 2017	Hong Kong Disneyland wins Travel Weekly Asia 2017 Readers' Choice Awards - Best Attraction.
Aug 2018	Hong Kong Disneyland Resort starts to create Hong Kong's single largest solar energy system by installing over 4500 rooftop solar panels on a number of attractions and backstage buildings.
March 2019	The brand-new Marvel-themed attraction Ant-Man and The Wasp: Nano Battle! officially opens. It is an attraction located in Hong Kong Disneyland featuring the Marvel Cinematic Universe characters Ant Man and the Wasp.
Nov 2020	The park's centerpiece castle- Castle of Magical Dreams, was officially unveiled.

Source: https://hkcorporate.hongkongdisneyland.com/about/our-company/milestones.html

USA, Fantasyland, Adventure land, Tomorrowland, Grizzly Gulch, Mystic Point and Toy Story Land. Main Street, USA is the first themed land inside the main entrance and themed to resemble small American towns during the early twentieth century. Adventure land is themed to resemble the remote jungles in Africa, Asia, South America, Oceania and the Caribbean. Fantasyland is themed after Disney's animated fairy tale films. Tomorrowland is themed lands featured in which each

Table 50.2 Sources of funding

Sources	Values in HK$ Millions
Debt	
Bank term loan	2275
Hong Kong government loan	6092
Subtotal	8367
Equity	
HK Government	3250
Walt Disney	2449
Subtotal	5699
Total	14,066

Source: HKITP Limited Offering Circular, September 2000

version of the land is different and features numerous attractions. Grizzly Gulch is a roller coaster themed attraction which provides a cross between the big thunder mountain railroads of the classic Frontier lands. Mystic Point is themed in a dense uncharted rain forest surrounded by scenes of supernatural events. Toy Story Land is a themed area based on the Disney Pixar film series Toy Story.

The debt component constituted 59.5% and the equity component 40.5% of the sources of financing. In the debt component, the percentage of bank term loan and government loan were 16.2% and 43.3% respectively. The equity component of Hong Kong government was 23.1% while that of Walt Disney was 17.4% respectively. The sources of financing given in Table 50.2 excludes the estimated HK$14 billion cost of land reclamation and infrastructure development provided by government to HKTP in exchange for non-participating convertible stock. The terms of Hong Kong government loan included 25-year final maturity with repayment initiating from 2016 and was fully subordinated to the bank loan.

HKITP and Walt Disney decided to raise a HK $2.3 billion, 15 year, non-recourse term loan for construction and a HK$1 billion nonrecourse revolving credit facility for working capital needs during the post construction period. In August 2000, HKTP and the Hong Kong government awarded Chase Manhattan Bank, the mandate to lead the HK$3.3 billion bank financing for the construction of the park. Chase Manhattan Bank was chosen among 17 major banks invited to bid on the deal based on its expertise and leadership position in syndicated finance. During 1999 Chase was the lead arranger for 34% of the total syndicated loans by dollar volume in US market.

The provisions in the Disney's proposal had 15-year final maturity for debt repayment and options for repayments to start as late as 3 years after opening of the park. From the banker's perspective, this was risky since normally the loans in emerging markets were fully repayable within 3–5 years. Final maturity or tenor and average life are key determinants of credit risk. Disney's insistence to use operating cash flow for expansion and unwillingness to subordinate management fees and royalties were not commonly observed in such projects. The collateral for the project was the oceanfront land which was yet to be reclaimed. However, based on the conservative capital structure and government commitment to the project, Chase bank took part in the mandate process. As a lead arranger, the general policy adopted by Chase was to hold 10% of the loan. This proportion declined in case the loan size or risk increased. Chase proposed an initial spread of 100 basis points over the HIBOR which could be stepped up to 125 basis point in year 6 and to 137.5 basis point in years 11–15.

The syndicated loan part for financing the park was oversubscribed 2.5 times and distributed equally among 32 banks. In the general syndication for bank financing, 32 banks received allocations. The seven lead arrangers received final allocations of HK$130 million, the 18 arrangers got HK$105 million, the three Co-Arrangers got HK$85 million and four lead managers were allocated either HK$70 million or HK$52.5 million based on their original commitment to HK$100 or HK$75 million. In terms of fees for the deal, the arrangers received US$94,000, the Co-arrangers got US$65,385 and lead arrangers got US$44,872 respectively. The general syndication produced commitments of HK$5.3 billion which was 16% more than Chase's original projection. Chase bank had merged with JP Morgan during the year 2003.

50.1 Economic Implications

During Disneyland construction, Hong Kong had become a booming business and tourism sector. Hong Kong has emerged as a world class tourist destination. The project would generate sizeable public benefits. It was estimated that the Disneyland project had the potential to create 36,000 jobs and contribute HK$ 148 billion (US $19) billion directly into the local economy over a period of 40 years. The target market for Hong Kong Disneyland consisted of family oriented Asian tourists from mainland China, Taiwan and Southeast Asia. The expansion and development of the project will bring around 3500 jobs and another 600 jobs in the year 2023 from HKDL's expanded operations. The government expected to generate financial return on its investment between 17% and 25% per annum and at least 6% in a worst case scenario.

50.2 Environmental Issues

The Hong Kong Disney land theme park project was based on marine land reclamation process. The process involved mining of substantial amounts of marine sand and earth from nearby places with cutter or trailing suction hopper dredgers which is then transported and discharged in the area to be reclaimed. The reclamation process has created environmental problems like habitat destruction and presence of fine oceanic sediments. There were opportunity costs related to reduction of marine biological food resources, loss of cooperative fishing and aquaculture rights. There has been decrease in marine leisure opportunities like pleasure boating and sports fishing.

Further Reading

https://hkcorporate.hongkongdisneyland.com

Terence Tsai, Shubo Philip Liu, Disneyland in Hong Kong — Green Challenge (A) Article in Asian Case Research Journal · December 2011 DOI: https://doi.org/10.1142/S0218927511001538.

Lee S, "Park still Viable if Visitors 70pc less than Estimated.", South China Morning Post, 11/11/99. p. 2

Benjamin Esty, Chase's Strategy for Syndicating the Hong Kong Disneyland Loan (A). Harvard Business School Case, 9–201-072.Pages 22.

Case 47: Jamnagar Refinery Project, India

Reliance Jamnagar Marine Terminal is situated in the Gulf of Kutch, State of Gujarat, India which is, about 35 km west of the town of Jamnagar. Jamnagar refinery is the world's largest refinery and petrochemicals complex owned by Reliance Industries. Reliance Industries, the flagship company is the largest private sector company in India. The Reliance Jamnagar is the world's largest refinery and aromatics complex. It is the largest industrial project implemented by Indian corporate sector completed by Bechtel. The first refinery was completed in the year 2000. The Jamnagar refinery project is the largest single investment at a single site in India. The Jamnagar complex is the first manufacturing complex of its kind with a fully integrated petroleum refinery, petrochemicals complex, captive power plants and a captive port. There are more than 50 process units in the refinery which carry out functions such as crude oil distillation, catalytic cracking, catalytic reforming and delayed coking. The refinery project incurred a cost of US$207 million and the first phase of the complex construction incurred a total cost of $437 million. The construction of the plant was initiated in the year 1996. The estimated completion period was of 30 months. However, the company was able finish the construction of the refinery plant well ahead of the schedule in 24 months. The contractors of the project worked on a two shift 24-h basis to speed up the construction activity. The first refinery plant at Jamnagar had the capacity to produce 15 million tonnes per year of refined crude.

The original construction of the Jamanagar complex for Reliance was led by Bechtel. Many Indian companies such as Larsen & Toubro (L&T), Dodsal, Punj Lloyd, Trafalgar House and Simplex were involved in the construction of the complex. The installation of the automation system was carried out by the Foxboro Company for both the Phase I of construction and its upgrade carried out in 1997 and 1999 respectively. The fully applied closed loop automatically controlled crude blending system for the refinery took 2 years for completion. This closed-loop crude blending system is based on Foxboro's I/A Series Process NMR (Nuclear Magnetic Resonance) analyzers and Simulation Science's powerful Connoisseur MPC (Model-based Predictive Control) package running on a Foxboro I/A Series control system. During the peak construction period, the project employed more than 70,000 workers. During the project, Bechtel had employed over 2800 engineers and other professionals in 19 offices around the world.

In 2006, Reliance Industries Limited (RIL) has planned to increase the crude processing capacity of the refinery from 33 MMTPA to 64.6 MMTPA, as part of the Jamnagar Export Refinery Project (JERP). The aim of the project was to maximize the number of processing units and add product portfolios of refined petroleum products for export markets. As a result, a second refinery in year 2008 was constructed thereby doubling the facility's capacity to more than 1.24 million barrels per day. The total investment for the second refinery project was over US $ 6 billion. The construction of the second phase was started in 2005 and completed in year 2008. The upgrade project at the Jamnagar Petrochemicals complex had enhanced the degree of vertical integration which facilitated Reliance to capture value across a broader spectrum of energy chain. The second refining unit can process approximately 29 million tons or 580,000 barrels per stream day. This crude oil throughput refinery was located in a special economic zone where only exports were permissible. The new unit was adjacent to the RPL's existing 33 MTPA export oriented refinery. The project was completed in a period of 36 months and had achieved a Nelson complexity index of 14 which enabled the refinery plant to process heavy and sour crudes to produce petrol and diesel complaint to Euro IV emissions norms.

The combined capacity of the two refineries is 662 million tons which catapulted Reliance's Jamnagar refineries into number one position among the top ten refineries in the world. The Jamnagar refineries have a refining capacity of 33 million tons per year and paraxylene production capacity of 1.5 million tons per year. The marine facility for the existing refinery consists of 2 SPM's for crude oil import and 4 Tanker Berths A, B, C and D for exporting products and a seawater intake facility for cooling water requirements. The marine facility also includes a Ro-Ro facility and unloading platforms for handling project construction cargo. The product pipelines from the existing Jamnagar refinery were routed from Marine Tank Farm (MTF) to Land Fall Point (LFP) on onshore RCC sleepers and steel frames.

The gasoline and diesel produced at Jamnagar is predominantly exported to the United States and Europe. The polypropylene is used to create products such as fibers, films and house old plastic goods.

The Britain based British Safety Council had awarded Reliance's SEZ refinery at Jamnagar with the "Globe of Honor award" for its policies in best environmental management practices. In 2019, Reliance Industries had secured the approval of the expert appraisal committee in the Ministry of Environment, Forest and Climate change to expand the capacity of its export oriented refinery in the special economic zone (SEZ) at Jamnagar by 5.8 million tonnes. The expansion project will raise the installed capacity of the SEZ refinery to 41 metric tonnes and increase the overall capacity of the Jamnagar refinery complex to 74 metric tonnes. In the fiscal year 2018, the Jamnagar refinery had processed 69.8 metric tonnes of crude. US firm Black & Veatch International Co; Kansas City, Mo participated in the project for the construction of sulfur recovery and gas treatment units. Dow Global Technologies

Table 51.1 Mandated lead arrangers for the project

ABN Amro
Bank of America Securities
BNP Paribas
BTMU
Calyon
Citigroup
DBS Bank
DZ Bank
HSBC
Mizuho Financial Group
SMBC
Standard Chartered
ICICI Bank
State bank of India

Inc. was responsible for providing licensing and services for the polypropylene plant process.

51.1 Ownership Structure and Financing

The expansion project was financed through IPO equity, commercial debt and ECA loans. The ownership structure of the expansion project is through the special purpose vehicle owned by Reliance Industries with 75% ownership, publicly owned shares with 20% ownership and US energy major Chevron with 5% ownership with an option to purchase a further 24% from Reliance Industries. The total project value was estimated to be US$ 6 billion. The total equity component was estimated to be US$ 1.5 billion. This included Reliance Industries equity of US$ 1.775 billion, Public shareholding of US$600 million and Chevron's equity investment of US$ 125 million. The senior debt component for the project amounted to US $1.5 billion. The project also used a US$500 million loan from the EXIM bank. Table 51.1 list the lead arrangers for the project.

Milbank Tweed was the legal adviser to the banks. The deal was characterized as one of the largest limited recourse financing deal in the Asian region. The deal had the longest tenor for a syndicated loan financing in India. The hedging risk based on the plant's rupee denominated revenues from Sulphur and petroleum coke were borne by the sponsors. The company RPL raised US$600 million through an IPO which was oversubscribed 51 times.

Further Readings

Expansion makes Jamnagar the world's largest oil-refining hub, https://www.bechtel.com/projects/jamnagar-oil-refinery/
https://www.hydrocarbons-technology.com/projects/jamnagar-refinery-upgrade/

http://teconsrl.it/Case-histories/Jamnagar-Export-Refinery-Project-JERP

http://archive.indianexpress.com/news/reliance-commissions-worlds-biggest-refiner/402999

P Manoj, Reliance gets green signal for Jamnagar refinery expansion https://www.thehindubusinessline.com/companies/reliance-gets-green-signal-for-jamnagar-refinery-expansion/article26063112.ece

Simon Ellis, Reliance Petroleum Jamnagar refinery, https://ijglobal.com/articles/34147/reliance-petroleum-jamnagar-refinery

https://www.exim.gov/news/us-exports-india-for-6-billion-refinery-and-petrochemical-complex-are-backed-ex-im-bank-500

Case 48: Big Dig Project

The Big Dig (Central Artery/Tunnel Project) was mega road infrastructure project which was undertaken in Boston, Massachusetts, USA to improve the flow of traffic and avoid travel congestion across Boston. The project replaced the outdated elevated Central Artery road. The Central Artery/Tunnel project was one of the most challenging project in the history of United States. The project replaced the six lane Central Artery (I-93) with an underground highway and two new bridges over the Charles River.

Major part of the project was completed by the year 2005. The project undertaken by the Massachusetts Turnpike Authority was initiated in the year 1991. The cost of the project was estimated to be US$14.8 billion. The project was completed in year 2007. The initial completion period for the project was estimated to be 1998. The technically challenging Big Dig project consisted of two major sections. The old Central Artery which was an elevated six lane highway was replaced by an extended subterranean highway and a 14 lane two bridge crossing of the Charles River at the northern end. The second section of the project involved the extension of the Massachusetts Turnpike (Interstate 90) from south of downtown Boston through a tunnel (Ted Williams Tunnel) under South Boston and Boston Harbor to Logan Airport. The six lane elevated Central Artery (Interstate 93) was constructed in the year 1953 and opened in 1959 with the capacity to accommodate 75,000 vehicles a day. However, the traffic flow in the region was in excess of 200,000 vehicles a day which led to severe traffic jams in Central Boston for more than 10 h a day. It was estimated that costs of $500 million were incurred on account of wastage of fuel burnt due to traffic congestion. The elevated highways were demolished and replaced by an eight to 10 lane underground expressway which led into a 14 lane, two bridge crossing at the Charles River. The demolition also freed up 29 acres for the construction of new parks in the region. The new road system was designed with the capacity to handle 245,000 vehicles each day. Eight lanes were opened by the end of the year 2003. The last two lanes were opened during early 2005.The 10 lane cable stayed hybrid bridge over Charles River (Leonard P Zakim Bunker Hill Bridge) was built at a cost of $100 million and serves the underground Central

Artery. The Leonard bridge which is the widest cable stayed bridge in the world is unique in the sense that it is the first "hybrid" cable stayed bridge in the US which uses both steel and concrete in its frame. The smaller four lane Leverett Circle Connecter Bridge (830 feet long) was constructed at a total cost of $22.27 million and connects the Leverett Circle area on the northwestern edge of downtown Boston with points north of the Charles River. The Massachusetts Turnpike (I-90) extension was opened to traffic in January 2003 and runs from Seattle Washington to Logan International Airport in East Boston. The complicated and technically challenging construction of I-90 involved tunnel jacking, construction of casting basin for immersed tube tunneling, cut and cover tunnel construction. The construction of I-90 facilitated reduction of traffic congestion through better traffic distribution and improved street system. The project included five major interchanges to connect the new roads and existing regional highway system. The four lane Ted Williams Tunnel was constructed at a cost of $1.3 billion and forms the part of the I-90 extension link. The undersea part of the link was built using 12 steel section and connects all the major routes along the project. Initially the Massachusetts Highway Department owned and managed the Central Artery project. Later it became a part of the Metropolitan Highway System (MHS) and was run by the Massachusetts Turnpike Authority (MTA).

The design and construction of the Big Dig project was done by a joint venture of Bechtel, Parsons Brinckerhoff, Quade and Douglas. The major heavy construction contractors of the project included Jay Cashman, Modern Continental, Obayashi Corporation, Perini Corporation, Peter Kiewit Sons, J F White etc.

The project was plagued by cost overruns, delays, leaks, design flaws and charges of poor execution management. There were problems of leaks in the ceiling and wall fissures which caused damages to steel support systems, fireproofing systems and drainage systems. An amount of $ ten million was provided as a cost overrun in order to repair the leaks. Over 200 complaints were filed by the state of Massachusetts as a result of leaks, cost overruns, quality issues and safety violations.

The project covered 7.8 miles of highway and 161 lanes miles. The project consumed 3.8 million cubic yards of concrete and excavated more than 16 million cubic yards of soil. The ten lane cable stayed hybrid bridge Leonard Hill Bridge was the widest bridge ever built and the first to use an asymmetrical design. This project was unique in the sense the project was completed in the middle of Boston without halting the normal work operations of the city. The project excavated a total of 16 million cubic yards of materials which were enough to fill a stadium to the rim over 16 times. More than 26,000 linear feet of steel reinforced concrete slurry walls were installed by the project. It was often said that the amount of reinforcing steel used in the project was equivalent to make one-inch steel bar long enough to wrap around the earth at the equator. The Ted Williams Tunnel interface in East Boston which was constructed 90 feet below the surface of Boston Harbor is the deepest connection in North America. The seven building ventilation system installed by the project is one of the largest highway tunnel ventilation systems in the world.

The project involved the largest geotechnical investigation, testing and monitoring program undertaken in North America to identify various conditions in the tunneling work. The project created more than 300 acres of new parks and open space. Over 2400 trees and 26,000 shrubs were planted at Spectacle Island. The carbon monoxide emission levels dropped 12% due to the adoption of the new highway system.

The project used 150 cranes during the construction work. The first 25% of the construction work was completed within 5 years whereas the second 25% of the work took 2 years for completion. By 2004, almost 94% of the work on project was completed. During the peak construction period of 1999–2002, calculations suggest that workers did $three million worth of work activity each day. During this period approximately 5000 workers were involved in the construction work. The project was structured with 118 separate construction contracts of which 26 were geotechnical drilling contracts.

52.1 Benefits of the Project

The project facilitated 62% reduction in vehicle hours of travel on I-93, the airport tunnels and the connection from Storrow Drive. The new underground route I-93 Central Artery has improved the peak period travel times through downtown Boston. For example, the average afternoon peak hour northbound travel time on I-93 through downtown had dropped from 19.5 to 2.8 min. The new project had provided approximately $168 million cost savings for travelers annually. This estimation includes $25 million of savings in vehicle operating cost plus a value of $143 million of time savings. The Massachusetts Turnpike Authority (MTA) has also implemented six emergency response stations for Boston highways which will further reduce delays. The fast lane automated vehicle identification program had speeded up the process of toll payment for travelers on the Turnpike Extension and Sumner tunnels to Boston. For Massachusetts residents, the average travel time from the I-90/93 interchange to Logan Airport during the peak periods had reduced between 42% and 74% depending on direction and time period. For example, the average travel times to the airport during the afternoon peak had decreased from an average of 16 min to 4 min. The opening of the Turnpike Extension to Logan Airport had added approximately 800,000 residents to Massachusetts population who could access the airport within a 40-min drive from home. The capital investments by MTA are supporting employment generation and business activity in the state. The MTA collects $3.5 million annually for leasing its corridor to four telecom companies. The operations of the MTA and its traveler service plazas resulted in the creation of 3565 jobs. Estimation suggest that the total impact on the Massachusetts economy is nearly $500 million of business sales which supports over 6000 jobs with a payroll of over $223 million. Over 45 parks and public plazas came into existence as a result of the Central Artery project. The project was able to complete the shoreline restoration in the Charles River Basin, Fort Point Channel and Rumney Marsh.

Table 52.1 Project milestones

Year	Events
1985	Final environmental impact report for the project approved
1986	Bechtel/Parsons designated as management consultants
1987	Congress approves funding
1988	Exploratory archaeology work undertaken
1990	Congress allocates $755 million for the project
1991	Construction contracts awarded and work begins on Ted Williams Tunnel
1992	Over $1 billion in design and construction contracts awarded
1995	Ted Williams Tunnel opened for commercial traffic
1998	Construction started on the Charles River Crossing
1999	New Broadway Bridge & Leverett Circle Connector Bridge opened
2002	Leonard P Zakim Bunker Hill Bridge construction completed
2004	Dismantling of the elevated Central Artery (I-93)
2005	I-93 South Tunnel fully opened
2006	Major completion of Central Artery/Tunnel Project

52.2 Project Financing Cost

The Big Dig was the most expensive highway project in the US. The original cost estimate was US$ 2.56 billion. By 1992 the project cost increased to US$ 7.74 billion. In 1994 the cost burgeoned to US$10.4 billion. According to Massachusetts Turnpike Report 2008, the project incurred a final cost of US$ 14.8 billion. According to The John W. McCormack Institute Report, many factors could be attributed to increase in costs such as the failure to properly assess the impact of unknown subsurface conditions, environmental, mitigation costs and inflation. The mitigation costs required 1500 separate mitigation agreements. The financial costs for the construction of the three major components of I-93, I-90, and the I-90/I-93 Interchange amounted to approximately US$8 billion. The design costs were estimated to be US$ 2 billion. The factors which impacted the Big Dig project's cost escalation included financing shortfalls and interest rates, shortages of materials and labor, technical and design complexity along with political and legal risk factors. The State had incurred over $100 million annually in debt service on account of the project and the debt maturity period is till 2038. The projects owe about $9.3 billion in both principal and interest. Table 52.1 list the major milestones for the project.

Further Reading

https://www.roadtraffic-technology.com/projects/big_dig/

Transportation Impacts of the Massachusetts Turnpike Authority and the Central Artery/Third Harbor Tunnel Project, The Turnpike Authority as a Transportation Provider, Vol 1 Feb 2006.

https://www.mass.gov/info-details/the-big-dig-project-background#introduction-

McCormack, J. W. (1997). Report to the Legislature on Managing the Central Artery/Tunnel Project: An Exploration of Potential Cost Savings. The John W. McCormack Institute of Public Affairs, University of Massachusetts, Boston.

Greiman, V. & Warburton, R. D. H. (2009). Deconstructing the Big Dig: best practices for mega-project cost estimating. Paper presented at PMI® Global Congress 2009—North America, Orlando, FL. Newtown Square, PA: Project Management Institute.

Case 49: North-South Corridor Road/Rail Project

The North South Corridor program is a major program aimed to enhance the economic potential of countries in Southern and Eastern Africa by improving the infrastructure in the region and increase the power generation capacity and trading potential. This multi modal (road, rail and ports) trans-continental interconnector project basically aims to connect Cape Town in the south and Cairo in the north. South Africa is the lead undertaker of this project and other countries taking part in the project include Botswana, Mozambique, Zambia, Zimbabwe, Tanzania and Malawi.

The North South Corridor project comprises inter-related projects involving road infrastructure; road transport facilitation; management of railway systems and rail infrastructure; physical and procedural improvements at border crossings; port infrastructure; management of air transport; and energy interconnectors. The corridor project was officially launched during April 2009.

The Regional Economic Communities (REC) of the Common Market for Eastern and Southern Africa (COMESA), the Southern Africa Development Community (SADC) and the East African Community (EAC) have focused upon the improvement of trade facilitation for deepening regional integration and reduction of costs for cross border transactions.

There are various phases for this project which are in different stages of the development life cycle. These include road, rail, bridge, border post and energy projects. In the first phase, 1041 km of road is aimed to be upgraded. In the second phase of 2–5 years, another 5156 km is planned for upgradation. The corridor will ease border restrictions for people and goods thereby increasing the efficiency and capacity of the transport sector. This would facilitate regional integration and increase the magnitude of regional trade. Approximately 90% of transport freight movement in the existing corridors in the region are through road while movement through rail account for only 10%. This imbalance between road and rail has resulted in significant road rehabilitation costs and environmental pollution. A single coordinated corridor would be able to address the modal imbalance between road and rail on the North South Rail Corridor. The corridor project highlights the cooperative efforts of five rail operators in South African Development Community (SADC) region to increase intra African trade. The North South Rail Corridor consists of a rail network which stretches over 3000 km from Durban in South Africa through Zimbabwe and Botswana and links to the Democratic Republic of Congo passing through Zambia. The corridor would be the SADC's main international rail gateway for transportation of inbound and outbound cargo. A memorandum of understanding has been signed between the rail operators on the North-South Rail Corridor which includes Zambia Railways Limited (ZRL); Grindrod/Beitbridge-Bulawayo Railways (BBR); Société Nationale des Chemins de fer du Congo (SNCC); National Railways of Zimbabwe (NRZ); Swaziland Railway (SR); Transnet SOC and Botswana Railways (BR). The North South Rail Corridor infrastructure and logistics study is being financed by the SADC Infrastructure Project Preparation Fund managed by the Development Bank of Southern Africa (DBSA). Nepad Business Foundation (NBF) is the project manager who facilitate the engagement between rail operators and appointed technical consultants. NBF had also received the regional and political support for the project from the SADC Ministers of Transport and regional bodies such as Southern Africa Rail Association (SARA). Government of South Africa have emphasized the completion of Beit Bridge Border Post as part of the North South Corridor on priority basis.

The Chirundu border crossing was opened in the year 2009. This facilitated the reduction of waiting times by an average 50% for freight transport and 83% for passenger transport. Kasumbela is the busiest border crossing between Zambia and DR Congo with about 500 trucks crossing per day. The border post was designated as a one stop border post. Kazungula, the border post between Botswana and Zambia on the NSC serves as the main alternative to the Beitbridge-Chirundu route from South Africa to the Copper belt. The Beitbridge border handles on an average 470 trucks per day and 800 passenger vehicles per day.

The existing performance of the railway systems in Eastern and Southern Africa is not according to standards based on budget and performance indicator achievements. The system is unreliable with high accident and failure rates. The operating costs remain high. The regional traffic volume of goods transported through rail system accounts for approximately 5%. The North South Corridor project focusses on phased restructuring process which involves the rehabilitation of the existing track and equipment. It was suggested to delink the rehabilitation of the track from the concession agreements in terms of provisions of rail service.

The ports located on the North South Corridor are the ports of Dar es Salam and Durban. The Tanzania Ports Authority is responsible for the implementation of the Master plan for the development of ports. Power generation projects are being constructed in the Eastern and Southern Africa region. The major power interconnectors on the North South Corridor which are being established are the Zambia Tanzania Kenya interconnector and the DR Congo Zambia interconnector.

Regional integration is a complex process with practical challenges in terms of implementation and inter agency coordination challenges between governments.

53.1 Financing of the Project

During the North South Corridor Financing Conference 2009, over $1.2 billion packages were announced for the implementation of North South Corridor and related projects. DBSA had pledged US$ 1.5 billion in loans over 4 years for projects in the roads, ICT and energy sectors. DFID UK have made commitments for £33 million technical assistance for the Trade Mark Southern Africa programme in support of the Tripartite regional integration agenda and £67 million grant funds for project investments channeled through the Tripartite Trust Account. World Bank have made commitments for US$500 million in loans for supporting activities related to economic development. African Development Bank have made commitments to a tune of US$380 million in loans for the North South Corridor and US$160 million in loans for the Nacala Corridor. European Union have made commitments for grants amounting to 115 million euros. DBSA have provided a grant of US$ one million to the Tripartite Trust Account in five annual tranches of US$200,000. DFID UK had disbursed a grant of GBP 67 million to the Tripartite Trust Account for construction and modification of building and prepare projects to Project Implementation Memorandum (PIM) stage. The World Bank's Africa Infrastructure Country Diagnostic for the COMESA region report suggest that sustained spending of US$ 5.5 billion a year is required for sustainable regional integration of Eastern and Southern African region.

The costs for upgradation and maintenance of the entire road network excluding South African roads was estimated to be US$6.9 billion of which US$ 4.5 billion was required for capital investment and US$2.4 billion as recurring costs.

53.2 Establishment of TTA

A Tripartite Trust Account (TTA) for North South Corridor was established by COMESA-EAC-SADC Tripartite Task Force along with Department for International Development (DFID) and the Development Bank of Southern Africa (DBSA) in year 2009. The TTA is designed as an infrastructure investment grant fund to leverage commercial and quasi commercial investments for supplementing member country public funds. The TTA fund is maintained in US dollars. A minimum contribution of 20 million euro is required for securing membership in the account investment committee. The investment committee consists of representatives of donors with contributions, three representatives of the Tripartite (COMESA, EAC and SADC), representative of the Tripartite Secretariat and three independent representatives. The Investment Committee will oversee and supervise the TTA Manager, shall report to the Tripartite Task Force and be subject to the strategic and policy guidance of the Tripartite Task Force.

Further Reading

https://www.nepad.org/north-south-corridor-roadrail-project

Report on the Infrastructure Components of the North-South Corridor. https://www.icafrica.org/en/knowledge-hub/article/infrastructure-components-of-the-north-south-corridor-100/

North-South Rail Corridor study: An example of what Africans can achieve when working together, https://www.tralac.org/news/article/11669-north-south-rail-corridor-study-an-example-of-what-africans-can-achieve-when-working-together.html

Case 50: Great Man Made River Water Supply Project, Libya

Libya's Great Man-Made River project consists of a long term plan to supply the country's water needs by drawing water from aquifers beneath the Sahara region and carry it through a network of huge underground pipes to the northern coastal belt.

In 1953, oil companies which were drilling in the Libyan desert for oil discovered basins with huge amount of fossil freshwater which had been stored underground for over 1000 years. Water was discovered in four major underground basins. The Kufra basin located in the south east covered an area of 350,000 km and formed an aquifer layer with a depth of 2000 m deep. The Kufra basin had an estimated capacity of 20,000 km^2 in the Libyan region. Sirte basin which is 600-m-deep is estimated to hold more than 10,000 km^2 of water. Murzuk basin is estimated to hold 4800 km^2 of water. Larger quantity of water lies in the Hamadah basin. The initial idea for the project was proposed in the late 1960s. The feasibility studies were conducted in 1974 and the work started in year 1984.

The Great Man Made River Authority (GMRA) project is one of the largest civil engineering projects in the world, involving the abstraction of ancient groundwater from the Sahara Desert and the transportation of water over hundreds of kilometers to the coast of Libya. Colonel Muammar Gaddafi, the late ruler of Libya had called the mega project the "eighth wonder of the world".

The Nubian Sandstone Aquifer System (NSAS) is the biggest fossil freshwater reservoir in the world, estimated at 373,000 billion cubic meters, which covers approximately two million square kilometers. The freshwater reservoir is located underneath the territorial lands in Sahara Desert which belongs to four countries- Libya, Chad, Egypt and Sudan. In the year 2013, these four countries developed a framework for the management of water resources.

The GMRA Water Supply project consists of five phases. Phase 1 covers 1200 km of pipeline from As-Safir and Tazerbo to the Ajdabiya reservoir and Benghazi and Sirte. The Phase II covered South Western aquifer (Fezzan) to Tripoli and Jeffra Plan. The Phase III involved expansion of existing Phase I system with 700 km of new pipeline. The Phase IV design consists of extension of distribution network and construction of a pipeline to link the Ajdabiya reservoir to Tobruk.

Phase V connect the eastern and western systems into a single network in Sirte. The average water flow rate is 0.95 m/s. In Phase I approximately 250,000 sections of pipe were laid each having a diameter of 13 feet and length of 23 feet. These pipes were made up of layers of steel reinforced prestressed concrete and manufactured in two large factories located in Libya.

The project duration is estimated to be 25 years. The total cost is estimated to be $27 billion according to 2004 estimate. The project is owned by Great Man made River Authority and funded by Government of Libya.

The first phase which is also the largest phase which provides two million cubic meters of water in a day became operational in year 1991. This phase consumed a quarter of a million sections of concrete pipe, 2.5 million tons of cement, 13 million tons of aggregate, two million kilometers of pre stressed wire and 85 million cubic meters of excavation. The total cost incurred for this phase amounted to US$ 14 billion. The Tazerbo wellfield is composed of both production and piezometric observation wells and generates approximately one million cubic meters of water daily at a rate of 120 L/s per well.

Phase II of the project was planned to provide one million cubic meters of water daily from the Fezzan region to the fertile Jeffara plain on the western coastal belt and Tripoli. This phase witnessed the installation of 127 wells which were distributed along the three east west collector pipelines. Phase III was divided into two main parts. The first part provided the planned expansion of the existing phase I system with additional 1.68 million cubic meters of water along with 700 km of new pipelines and pumping stations to produce a final total capacity of 3.68 million cubic meters of water a day. The second part of the phase involved construction of a reservoir south of Tobruk and additional 500 km of pipeline. The last two phases involved the extension of the distribution network along with the construction of the pipeline which linked the Ajdabiya reservoir to Toburk. Phase IV was put on hold on account of the revolution and civil war in year 2011.

The infrastructure of the project is owned by the GMR Project Authority. The primary contractor for the first phases in the Gaddafi era was the Dong Ah Consortium. Currently, the main contractor is Al Nahr. These companies are domestic construction companies. Korean and Australian firms have supplied technical parts for the project.

In the year 2001, GMRA awarded an $82 million contract for the construction of new major pumping facilities to a consortium led by Frankenthal KSB Fluid Systems. In 2002 the consortium led by Nippon Koei and Halcrow was awarded a contract worth $15.5 million for the preliminary engineering and design works meant for the phase III operations. Phase III operations were completed by the year 2009. This phase increased the total daily water supply capacity to 3.68 million cubic meters. This phase provided 138,000 m^3 of daily water supply to Tobruk and the coast. An additional 1200 km of pipelines were laid in Phase III of the project.

During 2011, Nato warplanes bombed water ducts in Brega and caused damages to a pipe making plant associated with the project. In 2017, the project witnessed repeated sabotage attempts on wells located at Jabal Hasawn. Table 54.1 discusses

54.1 Significance of the Project

Table 54.1 Milestones

Time period	Event
1984	Work on Project initiated
1989	Survey on initial soil resistivity survey
1990	First water flow received
1991	Phase 1 of the project from Sarir to Benghazi initiated
1995	Cathodic Protection System implemented
1996	Phase II—Tripoli Supply completed
2000	Phase II Jeffara Plain initiated
2002	Pipe production plant O&M contract awarded
2004	Pumping station completed

Table 54.2 Contract highlights

Original project design	Brown & Root/Price Brothers Cy
Main contractor in initial phases	Dong Ah; Al Nahr Co
Sub-contractors	Enka Construction & Industries; Thyssen Krupp Fordertechnik
Main contractor in Phase III	Nippon Koei and Halcrow
Pipe production plant O&M	SNC Lavalin
Pumping station construction/service and technical support contract	Frankenthal KSB Fluid Systems Consortium

the milestones of the project. Table 54.2 gives the details of the contracts for the project.

54.1 Significance of the Project

This "Great Man Made River" project is the world's largest irrigation project. The project had supplied the much needed irrigation and drinking water to the cities and farming areas in the North of Libya. The project consists of the largest underground network of pipes and aqueducts in the world. The pipes cover 2820 km. It consists of more than 1300 wells which are more than 500 m deep and supplies 6,500,000 m^3 of fresh water per day to the cities of Tripoli, Benghazi and Sirte. The pipeline system constructed runs through an underground network of pipelines from the Nubian Sandstone Aquifer System in the Great Sahara Desert to the coastal urban centers which include Tripoli and Benghazi. The project currently provides 70% of all freshwater used in Libya. The country is basically a desert with rainfall covering only 5% of the land surface area. There is no single river which have water presence throughout the year. In 1999, UNESCO awarded Libya a scientific research award for effective use of water in desert areas.

Some studies suggest that Libya's underground water could last for 650 years. Some other experts suggest that the aquifers would be exhausted in 250 years. The default age of pipelines is 50 years thus requiring replacement twice per every

100 years. Agriculture received a boost on account of this fresh water project. The government have made investments in seven big agricultural schemes. The agricultural project in Jafara plains consists of 3300 ha which are divided into 665 farms which cultivate citrus fruits, wheat, barley and vegetables. The project was able to expand the green areas in the north and west of Libya.

Libya has constructed this mega project without financial support from other countries or source of funding from financial institutions. The funding for the project was sources from fuel revenues and taxes on tobacco. The total cost estimated currently amount to more than $36 billion.

The environmental concerns include the potential changing desert environment of regions from where fossil water is sourced. The massive pipeline network may also affect the desert environment.

Further Reading

https://www.water-technology.net/projects/gmr/

https://www.canadianconsultingengineer.com/features/the-great-man-made-river/

Keys, D., 2011, Libya Tale of Two Fundamentally Different Cities, BBC Knowledge Asia Edition, Vol. 3 Issue 7.

https://www.britannica.com/place/Middle-East

Moutaz Ali, Fresh Water from desert, https://www.dandc.eu/en/article/libya-has-worlds-largest-irrigation-project

Printed in Dunstable, United Kingdom